Around the World on a Motorcycle

1928 to 1936

Zoltán Sulkowsky

English translation by
Noémi M. Najbauer

Octane Press books are also available at discounts in bulk quantity for
sales and promotional use. For details about special sales or for a catalog
of motorcycling books and videos, write to the publisher:

Octane Press
815A Brazos Street #658
Austin, TX 78704
512-334-9441
info@octanepress.com
www.OctanePress.com

OCTANE
PRESS

ISBN: 978-1-884313-55-4

5 4 3 2

Printed in the United States of America

Contents

Translator's Foreword

In *Around the World on a Motorcycle,* Zoltán Sulkowsky documents a daring voyage made by two Hungarian globe-trotters starting in 1928—one of the first successful and surprisingly little-known circumnavigation attempts on motorbike.

Zoltán Sulkowsky and his friend Gyula Bartha, two motorized Magellans, spent more than seven years discovering for themselves, and for future readers, our world during the deceptive lull between the two World Wars. The complete memoir, published in 1937 in Hungary, created great excitement and national pride.

Sulkowsky and his travel partner (refered to as Gyuszi throughout the memoir) had, during their journey, made every effort to raise awareness of the Hungarian presence in the world. They went out of their way to find compatriots in every country they visited and joined local Hungarian clubs for lectures and cultural events, thereby strengthening the global togetherness of their small nation. Yet Sulkowsky's memoir is much more than a record of the state of Hungarians worldwide; it serves as a historical document of encounters with citizens of 68 countries on six continents, and sheds light on an age when the large colonial empires were still intact and the pioneering spirit very much alive.

As Sulkowsky, somewhat tongue-in-cheek, describes in his memoir, round the world travel had reached epidemic proportions in 1920s Europe. This was due in part to the development of various media to follow travelers as they made their journeys and also to the availability of means of transportation—the railway, automobiles, and motorcycles—that allowed individuals to conquer larger distances. What set their journey, initially an alternative to unemployment, apart from the attempts of the many hundreds of other travelers was that it began in humility—Sulkowsky and Bartha could not be sure of the outcome, so they did not publicize their decision—and ended in well-deserved success and celebrity.

The two travelers met Mussolini, Prime Minister Hamaguchi, and General Chiang Kai-shek; hobnobbed with Charlie Chaplin and Greta Garbo; and were received by the President of the United States, Senator Borah, and Mayor Walker of New York. These encounters with foreign dignitaries and celebrities of the period reflect the great extent to which their efforts became known and recognized throughout the world.

Most of their time, however, was spent far from the comforts of human hospitality, in the jungles of Sumatra, on the red Australian earth or the pampas of Peru. Sulkowsky and Bartha were true pioneers, often forging roads where no roads had existed before and taking a whiff of exhaust-scented civilization to people who had never seen a motor vehicle in their lives. These were the same people and surroundings that Sulkowsky, a keen observer, described with great accuracy and sensitivity in letters and articles sent to Dr. Ervin Baktay, editor-in-chief of *Földgömb (The Globe)*, a Hungarian periodical in geography. Though not an expert in the field, Sulkowsky contributed extensively to the science of geography in Hungary both in his correspondence and through packages of animal skins, hunting trophies, minerals, and other valuable physical reminders of the places he had visited.

Sulkowsky and Bartha shared a lifelong friendship and professional partnership. Zoltán Sulkowsky, born in 1902 into a family of modest means, was raised by his mother (his father had abandoned the family and emigrated to Germany) until the age of sixteen when she and Sulkowsky's grandmother died in the 1918 influenza pandemic that swept through the world in the wake of World War I. Sulkowsky's grandfather and the Baroness Madarasi supported Zoltán and his brother financially and enrolled them first in Cadet School in Sopron, Hungary, then in the prestigious Ludovika Academy. Disenchanted with the prospects of a military career, Sulkowsky left the academy and studied engineering, but never received his degree. Like many talented but lost young people of his age, he sought opportunities abroad and left Hungary in 1927 to pursue them.

Sulkowsky's travel partner, Gyula Bartha, was born in 1898 in Transylvania to a poor Hungarian family. Bartha acquired very little formal schooling but had earned a certificate as a mechanic. The circumstances of his first meeting and evolving friendship with Sulkowsky are not known, yet in 1927 they left Hungary together, hoping to make a living in one of the countries of Western Europe. The decision to travel around the world came on a park bench in Milan, where they had arrived via Vienna and Venice. It was there, in the hours of the northern Italian dawn that they began planning the most remarkable journey of their lives.

A free-spirited young artist, Boriska Tila, known as Mimmy throughout the memoir, joined them in Paris where they purchased their 1922/23 J Model Harley-Davidson and sidecar, the motorcycle that was to carry them to what then seemed a very far-off and dubious victory. And the three of them left Paris on a sun-drenched summer morning.

The journey lasted almost eight years, until 25 June 1936, when

Sulkowsky and Bartha crossed the Hungarian border to the pride and ovation of their countrymen. On the money they had earned over the course of the journey (revenues of Sulkowsky's photographs, articles, and lectures) Sulkowsky went on to found two Hungarian film studios and built up a two-story villa in one of the finest districts of Budapest. The villa and the attached garage, which held the famed Harley until it was sold after World War II, remain standing to this day. Yet Sulkowsky's filmmaking enterprise went bankrupt during the war and a significant portion of his collections of art and travel memorabilia was stolen by prying neighbors and soldiers of the Soviet army. After the war, Sulkowsky tried to rebuild his life, but the verve and flair that had accompanied him around the globe were gone. He developed a chronic ulcer of the stomach and died at 48 on the operating table.

Gyula Bartha's fate was more fortunate. With a taste for the quiet, simple life, he invested his money in a fine piece of land on Remete Hill in Budapest, which he turned into a successful orchard and farm using the terrace technique he had learned on the island of Java. When Bartha died in 1972, Sulkowsky's remains were exhumed and the two urns containing their ashes were buried side-by-side in a small columbarium in the Farkasréti Cemetery of Budapest. Their shared inscription simply reads Világjárók, World Travelers.

But the journey doesn't end under the chestnut trees of the Farkasréti Cemetery. One Hungarian dreamer, Károly Kanyó, currently a resident of Daytona Beach, Florida, hopes to retrace Sulkowsky's and Bartha's journey and write his own story about what he observes in our much-changed world. It all started in Communist Hungary in 1983, when Károly, then in his teens, flipping through his grandfather's Car and Motorcycle Magazine found an article on Sulkowsky and Bartha's travels. Hooked from the start, Károly became determined to find the book version. He located a signed copy, which he bought from a fellow biker and soon read it to pieces. It was then that he made up his mind to retrace the author's travels and write his own memoir. Working as a truck driver for years after leaving high school, Károly scraped together enough money to buy his own (then somewhat decrepit) Harley-Davidson.

He has since befriended Sulkowsky's relatives and, in 2004, moved to the U.S.A. to earn enough funds and find sponsors to realize his dream. The English translation of this memoir is a strong link in the chain of events that Károly hopes will facilitate his travels.

There is traditional wisdom that man has two contradictory impulses: to find his home in the world and to make the entire world his home. Eighty years ago Zoltán Sulkowsky lived this wisdom. By traveling the world and raising Hungarian awareness globally, Sulkowsky and Bartha made the entire world their home. By returning to inter-war Hungary and publishing his memoirs of world travels there, Sulkowsky found his home in the world, and brought the rest of the world to his people. And today, at least one more man hopes to do the same.

A Final Note

As all translators inevitably do, I faced a series of difficult decisions as I progressed through the work, the most pressing of which was the question of verbal tenses. Sulkowsky's book is based on a journal, pastiche-like and composed in the present tense, lending a sense of presence and urgency to his writing. The seventy years that have passed between the publication of the book in Hungarian and the birth of its English translation have been more than enough to make it a historical document. To convey a sense of a historical perspective, I opted for the past tense throughout the book, except where the author was describing natural and architectural phenomena that remain intact to this day. I hope the sense of presence conveyed by Sulkowsky's use of the present tense will be palpable in my rendition of his engaging style.

Noémi M. Najbauer, translator

Born in Budapest, Noémi Najbauer received a B.A. in English Language and Literature from Yale University. Since 2005 she has been teaching English literature at the University of Pécs in Hungary. Her other English translations include The Gift of the Wondrous Fig Tree *by Magda Szabó.*

Introduction

Budapest, Hungary, November 1937

This book was not written by a scholar. Neither did I set out on my adventurous journey after thorough scientific preparations or precise planning. What I did pack in my proverbial rucksack was an intense desire to see and to learn, and a healthy helping of determination. I could never boast of prestigious social connections or doors opening wide as a response to letters of recommendation by the rich and famous, and therefore my impressions and knowledge of far-away countries and strange peoples were not one-sided, gathered at the same influential source, but by myself, day by day. It was my determination and the work of my own two hands that sped me along; not open checkbooks and well-stuffed wallets. My determination, hard work, and a well-chosen vehicle, the motorcycle, carried me not only to railroad junctions and busy sea ports, but also off the "ridden" path, hummed its way into the real lives of real people, into isolated villages, forests, and untried mountains.

What I saw, I saw through my own eyes, not the pages of a guidebook, and what I wrote, I wrote based on my own experiences, gained at my own expense.

I hope to bring those far-off places just a little closer through first-hand observations, exacting detail, and a sometimes sad, sometimes cheerful, but always truthful description of our adventures, great and small.

There is no beauty and no place on earth without a flaw. I haven't gone out of my way to find fault with foreign cultures, but neither have I glossed over negative impressions. Those who have traveled a great deal already know that no place is as wonderful and ideally perfect as travelogues make it out to be. Life is not the movies. Seasoned travelers also know that we have no reason to idolize any nation or country, because we have yet to find heaven on earth.

Finally, this book was not born on a writing desk. The journal upon which it is based was a work in progress throughout our travels, often written while we sat on our moving vehicle, sometimes during brief stops or in luxurious hotel rooms, other times, while sitting in our small tent, or in the desert sand, or in virginal rainforests, where a group of curious monkeys listened to the steady tap-tap of the typewriter.

Traveling around the world no longer means what it meant a few decades ago, however, wandering around the highways and byways of the world for eight years straight remains a daring accomplishment. I would bet that very few cyclists or other species of travelers would be up for such a trek, and the difficulties of the venture are underscored by the fact that nobody before us ever undertook a similar journey.

Trials and dangers were our constant companions. Think of countries with no roads to speak of, think of narrow, precipitous mountain paths, which, in a few hours, carry you from the green lap of summer into whitest winter. Think of bitter cold and even more unbearable heat. There is nowhere to hide from the elements when you're riding a motorbike. Rain and blizzards, mud and ice hinder your progress, or you may find yourself riding through the most desolate of deserts, wide, open lonely spaces, several days' journey from any sign of civilization. Think of pushing, pulling a well-laden bike through deep sand, your supplies on your shoulders, one eye always worriedly gauging the gasoline level, even as you contemplate how to eat and drink less while traveling more and pray that you are spared any major accidents or breakdowns, which could very easily lead to complete isolation and a slow and painful death. You cross fever-ridden tropical countries, entire epidemic zones, where trying to find a doctor is a lost cause. You traverse through ancient lands belonging to wild and uncivilized people, where hatred of white man can have a deadly outcome. You spend sleepless nights worrying about your reptile neighbors in the swamp, wild creatures of the forest, or bands of outlaws lying in wait.

Was it all worth the price? Was what we saw and experienced worth eight long years of our lives? These are questions best left up to you, the reader!

Zoltán Sulkowsky

Still in Europe

Sicilian Roads

"We're going to need that book after all," said one cyclist to the other, sighing.

"All right, but pour in a little more gas first," answered the other, his voice unsure.

Two sweaty young men, clad in sportsman's gear, bustled around a huge motorcycle with a sidecar parked at the edge of the road. This would have been a familiar scene to anyone used to European roads in the summer, when the power of the sun draws hundreds upon hundreds of cyclists into the open air, or else, business matters force travelers of all sorts into cars or onto motorcycles. Nevertheless, the sight was slightly unusual on the roads of Sicily, where donkeys are the preferred, if not the only, mode of transportation.

The heat was merciless, and not a dusty leaf stirred on the few visible trees, seeing as there was not even a breath of a breeze to speak of. It took long minutes for the dust to settle after every donkey-riding traveler passed by.

The few words had been spoken in Hungarian, and it's time for me to reveal that I was one of the sweaty young men standing there. Such helplessness is embarrassing, but I cannot tell a lie; our bike had broken down, and we had no idea what on earth could have gone wrong. We'd scanned the whole machine for anything out of place but had discovered nothing. The tires hadn't deflated; heck, even the horn was working well. And still, our motorcycle refused to start up. Our last, desperate hope that we had merely run out of gas had just been dashed. There's not much chance of a friendly automobile coming to our rescue on the dusty road somewhere between Marsala and Trapani.

I am entirely familiar with the mechanisms of the motorcycle, down to its nuts and bolts. I had learned the names of all the parts while still in college, I knew rpms and pistons, but I had no idea what to do when the engine shut down.

And so we consulted our book, troubleshooting systematically, part by part and line by line, and still, we found nothing out of the ordinary. Then we gave the bike a push, desperately: nothing. Two helpful *amici*, wearing long

13

scarves despite the blazing heat, pushed with us: still nothing, and then…
"Grazie Signori," we cried. *"Niente, buon viaggio!"*

Our motorbike was a beautiful sight after all, bearing on itself signs of past and future miles. The shiny sidecar was decorated with three or four badges from various biker clubs; its comfortable, springy seats were an inviting sight. The presence of a passenger seat behind the driver's seat made even the casual observer suspect there must have been a third traveler.

Considerable time had passed; the sun was setting behind the hills when our cries of joy were peppered by the healthy hum of the engine. And it dawned on us what had been wrong all along. In all the heat and haste of the Sicilian noon, the poor engine had refused to start without the switching on of the electric current. In other words, the *key* had turned without turning anything.

The third passenger suddenly appeared upon hearing the engine rev. Our companion was a blonde young woman with smiling eyes, bursting with energy and *joie de vivre*. She soon disappeared for the second time in the cloud of dust that accompanied our thankfully functioning bike.

Who were these travelers and where were they headed? It was the year 1928, when Marsala aristocrats weren't too proud to indulge their curiosity alongside their donkey-riding compatriots in Sicily, where the passing of every foreign motorbike was a social event.

The bike was a two-cylinder American motorbike, a Harley-Davidson. The sidecar was severely oversized, and at any given moment the passenger sitting inside was wedged in by mountains of suitcases and packages. The other two travelers rode the bike proper. As I mentioned before, one of the passengers was myself, while the other was my loyal companion, Gyula Bartha. The young woman in the sidecar was Mimmy, a Hungarian painter, to whom foreign travel was no novelty. We were three travelers, united in our youth, world views, social and economic status, even in our varying moods and great enthusiasm. As evidenced by the scene described above, we were also sorely inexperienced in motor sports, though we sought to hide this sad fact from lookers-on. The adventure of the engine that would not start was the first real "danger" we had faced on the road.

And where on earth did our destination lie, you may wonder. It could hardly have been Trapani, and not even Palermo seemed highly likely. To the casual observer, the direction in which we were headed made little or no sense, unless our plan was to wander about Italy aimlessly.

Our excursion, however, was a much more serious affair than outsiders could have suspected, outsiders who envied us the prospect of a pleasant journey through a few foreign countries, the exhilaration of summer travel, the speed, the redness in the face, and then the enthusiastic sitting down to a well-deserved dinner after having put hundreds of kilometers behind us. Our lot was enviable indeed, travel for the sake of travel past an endless stream of new faces and new cities, and the beauty of nature our constant companion.

But how far could a little company like this go before it was turned back by... what, the sea? Lack of time? Of money? Perhaps satisfaction with having already accomplished enough, creeping boredom or responsibilities at home? My two companions and I, however, imagined we would rise above all these dangers. Our determination was louder and stronger even than the hum of our engine as we sped along, and it was fed with the fuel of enthusiasm and gritty determination. The three Hungarian cyclists were letting the lousy Sicilian roads shake the living daylights out of them in the name of a noble cause—that of traveling around the world on a motorcycle!

Although many people had merely laughed and shrugged it off, our plan was on its way to becoming realized. The roads had not shaken our enthusiasm, our determination was exemplary, and "incidents" like the one above were few and far between.

Around the world on a motorbike!

50-60 countries to explore!

Across five continents!

It had taken so long for the idea to mature in our brains. We had filled numerous days with feverish plans, so many maps with our unintelligible scrawls, and had anxiously scanned the pages of several volumes of encyclopedias before getting started.

We had calculated the odds, measured the length of the entire trip, bought all the necessary supplies (or at least, all we thought was necessary) and made up our minds to stick with our plans for the four long years their realization would require, because we hoped to be home after four long years, at the very most. And we were off.

At the time of our forced stop somewhere on the dusty roads of Sicily, we had been on the road for just a few weeks and were intensely proud that we were in the third foreign country already.

Beginnings

But how did we ever get from Budapest to Sicily? How had the idea of the unconventional journey come to us in the first place?

In the life of Hungarian youth 1927 was one of those fateful years. Although only twenty-five years old, I had started down several paths in life, which had all proven to be dead ends. I had tried my luck at the military academy, officer cadet school, and the Ludovika Academy. Later, deciding to steer back to civilian life, I had become a student at the Technological University, where I supported myself by working as a student counselor. Afterwards, I sought work opportunities in the country, where quiet life in farm and field reawakened my interest in travel. My friend and I had saved up for years in order to realize our dream, but it wasn't until 1927 that we finally said good-bye to Hungary.

We had left for Italy carrying enormous suitcases, unsure of what exactly we were seeking in that southern land. The possibilities of further study, university degrees, working in factories, improving our language skills, and the sheer joy of trying our luck and satisfying wanderlust drew us on, and we weren't expecting to return to Hungary any time soon.

Flipping through my journal from those Italian years, I fail to find one specific driving force behind the decision to leave our country. The following words begin my journal of ten years ago:

"I wish to record every movement of our foreign travels, in order that I may have written records of the bitter and the joyous days to come. If ever my journal is read, I wish the reader to learn from it what it means to leave your homeland on a whim, going against the good advice of all and your own better judgment". My goal was simple, to ride possibilities as they came along, harnessing my youthful desire to see and to learn.

"I cannot know how long my journey will be. I might not fill even half of this notebook, or my journal entries may span the length of years."

We boarded the train on a grim, overcast day. Although our numerous suitcases weighed us down, we took the streetcar to the railway station, wondering what we would ride on our way back. (Little did we know that we would return by motorcycle.) The heat of my excitement was exchanged for cool sobriety when my friend pointed at the porter struggling with our bags and quietly remarked, "Take a good look; that'll be you soon enough." Only after we had actually boarded the train did we realize it was Friday the thirteenth.

We rode through Vienna and Venice and arrived at our first destination, Milan, where we spent four depressing weeks, filled with sad memories and one bitter disappointment hard upon another. We had learnt that college tuition was much higher than in Hungary, that we weren't legally permitted to work in Italy, and even if we had been, there were no jobs to be had. We ran into numerous Hungarians who were all complaining and miserable. After a tour of the city, we went from company to company and visited one factory after another, all in vain.

We actually spent the lion's share of our time at the Hungarian Club, which was the fancy name for old Mr. Rosenfeld's little pub. We were glad to see other Hungarians and realized they had not fared much better than we. In fact, we seemed to have an advantage over them, because we still had our savings from home, savings that we weren't so anxious to spend, however, as we hoped to stay abroad for at least a year. And something could very well turn up in that time. How we pitied the others, who often had nothing but thin soup to fill their stomachs! Hungarian guests at the Club could earn a meal by rolling up their sleeves afterwards and washing dishes.

People at the Club came and went; a single afternoon at Mr. Rosenfeld's pub was filled with more novelty and possibilities than weeks in the company of the Italians. It was a brave new world for us consisting of n'er-do-wells, parasites with an aversion to all forms of work, new arrivals in Italy, a few college students, and travelers who remained strangers even after their departure. Somehow, all Hungarian emigrants found out about the pub and went there just to chat in their native tongue, to sample some traditional dishes, brag about their accomplishments, whatever they may be, in front of other Hungarians or remain on the constant lookout for good advice and patronage.

Our mood got progressively darker as the weeks passed. We hadn't quite reached the depths of despair; we knew, even before coming to Italy that it would be no walk in the park at first. The trouble was that we never made it to the proverbial park, and we were not alone. We had compatriots who had been there for years, still with no prospects in sight.

To make matters worse, we were running out of money, so we seriously began to consider leaving Milan. But where to go next? And how?

I must mention here that the Club was also the favorite meeting place of a curious, bohemian caste of young men who took nothing in life seriously, a special breed of globetrotters. They wandered from country to country, city to city, or simply the streets of Milan and made their money by selling their own photographs and samples of their correspondence. They often made a fair living, got all sorts of discounts at a variety of places and got most of their funds from restaurant and coffee house guests.

Many of the globetrotters were Hungarian youths. Some had been traveling for five or six years, but had hardly three or four countries behind them. They wore elaborate clothing, somewhat reminiscent of Boy Scout uniforms, short pants and tropical hats. Furthermore, multitudes of them boasted that they were traveling around the world on foot; however, they were mostly too lazy to walk to the street corner and back. They complained of competition in their "profession," however, they all managed to make a living one way or another, and altogether rather pleasantly.

There were few parks in Milan, with even fewer benches. In fact, there were two benches to a park at most, but, through a stroke of genius, this proved to be enough. Each bench was constructed of two planks with a space of about 8-10 cm in between, which resulted in sore behinds for those foolish enough to brave sitting down, and even the hardiest did not remain for more than half an hour. And yet our plan to travel around the world on a motorbike was born on just such a bench.

My friend and I had never brought it up in conversation, but the idea of such a journey had crossed each of our minds on numerous occasions. Then one evening, while sitting on a back-breaking bench in Milan, I popped the question to my friend. "What do you think of traveling around the world?"

"I've been thinking about it for a long time, only I didn't dare bring it up," exclaimed my friend Gyula.

Everything went smoothly from then on. Our plans became clearer, and the prospect of the journey loomed large and sure. We realized that with a little skillful planning, we could raise significant funds at the hands of a variety of sponsors. We threw ourselves into feverish planning and the foggy Milan dawn found us still sitting on that awful Milan park bench!

The next day, our planning took a serious turn, and the trip began to seem more and more likely. We decided on the motorbike as our mode of transportation, and we thank our lucky stars to this day that we did. The motorbike seemed like the best choice from the start. We considered both the bike and automobile as possibilities, but while the former promised to be slow and uncomfortable, the latter gas-guzzler was going to be too expensive. But it wasn't until after the trip that we realized just how fortunate our choice had been. In choosing the bike, we would have had to leave a significant amount of supplies behind, and we would not be able to carry all the food and water we desperately needed on the long stretches of our journey far from civilization. But the automobile would simply not have gotten us everywhere we needed to go. You couldn't take a car apart and carry it across a river, the way we did our motorcycle on numerous occasions. And then, the sheer sport value of circumnavigating the globe on a motorbike was far more enticing than simply driving.

Arguments for and against the success of our venture followed in close succession, but somehow, arguments in favor seemed to dominate. We still had enough money to buy a great bike and food and supplies for the first six months of the trip. We planned to be in far-off Asia by the end of those six months, at which point we could begin to make a profit off the materials we had assembled thus far. We planned to sell our photographs, contact various journals and periodicals, and give lectures. Also, once we had a significant number of miles behind us, we could count on the support of the motorcycle factory and various gas and oil companies, as well as the backing of biker clubs and associations.

The next week found us sitting in one of the cabins of the *direttissimo* train, saying farewell to Milan and to all of Italy—at least, for a while.

It wasn't hard for us to leave Milan. We had become painfully aware that we had no prospects there, and the smartest thing for us to do at the time was to start the journey we had been so carefully planning. Our first task was to purchase the right motorcycle. We had visited all the bike shops in Milan, but disappointment followed disappointment. We needed a serious bike for a trip around the world, a brand of bike known the world over, so that no matter where we broke down, we would be able to find replacement parts at local shops. Italian bikes simply did not qualify, and so, although they were cheapest, we were forced to look elsewhere for the perfect solution. American motorcycles seemed the way to go, as they were the most popular and the toughest. Also, to our sorrow, the most expensive. After considering a variety of brands, we agreed that the best choice would be a Harley-Davidson or an Indian.

The high import tax in Italy, however, made it unreasonable for us to buy our bike locally, and after hearing from a number of independent sources that prices were much better in France, we made up our minds to travel to Paris. And motorbike or no motorbike, Paris was an attractive destination. Who said we had to start our bike odyssey in Italy, anyway? Couldn't we choose Paris as our starting point instead, Paris, where motorcycles were cheaper to boot?

And so, on to Paris!

It took us a few days to get our bearings at our new location, but we purchased our bike very soon after becoming acquainted with the City of Lights. Little did we know that we would meet the third member of our company in those few short days. We ran into a nice Hungarian girl in front of the *poste restante* counter at the main Paris post office. The accidental encounter was followed by a pleasant chat, the chat followed by dinner, the dinner by a *rendezvous* the very next day, and the *rendezvous* by the mutual decision to travel together. "Why not?" she asked, and we agreed, "Why not?"

Mimmy, our new friend, was a painter in training from Budapest. She'd left Hungary on a scholarship, afterwards, she was supported by her talent alone. Mimmy had lived in all the major cities of France and Italy, and had visited a number of other European countries and had even made it as far as North Africa. She was a talented artist and had always managed to sell enough paintings to support herself and her inordinate wanderlust. Mimmy was familiar with foreign customs and had a knack for languages. What's more, she was young, modern, and a boyish sportswoman, not one to be deterred by the possible difficulties of our projected journey.

If she was to join us, however, a sidecar was an absolute must. In the end we agreed that a sidecar would do a lot to balance our bike on the lousiest roads, and of course, we could use the extra space for packing significantly more supplies. We chose a Harley-Davidson in the end, and were I to make the journey all over again, I would chose a Harley again with the greatest confidence. It's funny, but I must admit that the sidecar hasn't been paid for to this day. When purchasing the bike, we were drawn to a much more spacious sidecar than came with it, but the sidecar we knew we needed was severely used. We made a deal with the company in the end; they gave us the old sidecar nearly for free, for 50 francs in all, with the condition that we would one day exchange the bike itself for the newest model on the market. Come to think about it, we don't actually owe the company anything, because we never got that new Harley. Nevertheless, we own and use the old sidecar to this day.

Weeks passed with planning and preparations. My first task was definitely learning how to drive a motorcycle. After a few practice sessions, however, I obtained my license with ease. What the driving school officials didn't know was that those practice sessions had involved my close encounter with a wall and a woman cyclist's arched flight into the puddles dotting the road, but after seeing my graceful figure eight, they made out my license without further ado. With the license in hand, I was able to apply for the necessary official documents for international travelers issued by the Automobile Club.

And we were off! We had only what we thought were the most important supplies on board, but who could blame us; we had no experience as world travelers. Who would have thought, for example, that a spade would prove to be much more necessary than a telescope, or that the revolver and small radio would in no way make up for the lack of pots and pans and a strong axe? At the same time, we sported splendid goggles and did not forget to pack the sponges and deerskin necessary for keeping the glorious shiny bike at its shiniest. After all was said and done, no power on this earth could have held us back from our voyage.

Getting Started

In hindsight, I can't even imagine what those few passers-by on the Bois de Boulogne would have thought on that sun-drenched morning had they suspected the extent of our travel plans. I can't help but smile when I remember that the first short stretch of our trip was traveled by taxi and not by motorcycle at all. Our hotel was on Rue de Louvre, but we had left our bike outside the city, in a garage in Neuilly. Neuilly had been the scene of my first attempts at driving the bike, as well; I would never have braved Paris traffic on a bike. Getting out of the taxi, we heaped all our supplies on a bench in the Bois, and I hurried off to get the motorcycle and parked it next to the bench. We finished our packing and got into the saddle of our three-wheeled "iron horse," carefully avoiding Paris and making our way along the outskirts of the city to the road leading south.

Everything went smoothly. My driving was far from professional; however, I was all the more careful. The engine was running well in the brilliant sunshine, and the three of us were ecstatically happy to be on the way at last.

We had not publicized our destination, so nobody knew of our daring plans. In reality, we weren't very sure ourselves of the outcome of the journey. We were curious to know how far we would get, and if we didn't get very far, we weren't very keen on being laughed at.

After a few days of traveling, we were approaching the French border. The quality of the roads got progressively more varied, and we found ourselves being jolted along increasingly as we neared Italy. The quality of the road changed from one kilometer to the next; one moment, we may have been riding along asphalt, then we suddenly found ourselves on a smooth, gravel road, then concrete, then macadam, occasionally a stretch filled with potholes, and these variations followed one another in quick succession. After having made the acquaintance of numerous friendly and courteous Parisians, we encountered the opposite qualities in rural Frenchmen, whom we weren't at all regretful to exchange for the friendly Italians we met in the Alps.

After crossing the Alps, we explored nearly every corner of Italy. Traveling down one side of the large boot-shaped peninsula, we arrived in Sicily via Milan, Bologna, Ancona, Bari, and Brindisi. This was a pleasant journey of exceptional beauty. Our bike was holding out splendidly, and all three of us were becoming progressively better drivers. The weather was ideal, and I can honestly say, never before in our lives had we felt this free. All we needed was on the bike, and we could take the bike anywhere we wished.

We were enchanted by the countless historical monuments and spent entire days within ancient walled cities, visiting every museum and gallery without ever being sated.

And so we journeyed on!

The roads were worst in the south but not even the bumpiest stretches could shake our enthusiasm. We grew to know the country better than any foreigner and the many-storied villages of South Italy no longer held any charm for us. They gave the impression of having been thrown together from scraps of stone left after a great battle. Most of these villages were built on hilltops, and we were forced to exchange the mild, almost spring-like winter days for cold city night and the depths of winter. The smaller towns were absolutely filthy. Those who don't believe our description are advised to visit Chienti, Serracapriole, Torremaggiore, where the conditions will shock even seasoned travelers familiar with the Balkans. In small shops, a wall of thin boards, no higher than a man, separates the counter commercial area from the shopkeeper's bedroom, which is often located right next to the stables, the home of the ubiquitous donkey.

"Where do I empty the dirty water?" I asked the innkeeper's wife after washing up. "Out the window, of course," she answered, astonished at my question, and she hurried over, bucket in hand, to show me how it's done.

A great advantage of country life was all the fresh milk. Cows, or in poorer families, goats, were driven home along the street every evening. Whoever needed milk simply stood at the side of the road, and the animals were milked as they passed by. The cow that ran out of milk was then taken home.

We fell in love with the Italian people. They were good-hearted and altogether lovable. We marveled at the cleanliness and order in larger towns and admired their beautiful castles and churches. *Bibitas,* sparkling in the various colors of the rainbow, quenched our thirst, and we were delighted by the magnificent fruits. Whenever we had worked up our appetite for sweet grapes or golden oranges, we simply stopped at the side of the road, and my friend, Gyuszi, cried in his deep bass voice, *"Un poco de frutta, Signore or Signora!"* Locals bearing the choicest fruits soon surrounded us, and only upon repeated urging would they agree to accept any money in return. After a while, we stopped being so adamant about paying for our fruit.

We crossed to Messina at Reggio Calabria and circumnavigated the entire island of Sicily. The roads were neglected; giant cacti and wild geraniums lined the stone fences. Making our way across veritable forests of olive, orange, and lemon trees, we finally arrived in Taormina, whose beauty surpassed that of any sight we had seen up to that moment. The blue of the sky and the blue of the sea, flowers of a thousand hues in between, the green of the palm trees lining countless tiny inlets between the cliffs jutting out to sea, harmonized in a symphony of color. It seemed to us like a fairy-tale world made all the more beautiful by the work of human hands in the form of magnificent hotels, whose terraces jutted out over the tremendous depths. The snowy peak of the Etna, looking very much like the head of an old man peacefully puffing at his pipe, presided over the whole scene.

Of course, later we encountered landscapes that were much less attractive. The mountains of Sicily aren't always green; in fact, most of the time, they are bald and barren. It seemed to us that God himself had shaved those ugly peaks with a giant razor. It was in Palermo that we stopped to rest, after the "dangerous" adventure described at the beginning of the chapter. We visited the Hungarian consul, whose hospitality and kindness were notable, whose children, however, although born in Hungary of Hungarian parents, spoke little Hungarian. We were also struck by the consul's ignorance of which parts of Transylvania our country lost as a result of the Trianon Peace Treaties.

Following our stay in Palermo, we traveled up the opposite shore of the boot-shaped peninsula, making our way north. The geographic layout of

Naples was grand, but we must note that the roads in Pompeii, surviving from the Roman times, were better paved than the streets of Naples. The countless beauties of Rome left a permanent mark in our consciousness. It was in Rome that we realized how unique our travel plans were, because we were able to obtain a short audience with Il Duce without much ado. We only spent a few minutes in Mussolini's presence; and he duly wished us a *"buon viaggio"* after a few polite questions, but we did come away with a precious autograph, which is now one of the prize pieces in our collection.

Our next few days were spent on the island of Sardinia, and we returned to France via the Riviera. A road lined with cities and landscapes of indescribable beauty led us through Menton, Nice, Cannes, and Toulon. We soaked in the charm of each city for a few days before entering Spain via Marseille.

Entering Spain was no easy matter. We very quickly found out that all foreign vehicles were subject to fees of two pesetas per day. Little did we know that we would make a second tour of Spain eight years later, towards the close of our odyssey. When we first entered Spain, however, the country was still ruled by Alfonso XIII and cut a vastly different picture from the one today.

The best roads were in the northern regions of Spain. As we progressed towards the South, the roads got gradually worse. In some parts, huge construction projects made the going more difficult, but mostly, it was the numerous potholes that hindered our progress. Road repair meant filling the potholes with large stones and waiting for passing automobiles and time to wear them down to perfection. Even in places where the roads were acceptable, we were greeted by a veritable deluge of mud every time we left a town or village, and thus, making our way across any type of human settlement was a struggle. Occasionally, even the townspeople worked against us; to prevent cars from speeding, they would dig large holes themselves along the stretch of road that led through the town.

We reached the southern lands in orange season. The roads were filled with giant, two-wheeled carts brimming with ripe fruit. The wheels of the carts sank deep into the mud of the roads, leaving break-neck furrows behind them. Although the kind carters often filled our sidecar with free oranges, this did not help the road situation in the least.

Our travels took us to the land of the Basks and Catalans, and on to Andalusia via Galicia. Cart and horse drivers did not observe any driving rules we could discern, so we were forced to be extra careful on the roads.

On the whole, Spain was an ugly land, with very little natural beauty. The cities, however, were splendid and well-kept. Almost every city and town was the site of ambitious building projects; the Spaniards were striving hard to catch up with the rest of Europe. New and old mixed in charming and unexpected ways; we were forced to smile upon entering an avant-garde café where old men wrapped in scarves perched on futuristic furniture, and chattered endlessly, occasionally turning to spit on the shiny floor without showing the least sign of remorse. A waiter was forced to stand guard in front of the new revolving doors to prevent hordes of street urchins from using it as a merry-go-round.

The only hotels proper we found were located in the cities. In rural areas, the inn-like, but run-down *posada* took the place of the urban hotel. Our nights in the *posadas* were peppered by the sounds of horses and donkeys from underneath, but what really kept us awake was the overwhelming smell and, of course, the bedbugs.

The poverty of the people was especially remarkable in the southern regions. Most of the land was barren, and the landowners, who often ruled over territories the size of counties, used the entire area for raising bulls. Long lines of beggars filled the streets, grabbing every foreign-looking passer-by.

We always had to make sure to stock up on gasoline while we were still in the big cities. Although many Spaniards owned automobiles, country roads were virtually empty of cars. The dearth of car traffic in rural areas made Madrid and Barcelona seem even more cosmopolitan. The largest cities were wealthy and crowded; the shops were filled with people, whose pockets were, in turn, weighed down with silver coins. Countless street vendors used amplifiers to lure customers and made very good money.

Spanish people were, on the whole, honest, and contented despite their poverty and kind to strangers, although by no means subservient. They never allowed the arrival of foreigners to affect the rhythm of their daily lives. The barber, while giving us a shave, ate two bananas, then proceeded to clean his teeth and smoke a cigarette.

Spaniards woke late and went to bed late. Not a single store opened before ten in the morning, and most people ate dinner around 10 p.m. Shows at the cinema or in theaters often lasted until past midnight, occasionally ending at one-thirty in the morning.

Coffeehouses brimmed with people all day long. Women, however, were a rare sight after a certain hour in the evenings; we saw very few walking about on the street and none at all in the cafes. Spanish men rarely took their families out in the evenings and often made remarks or joked around with women who happened to be walking by at a later hour.

It didn't take us long to get used to our newfound popularity. We began to taste the sweetness of being "somebodies." As the first newspaper articles detailing our plans appeared, our hotel rooms began to fill with journalists, and the curious crowd that greeted us every time we arrived in a new place grew progressively larger. Even though our bike did not yet stick out the way it would later in our journey, the foreign license plate and the layers of dust or mud made the extent of our plans clear. We were the center of attention especially when Mimmy drove the bike. *"Chico o chica?"* people asked, boy or girl?

Our *chica* was just as happy with our progress thus far as we were. On the whole, we had no reason to complain; we had covered good ground and perfected our driving skills. Whenever something did go wrong with the bike, we quickly fixed it and were on our way before we knew it.

We did have two significant incidents in Spain, however. The first occurred somewhere on the road between Alcoy and Alicante. Mimmy was driving and, after reaching the base of a sharp decline and encountering a sudden bend in the road, she completely lost her head. The sudden twist in the road happened to be on the sidecar side of the bike, so the entire vehicle tipped over in the other direction, and, within a split second, all three wheels were spinning in the direction of the sky. Mimmy had enough time to jump to the side, and I slid off the back passenger seat just in time, but poor Gyuszi flew out of the sidecar and traced a graceful arch all the way to the ground. To our great good luck, nobody was hurt, so we simply righted our vehicle and were soon on our way again. Only Mimmy's pride was hurt, and so she had no inclination to drive for the next couple of days.

The second incident happened in a tiny village where we had stopped for lunch. The restaurant owner was demanding that we pay 25 pesetas for the three lunches, a sum we considered ridiculous. Meals were cheaper in Madrid's finest hotels; at a place like this, we were expecting a sum of 6 to 8 pesetas at the very most. And so, I refused to pay.

"Take me to the police!" I told the woman.

"Let's go!" she answered.

The lieutenant wasn't at the station, and so the single policeman present had to keep one of us under arrest until his boss arrived to make sure we didn't get off without paying. That "one of us" was myself, and I sat under lock and key for an hour, meditating on my run-in with the law in my dirty, narrow little cell. I showed no remorse, however, and doggedly waited on for the lieutenant.

The interrogation began as soon as he arrived. We were asked to show our passports and other personal documents, and the restaurant owner filed her complaint. Then I filed mine.

"How much would you be willing to pay?" asked the lieutenant.

"Two pesetas per person, at the most," I responded.

"What price did you have in mind?" he asked, turning to the woman.

"Twelve pesetas, at the very least."

"Are you willing to give this woman what she is asking for?" he asked me.

"Most certainly not," I answered.

This interchange was followed by a long argument, during which the lieutenant alternately painted a picture of the direst poverty for us and sharply rebuked the woman in a torrent of Spanish. In the end, we gave the woman ten pesetas, which seemed to satisfy both her and the police. After we left, I reflected on how unlikely it was that she got even half of the money after the policeman was through with her. She may even have been fined.

The most beautiful region in all of Spain is Andalusia. We arrived at the time of the great festivals. There are festivals and holidays to be had all over Spain, as every little town and village has its own patron saint and all events in the Church calendar related to that saint are holidays. All the townspeople take part in the procession; the more religiously inclined drop to their knees on the street, even in large towns like Bilbao, everyone in the street, from passers-by to merchants, policemen, soldiers, all genuflect with reverence. Young people dance around the statue of the saint, peppering the celebration with salvo after salvo. While a portion of the population attends mass, a brass band stands outside the church and enthusiastic young people dance to the newest foxtrots. The dancing is followed by bullfights in the afternoon and fireworks in the evening.

We made our way through Seville, Malaga, Granada, and Alicante, marveling at the loveliness of the land, the Mediterranean temperament of the people, the beauty of the women, and the roses, which filled not only the gardens, but spilled out onto the street through the windows and crept up the walls of the houses. Above us shone the ever-blue skies of Andalusia!

We made time for a few grand bull fights and did not forget to get a shave from the barber of Seville before crossing the bridge over the River Guadiana and entering a new country altogether: Portugal!

Portugal is, without a question, the westernmost country of Europe, yet we were at a loss to find traces of the cultured European West. After having visited Spain, we were prepared for even greater poverty and backwardness, both of which were present, yet in the eyes of the people, immaterial. The Portuguese were a cheerful and outgoing people. They were happy, because they contented themselves with the simple things in life and let tomorrow take care of today's worries, living every day to its fullest, one day at a time. In the central regions of the country, we encountered numerous deserted little villages, with hardly any people and no shops at all. We had no access to food or even a glass of water, unless we made up our minds to knock on a family's door. The coast, however, was paradisiacal, lined for hundreds of kilometers by soft yellow sand. We passed seaside resorts of the highest quality but entirely without a sign of a single tourist.

Wherever we stayed, we were stuffed to the gills with salt fish. Salt fish is the national food in Portugal, or, we might even say, wine is the national food, complimented by salt fish, sausages, sardines, cheese, rice, and potatoes. After a short stretch back in Spain, we arrived at Gibraltar, only to be disappointed. In place of the awe-inspiring British military post, we found a sleepy little Spanish town. There were, nonetheless, numerous British soldiers stationed at Gibraltar, but only a few of them could be seen walking about on the streets, because the barracks were located on the outskirts of the town and the fortress seemed to seamlessly melt into the cliffs overlooking the strait.

We could see the opposite shore from where we stood, the blue hills of Africa from a distance. After sailing across the strait, we landed in another small Spanish town by the name of Algeciras, from which we traveled on to Ceuta, located in Spanish Morocco. Our ship was small, but we made good progress and crossed the strait in a mere hour and a half. The ocean was quiet, and we had ample time to reflect on our journey as the keel of the ship sliced through the waves.

We were soon to land on a new continent, and our dreams would continue to unfold in their realization. In just a few weeks, we could be in Asia, or the Near East, at the very least. We were thankful that no great obstacles had hindered our progress until that moment, and that we had been able to follow our meticulous travel plans. We all realized, however, that as soon as we set foot in Africa, we would be in a different world. Our plan was to cross Northern Africa by bike, and make our way into Egypt, then through the countries of Asia Minor until we reached India. The year was 1928, and we were very anxious to reach Asia.

Counting Hungary, we had crossed six countries, so we had something to be proud of already. Then, we imagined, few people had undertaken extensive motor travel in Africa. Our Harley was working great, my journals and notes were extensive and our knowledge of foreign languages was steadily improving. Then there were two treasured memories we could always be proud of: our short audience with Mussolini and our visit to our own Queen Zita in Lequeitio.

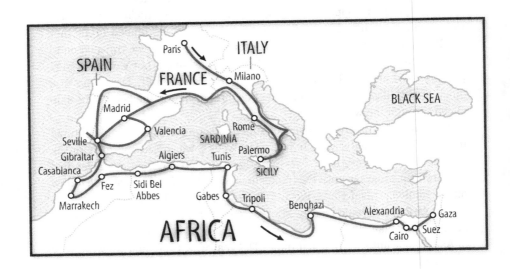

Across Africa

Moroccan Trails

Our small boat, *Miguel Primo de Rivera* (although someone must have painted over the white letters of its name since we last sailed in it) floated serenely into the harbor at Ceuta. A whole new world opened before our wondering eyes. Although only a narrow strait separated it from familiar Europe, we were overwhelmed by the novelty of Africa. Even while we sailed on the boat, the feeling that we were entering a new world never left us. The crowns of tall date palms waved gently to and fro in the wind, as if in greeting. In the harbor, the brown of storehouses and piers set off numerous moving white dots, which were Arabs, clad in flowing, white garments. Their robes flapped noticeably at every move, and movement there was in abundance, because our ship was just landing.

As soon as our feet touched dry land, we were inundated by hundreds of eager Arabians, as were our fellow passengers. Arabian porters, tour guides, hotel receptionists, shoe shiners, money changers, and a vast assortment of people belonging to other professions surrounded us, until we could hardly move. Our bike was unloaded shortly after we had landed, and then we were ready to tackle the highways and byways of this new continent.

Things weren't as simple as we had hoped. We had travel documents granting us free movement throughout the territory of tiny Spanish Morocco, but our passage into the French regions was not assured. Although the World War had been over for ten whole years, the French were still hesitant when granting travel rights to their former enemies. We were forced to send a telegram to the governor stationed in Rabat.

Our difficulties were soon solved when we received papers granting us access to all French colonies and protectorates in Africa. With our new documents in hand, we headed east. Our hope was to travel around the world of course, by keeping due east, but we were forced to travel north on south on various occasions, and we anticipated that a time would come when we might have to "regress" towards the west.

Although anxious to progress, we were in no hurry to miss the beautiful sights along the way. We visited nearly all the regions of Morocco and passed through every city or town worthy of mention. After Ceuta came Tetuan, then we headed south to Casablanca via Tangier and Rabat. Following this portion of our journey, we found ourselves near the desert—real Africa—upon visiting Marrakech at the foot of the great Atlas Mountains. From Marrakech, we were forced to turn back for a stretch, and it wasn't until we arrived in Meknes that we were able to head due east again, passing through Fez, Taza, Algiers, and Tunis.

It was in Tangier that we readied our bike for the long, arduous journey. Belongings we no longer felt were necessary we mailed home. We carefully weighed the importance of each item and kept only what was indispensable. On the other hand, we were also forced to buy a few items we felt we would need in the coming weeks and months: lengths of strong rope suitable for towing, an enlarged gas tank and water, in large amounts. The best way to transport water was in water sacks, which boasted a natural and infinitely simple self-cooling mechanism. As the water seeped out in tiny quantities, the sides of the sack remained wet, and so, however hot the air around us, the constant evaporation kept our water supply at a very acceptable temperature. It was really as we traveled Africa that we realized what a blessing the sidecar was proving to be. There was much more space for our supplies, and the bike remained balanced even as we rode across unsteady sand.

Then again, the sand roads caused us little trouble at first. We left the worst roads behind us as we crossed the border from Spanish into French Morocco. French roads were first class, almost without exception. Most of the main roads were covered in asphalt or stone that had been beautifully flattened by a steamroller, and we often reached our Harley's speed limit while riding them.

A hundred kilometers before reaching the French-Moroccan border, we remembered that we needed to be careful, because Morocco was far from peaceful. The Riff-Kabil uprising was in full swing, and both the Spanish and the French were thoroughly engaged in countering local guerilla attacks. Both the French and the Spanish were reluctant to risk the lives of their own, yet the nearby hills were the sites of daily bloody battles. We came within 60 km of Ouezzan, which was then the site of another fierce encounter between the Riffs and the French. The roads were filled with army vehicles; buses carrying civilians were heavily guarded by soldiers armed to the teeth.

In the vicinity of Marrakech, we no longer knew what exactly to expect. Roads leading into the Sahara were deserted, the local Arab population unpredictable. We were given the friendly suggestion to cover our tropical hats with white headscarves. As the rest of our clothing was white, we hoped to pass as fellow countrymen to Arabs on horseback, who might be viewing us from a distance.

We were enriched by numerous experiences on the way. After arriving home in Hungary, we often remembered the African portion of our journey fondly. In Africa, every moment of every day brought something new. European travelers to Morocco were never bored.

It didn't take us long to develop an affection for Arabs. We felt very close in spirit to these noble-minded people, who bore in their hearts a great love for their country. They showed respect to each other and deference to their elders; their polite, quiet way of speaking and serious, almost aristocratic gestures won our hearts. We were filled with regret that this race, which had immense territories to call its own, enjoyed self-determination in none.

We encountered black Africans everywhere, although they were most common in port cities. The mingling of black and Arab blood produced skin colors ranging from almost jet black to a light brown. Those of mixed race did not prove to be half as likeable and or to possess even a portion of the excellent qualities of pure Arabs. Nevertheless, they were clad in the same burnooses. Arabs, on the whole, were lanky and large, almost fearful to look at, although this fearful quality mostly proved to be skin deep, as they were truly gentle on the inside.

Both their towns and their villages were vastly different from those we were used to in Europe. Most large settlements were comprised of three parts. The *Medina,* or old town, was the Arabian quarter, which was often surrounded by a modern new town, made up of a few European-style houses and shops. The third district, the *Mellah,* was where the Jews lived.

All the houses were white, as well as the city walls. In addition to the four- or five-layered walls surrounding each town, smooth white walls lined even the narrowest of streets. Windows and doors faced inward, onto the courtyard, and so it proved to be difficult indeed to see the city for the walls. Had it not been for the occasional tiny shop carved into the monotony of the white walls, we would have been surrounded by walls on all sides.

Tangier, Marrakech, and Fez were the three most interesting Moroccan cities, the latter two being the most Arabian in character, while Tangier was the most mixed. We traveled to Tangier from Tetouan along the winding paths of a mountainous district. The city and its vicinity belonged to a neutral zone, an area in which all the superpowers strove to maintain their neutrality. In other words, Italy, Spain, France, and England all feared that strategically important locations would pass to the enemy. They all would have loved to have control over Tangier. Tangier was a city that had changed hands many times throughout history. Besides Phoenician and Roman rule, it had experienced Byzantine, Spanish, Gothic, and Arabian dominance. In the fifteenth century, Tangier briefly passed to the Portuguese, who lost it to the Spanish, who in turn were forced to relinquish the city to the English. It wasn't until

1860 that it came under Arabian rule yet again. At the time this book was written, it belonged to everyone and no one. Although the official languages were Spanish, French, and English, Arabic proved to be most common.

We had a choice between the postage stamps of three nations when we mailed our letters from Tangier, and paying for the stamps proved to be no problem, as over a hundred types of currency were in use. Money changers set up their stands on each street corner and in front of every shop. Arabs from the interior of the country brought entire sacks filled with a variety of foreign silver coins.

The confusion in stamps and currency reflected the mixed quality of the people who inhabited this region. The few European outfits were lost in a sea of burnooses, caftans, rags, or near nakedness; turbans and hats were outnumbered by a veritable sea of red fezes. All this confusion in dress and currency was complemented by the jumble of languages reminiscent of the Tower of Babel.

One striking feature of this new world was the constant attention given to tourists. It proved to be a good idea to pick up a few words of Arabic and attempt to use them, even if our knowledge was severely limited. A single well-placed word in Arabic could prove to be very useful to us in our attempt to rid ourselves of overly helpful would-be tour guides. In this respect, Tangier was no different from any other African city we visited. *"Tzirer, tzirer"* the shoe shiners cried every step of the way. Hotel receptionists and innkeepers loudly promoted their respective institutions. Others offered to change our money or enthusiastically described the important sights of the city; still others suggested we board boats, visit the theater, or enjoy the graces of beautiful girls. Certain street vendors followed us around hours on end in an attempt to sell us their tiny pearls, old coins, silk, "genuine" ivory, carpets, ties, or linen clothing. I would tire myself more than they tired me, were I to attempt to describe how many different people we had to rid ourselves of during our stay in Africa.

The crowds, the color, the hustle and bustle of Tangier were characteristic of all the cities of Northern Africa; Tunis, Algiers, Tripoli, and Cairo were no different. As we gradually got used to the busy streets, we stopped hearing the cry of the vendors and would-be tour guides, and our hands reached almost mechanically into our pockets to take out the small coins we had prepared for the beggars or shoe shiners. It took only a moment for our shoes to be just as dusty as before the cleaning, but there were crowds of Arabian children anxious to dust them every step of the way. They did their job whether we liked it or not, whether our shoes were dirty or not. There was no way to evade them, but in trying to shoo them off, we would simply have exasperated ourselves.

We left this wonderful city without visiting any of the casinos or opium dens. Leaving the clusters of white houses and the blue of the sea behind, we made our way across Morocco's green belt, its mountains covered with lush vegetation. The only color constant on our trip was the deep blue of the cloudless sky.

We made our way south and reached the capital, Rabat, after crossing the dry basin of the Oued ben Regreg. Leaving Rabat, we headed to Casablanca. The roads were a joy to travel. There was no sand to worry about; the weather was a bit on the warm side, but our thoughts turned to winter in Hungary in an effort to appreciate the warmth of Morocco.

It was in Rabat that we got a glimpse of the sultan of Morocco—an unforgettable experience. The palace stood behind a dusty, uneven open area that looked like it might have been used for cattle grazing, but had historically served as an extensive parade ground. Had it not been for the Moorish architectural style, we might have mistaken the building for a medieval castle. The guards stiffly saluted our old French patron, and we soon found ourselves inside the impregnable complex. Flowers, roses, fountains, and black guards in colorful uniforms framed the castle, while the corridors were crowded with visitors. There was a celebration about to unfold, and we were only a small part in the vast audience.

We stood before the sultan in a crowd of Arabs, Frenchmen, American tourists, and handful of consuls and officials. After a few moments of head-nodding and well-placed phrases in Arabic, we all marched out into the courtyard. The sultan was dressed in simple traditional attire. Those who passed by him and managed to get close enough covered his hands, feet, and clothing with kisses.

The celebration was exotic and chaotic. It began with a parade of soldiers in colorful uniforms and sizeable bands of musicians followed by spearmen with drawn swords, riding horses of impressive beauty, who were in turn followed by courtiers. The courtiers were a motley crew; in fact, we had trouble deciding whether they were clowns, priests, or ministers. Their long, flowing shirts were brilliantly colored but showed wear and were visibly torn.

The sultan sat in a gorgeous glass carriage. The Arabian onlookers threw themselves to the ground emitting loud shouts wherever he passed. The sultan entered the royal mosque. His entire retinue followed, but foreigners weren't allowed inside for the religious ceremony. As we left the palace the uproar emerging from the mosque grew in intensity and sounded to us like a furious quarrel, but in the end, it was probably nothing more than the enthusiastic response of the crowd to the sultan's greeting.

Leaving Casablanca, we traveled 240 km before reaching the southernmost Moroccan city on our journey, Marrakech, population 100,000, which was, without a doubt, the most fascinating city in the country. At first, we rode through fertile land, where the green of various crops made waves like the sea, but as we progressed, the degree of poverty and desolation increased. Crowds of beggars lined the streets of tiny, insignificant Arabian villages on our way to the gigantic forest of 90,000 palms, behind which lay the renowned city of Marrakech.

Beyond Marrakech lay the Atlas Mountains. It was not advisable for foreigners to enter the mountainous regions. The snow-capped mountains were an enchanting sight in the unbearable heat. Behind the mountains, we knew, lay the vast Sahara...

Marrakech and Fez had retained their Arabic character, because they were the Moroccan cities with the smallest European populations. In Casablanca and Morocco, the ratio of European foreigners to indigenous Arabs had been one to one, but in Marrakech and Fez, there was a total of 3,000 white Europeans out of a population of 100,000. We were virtually run down by black African and Arabic locals upon our arrival. As we stood on the main square, we were slowly ringed in by a huge crowd of curious onlookers and had difficulty getting to our hotel. Thousands of Arabs milled about on the main square, which was framed by numerous tiny stands, where buying and selling, trading, recreation and good cheer took place. Occasionally, a herd of camels would pass through. In other corners of the square, a few small children stood guard over a hundred donkeys. The Arabs in their white burnooses walked about or squatted in large groups, listening to storytellers, watching and laughing over a monkey at his tricks or listening attentively to the simple melodies of a primitive band. To us, this was unsurpassed Africa! Vendors in long rows attracted customers with their ear-piercing cries, others recited prayers standing next to camels. The crowds and the hubbub, the desert Arabs on their horses, Jews and black Africans riding donkeys, the numerous tiny houses and shops, and the winding, labyrinthine streets made a lasting impression on us.

The Arabian bazaar, or *souk*, was the inescapable highlight of every town or city. Those of one profession clustered in the same street; for example, there was a street lined with what seemed to be hundreds of tiny slipper shops. Slippers were perhaps the most popular and best-selling items in the entire bazaar. There were *souks* in every Arab city, but the biggest and the most varied was located in Marrakech, which was the commercial center of the entire South. Arabs wore slippers, most often made of yellow leather, occasionally enhanced by artistic embroidery. The next street over belonged to the bakers. The shops were so tiny that it was often impossible to enter; the vendor sat in his tiny corner and held out his wares for sale. There were a few women among the bread-vendors, but the other professions were, without exception, in male hands. Later, we strayed among the fruit-sellers and cut our way across heaps of lemons and dates and entire mountains of St. John's Bread. Most spice shops and vendors selling household goods were best stocked in soap, and, unexpectedly, kerosene lamps. The kerosene vendors, however, were located in a different street. The chandlers' row was hard upon a street full of haberdashery and dry-goods stores. Most haberdashers carried large quantities of silk and linen. The fine linen for burnooses came in a variety of textures and varied in quality; however, striped or plain burnooses of the simplest cut sold very well. No European tourist can walk down the street of leather workers without investing in their beautiful pillows, wallets, tobacco pouches, or any other wares imaginable that could be made of leather. Most of the leather goods were embellished by embroidered designs in silver and gold.

The *souk* belonging to the jewelers, gold- and silversmiths, was located at the center of the bazaar complex and usually manned by Jews. The blows of their hammers could be heard entire streets away. Most of the jewelry available was of silver, but beside the masterful necklaces, bracelets, anklets, and earrings, we were amazed to discover harnesses and intricate swords, including the famous Berber scimitars. All Arabs had scimitars at their sides; the weapons of the poor were made of copper or steel, while the swords of the rich were gold or silver. Earrings, most popularly of the large, round variety, and rings, occasionally fitted with large precious stones, were mostly carved in front of the passers-by.

But who could list all the sights of a real, Arabian bazaar? We ourselves spent hour upon hour in the *souk* and felt we had seen but a portion of all there was to see. Our next stop was the street of the blacksmiths and braziers, streets that resounded and veritably trembled with the constant blows of hammers. This was where large cauldrons as well as pots and pans for every day use were made, mostly out of a reddish copper. The street of the perfumers was much more discrete. Walking along, we were enveloped in a thick cloud of heady eastern fragrances. The perfumeries were very fine; as we entered, we found ourselves treading on delicate Persian rugs and were promptly served coffee by the shopkeeper. There was no sign of the hawkish commercial spirit of the rest of the market. Here we were allowed to browse through the wares at our ease, and even if we chose to leave without purchasing a single thing, we were treated with respect and urged to down another portion of coffee on our way out. The shops of the incense vendors were located close by; these tiny shops sold both incense and a variety of meticulously crafted little censors. After passing through this fragrant sector of the market, we passed the rug makers, ivory carvers, and vendors selling strings of pearls or simply souvenirs. The tiny shops we encountered doubled as workshops. Then came the tailors, the shoemakers, the saddlers and harness makers, potters, and mat makers. As we made our way back to the hotel, images of vendors and exotic wares followed one another in rapid succession in our dizzied and overwhelmed minds.

We devoted the next day to the exploration of the Djemaa El Fua, the largest square in Marrakech, which also served as a marketplace to all the inhabitants of Southern Morocco. The Djemaa El Fua was an immense, treeless space where tens of thousands of Moroccans gathered every night to enjoy themselves or simply walk about. When we arrived, the entire square was white with Arabs, and this great mass of white wasn't still for a moment, but heaved from side to side, very much like the waves of the ocean. Hundreds of curious onlookers surrounded the merest clown, who hoped to attract further attention by screaming as loud as he was able. When he ran out of breath, he would resort to a drum or a whistle to do what his tired voice no longer could. The racket of drums and whistles heralded every performance, which could not begin until a crowd of decent size stood by in anticipation. In the end, the most common performance was the passing round of the collection plate, which occurred with great frequency before, during, and after the performance. The audience was ideal; they were grateful, generous, and amazingly easy to please. Thirty to forty such performances could be in progress at any given time on the square; the performers varied from strong men to storytellers, dancers and musical ensembles, but fakirs, men bearing monkeys, and snake charmers did not pass as rarities either. We ourselves waited twenty minutes next to a snake charmer, but at the end of the twenty minutes, it seemed we were no closer to seeing his performance than we had been at the beginning. On the other hand, the snake would "accidentally" run loose every three minutes, which resulted in much excitement and running on the part of the audience and considerable wailing and screaming on the part of the snake charmer. He caught the snake every time, and, after sighing heavily and placing the snake back in its narrow box, the charmer would pass his plate around for the umpteenth time. As soon as the plate made its way back to the snake charmer, the snake would mysteriously "get away" yet again.

Besides the snake charmer, we were entertained by fire-eaters, strong men who tore apart chains with their bare hands, and very amateur magicians. The fakirs mostly prayed unceasingly, except for the brief intervals of time during which they passed around their collection plates. There were also tiny theaters, manned by one or two actors, who nevertheless drew a crowd.

The square was crowded until late into the night. Occasionally a flute player, with his quiet melodies, or a storyteller managed to retain the attention of his public until dawn, but finally the square filled with quiet, and the remaining loiterers departed, wrapped in their shawls. Then darkness and

Moroccan snake charmer

silence prevailed for a few hours on the great square in Marrakech. Although we left Marrakech and all of Africa a long time ago, I can still see the Djemaa El Fua when I close my eyes.

Following our visit to Marrakech, we headed straight for the sea, because our intention was to make the necessary return trip along another route, via the cities of Mogador, Safi, and Mazagan. We reached Mogador after riding 185 kilometers through a barren wilderness. Every time we stopped, our vehicle was immediately surrounded by a crowd of emaciated beggars whose wails were heartrending.

It was in these three cities that we became better acquainted with Moroccan Jews. Every Moroccan city thus far had had its own Mellah, or Jewish quarter, but in this corner of the country, almost half of the population was Jewish. We ourselves lodged at a Jewish hotel across from a row of synagogues.

The Moroccan Jews we met were poor Sephardim, anxious for a chance to immigrate to Europe. Very few of the Jews were merchants or worked in the commercial sphere; they were mostly quiet and hard-working. Things had gone poorly for them before French rule, and even at the time we passed through, Arabs hated them with fanatic hatred. Under the French regime, however, Arabs no longer had the power to divest Jews of their property or wares, as they had done before, under Arab rule, when no day passed but a Jew or two were beheaded. Jews were easy to recognize by their clothing. Their shirts reached to their knees and were complemented by white pants.

Over the shirt, most wore a small coat or a vest; men covered their heads with red fezes. Stockings and shoes completed the outfit; the stockings of the well-to-do were of silk and their shoes patent leather.

Industries involving exotic oriental goods (leather goods, ivory carvings, metal works) were in the hands of the Jews, who, for the most part, did not speak European languages; many spoke only Hebrew and were entirely ignorant of the Arabic spoken around them.

Jewish women were, for the most part, fat and ugly. Young people, however, tried to keep abreast of the times, and so Jewish girls were modern, attractive, pretty, and amiable. All Jewish women, young and old, were heavily made up; in this they differed from the Arab counterparts, as well as in their lack of a veil. Their clothing was otherwise similar to that of Arab women: baggy, Turkish style pants on the bottom and burnooses on top, mostly made of silk rather than linen.

Upon our arrival in Mazagan, which lay 320 km north of Safi, we were once again generously welcomed by curious young Jews, who showed great interest in Hungary, especially in the capital, Budapest, which for them was synonymous with heaven. We were hard put to answer all of their enthusiastic questions.

In the evening, a few Jewish boys and girls visited us at our hotel. We spent some very pleasant hours together and broke out in song sometime towards dawn. After a few French chansons, they treated us to Jewish melodies and then unanimously agreed that we should teach them a Hungarian folk song. "Something cheerful, Mademoiselle," they cried, turning to Mimmy.

Mimmy had a mischievous idea. She wrote out the Hungarian text for them, using French phonetics and hummed the melody again and again, until it stuck. Soon, young Jews of the entire city were glibly singing, *"Erguère, berguère, chocheberguère..."* When we translated the Hungarian text into French for them at the time of our parting, they laughed uncontrollably.

We headed north from Mazagan in an excellent mood, turning our steering wheel in any direction we pleased. With the passing of each day, we felt ourselves just a little bit closer to achieving our ultimate goal, but at the same time, we strove to seize the day each and every day. The thought of traveling by boat or train became more and more outrageous. We would never have enjoyed so many opportunities to meet new people and discover new lands had we traveled by any other mode of transportation, and neither would we have had this sense of liberty.

Then again, riding African trains was no tempting prospect. The tiny locomotives, puffing and wheezing along, seemed like mere toys in our eyes. The rails were inconceivably narrow and schedules erratic at best. Most trains were comprised of freight wagons, yet they were invariably filled with people, who squatted on the steps, the roof of the train, and even on the links between the cars for lack of a better way to travel. We saw Arabs and soldiers sitting on heaps of wares, sometimes literally on top of each other. The delicate rails weren't even attached to the ground; they were simply laid down wherever the train needed to go, however, this instability in the rails posed no danger considering the speed at which the trains generally traveled. What's more, trains never traveled at night; they slept at the various stations along with the passengers waiting for morning. Our motorbike, on the contrary, went where we wanted it to go, and when we wanted it to. Very few mechanical problems arose, and they no longer frightened us.

Passing through Casablanca, we paid special attention to the luxurious European quarter. Such European quarters, referred to as "new cities," sprang up next to almost every African city, generally outside the established city walls. Of course, they could not be compared to European cities; they were colonial settlements only a few years old. The new houses were built in the native style; the roofs were flat, the walls a brilliant white and the gardens filled with palm trees and other southern flora. Some of these new houses were veritable palaces, but they were never more than two stories tall, but they were modern, bright, and brand new. The streets were wide and very straight, often lined with great metropolitan shops. The only thing missing was perhaps the occasional streetcar, but hoards of cars and buses made up for the lack of streetcars. The flow of urban cars and buses was interrupted by the occasional appearance of a colossal, dusty, long-distance bus so crowded that some passengers were forced onto the roof. Out of a population of 120,000, there were 50,000 Europeans residing in Casablanca, but the size of the "new city" far exceeded that of the old.

We were charmed to discover two threshing machines that had come all the way from Hungary; parked side by side, they were reminders of the economic expo that had taken place the week before.

After leaving Casablanca, we found ourselves in Spanish Morocco once again. Before reaching the border, we encountered a European man wearing a sports shirt and linen pants and waving at us frantically. We pulled over, and he addressed us in faultless English, "Take me to Ceuta, please."

"To Larache, if you like," I answered him, switching to French to explain that we were hoping to return to Fez via Larache. His French was poor, and his English became more and more suspect as we traveled along, although he claimed he was an Englishmen from Gibraltar who had run out of money and was desperately trying to find a way to get home.

We couldn't find it in our hearts to refuse him. The way wasn't long, there was space for another passenger in the sidecar, and besides, Europeans outside Europe tended to stick together much more than in the Old World. We even gave him something to eat on the way, as he looked like he hadn't eaten in a very long time. When we reached the border, we were greeted by a French official, whose presence seemed to make our new passenger nervous. The official looked at our man in his sports shirt, ripped his shirt at the collar and shouted, *"Deserteur!"* His cry brought two armed soldiers running. They headed straight for our companion.

And so we found out we had encountered a deserter. The only institution a white man in Africa could have deserted was, of course, the Foreign Legion. It had taken the border patrol a single glance to determine that he did not truly belong to our party; he might even have received word of the desertion beforehand. The matter had become as clear as day when our companion's white sports shirt was torn away to reveal the typical striped shirt of the legionnaires. We soon found out that the poor man was actually German, but he had been too afraid to tell even us. This was his downfall, because had he told us truthfully who he was, we could have told him which way to go. He had been overbold in assuming he could get to Ceuta without maps or a backup plan. On the other hand, had he reached a port city, any German ship would have taken him on board, and he would most likely have been safe on Spanish territory as well. But our poor legionnaire wasn't even aware how close he was to the border, and that he could have avoided the patrol and having his passport examined had he crossed the border on foot instead of asking us for a ride.

Once they had identified him, the next step was to take him back to the Legion. We saw his probable fate: a horrible beating followed by months of imprisonment, unless the riff wars were still raging, in which case the Legion would be in a state of military preparedness and he would be shot immediately.

The incident ended luckily for us, because our mysterious traveler had the integrity to admit that we had known nothing of his true identity. We made up our minds to be more careful the next time.

Three hundred kilometers later, we found ourselves in Meknes, and soon after, in Fez. Fez reminded us of Marrakech, because it was peopled almost entirely by native Arabs with very few Europeans, and was surrounded by monumental walls, as Taza and Meknes had been. The walls were four-fold in both cities and lined with impressive *babs* or gates. We found it hard to navigate the old city, because the walls of all the buildings were bare, and we saw nothing but walls, no matter where we looked.

The famous Bab Mansur gate in Meknes is known the world over for its beauty. The gate was covered with artistically carved stones and intricate mosaics and embellishments. It was in Meknes that we first saw pony-tailed Arabs, men who shaved their heads leaving a single tuft of hair in the middle.

Fez was the de facto capital of Morocco, serving as the religious, political, and economic heart of the country. It was a city that had been flourishing since the ninth century. Its first university was founded in 1325. Two famous routes intersected in Fez, the first connecting Algiers with the Atlantic Ocean, the second serving as a link between the Sahara and the Mediterranean Sea. There were no less than seventeen synagogues in Fez, even though its entire population, comprised overwhelmingly of Arabs, did not exceed 100,000. Its largest mosque could hold 20,000 Muslim worshippers, and its famous library was home to 16,000 Arabic manuscripts.

There wasn't much to look at on the way out of Fez. We passed the usual tiny villages, clusters of tents, and large, desert spaces. The land would have been excellent for grazing, but disregarding the occasional small herd of goats or sheep, we didn't encounter many signs of animal husbandry.

We encountered the tiny African train for the second time between Fez and Oudjda. It took the train three excruciating days on its 60 cm wide rails to cover the distance between the two cities, while we arrived in Oudjda, our last Moroccan city, after a mere day spent on pleasant roads. There was another international border near Oudjda, which we crossed that very day to find ourselves in Zoudj-el-Baghat, a village belonging to Oran.

Continuing through Arab Lands

We had left yet another country behind, only to realize that we had traveled in the wrong order; Morocco was much more Arabian and interesting than the territories we were to pass through afterwards, and it wasn't until Tripoli that we would encounter real Africa again.

Algeria was the oldest of French territories and had been in French hands since 1840. When we traveled through, it was an official French colony ruled by a French governor. The old culture and established native customs were of course better preserved in countries that had not been under European rule for so long. Algeria had been divided into three provinces, each province bearing the name of its largest city: Oran, Algiers, and Constantine. Tunis was a fourth territory, conquered by the French in 1880, but its status was somewhat different. It was a protectorate ruled over by the *Bey* of Tunis.

Morocco was a relatively recent French acquisition and also enjoyed the status of protectorate. Though it had been conquered gradually by the French between 1908 and 1917, its status as a protectorate was established by 1911. In the roughly two decades from 1911 to the time of our travels through Morocco, numerous exciting developments had taken place. Morocco was a rich land, especially its northern half, which was clad in lush green vegetation and comprised mostly of fertile arable lands in contrast with the southern deserts. The land was rich both above and below ground; copper, iron ore, zinc, lead, phosphate, and salt mines contributed significantly to the flourishing economy. The land was further dotted with marble quarries and heavily forested.

Algeria and Morocco shared the common characteristic of an indistinct southern border. This was because the border had to be drawn through a desert, and deserts had never been of much interest to the European superpowers—at least up to that point. All roads, even the railroad, came to a sudden halt where the desert began. The military zone also ended where the desert began; the rest belonged to the Arabs.

We passed mostly wheat fields and almond orchards on the roads of Algeria, where local Arabs were, almost without exception, to be found on horseback. They often appeared unexpectedly, but we had no idea from where. A nearby village or oasis perhaps? The sight of the tall, stately, somewhat grim riders fascinated us. Their horses were equally splendid, equipped with intricately decorated, sizeable, comfortable saddles, harnesses in gold and silver and large, boxlike stirrups. I never knew whom to admire more, the rider or his horse.

All Arabs wore guns at their sides. Guns were of the essence for these men, and not a single Arab could be seen without them. Arabian men were passionate about their weapons, and those who had none felt themselves to be outcasts, social pariahs. A popular Arabian proverb reflected this unusual love: "Guns first, horses second, women third."

It was impossible not to grow to love these modest, unassuming people, who nevertheless possessed true inner nobility. We felt ourselves to be especially close to them in spirit. What a pity that they were so underdeveloped. Had they at least been on the level of their fellow Arabs in Egypt, they would not have been living in a protectorate for long. Protectorate was a strange, phony word! Arabs had both endurance and hope. Their souls turned to Morocco as the expected source of their liberation. They hated the French and Spanish with a passion, but showed a great deal of kindness and hospitality to other foreigners.

Millions and millions of Arabs lived in the lands surrounding the Mediterranean, yet such little land was actually in Arab hands. We had the feeling, and the hope, that this state of things would not be permanent. Woe to the colonists if these people ever unite against them.

Propaganda in favor of Arab independence was robust at the time, and stemmed mostly from the non-French and Spanish parts of Europe, especially from Communist circles. Jews had nothing to do with this propaganda, because they were terrified by the prospect of Arab rule. Under the Europeans, Jews enjoyed a number of privileges, but Arabs considered them intruders and looked down on them. Arab and Jewish children fought daily in the narrow streets of every village.

I observed, on numerous occasions, how Arabs, presumably belonging to the higher social classes, greeted one another. Their gestures were filled with pride and respect, and were so different from the western handshake and perfunctory pat on the back. They would embrace one another gently, and then kiss the other on the shoulder. If they did shake hands, they raised their hands to their lips afterwards and began a short, formal, and polite conversation. "How are you? How are your parents? How is your wife? And children?" they would ask, taking great pains not to leave anyone out.

We passed through French North Africa relatively quickly. Oran, Constantine, Algiers, and Tunis were four large cities, on which the long years of European control had left their mark. Some of their boulevards would have passed for those of French cities, had they not been filled with Arabs.

The roads we traveled on were wide, smooth, and well-constructed. A layer of tar protected long stretches of the road from the dust, which formed an intrinsic part of all African roads. The fields around Oran were beautiful, but we soon learned that crop failure was a common occurrence due to the sultry sirocco winds, which swept out of the desert and turned the flourishing fields into a wasteland. There was no mediocre harvest in Algeria; it was either bountiful or pitiful.

We dined mostly at French restaurants and left local food for times of necessity. We avoided the expensive places and thankfully found that the French had a genius for affordable but tasty dining, which left us fully satisfied. In the end, it's just as easy to get used to great food as to poor dining, and we soon found we were spoiling ourselves.

"This was nothing to write home about," exclaimed Gyuszi on one occasion, as if he'd just eaten some watery vegetable soup and nothing else. In reality, we'd been enjoying a full meal of chicken soup, fish with mayonnaise, roast pig and salad, beer, and dessert.

We will never forget the crooked streets of Oran. The entire city was nothing but hill upon small hill; it was impossible to walk more than twenty steps on level ground. The Arabian quarter was filled with stairs going every which way, far from ideal terrain for a motorbike. Later, we touched on the city of Orleansville, which is renowned the world over for its unbearable heat waves. Temperatures between 50 and 55 degrees C were not uncommon.

We didn't spend much time exploring Algiers, either. We weren't interested in the wide, cosmopolitan avenues, the hustle of streetcars and automobiles. Everywhere we looked, we encountered only too obvious signs of a hundred years of European rule. There were few native Arabs there; they didn't even have their own quarter, and the *souks* to which we had become so accustomed, had been replaced by rather prosaic market halls. On the other hand, much could be said of the lively night life and immorality, which were hallmarks of this beautiful African town.

The land of the Kabyles was our next destination. Many of them wore European work clothes, known as *combinaisons,* but their red turbans marked them as distinctly non-European. Most of the Kabyle villages clustered around the Isser River valley. The snow-capped peaks of the Kabyle Mountains were our constant companions as we neared the city of Constantine. Constantine was a fascinating place, perhaps one of the world's most beautiful sights, thanks to the curious lay of the land. We arrived at night and encountered numerous bridges and tunnels, which, however, did not prepare us for the sight that greeted our eyes in the morning.

Constantine was built on a hilltop, and the hill was surrounded nearly on all sides by the Gorges du Rummel. The river was insignificant in size, but the gorge it had carved out for itself on all sides was unbelievably deep, its tall sides steep, nearly perpendicular. It seemed to us that the water was flowing between two giant cliffs. The city began at the top of these cliffs, so much so, that the windows of the first houses overlooked the abyss, which was spanned by numerous bridges. The bridges were a beautiful example of the wonders of technology harmoniously cohabiting with the exquisite beauties of nature. Four splendid bridges linked the two sides of the gorge, and under them, the waters of the unruly little river thundered and roared. The most magnificent bridge was the El Kantara, which led straight to the train station. The El Kantara, a gorgeous arched stone bridge, was 127 meters long and built 125 meters above the waters of the river. We couldn't get our fill of the stunning view from the bridge. The next bridge over was the Sidi Rached, which hung by ropes of steel, viaduct-like over the water. It was so narrow and finely built, that it swayed under the lightest of steps. The third bridge was in the shape of a giant semi-circle and spanned the gorge at a height of 120 meters.

The first houses were built at the extreme edge of the cliffs. The bold terraces, which jutted out over the abyss, took our breath away; the inhabitants of these houses must have heard the rumbling of the water continually. This city, originally built by Phoenicians, was demolished by armed rebellion before being rebuilt during the reign of Emperor Constantine in the fourth century A.D. In 1834, it took the French three attempts and ten thousand men to conquer this virtually impregnable aerie.

We descended to the Tourist Path, which was a gorgeous, two-kilometer trail, created with the intention of acquainting the visitor with those hidden beauties of the Rummel Gorges, which were perhaps less visible from the bridges and lookouts above. The narrow path, which followed the windings of the capricious little river, was carved into the cliffs and reinforced with steel handles, which had been drilled into the rock. We discovered new wonders every step of the way; waterfalls, large and small, alternated with cataracts, whirlpools, the ruins of Roman baths, and dramatic ledges. Twice during the trail, we disappeared underground with the river, and as we gazed upwards, the sight of the bridges was just as magnificent as the view from atop them had been.

After leaving Constantine, we soon found ourselves on the territory of Tunis. We reached the border after passing through Souk-Ahras, leaving behind a mineral quarry and surrounded on all sides first by forests, then by vineyards. The roads were still excellent, and the countryside was brilliantly colorful. After a stretch of olive trees, we unexpectedly reached a clearing filled with storks. We concluded that our Hungarian storks had very good taste when choosing this pleasant, warm land in which to pass the winter months. Musing over the familiar birds, we wondered how many of them had come all the way from the villages of Hungary.

We left Bizerte just after the cannon shot. There was a custom in most Arabian towns, including Bizerte, of firing a cannon at the rising of the first star each evening. The custom was Jewish in origin, and there was a significant Jewish population in most Arab cities.

Tunisia, too, was a fertile and magnificent country. Those who owned a bit of land lived well, regardless of race. We often encountered, especially in urban hotels, wealthy Arabs, whose social status was made evident by their fine, spotless burnooses. Their ebony walking sticks were capped with silver and their fingers crowded with diamond rings. Although it was February, the grain in the fields was lush and green, sometimes exceeding the height of a man.

We didn't spend much time in the capital, Tunis, because we were secretly drawn to Tripoli and the real Africa. Tunis, although much more Arabian in character than Algiers had been, was, nevertheless, overwhelmingly modern, clean, and European. As in other parts of Northern Africa, prices were generally low, especially in comparison to France or Italy. A night at a fine hotel cost ten francs per person, which was also the price of a magnificent meal. However, on the cheaper end, there were some very satisfactory hotels where we paid a mere fifteen francs for the three of us and enjoyed a six franc meal. The cost of animals was cheapest of all. A fine horse, the most expensive of farm animals, cost 1,000 francs in Tunis. Cows, however, could be bought for 500 and camels for 400 francs. Sheep and goats sold for a mere 50 to 60 francs.

The old city lay on a hilltop, but it, too, showed signs of Western influence. There were numerous mosques, but their accompanying minarets were square and unwieldy, instead of slender and rounded. We were struck by the amount of Italian we heard, while French seemed to be the language of preference for the merchant class. The traditional *souks* were located in the capricious, winding streets, and were made up of tiny hole-in-the-wall shops, where the shopkeeper lay or squatted day after day. Reed mats or veritable forests of twigs protected customers from the heat of the sun, often covering entire streets with their shade.

We had picked up a few words of Arabic by the time we arrived in Tunis. Most foreign settlers, aside from the Brits and the Americans, learned Arabic quickly and well, since they were forced to use it every day. We, on the other hand, never spent enough time in one place to truly learn the dialect. By the time our ears grew accustomed to the language of a certain region, we were ready to move on to our next destination. Dialects varied significantly from region to region. Mimmy and I had great fun teasing our friend Gyuszi about his poor language skills. He was a true, blue Hungarian from Transylvania, and he mangled every language he came across, whether French, Arabic, or Italian, but nevertheless continued "speaking" them with unflagging enthusiasm. When nobody understood his heavily accented attempts at communication, he would revert to his favorite universal expression, "Speak English?" even though these two words comprised just about his entire English vocabulary.

We didn't leave Tunis without visiting the ruins of Carthage outside the city. Very little remained of this once glorious city; the hillsides surrounding the ancient site were lined with the attractive villas of the wealthy.

From Carthage, we headed south, traveling 300 kilometers to Sfax, the largest city in Southern Tunisia. The roads grew progressively worse and less crowded. The green of farmlands was interrupted more and more often by yellow patches of desert sand. We passed tiny Arab villages, whose lovely names made up in length for the insignificant size of the villages to which they referred; Funduk-Djedid, Bir-Bu-Rekba, Bu-Fisa held little worth remembering, aside from their names.

Sousse was the first sizeable town we encountered. Here we stopped for coffee, as had become our custom ever since we landed in Africa. Coffee was best in the tiny, typically Arabian coffee-houses, which were duly filled with Arabs at all times of the day, because Arabs were a people who always seemed to have time on their hands. Merchants, waiters, artisans, and barbers gathered for their hourly cup of black coffee. Short young waiters, assistants to the coffee brewers, carried the pleasant-smelling concoction on copper trays. We grew accustomed to Arabian coffee just as we came to enjoy Arabian music. Arabs loved to sing, mostly quietly and monotonously repeating the same fragments of melodies. What seemed boring and irritating at first soon grew familiar, even pleasant. As we got to know more and more of the indigenous melodies, we often caught ourselves humming them under our breaths.

Sfax was three times the size of Sousse, but despite its population of 80,000 and significant hustle and bustle, it was home to merely five hotels. To make matters worse, we had arrived on the first day of Ramadan and were therefore fearful of not getting a room. Ramadan was the most important Muslim holiday, and most foreigners arriving in Sfax were simply forced to move on. Founding a hotel in Sfax could be a potentially rewarding venture, unless many people have since had the same idea. Sfax was in many ways the heart of Southern Tunisia, often inundated with visitors traveling by boat, train, car, or caravan. Ramadan lasts for four weeks, and Muslims are only allowed to eat and drink after nightfall. We were struck by the frequent shouting and unrest on the streets. We later found that the to-do was caused by the occasional appearance of an intoxicated man. The man logically drank to become drunk, and therefore, it was obvious to all that he had broken the religious laws regulating Ramadan. Drunkenness was not punishable by law, but the unfortunate drunkard was instead punished by the children who crowded onto the street. Hundreds of children would crowd after him, followed by groups of adults, all of them laughing at, scolding, ridiculing and, occasionally, throwing objects at the poor wretch. Needless to say, after such public disgrace, it would take a long time before the poor sinner worked up the nerve to get drunk during Ramadan again.

After passing by Gabès, we reached the border of Italian Africa, or Tripolitania. Before leaving the French territories, however, we had a memorable encounter with a rather mysterious institution often romanticized in the cinemas: the French Foreign Legion.

Legionnaires could be found everywhere from Morocco to Tripoli, often gathered in small groups or simply strolling through town. Occasionally, we caught sight of their sizeable barracks, but it was in Sidi-Bel-Abbes, in the province of Oran, that we first understood the Legion and familiarized ourselves with the legionnaire's daily life.

Sidi-Bel-Abbes, a small but modern and rather beautiful town of 27,000, was literally swarming with legionnaires. Walking down the street, we ran into a Hungarian member of the Legion who invited us to visit the barracks outside of town. At this point, we were still under the influence of over-mystified impressions of this institution, so only Gyuszi accepted the invitation, while we stayed behind, in case our friend got captured and we were needed for the rescue operation.

Of course, there was no such rescue operation needed. When he got back to us in the afternoon, he told us that the legionnaires had given him a warm welcome and lunch, and the Hungarian members had asked all three of us to dinner.

As the afternoon progressed, we arrived at the site of the huge barracks and were immediately struck by the exercises of the novices, which didn't seem to differ much from one institution to the next. We were also quick to note that discipline wasn't nearly as harsh as one would have expected.

The African branch of the French Foreign Legion was comprised of five regiments, four infantry and one cavalry, but the actual number of legionnaires far surpassed the official count, so much so, that the men stationed in Africa could have been divided into eight whole regiments. One of the five official regiments was stationed in Sidi-Bel-Abbes. Our new friend led us straight to the mess hall. On the way, he explained that he was a veteran legionnaire who now worked in the cafeteria with two fellow Hungarians. There were only twenty Hungarian legionnaires in their regiment, but in the years 1919 and 1920, following the collapse of the Commune, there had been enough Hungarian Commies to fill an entire battalion. That "army" of Hungarian reds had since dispersed, many had served their terms and returned to Hungary, others had died in the Riff Wars or been imprisoned, a small minority remained active legionnaires.

"And how do the Hungarian boys behave themselves?" I asked Sergeant Major Bakács, who ran the entire mess hall. "You might not believe me," he replied, "but Hungarians have a very good reputation around here. Of course, the Legion is an international organization, but Hungarian members enjoy special respect. They are, for the most part, skilled, disciplined, and always ready to help, that is why they get some of the best positions. Out of the twenty Hungarians in our regiment, three work in the mess hall, a few in the offices; others have been assigned to the workshops and storehouses. What's more, the master gunsmith is Hungarian. They are, for the most part, former Communists, and although it's 1928, a few of them still cling to their old beliefs. Then again, most of our former Commies would love to see Béla Kun himself rot in hell."

Our hospitable sergeant major was somewhat reluctant to explain his own political views. As we stood there talking, the mess hall filled with people and the tables with food. Mimmy very quickly became the center of attention as the legionnaires walked in and gallantly, somewhat in the French manner, touched their fingers to their caps. As we sat in the mess hall, we heard most of the major languages of the world being spoken around us. Most of the boys bought tobacco, which, unlike food and drink, was not a regular part of their allotment. They were paid laughable wages, 30 centimes a day, which, at the time, was the price of a box of matches; their sorry earnings reminded me of the pittance soldiers in Hungary made during peacetime.

German legionnaires were in the majority, followed by Russians, then fair numbers of Austrians, Hungarians, Italians, Swedes, and Japanese. There was also a decent crowd of Brits and Americans, as well as French, who were officially listed as Swiss. No form of identification was necessary for acceptance, so a new legionnaire could go by any name and belong to any nation he chose. After providing the Legion with some basic information, the would-be legionnaire was asked to sign at the bottom of the page, and he was in for five years, which was the minimum. These five years were an assurance for those fallen out of grace in their own countries. The Legion never turned their members over to any earthly power, and five years was a long time, enough time for things better forgotten to be thoroughly forgotten. As a consequence, the legionnaires were hardly an innocent bunch. Not all of them were criminals; there were youths in search of adventure or looking to forget an unfortunate love-affair, others had joined almost by accident or been dragged into the Legion by a friend, but the overwhelming majority of members had something to hide.

"You should tell everyone that we are all here out of our own free will; nobody is forced to join the Legion," explained a nice-looking young German, who happened to be sitting next to us. A fellow Hungarian chimed in, "Precisely! There are plenty of volunteers, especially in the fall, when the weather gets cold and the benches in the city parks mysteriously empty of tramps." At this point, a new guest arrived and introduced himself as Sergeant György. The privates around us leapt up and saluted stiffly. Lower-ranking officers belonged to a class by themselves. They were the heart and soul of the Legion and legionnaires were more frightened of them than of the highest-ranking officers. You had to work hard to be promoted. Those who signed up for another five years after their first term of service was over often received a low-ranking officership. That was how most officers were made, although legionnaires could occasionally rise to office receiving an academic degree. Sergeant Major Bakács was a seasoned veteran; he had been with the Legion for twenty-five years, received numerous medals, and fought for the French during World War I.

These lower-ranking officers had it good. Sergeant György, for example, made 700 francs a month. He spent 180 francs on food, and as he had clothing and a place to sleep for free, he was able to save a nice sum of money during his years of service. "What would we do if there was no mess hall and no wine to drink in it?" cried the sergeant in a jaded voice.

None of the legionnaires complained about the high-ranking officers, even though there were over a dozen of them, but they had a lot to say about the brutality of the lower-ranking officers, who were often cruel even to their fellow countrymen. Physical manifestations of this brutality were the frequent beatings and whippings. Those who had been officers in another army were stripped of their rank once they joined the Legion and made to start over, re-earning their ranks through years of dedicated service, like the others. There were no Hungarian officers in Sidi-Bel-Abbes, but our friends knew of a Hungarian colonel stationed in Morocco. Then there was an Austrian artillery officer who had been made captain after successfully working as a French spy.

There were Legionnaires stationed in Tunisia, Algeria, and Morocco, as well as Syria and Indochina. Indochina was a Legionnaire's paradise with high wages and native servants, but only those who had served faithfully and well for three years got the opportunity to go.

After World War I, all new legionnaires were transferred to the battlefields of Europe, but so many legionnaires switched sides, that after a while, only those belonging to nations allied with the French were taken to Europe, the rest took part in the colonial wars, often fighting in the front lines.

Service in the Legion was very difficult. Life was hard, rules strict, and the climate sweltering hot, especially in the summer. Legionnaires, because of their high level of military training, were deployed in the most dangerous war zones. But not all aspects of a legionnaire's life were as horrendous and full of suffering as popular belief held them to be. A soldier's life never was a bed of roses, especially not in the desert, where you'd be hard put to find a single rose. Novices were allowed to leave the barracks after their exercises were complete, and after a few months of service, even the most inexperienced greenhorns were allowed to go into town every afternoon. Of course, each man had to decide for himself whether it was worth leaving the barracks in search of the sorry excuses for entertainment the small Arab towns offered.

Desertion attempts were common but rarely successful. Those who had been with the Legion for some time did not even attempt it. Most would-be deserters were novices, who, after a few months of service, experienced deep regret at the thought of their five-year contracts. Even if they did manage to escape, they couldn't get far not speaking the local dialects and without a penny in their pockets; what's more, deserters rarely had civilian clothes to change into, so they were caught and brought back. In the end, all they accomplished was the privilege of a thorough beating and a few months of jail time added to their five-year period of service.

They were all dreadfully homesick. Our seasoned Hungarian veterans grew teary-eyed as we spoke of our mutual homeland. We were all so far from home! Most legionnaires could hardly wait for their years of service to be over, at which point they would receive their monetary compensations and return to their own countries. Others did not plan to return but hoped to settle in the colonies instead. Five years were enough to learn both French and Arabic, and many grew accustomed to the climate and the local culture. With their newfound French citizenship papers in hand (all legionnaires automatically received French citizenship after their fifth year) some decided to try their luck as civilians in the land where they had completed their service. A good number of urban artisans and merchants had originally come to Africa under the auspices of the Foreign Legion.

The evening grew progressively more cheerful. After we consumed considerable amounts of alcohol and cigarettes, the Foreign Legion barracks in Sidi-Bel-Abbes resounded with the sound of Hungarian tunes. The first to hear the call of duty and leave us was a grim man of about 50 or 55 years, who nevertheless had an honest, even kindly face.

"Do you know who this man is?" asked the head of the mess hall, as soon as the older man was out of earshot.

"I haven't the slightest clue," I answered, "Am I supposed to know?"

"You bet, but don't tell him I told you, because he's not fond of discussing his past in public. He's a master sergeant, which is the highest rank you can achieve as a member of the troops. He's being transferred to China next month. He's a good soldier, well established in the Legion and favored by fortune. His superiors are all fond of him. I'm sure he'll be an officer soon. We Hungarians call him "Doc" for short."

"Is he really a doctor?" I asked.

"No, not quite," our friend answered, "but he specializes in, shall we say, canned goods. You must have heard of him, although what he did to become famous happened a long time ago. Does the name Béla Kiss of Cinkota ring a bell?"

A grim realization suddenly dawned on the three of us as we called to mind the gruesome case of the tin barrels containing women's corpses, which the police had dug up in the town of Cinkota. The perpetrator had fought in the front lines during World War I but disappeared shortly afterwards without leaving a trace. So this was Béla Kiss! Now we understood only too well why he was reluctant to talk about his past.

I wrote a sensational letter to the newspapers in Budapest the very next day and longed to meet with the "Doc" again. Who knew, we might encounter him in Indochina! What I wouldn't have given for a photo of the master sergeant, but somehow, none of the legionnaires seemed anxious to help me secure one.

The next morning, before we set off from Sidi-Bel-Abbes, a few Hungarian legionnaires came over to say goodbye. The afternoon and evening with them had been a memorable one, and their goodbyes were enthusiastic. Although many of them were criminals, for that moment, I looked at them simply as fellow Hungarians, who had, through our visit, recalled and in a sense revisited the homeland they had somewhat carelessly left. A young legionnaire named Buduka, who had only a few months of service left, had remembered that my friend Gyuszi's shoes were hopelessly worn and brought along a brand-new pair of legionnaire boots. We felt we had to accept the generous gift, even though we remembered from our visit the day before that Buduka worked in the storehouse and finally left to cries of "Au revoir!"

The Sands of Tripolitania

We crossed the border into Italian Africa well after passing Gabès. Although the road leading to the Egyptian border was a short one, its quality was reminiscent of the first African roads we had encountered. We had hardly left Gabès when we got a taste of the true desert experience. Up to that point, we had been traveling through civilized country, but the last remaining signs of European civilization disappeared on the road from Gabès to Tripoli and Benghazi to Egypt.

Palm trees lined the first stretch of the road, but as we neared Egypt, they decreased in number and grew progressively uglier. The first palm trees had been lush, their mighty leaves serving as excellent protection against the merciless sun, but later, we encountered only a single tree here and there, each tree sticking out like a sore thumb. There was not a living creature in sight. Occasionally, we saw Arabs with camels or a few tents, witnesses of the nomadic way of life, or tiny settlements comprised of windowless huts dug deep into the ground. The only feeble signs of civilization were the telegraph wires lining the road. Fertile land alternated more and more often with vast stretches of yellow sand. The sand was dotted with clumps of dried grasses; the only other sight for sore eyes was the occasional oasis, recognizable from afar by the lushness of its greenery, the life-giving well and a cluster of homes.

Fortunately, our motorcycle bore the heat exceptionally well. We sped along at a very satisfying pace, disregarding the few lengths of road where the going was sandy and tough. Things were going so well that we hardly noticed the hot desert wind picking up and beginning to thrust us with great force from the side. It was a while before we realized we were in the middle of a rising sandstorm. Since we had no relevant experience to work from, we decided to wet our handkerchiefs and tie them in front of our mouths and noses. With this slim protection, we started frantically looking for the nearest house or, at the very least, natural shelter of some kind. The wind had swept up the fine sand surrounding the road, and the air was filled with the tiny, flourlike grains, which whipped and stung our faces. The horizon grew darker, as if night had descended, or as if we had been wading through a thick fog. The wind grew so powerful that it kept pushing our packed vehicle, sidecar and all, off the road. Wet handkerchiefs, as we found out, weren't much use. Our

Oasis in Tripolitania

eyes, ears, and mouths filled with sand, but there was sand under our clothing, in our shoes, and in the tiniest compartments and crevices of our motorcycle. Standing in one place didn't help either; we couldn't see further than
our noses.

In the end, we got lucky and discovered a hut by the side of the road. We
stopped, covered our motorcycle with tarps, and got under shelter as quickly
as possible. The tiny house was comprised of a single room, and from the

looks of it, the building must have served as a wayside shop or tavern at one point. When we entered, it was nothing but a simple shelter from the storm. In the prevailing gloom, we greeted our fellow shelter-seekers, 8-10 Arabs who were sitting on reed mats and rugs along the floor, waiting anxiously for the storm to pass. We were greeted by curious, but not terribly friendly faces. We settled into the quiet and almost devilish calm of the place. As we looked around further, we discovered a number of chests, sacks, and packages scattered about the room. One of the Arabs squatted for hours, staring into space, another lay on the ground, wrapped in his burnoose. A few were having a quiet conversation, and we heard the muted strains of an Arabian melody from another corner.

It soon grew dark. We attempted to create something of a bed in one corner of the room, but we knew that we would hardly be getting a full night's sleep that night. We didn't know the strange Arabs in the hut, and, not knowing the language, had nothing to say to them. At the same time, we grew progressively more and more hungry, but there was no food to be had. We ran out of cigarettes too, and I had plenty of time to debate what would be better: food or another pack of cigarettes?

As the hours passed, it grew more and more chilly. Our tiny hut, pretty much open to the buffeting of strong winds, was no great protection against the cold. We had used our tarps to cover our motorcycle, so the only thing left was to huddle close and hope for the best.

Suddenly, one of the Arabs walked up to us, a rug in either hand. With a face beaming with generosity and courtesy, he explained that we should use the rugs to cover ourselves against the cold. We sighed with relief, not so much because of the rugs, but rather because we realized that a man who cared so much about our comfort could in no way be a desert bandit. We smiled up at the bearded old man with gratitude and soon drifted off to sleep.

When we woke in the morning, the wind had died down completely; the skies were blue and cloudless, and we continued on our way in the cheerful sunshine. We said our goodbyes to our curious bedfellows, who were astounded at the sight of our motorcycle.

As we got on our way, we soon discovered that the wind had blown great quantities of sand onto the road. Occasionally, we were forced to make our way through a layer half a meter deep, but we reached Tripoli without any further incidents. There wasn't a single town along the long stretch of road. Upon our arrival, the sandstorm seemed dreamlike and unreal; we hardly would have believed it ourselves had we not been forced to subject our bike to a very thorough cleaning. As the motorcycle was being cleaned, we reflected on how fortunate we had been that the storm had overwhelmed us when we were on the road and not, say, in the middle of the desert, following a caravan route.

Tripoli was in many ways inferior to the towns of French Africa, partly because it was so new and partly because it wasn't located in one of the wealthier regions. The city was built at the edge of the desert, hard on the sea, and surrounded by sand or water in all directions. The streets and the buildings lining the streets were obviously very new, yet, as we made our way into the heart of the city, we discovered it to be a rather sizeable and very busy place. The vast majority of the population was made up of Arabs, and the streets, even the main ones, were filled with their donkeys and camels.

We were pleasantly surprised when we discovered a copy of the *Budapest Daily* at a date-vendor's in Tripoli. Upon buying a kilogram of the sticky fruit, we were astonished to find our purchase wrapped in the newspaper so familiar to us. The vendor honestly admitted that he had no idea where the paper had come from.

As we walked through this typically Arab city, we were amused once again by the curious Arabian customs. To those who wish to see true Arab Africa, I would recommend Tripoli over both Tunis and Algiers as a city where the indigenous culture has had minimal exposure to the West. The narrow streets were lined with tiny houses hundreds of years old. There were no windows overlooking the street; the flat-roofed homes got their sunlight from above. The city was filled with mosques and their minarets, topped with the typical crescent moon and resounding with frequent calls to prayer. There were naturally many Jews as well; they had their own quarter and synagogues.

Street signs were all in Arabic. We were soon forced to learn Arabic numerals, because, although we call our own numerals Arabic, they are in reality rather different from the numerals the Arabs use. Of course, there were many similarities, but out of all ten numerals, only the nine was exactly identical in both systems. What looked like a flipped three was actually a four, and what we thought was the four turned out to be the five.

We took a good look at Arab women. Most men kept 3-4 wives, buying women from their parents. Formerly, the husband had full control over his wife and could even kill her if he pleased. Nowadays, this is no longer possible, but because most marriages went unregistered, men mostly had the power to chase away the wives with whom they were no longer pleased. The richer the man, the more wives he has, but most men kept a watchful eye on their wives, because the winds of Western culture had reached even the most cloistered of Arab women.

Arab women were undeniably beautiful. For the most part, they went about in veils, or covered their heads and faces with the long, sheet-like material in which their whole body was wrapped, so thoroughly, that their black eyes were framed with the white of their linens. Some women cut small holes in their veiling, in such a way as to enable them to observe men while they themselves went unobserved. They loved jewelry, and would occasionally wear silver hoops 10-15 cm in diameter in their ears. Silver bracelets and anklets complemented the feminine look. Jewish women did not cover their faces, but they were heavily made up, most likely in an attempt to make up for the lack of covering.

Not all Arabs shared the same customs and dress. In the countryside surrounding Tlemtsen, for example, the women belonging to Berber tribes did not always cover their faces, wore brilliantly colored silk garments and went about bedecked in ribbons, jewels, and pearls.

Arab girls blossomed early and faded just as fast. Twelve-year-old girls counted as grown women and looked, indeed, fully developed, only to become wrinkled and ugly by the age of thirty.

The impression we made on the inhabitants of Tripoli was perhaps stronger than the impression they made on us. Not a day had passed before the entire city seemed to know who we were and where we were going. We were greeted by friendly faces every step of the way; Italians and Arabs competed to make us feel welcome. Shopkeepers invited us into their shops, served us coffee and sweets and showed us their wares, not showing a bit of disappointment when we refused to buy a single thing. Mimmy very quickly became the center of attention. With her boyish haircut, sporty clothing, and the charm of her exotic undertaking, I believe she was on her way to becoming every young Arab's dream woman. Our hotel was surrounded from morning until late evening by patient and enthusiastic locals. Occasionally, in the manner of generals or dictators of sorts, we were forced to make an appearance on the balcony, and each appearance was greeted by cheering and applause.

We spent hours in the Old City and were barely able to rid ourselves of our enthusiastic would-be tour guides. Trusting in our fine-tuned navigational skills, we proudly sent all hangers-on away, which resulted in our getting lost again and again in the maze of the narrow and crooked streets. Although we soon found we were walking in circles, we nonetheless refused to accept the offers of potential tour-guides. The streets were filled with crowds of people and even greater numbers of donkeys. Donkeys carried straw, wood, and crops, occasionally disappearing under their bulky burdens. Cries of "Barra! Barra!" resounded from all sides, warning us to make way for the donkeys.

The bazaar in Tripoli was just as impressive as those of Morocco. We found all the usual wares in place, yet there was a spirit of resourcefulness about the Tripoli bazaar that surpassed that of Morocco. Not only did we encounter entire chains of *souks,* but we were also astonished when we walked right into the African version of a primitive stock-exchange. A huge crowd of people, shouting at the top of their lungs, milled about the narrow street and filled it so completely, that it was impossible to pass through. They were all selling

Young Arab beauty

something: a pair of slippers, a kettle, an outfit, trinkets, a rug or two, or a variety of other wares. People ran to and fro, shouting out their wares and prices.

We gained a new addition to our small collections of souvenirs. I received a Hand of Fatima made of pure gold. These amulets, mostly made of gold, silver, or copper and representing the hand of Mohammed's daughter, if I am not mistaken, were believed to bring good luck. The amulet was worn on bracelets and watch chain, but some went so far as to paint it on their fences, the walls of their houses, or even shop signs. The symbol was widely recognized in Morocco, Arabia, Palestine, and Tripoli.

I got my Hand of Fatima from a local girl. I entered into the short "affair" with a great deal of caution. Sitting in a fancy Arabian coffee house, I spied a beautiful young woman dressed in modern but elaborate clothing who was showing obvious interest in my person. As she smoked her cigarette, her veil lifted at every puff only to reveal her beautiful face and shining black eyes. I sat down next to her. She spoke a few words of Italian, so we struck up a conversation. The conversation was followed by an evening rendezvous, which was followed by a moonlit walk along the beach. This beautiful young lady gave me the golden Hand of Fatima to keep as a memento.

The art of ivory carving was highly developed, industrialized even, in Tripoli. Walking along the *souks*, we encountered marvelous works of art: cigarette-holders, figurines, boxes of all shapes and sizes, even a walking cane, carved of a single piece of solid ivory. Ivory was very cheap. We could have bought an ivory chess set for a laughable 200 Italian liras, but since we couldn't have taken it along on account of the numerous borders we were still to cross, and sending it home would have been complicated, we decided to take only the memory of it with us.

The streets of Tripoli were filled with soldiers, not only Italian, but indigenous soldiers: both black Africans and Arabs. The black soldiers were clad in especially fantastic gear. Although their uniforms were worn and ragged, they were covered with decorations, gold braiding, and other fancy touches. The soldier look was completed by the red, tasseled cap and the textiles wrapped around the calves of legs ending in bare feet. Some of the officers and those with better taste wore elegant wooden sandals. The coffee houses and the single movie theater were filled with these colonial soldiers. Mussolini spoiled the indigenous soldiers with high wages and heaps of medals and decorations. There was hardly a soldier without a decoration of some kind. *Il Duce* was fond of Arabs, left them at least a feeling of liberty, allowed them to build Arab school after school, post signs entirely in Arabic, and even promoted the more educated Arabs to higher posts in the bureaucratic system. On second thought, maybe these weren't signs of love on the part of Mussolini. Perhaps the Arabs who greeted their colonizers in the Roman manner weren't doing it out of love, either.

We enjoyed numerous holidays during our stay. The Arabs have their own holidays and set Thursdays aside as holy days; the Jews keep Sabbath. A number of Christian feast days, outside of every Sunday, were celebrated alongside Italian national holidays. The city was beautifully lit up for every festival, and all its inhabitants received a day off.

Our few days in Tripoli passed very pleasantly. During our stay, we encountered many of the brand names known the world over: Singer sewing machines were ubiquitous, other common brands were Odol, Bayer aspirin, Vacuum, Mobil Oil, and Zerkovitz. Zerkovitz melodies were much beloved by both the pianists and the larger orchestras of the African cinemas.

We also had the opportunity to go to the mayor's house to pay him a visit. When we arrived at the elderly Arabian prince's palace, just outside the city limits, we were surprised to find not a soul in sight. We passed through the gate and entered the stone-lined hall, which opened onto a series of rooms furnished in the usual elegant Arabian style. Although we had been standing inside for some time, we still encountered no one. The spooky quiet reminded us of an enchanted castle. We walked in, turned left, then right, opening doors at random, coughing politely and calling out greetings, but all to no avail. Next, we climbed the stairs to the second floor, where, behind one of the doors, we were greeted by a strange sight. I cannot decide to this day whether we were lucky or not, but we had happened upon a group of 10-12 gorgeous Arabian women in baggy clothing, mostly scantily clad in a transparent, veil-like material. Their faces were uncovered, and this was the cause of their consternation. We had only a brief moment to take in all this beauty, because the shocked silence was soon peppered with screams, the sound of curses, and footsteps coming toward the room we were in. Although we knew we were innocent, we rushed for the gate as quickly as our feet could carry us and didn't return to the palace ever again.

Of course, at the time of this incident, we were still very much beginners in intercultural interactions. As we made our escape, we weren't worrying about our poor European manners, rather, it was thoughts of the mysterious institution of the harem and torture chambers awaiting all transgressors that made our flight almost superhumanly swift.

Our next visit was to the governor, Emilio Bono, who made every effort, within the limits of courtesy, to dissuade us from continuing our journey. He told us that the road to Benghazi was highly unsafe, and the Italians could in no way be made responsible for our safety. Upon witnessing our stubborn refusal to travel to our next destination by ship, the governor allowed us to proceed at our own risk. We were asked to sign some governmental papers documenting that we were thenceforth responsible for our own safety.

The road to the Egyptian border was, as the governor had predicted, far from pleasant, but not so much because of possible dangers (in reality, we were not aware of the danger we were in) but rather, as a result of the poor quality of the roads.

As we left the city, we were immediately greeted by an unsurpassed African countryside. Palm tress grew more and more rare, there were fewer and fewer houses, and, after passing a few caravans, we suddenly found ourselves riding in a barren, unpopulated wilderness. By the sides of the road, we saw signs of pitiful attempts to hold back the sand, while in the distance we spotted a few tiny fortresses surrounded by giant tangles of wire. Our motorcycle sped through the dry riverbeds, or *wadis,* which rarely contained any water.

The first larger town we passed through was Homs. With a population of 1,000, it was the largest town in Tripolitania, after Tripoli itself. The "highway" came to an abrupt halt outside of Homs, where archeologists were digging up the remains of a Roman settlement, known as *Leptis Magna* in the original Latin. The outlines of the antique city were becoming more and more visible as the layers of protective sand were removed. Paved roads, entire houses, palaces, a huge square, baths, even an imperial palace lay bathed in sunlight. Exquisite statues, competing with the beauties of Pompeii, lined the city. Although much of the town was yet to be excavated, what the archeologists had found thus far boded well for the future of tiny Homs.

What a contrast there was between the Roman city, decorative and repre-sentative of the height of antique civilization, and the dusty, miserable twenti-eth century settlement. Had humanity progressed or regressed in the centuries separating *Leptis Magna* from Homs? There was a series of tiny mills surrounding the ruined palaces; patient camels, their heads bound, trudged in circles moving the millstones. Maybe they were reflecting on the newest developments of modern technology!

The road to Egypt was long; we attempted to stay close to the sea on the stretch leading to Benghazi. Wherever possible, we rode the coastal sands, which had been packed down by the crashing waves. We raced along this un-usual speedway, the sea to our left, an immeasurable sandy wasteland to our right. Occasionally, we were forced to slow down upon encountering a dry riverbed, a gully or a stretch of softer sand; sometimes, it took us hours of hard work to free ourselves from the clutches of the sand. When our way hard by the sea proved jagged or otherwise dangerous, we were forced to retreat to the caravan routes further in the desert.

Riding a motorcycle in the desert sand was no easy feat, and there were many more such stretches of road to come. The way from Egypt to Palestine also led through a desert and proved just as difficult. The deserts of Western Australia, the sands of Arabia, the sandy pampas of Peru and Northern Chile all posed their own formidable challenges. When we rode towards Egypt, we were mere beginners in desert travel; by the time we reached Chile, years later, we had years of experience behind us and were able to conquer the sandy terrain with relative ease.

Motorcycles were very rare in this part of the world, as evidenced by the astonished glances we received each time a caravan passed by us. Even the camels seemed surprised and confused by this motorized competition.

Sometimes we were tempted to play a practical joke or two. Knowing how scared camels were of motorcycles, we'd wait until the animals got relatively close, then, I'd rev the engine, and we'd all start shouting at the top of our lungs. The poor camels would run wild; their riders dropping off their backs into the soft sand like bags of grain. We listened to their scolding and were pretty sure they weren't asking Allah to bless us all our days. Of course, we kept a safe distance every time we decided to play our joke.

The sands of Cyrenaica proved to be the greatest challenge of all. We struggled every step of the way, the brilliant blue sky above us, the yellow sands below. When the winds picked up, light sand quickly covered everything. The "road" was no longer visible; only our compass, the sun, and the occasional posts driven into the ground helped us navigate the desert sands. The posts were initially intended to help caravans find their ways, but they weren't to be trusted without some reservations. Occasionally armed and determined Bedouins belonging to various desert tribes, knights-errant of the desert, would pull up the posts and rearrange them to lead the unwitting caravan straight into the desert. The caravan following the changed signposts would then make its way deeper and deeper into the desert, further and further from the last signs of civilization. Then, kilometers away from the correct route, the poor travelers would stop and look about in consternation, only to find themselves surrounded by Bedouins, who would swiftly take everything worth taking, drive the camels into the desert and ruthlessly kill anyone who resisted.

We weren't afraid of being attacked by Bedouins ourselves, because they usually stayed away from white travelers, knowing full well that the consequences of such an attack could be grave. Besides, they were more interested in camels and merchandise than the cash or checks white men usually carried.

Our real worry was the sand, because getting stuck in the desert could very easily end in death. The soft sand was merciless. We tried binding chains around the wheels, then rags and bits of rope, but the wheels continued spinning around helplessly. Although the engine was guzzling gas, the wheels were spinning, and the kilometers were adding up on the odometer, we were not making the least bit of progress.

We had to think of a different method. Deciding to lighten the load as much as possible, we removed everything from the bike and carried our belongings on our shoulders. Then, dropping them off on sturdier terrain, we walked back to get the sidecar. After we had carried our sidecar across the worst stretch, we returned for the motorcycle. This new method, although it worked well, was nevertheless tiring and unpleasant, as we were forced to walk for kilometers before we found terrain sturdy enough to unload. On our lonely trek to and fro, our brains clouded over with worry. We wondered how many more times we would be forced to a halt by the sand, whether we would have enough water and food for such unforeseen incidents, and, most importantly, whether we would have the strength to repeat this again and again. Vultures circling overhead reminded us of the very real possibility of failure.

In the end, we reached the Egyptian border with a set of new experiences under our belts. Although we had lost weight and our clothing and motorcycle showed signs of wear and tear, nevertheless, the thought that we had crossed the African continent, from Morocco to Egypt, on a motorcycle, was very uplifting.

In the Land of the Pharaohs

We cut our stay in Egypt relatively short, yet we took the time to visit the best-known cities and get to know this interesting country and amiable people as well as possible. Leaving the Italian sector at Es-Sollum, we rode on through a desert landscape that was relatively unchanged from what we had just traveled through. The same sea and the same sand lined our way. Our progress was slow, but we gradually left the unfriendly Libyan desert behind and made our way into a more populous and civilized portion of the country. Once we reached the El-Iskandarian, or Alexandrian railway, we were back in civilization, but we didn't reach Egypt, as marked on our maps, until we got very close to El-Iskandaria.

We arrived in a marvelous country, the land of the Nile, a land that, millennia before, had played a leading role in the drama of mankind, and which had given birth to civilization after civilization. The Nile had always been and will always be the heart and soul of Egypt. It was an artery, 3,000 kilometers long, carrying the lifeblood of the delta region. The river was like an unending silver ribbon, causing the yellow desert to bloom, and towns and cities to spring up. Egypt was the Nile and the fertile lands surrounding the Nile, which were expanding due to widespread irrigation. The rest was just desert.

Passing through Egypt's cities was comparable to entering and exiting the doors of a dream. El-Iskandaria and El-Kahira (Alexandria and Cairo) were the meeting places of East and West, where the Orient and the Occident lived side by side, inextricably intertwined. These are the cities of caliphs, *khedives,* and kings—wide, cosmopolitan boulevards and narrow alleys reminiscent of the *One Thousand and One Nights.* Luxurious hotels and tiny, Arabian coffeehouses and bazaars, camels on concrete intermingle to create the unique atmosphere of Egyptian cities. Even the people living in Egypt seem to have been born of an intermingling of many different nationalities. All the nations of the world have a part in Egypt, just as the past has a part in the present.

We visited many of the smaller towns as well during our Egyptian stay. After Tanta, Zagazig, Kafr-el-Zayat, El-Mansura, and Damanhur, only Bor Said (Port Said) and Suez turned radically different faces to the world, both of them being important rest stops for those crossing the canal.

Egypt was very different from the Africa we had encountered up to that point. Its cities did not have separate Arab and European sectors; the streets were just as mixed as the people themselves. Locals could be split roughly into two groups: descendants of the ancient Egyptians and Arabs, but because of the mingling of races, most people did not clearly belong to one group or the other, and many had European blood as well. Skin hues ranged from white to the darkest brown. Some Arabs were whiter than most Germans or Brits, and many Europeans had been tanned beyond recognition by the African sun. Few people wore turbans or burnooses; shopkeepers, servants, shoe-shiners, newspaper vendors, and other simpler folk wore the traditional Arabian style garments and went about clad in striped or brilliantly colored, ankle-length robes. Those belonging to higher classes, officials, merchants, and the like opted for European-style clothing; however, no one went without the *tarbus,* or traditional red fez.

Some women wore veils, others did not; most veils were of a thin, transparent material complementing somewhat European outfits. Most women wore long, black, loose robes, which sometimes covered the most brilliantly colored pants. Veils were black or white for the most part, held together by a copper pin, which lay on the forehead. The veils, which covered women to their noses, weren't attractive, but the eyes gazing from behind the veils were beguilingly beautiful. Egyptian women, although hidden by veils, looked at strange men in a way European women never will.

If we hadn't known we were in Egypt, we never could have guessed based on what we saw on the street. Most street signs, inscriptions, newspapers, and names of stores, were in French; writing in Arabic was relatively rare, but we were surprised to find quite a bit of Greek, especially in the cities of central Egypt. The streets were filled with a motley crowd of vendors, shoe-shiners, and freeloaders, not a very inviting group of people, especially in comparison to the noble Arabs of Morocco or Tripolitania. Many were dirty, loud, and argumentative. The international quality of the place reminded us of Tangiers.

Our knowledge of French was endlessly helpful, although we heard plenty of Arabic, Italian, English, Greek, and even German being spoken all around us.

Cries of *"Baksheesh, baksheesh!"* resounded nearly every step of the way. Baksheesh was the Egyptians' favorite word and signified something that was very important to them. We first encountered the word while going through customs. We spent a lot of time at the checkpoint, and the customs official on duty beamed with satisfaction each time he matched another one of the long numbers on our documents with a number on our motorcycle. He made no secret of his delight and spent what seemed to us like an eternity examining our belongings, circling the motorbike like a buzzard.

By the Egyptian pyramids at the beginning of our journey

"It says here, Monsieur, that there are not one, but two cylinders…"

"Voilà," I answered, pointing to the cylinder, "one, two."

"Are you sure there are no other cylinders?" he asked with a strict face, which soon melted into a joyful smile that we had hidden no cylinders from him. Although the encounter ended on a pleasant note, we had to pay *baksheesh* anyway, just as we paid extra after every purchase we made. We even paid police *baksheesh* when asking for directions.

While in Egypt, we wouldn't have missed the pyramids for the world. We were anxious to take photos at these famous sites. The incomprehensible labor that must have gone into building up the Cheops Pyramid, for example, was astounding. This pyramid alone, built entirely by human hands, was comprised of 2,300,000 stones, each weighing an average of two tons.

Entire crowds of tourists were quickly surrounded by would-be tour guides. An American woman was almost crushed between two such Arabs on camels. Had it not been for the British police, she would have met her Maker there, in front of the pyramids. British police, however, had more power than King Fuad himself. The humble crowds receded at a wave of their hand. We

Statue of Ramses II near Bedrasein

took the opportunity to marvel at the British knack for keeping order. The British police were never aggressive, did not use their batons, but still managed to create order in the midst of chaos. The sure gestures that quieted the crowd were the same gestures that governed the Empire. British police around the world were a credit to all of Britain.

The respect that the people of the world felt towards British policemen was made manifest before our eyes, as the crowds that were threatening to crush the tourists they came to serve, grew quiet and drew aside without the policeman having to speak a single word. But it wasn't only human beings who were awestruck in the presence of these champions of order. Upon seeing the policeman, a huge chimpanzee, which had broken away from one of the Arabs, jumped back five or six meters and crouched quietly on the ground. The chimp wouldn't have repeated this act before the mightiest king in the world, yet it felt constrained to retreat before the policeman, even though the Brit would never have so much as touched it.

If there hadn't been a single shop in Egypt, we still could have managed, simply buying what we needed from street vendors instead. Caution was in order, however; not even the savviest shopper in the world could avoid being cheated at least once by the local Arabs. Prices were high, especially the prices of all things having to do with tourism. The smallest currency was the half-piaster, which therefore was the amount of the smallest *baksheesh*. The name of the currency changed whether those using it were Brits, Arabs, French, or Greeks. There was the *piccolo* and the *petit* piaster, as well as the *tariffa*. Five piasters equalled a shilling, twenty a dollar, but there were other relevant currencies, such as the small and large *girsh* and the *milliem*.

Everyone was out to make money; there were no set prices whatsoever, and so, we had to haggle every time we made a purchase, whether it was a newspaper or cigarettes; even ticket prices to museums and performances as well as customs duties at the border were negotiable. I bought three twenty piaster tickets to a banquet for five piasters total; a ten piaster box of cigarettes was more often than not intended to be sold for seven or eight piasters. Official prices were intended to confuse the inexperienced. Experimental prices were the hallmark of the entire experimental Egyptian economy, the motto of which was: take as much as you can from whomever you can.

Foreigners arriving in Egypt are lectured on proper haggling techniques even before stepping off the boat. The tourists in turn, fortified by what they have heard, step off the boats with a gleam of determination in their eyes and head straight for the markets, where they are immensely proud to pay only half of what the vendor originally asked, not realizing that the locals put one over on them when they named a starting price that was ten times the going rate.

We spent hours in the coffeehouses. We needed to go no further than the nearest coffeehouse to make all necessary purchases, as street vendors peddled from table to table, selling postcards, cigarettes, beads, and shoe polish. Basic wares such as these were for sale in the simplest of coffeehouses, but Cairo coffeehouses were so well stocked that we could have clothed ourselves from head to toe, bought raffle tickets and fine rugs, soap, brushes, and walking sticks, tropical hats, ties, and socks. One vendor carried men's shirts, but in case you weren't interested, he also had a basket of juicy oranges for sale. Another carried newspapers, cigarette holders, toothbrushes, and cuff links. There seemed to be no end in sight. The cigarettes we bought from street vendors were mostly hideous and of poor quality. Fine Egyptian cigarettes were only available in official places.

There was a group of Americans sitting one table over. A jeweler walked in, his basket spilling over, his arms, neck, and waste wrapped in strings of beads. If anyone so much as glanced at him, the strings of beads were as good as sold. Stopping by the American table, he offered those sitting there a "genuine scarab," and refused to leave, despite vehement protests and rude gestures.

"Please buy just one, sir, help me out," he said.

"How much?" asked one of the Americans, and we knew the "scarab" was as good as sold.

Ancient irrigation canals in modern Egypt

"Sixty piasters, sir, because this is my first sale of the day," answered the vendor. The American had obviously received the haggling lecture upon arrival, because he sank into silent thought for few moments. We saw that he found the jewelry attractive and had plenty of money at his disposal, but he had no idea how much the scarab was worth.

"Too much," he said cautiously, still refusing to name a price. The Arab then posed the question we had heard all too often, "How much will you give?"

"Well, let's see, would you sell it for ten?" asked the American. The eyes of the vendor lit up, but as he started wrapping the necklace, he pretended to grumble at the proposed price and finally announced that he would not part with the necklace for under forty piasters. The end of the story was that the American bought the necklace for twenty piasters, smiling with the assurance that he had refused to be taken in by the wretched Arab. What he never found out was that a necklace like the one he bought usually sold for five piasters, was actually worth only two, and the vendor had bought it himself for a single piaster.

One evening I proudly carried my own purchase home. I had bought a beautiful scarab necklace for five piasters at a remote bazaar. I was convinced I had made a great deal, until Mimmy showed me three identical scarabs she had bought for a total of five piasters!

As I have mentioned, the largest cities of Egypt resembled each other to a great extent. Traffic cops stationed along the largest cosmopolitan boulevards directed the flow of traffic; those working in the downtown area wore white gloves, while the cops in the outskirts controlled traffic with the help of red and green flags. Those with the flags were especially enthusiastic about their jobs, often stopping six to eight cars to let a single cart rattle through. There were a large number of horse-drawn carts, aptly fitting into the Middle Eastern context. The narrower streets were always filled with huge crowds of people, camels, buffalo, donkeys, cows, and sheep.

We couldn't complain about the roads. Life-giving irrigation canals crisscrossed all of southern Egypt. The main canals were 30-40 meters wide, and most roads led next to such canals. The wider canals branched out into a network of thinner and thinner canals, ditches, and wells. When the water reached the fields, it was lifted out by various devices, some as ancient as the pyramids. In other places, the hard-working peasants themselves scooped out water from the ditches, using their hands or any containers they happened to own.

King Fuad the First was the one who began constructing roads throughout the country. Before his reign, there had been no roads to speak of, aside from the paths trodden by donkeys and camels. Most of the roads we encountered were simple sand roads, which were kept wet by the water from nearby channels. By watering and flattening the sand, the Egyptians created outstanding roads, suitable for automobiles even. There were no stone markers; in reality, the road formed a continuum with the desert sands to the right and to the left and was identifiable only by its relative hardness. Most roads were strictly straight and therefore, allowed travel at high speed, however, the dust and almost unbearable heat combined to make traveling difficult. Although we were there in the spring, temperatures of 40-45 degrees C were common. Most tourists refused to ride cars in the heat and dust, opting instead for trains and boats. The dusty roads were therefore usually filled with locals riding ancient-looking bus-like vehicles from one village to the next. The four wheels of these "buses" seemed to be constantly headed in four different directions; there wasn't a drop of paint or varnish to protect the metal sides of the bus, and travelers hung from its roof and sides in grape-like bunches.

We passed through scores of tiny villages. Most villages were nothing but a clump of primitive huts, built of adobe or pounded earth, with a single opening to the world. There were no streets to speak of. From a distance, the clusters of houses looked like giant molehills, occasionally shaded by a dried out palm tree or two. The villages built near canals boasted a number of trees and water-lifting devices powered by cows, buffalo, and camels. A good portion of the water was meant for the roads, which had to be kept wet constantly.

A glimpse of Old Memphis

We explored the ruins of the city of Memphis, climbed the pyramids yet again, and made sure to see the treasures of Tutankhamen at the museum. After Shepheards and Mena-House in Cairo, we found ourselves drinking black coffee at the tiniest, hole-in-the-wall kinds of places. As we headed towards the Suez Canal, the Eastern luxury and pomp, the loose morals, drugs, and orgies of the beautiful cities we had visited passed before our eyes like a wondrous dream.

The heat was relentless; there was not a drop of rain to cool the parched traveler. Although it was early spring in Egypt, we had never experienced such heat in our entire lives. We were forced to rest an entire day after completing the Cairo-Suez stretch of the desert road. We must have drunk vats of iced beverages in all that heat, but the most pleasant memory of all involves Egyptian beer.

A glass of beer, usually imported from Germany, cost only two piasters, but more often than not, we received a few bites of food to go with the beer: bread, fish, a bit of salami, a baked potato, and sardines. With all these delicious food samples complementing our beverage, we usually ordered two or three beers for dinner.

While still in Suez, we had difficulty deciding which road to take to Palestine. Those we asked for suggestions gave varied advice. Nobody seemed to know the way in reality, so we decided to use the railroad as our guide, and ride along the El Kantara-Gaza line.

We took a small ferry from El Kantara across the Suez Canal. Our companions on the three-minute ride were morose, not very welcoming looking Bedouins. We knew that we were traveling into a region where we would encounter more and more Arabs who didn't always look upon foreign travelers with approval. It took us a mere three minutes to go from Africa to Asia; as we left Africa for good, we reflected that we were setting foot on our third continent.

The only road, if it could be called that, to Palestine was an obscure caravan route that had partially disappeared in a sea of sand. We had arrived at the northernmost part of the Sinai Peninsula. The land once trod by Moses himself was very unfriendly country.

There were still 200 kilometers to the Palestinian border. Because of the inland seas, we had to keep to the desert roads, which mostly led through a maze of dunes.

The wind had arranged the sand in various ripples and waves, and as we looked upon the desolate landscape, we grew less and less certain that we would successfully cross the desert. After leaving our old guide, the railway, we soon found ourselves riding on the typical yellow sands of the Sinai Desert. We had enough water to last us days, because we knew that the water sources marked on our map were usually dry. The map wasn't much use in the desert; we were forced to rely on our good navigational skills and instincts, which often proved to be the best guides.

Our struggles with the sand were renewed. Some days, we barely made ten kilometers. Whenever we reached the railroad, we rode along the tracks as far as we could, despite all warnings to the contrary. There were stretches where the tracks showed distinctly; here we were forced to slow down, but

Somewhere between Cairo and Suez

whenever they were covered by a layer of sand, we sped up and made some progress.

There wasn't a single human being in sight. Railroad stations were few and far between, usually consisting of run-down wooden shacks, inhabited by a single Arab. At the same time, we could always count on fresh water at these stops, and one train per day, should all else fail.

On our trek through the desert, we encountered a number of unpleasant signs, silent witnesses to those who had passed through. Bones white as chalk, and who knew whether they had belonged to a camel or a human being, occasionally stuck out of the sand, calling to mind hair-raising stories of Bedouins, jackals, vultures, and slowly dying of thirst. We redoubled our efforts to leave the desert behind as soon as possible.

We spent our nights in the sand. Cool nights followed sweltering days. As soon as the sun set, the air grew colder and colder. During the day, the sun was so strong that it would have been risky to remove our tropical hats for a single moment; the metal parts of our motorbike were so hot that we couldn't touch them with our bare hands. Whoever was driving had to do so wearing gloves, and we shielded our lungs from the waves of unbearable heat by tying wet cloths in front of our mouths. It was in the Sinai Desert that we first made use of our new water sack, which we had purchased in Cairo. The sack could hold sixteen liters of water, and we hung it from the front of our motorcycle. As a small amount of water was continually seeping from the sack, our water was kept relatively cool through the process of evaporation despite the 50 degree C heat.

We grew to admire our motorcycle. Although we were making slow progress, it seemed to bear the heat very well. Then again, we did make numerous stops, so the engine wasn't in constant use.

At night, we were all cold, as temperatures often approached freezing. Our tent wasn't warm enough, so we tried a different solution: burrowing in the sand. The sand retained much of the heat it had absorbed during the day while being incredibly soft. All in all, it would have been the ideal bed, had we not been forced to be on constant guard against a new enemy: the scorpion. We had met our first scorpions in Egypt and observed their curled up, sinister tails, the tips of which were filled with poison, deadly poison in the case of most species. Before settling down for the night, we had to be sure to scan, then thoroughly examine our beds while it was still light, to avoid unpleasant surprises.

Our nights were far from restful; we were constantly on guard against not only desert animals, but Arabs as well, and took turns watching through the night, weapon in hand. We never made a campfire for the simple reason that there wasn't a tree in sight.

After three days of desert travel, on the fourth day, we crossed the border into Palestine and arrived in Gaza, which was the first larger town we encountered.

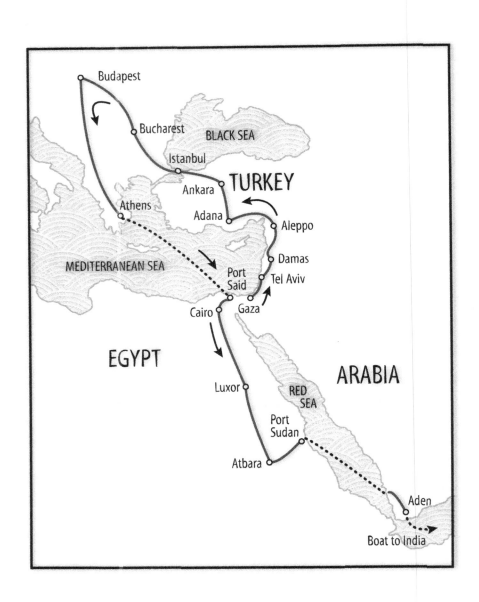

The Roundabout Way to India

The Ruthless Roads of Asia Minor

We had been longing to visit the Holy Land for as long as we could remember; the charms of the biblical countryside were palpable to everyone with at least a mildly elevated spirit.

And we had arrived. The first small Arab town we passed through did not differ much from many other similar towns, and the lousy sandy roads managed to dim our exhilaration upon reaching this famous land. Despite efforts to the contrary, all signs of civilization were stamped with an undeniable Arab character. The only sign that this land was different from those we had visited so far was the presence of Hebrew writing, Hebrew being the third official language in the land, beside English and Arabic.

We rattled along for quite some time, encountering camels and entire caravans, as well as Arabs on donkeys, with their wives walking patiently behind them. Although we had become used to the sight, our European sensibilities could not grow accustomed to the idea of large Arab men comfortably perched on tiny donkeys, smoking their pipes as their wives walked beside them, trying not to fall behind while carrying a child on their backs and packages on their heads.

While in Palestine, we visited all of the important sites, taking care not to leave out any attraction worth seeing. Jerusalem, Bethlehem, Nazareth, Haifa, Hebron, Tiberias, Kaffarnaum, and Jericho remain strongly etched in our memories. We spent a number of days immersed in the pulsating rhythms of the new Jewish capital, the almost American Tel Aviv. We climbed the Mount of Olives, visited the Garden of Gethsemane, bathed in the Sea of Galilee and even managed to cross the River Jordan.

At the same time, some of the sights were disappointments. There were a great number of churches, each of them built up around a site of biblical significance. The churches were for the most part large and somewhat archaic; we had expected them to be more beautiful. To make matters worse, they were mostly under the auspices of the Greek Orthodox Church and very neglected. Christendom, which had created marvelous, monumental churches throughout Europe and cathedrals outfitted with some of the wonders of

The Mount of Olives in Jerusalem

modern technology at sites of pilgrimage, had neglected the holy places of Palestine. The churches in the Holy Land were lit by candles only; beautiful works of art hung on the walls, held there by mere strings, the myriads of donations, jewelry, and precious stones were stored in beat-up glass cupboards.

Then we thought, perhaps this was the way it was meant to be. Maybe the Christian soul could find more peace between these old, worn walls than in the most shining of cathedrals. Most of our guides were bearded Orthodox priests, who opened the churches only when a visitor expressed interest in going inside. *Baksheesh* was not exactly obligatory, but it would have been considered very impolite had we passed through the holy places for free.

At the tomb of the Virgin Mary, a young Arab brought us the key to the ancient chapel. There was a deep well inside. "Are you Christians?" asked our guide. "If you are, you should drink some of this water. The Virgin Mary herself drank from it." We were happy to try the water; the problem was, we had no cup. The young Arab, however, was certainly not at a loss, because he marched up to the altar, opened the tabernacle and took out a golden chalice, filling it with the crystal clear water for us to drink.

As we were leaving the chapel, he held out a collection box. As soon as we placed a few coins in it and stepped outside, he ran to the altar and emptied the box of donations.

The only good road we found in the land of Palestine was the modern asphalt road connecting Jerusalem and the sea, leading from Jerusalem to Jaffa and Tel Aviv. Other roads were under construction; automobile traffic was minimal. The preferred mode of transportation, as in the days of Christ, was the back of a donkey.

We couldn't access the Old City in Jerusalem with our motorbike. The narrow, winding alleys, tunnel-like arches, and steep inclines were crowded with people, on foot and riding donkeys. Arabs and Jews, sheiks and Christian priests hurried in all directions. The number of long, thick beards sported by the men was astounding. Women were dressed according to a variety of fashions, but there was a clear majority dressed in all black, covering their bodies with large, white sheets and their heads with flowery or lacy white scarves.

The land itself was not conducive to the formation of a Jewish state. Most of the country was a vast desert or stony wasteland. Rain was virtually unknown and all forms of agriculture seemingly impossible. We expected the land to flower only if an irrigation system resembling that of the Egyptians could be built, turning the Promised Land into a land of promise. The construction of such a system of canals and ditches would take unforeseen sums of money and vast stretches of time.

There were territories within the Holy Land, however, that had already begun to flourish. These were the strips of land closest to the sea. As foreigners, we were amazed by the enthusiastic efforts the Jewish settlers made to cultivate the land. Everyone worked hard. We met a few Hungarian Jews; one who had been a banker in Hungary was pushing a cart, clad in shorts and boots. Others, former merchants, proudly showed off their calluses caused by handling rough farm implements. Hungarian university students working as porters at the railway station beamed with the happiness of being able to take part in the building up of their new country.

The situation of the Jewish settlers, however, was far from enviable. There was an overwhelming Arab majority entirely disinclined to stand by and witness the birth of a Jewish State. Arabs were just as skilled and resourceful businessmen as the Jews, and their love of their homeland and independence burned strong.

The Jews themselves were dissatisfied. Life was hard, work was strenuous, and hope waning. To make matters worse, Jews did not enjoy the independence that had been promised them by the British. They didn't stand a chance against native Arabs when it came to cheap labor; official positions were few and the amount of arable land minimal. Many who had formerly arrived armed with funds, hope, and creative promise left Palestine destitute.

It felt like the Jews had come face to face with the inspired colonial politics of the British. Although Palestine was promised to the Jews, the Arabs could not be expected to give up their homelands. At the same time, full Arab control of Palestine could not be reestablished, because any attempts in this direction would trigger Jewish discontent the world over. It seemed the two peoples were sentenced to life-long conflict and strife, unless the British magnanimously stepped in to create order. And of course, the keeping of order was a profit-oriented undertaking.

We received a warm welcome in Tel Aviv, a modern metropolis that had sprung up almost overnight, carving out a place for civilization in the desert sands. Tel Aviv was inhabited solely by Jews, and Hebrew was the only accepted language. This rule caused Hungarian Jews a lot of grief. Hungarian Jews were far superior to their fellows in many areas of life and were therefore not very well liked. To make matters worse, they were forced to give up their mother tongue and learn Hebrew directly upon arrival.

Elderly, bearded Orthodox men stopped us a number of times, admonishing us to speak Hebrew. When it got out that we were foreigners, we were greeted enthusiastically by curious young people. One university student went so far as to introduce us to the local notables. Although we didn't understand a word of the speech, which was in Hebrew, we were nevertheless overwhelmed by signs of admiration and affection. It was only on our way back to the hotel that our young Hungarian patron admitted he had introduced us as fellow Jews.

The first time we got truly sick on our trip was in Palestine. After being stung a number of times by a species of tiny fly, we developed a rash on the entire surface of our bodies. Scared, we ran to the doctor, who assured us, after a brief examination, that we had contracted an illness that was very widespread but easily cured by the sea. Sure enough, after taking a bath or two in the salty waves, we were as good as new.

On the road to Haifa, however, we ran into trouble. Still weak from our illness, we were shocked to discover that our sidecar had broken off from the motorcycle. With all our bags in the sidecar, it was impossible for us to continue the journey. We were still 50 km from the city, but fortunately, we received a cart and loaded the entire sidecar, all our packages and Mimmy onto the cart. Gyuszi and I rode the motorcycle. Our progress was slow on the hilly terrain; we hadn't fully recovered from our illness, the sidecar was heavy, and our experience with carts limited, at best. Although the entire cart and sidecar tipped over three times, we somehow managed to reach Haifa by the evening. We were delighted to find that the shop to which we took our motorcycle and broken sidecar was Hungarian-owned.

We left the Holy Land via Damas, or Damascus, but not before experiencing what was to become one of the most serious adventures of our entire journey. This was an incident that could have ended in death, and it therefore remains deeply etched in our consciousness.

An Encounter with Syrian Bedouins

The way from Nazareth to Damascus was rather dull. The road led through the Syrian Desert, a wasteland of scruffy bushes and rocks, infamous and unpopulated. Automobile drivers undertook the journey of about 300 km only in larger groups, but we weren't about to wait for an automated caravan.

The heat was stifling; although we were sitting on a moving vehicle, we felt like we were riding through a sauna. I was driving; Gyuszi Bartha sat in the sidecar, and Mimmy opted for her favorite place: the passenger seat. The oppressive silence was broken only by the puffing of the engine. Occasional cacti, twisted in fantastic shapes and white with desert dust, peppered the otherwise monotonous landscape. There wasn't a single tree in sight except for a sorry looking withered palm, whose dried fronds waved in silent reproach to the Creator.

Our conversation was just about as dull as the landscape around us. A violent bump shook Bartha up, and he exclaimed: "This road must have been built around the time of Christ!" He was overly critical, however. We were making decent progress at forty kilometers an hour, despite the occasional bumps. In any case, the road was much better than your random sandy caravan route.

We took a short stop at a bridge spanning the Jordan River. A few green bushes lined the narrow ribbon of water on both sides and were a refreshing sight in the gray and yellow landscape. We continued on.

"I see people," Bartha cried suddenly. We all looked back. "Arabs on horseback!" one of us cried, "Bedouins!" Suddenly, we called to mind the warnings, the tales of desert robbers and of sheiks who were skilled in much more than love.

"Faster! Let's go!" cried Mimmy from the passenger seat. I had a feeling she was right but tried to reassure her by saying, "Be sensible. What could they possibly want from us?" Nevertheless, I upped our speed to 50 kilometers an hour.

The sidecar was literally leaping over potholes. We spent more time looking behind our shoulders than forward in the direction we were going. The horsemen seemed to be getting closer and closer. The magnificent horses and those riding them became visible in more and more detail; soon we could make out the weapons the riders were waving and heard their shouts. It didn't take us long to realize that they did, indeed, want something from us and were pursuing us at top speed. "Faster! Faster!" Gyuszi and Mimmy cried. I took a moment to think things through. If they were determined to catch up with us, we had no chance of escape because of the poor quality of the road. Maybe it would be better to stop and try to negotiate? After all, there were at least ten of them, and our two guns and one revolver were no match for their weapons. We also knew that our life wasn't in danger if we didn't resist; Arabs didn't kill without reason.

My reverie was broken by the sound of gunshots. We were still far enough away that their chances of hitting us were small; I conjectured these were warning shots to get us to stop. I gave Mimmy the revolver, saying "Hold on to it, but don't use it just yet."

I didn't stop the motorcycle. I didn't think of the loaded guns but speeded on, come what may. We had too much to lose: weapons, packages, and supplies, but first and foremost, Mimmy, who would have been a prize for these pirates of the desert.

Seconds passed like minutes. I couldn't get the speed past 50 kilometers per hour; we all leaned forward excitedly, Gyuszi climbing out of the sidecar and onto the bike to speed our progress. We couldn't convince Mimmy to hide in the sidecar. We sat in line on the bike, and it came to me how a single bullet, if aimed well, could kill the three of us. Our pursuers were still hot on our track; Damas was 50 kilometers away, and we knew the bike wouldn't last an hour at this speed. Then again, neither would their horses! All we could do was hope the roads would get better...

The roads did not improve, but the cries of the approaching horsemen got louder and louder. I even had to put on the brakes as we encountered a series of ditches. Our hearts were pounding almost audibly, and we started to give up all hope as the grim, bearded faces came into view. Then, I made one last attempt.

"Hold on tight!" I screamed, giving the engine full throttle. The hand on the speedometer showed sixty, seventy, then eighty! We were gaining on them, but the bike could have broken down at any moment. The whole contraption was shaking; occasionally, we found ourselves a full half a meter above ground, clinging to the seats for dear life. The distance between us and our pursuers grew, and soon after, we reached a smooth stretch of road, where we were able to speed along at a hundred kilometers per hour. By then, the horsemen were a full kilometer behind, out of both ear- and gunshot, and soon, out of sight.

Horsepower had defeated the horse. On good roads, this would have been no miracle, but the four or five minutes of pursuit had exhausted us more than a whole day's journey in the desert.

Upon our arrival in Damas, we made our way to the French officials and explained, excitedly and with flushed faces, what had happened to us on the way. They made a note of the incident, which was just one of many, without showing the least bit of surprise.

Heading in a New Direction

Our original intention had been to take the long land route from Damas to India, via Baghdad, Teheran, and Afghanistan or through Baghdad, Southern Iran, and Baluchistan. Both were difficult prospects, and we spent a great deal of time mulling over which would be the less risky of the two.

Upon our visit to the British consulate, however, our eyes were opened to grim reality. We quickly found out that the British weren't allowing anyone into either Afghanistan or Iraq as a result of the bloody events that had taken place in the former and the rebellion that had shaken the latter country. The officials at the Consulate told us point blank that they would make no exceptions. Our only chance was to wait a few weeks in the hopes that the situation would improve and a new set of ordinances would come into force.

"Should we return to Egypt?" we asked ourselves, quickly rejecting the idea, as our entire trip was centered on the notion of moving from one new place to the next. We had made ourselves a promise that we would never travel down the same stretch of road twice, and we intended to keep it.

In the end, we decided to travel to the Balkans, which were nearly as novel to us as the African countries we passed had once been, via Eastern Turkey. From the Balkan Peninsula, our project would be to reach India by traveling south, through Upper Egypt, Sudan, and Arabia. Our plan to briefly return to Europe seemed especially wise in the light of Mimmy's poor health; she had been suffering from frequent fevers, which we feared were indicative of a developing case of malaria. In case she really did come down with the disease, her traveling to tropical countries would be out of the question.

For the time being, we explored Syria. Although its political ties with France were stronger, it didn't seem nearly as "French" as Egypt and Palestine had been. The population was very mixed, comprised of Arabs, Druze, Bedouins, Syrians, Armenians, Persians, Circassians, and Turks. The most varied and fascinating of all its cities was Damas. The roads were filled with horsemen on magnificent steeds, both the men and the beasts uncannily reminiscent of our pursuers in the desert. The city itself lay surrounded by lush vegetation; the waters of the earth were kind to "the oldest city in the world." Streams of water ran along the streets and parted into narrow, man-made channels, which branched out into as many streets as possible to bring water and coolness to as many places as possible. There were fountains in the shops, and although the heat was stifling, the locals had developed a number of ways to keep cool. We especially grew to love lemon ice, which was kept in huge barrels and thankfully cheap; for an insignificant sum, we purchased more lemon ice than the three of us could handle.

Making our way through the immense bazaar, we were especially drawn to

Water wheel in Hama, Syria

the splendid Persian rugs, which had been brought to Damas by the caravans, were available in an infinite variety of patterns, and were most likely sold for less than in any other city in the world. The furniture-, weapon-, and jewelry trade were also booming.

After Damas, we traveled on through Beirut, Homs, Hama, and Aleppo. Beirut, the capital of the Republic of Grand Liban, was in the proximity of the Mountains of Lebanon, which still gave shelter to over 400 of the ancient cedars of Lebanon. Beirut was full of nightclubs and had a distinctly French flavor. We even ran into some Hungarian acrobats, who had been invited for a few performances.

Hama and Homs were very Arabian in nature, and Aleppo was the queen of the desert and the destination of many Persian caravans. In the past, all caravan routes between Baghdad and Teheran had met in or passed through Aleppo.

We were forced to spend two weeks in Beirut, waiting for our ten pound deposit, which we had made at the British customs upon reaching the Palestinian border, to be returned. We experienced British bureaucracy at its worst; day after day we waited, without any indication that we would ever see our ten pounds again. After our telegraph produced no results, our only option was to retrieve our money personally. I made my way back to Jerusalem by car and train and returned with our ten pounds, which I secured after a great deal of footwork.

The trip from Beirut to Jerusalem and back to Beirut had cost us seven of our ten pounds, but I still felt justified in my efforts. After all, we needed the money much more than the British did. We made up our mind to be more cautious about making deposits and to try to avoid them altogether whenever possible.

Our troubles with the gasoline prices continued. There were no set prices, and if we didn't take care to stock up in larger towns, we soon found ourselves paying exorbitant sums in the villages. In all of Northern Africa, as well as in the Far East, as we later found out, gasoline was sold in closed tin containers rather than from a pump. One such container fit four gallons, or sixteen to eighteen liters of gasoline, which got us 200 to 220 kilometers. Used containers had no value and were often tossed out by automobile drivers, only to be picked up by the resourceful natives. We saw the tin containers put to the most amazing variety of uses in the smallest of villages and the largest cities alike. Some used them to carry water; others stored grain or other foods in the handy containers. The shops were lined with them, as they proved to be the ideal storage bins. The most creative envisioned ideal basins, watering cans, even building material made of the tin containers. There were entire warehouses, even small homes, built of tin. After seeing the widespread uses to which these ubiquitous containers were put, we wondered how the Arabs had survived before the advent of the automobile and the gasoline container.

We hadn't been able to secure directions or maps for the Turkish portion of our trip. This did not bode well. Another problem was the quality of the roads, which deteriorated sharply as soon as we had left Aleppo. The roads were not only poor, but entirely deserted as well. We didn't encounter so much as a donkey or a cart and saw very few signs of life. Forced to rely on our eyes, instincts, and the tracks of those who had gone before, we made our solitary way to the Turkish border. The closer we got to the border, the more deserted the road and countryside grew. Nearing a mountain range, we discovered an old Turkish military road, or rather, the remains of the military roads, as all that was left was the foundation, built of large stones. The smaller stones and the earth had long since been swept away by time. The stone foundation wasn't strong enough to allow modern vehicles to pass, but the old road did provide an excellent guide, and we decided not to stray very far from it. There were traces of a new earth road, but to our greatest consternation, it was entirely overgrown by grass. We conjectured the last time it saw any traffic must have been during the war.

Our destination was Seyhan, or Adana, and we crossed the border at the village of Meydanaliz. The border station was comprised of a wooden shack. Two grimy guards stepped outside when they heard us coming, their eyes growing round with wonder at the sight of our motorcycle. We were pretty sure they had never seen a motorcycle in their lives. They were so taken aback that they didn't ask for any documentation regarding the vehicle and returned our passports after one quick glimpse inside. A third guard stepped up to us and read the contents of our visas to the two previous guards, who immediately saluted and let us through. The Eastern Turkish chapter of our journeys was just beginning, a chapter that would be filled with miserable roads and unforeseen hardships.

Unless new roads have been constructed since our own travels, I would strongly advise any motorist against undertaking such a journey. At least for some time, until the ambitious plan of building a land route to connect Great Britain with India is accomplished.

The troubles began as soon as we had crossed the border and continued for some time. We were driven by our hopes. At first, we were hoping the road would improve once we reached Seyhan, but as we neared our destination, we were forced to imagine that the place the really good roads began was Nigde. Then Kayseri. Then Kirsehir and Ankara. Leaving Ankara we were shocked to discover that there was no road leading to Constantinople. Never in our wildest dreams could we have imagined that there was no road connecting the large, historical metropolis, Constantinople with the modern Turkish capital, Ankara.

Nobody traveled on wheels, and nobody was able to give us any directions worth following. We weren't even sure of the direction in which to get started. We marked what seemed to us like a reasonable route on our inaccurate, nearly useless maps, and traveled village by village, asking the villagers for directions to the next village on our route. Although we had acquired a basic Turkish vocabulary, our attempts at communication proved futile. We were not being understood. If we asked three different people for directions to the same location, we received three different answers. The more villagers we stopped the more "answers" we got.

"Nerde vahr youl ne Angorada ghidior?" we mumbled, "Which way to Ankara?" *"Sahl? Soul?"* "Right? Left?"

The usual answer was *"Evet,"* "Yes" and we continued on after polite thank-you's, *"Teshkuer edereem."*

Even before reaching Seyhan, we were forced to cross the Gyaur Mountains, which towered above us at 2,200 meters, as well as the monumental Taurus Range. It took us fourteen hours to travel forty-five kilometers, and after passing the village of Osmaniye, our pace slowed to a total of sixty kilometers in three days as we crossed the Taurus Range.

For the most part, we stayed on the old military road, especially in the mountainous regions, where the road proved absolutely indispensable. Only the foundations of the road remained; most of the actual road was covered with earth or giant rocks. We were forced to stop a number of times to clear

Three days on the road in the Taurus Mountains of Turkey

the road of the layers of earth and large rocks; on other occasions, we took it upon ourselves to build up a stretch of the road that had slid into the depths to avoid the same fate ourselves. Gullies and mountain creeks further obstructed our way. Each time we encountered water, we faced having to build a small bridge and carrying, pulling, and pushing our motorcycle along and what seemed like a snail's pace, hoping with each step that we were that much closer to the "good" roads.

We never met a soul outside of the villages. The countryside was desolate all the way to Ankara; we had nothing to fear. Aside from insects, no wild animals confronted us. Myriads of mosquitoes made our evenings miserable, and two nights in cheap small-town hotels brought us face to face with worms and bedbugs, whose insistent presence convinced us to opt for our tent instead.

The people and the conditions in which they lived were miserably backward. Back in the worm-infested hotel, we had asked the receptionist where we could wash up. Astonished at our questions, he pointed to the creek running just outside the hotel and explained that everyone bathed there.

We never ran out of water. Although the mountains seemed dry and barren from far off, they were nevertheless filled with life-giving creeks. Not a bit taken aback, we stripped and bathed in the crystal clear water at least twice a day, washing our sweaty clothes each time.

The villages were very poor, comprised only of tiny wooden huts, with not a single shop in sight. Each village was built around a creek that ambled through the various streets. If the village was built on a slope as well, there wasn't a single house without its own personal branch of the creek flowing by the front door. The Turkish towns in the Eastern, or Asian, half of Turkey were in no way superior to Arabian towns of a similar size.

In the larger towns, we encountered Hungarians who mostly made their living as industrial workers and complained unceasingly of present poverty while fondly reminiscing about a wealthier, happier past. Ankara especially was home to numerous Hungarians, although many more had been living there in the past. A lot of immigrants, however, were forced to move on as a result of the working of the Turkish system. The Turks essentially welcomed and respected strangers, as long as they needed them for something. The citizens of Turkey, especially those living in Ankara and Constantinople, had the immigrant workers to thank for a lot of positive developments. However, as soon as the Turkish workers mastered the methods that had produced so many positive results in the hands of strangers, foreign workers very quickly found themselves without a job. For example, a Turkish carpenter might hire immigrant workers for some time, only to fire them ruthlessly as soon as he had learnt the tricks of the trade. And it wasn't only the carpenters who resorted to these less than fair methods. The Greeks had made Constantinople what it was, and what did they get in return? They were thrown into the sea. It was a common occurrence for a foreign worker to go without his wages for a long time; even the government issued promissory notes instead of paychecks. Some Hungarians complained of having waited years for their wages, which, after all that time, should have added up to a considerable sum.

The Turkish people, as a whole, were a warm-hearted people. Our pity for them exceeded our anger at the unfair treatment of immigrant workers. The Pasha Kemal had a difficult time reforming them, because they had an almost innate horror of change. Generations of Turks had been perfectly contented with an unassuming existence, a life of restful poverty, and the prospect of having to learn a new alphabet and work hard for a living did not appeal to the people. Turks had a deep love of tradition. When Kemal Ataturk forbade the wearing of the red fez, men opted for caps and hats, but only in public. As soon as they reached home, they laid aside their hats and affectionately redonned their fezes, sometimes refusing to take them off even in bed. Women weren't allowed to wear veils; in fact, police who caught women with their faces covered simply ripped off their veils. Nevertheless, women continued to wear their veils, if not over their faces, than bound to the tops of their heads.

Kemal had built up an entire new district in Ankara, a district filled with modern, stone houses with proper windows and doors. Then the citizens were requested to leave their wooden shacks and move into the new stone houses, so the construction of modern homes could begin in all parts of the city. There wasn't a single Turk willing to exchange his old, tumbledown hut for a new stone house. Then, one night, a fire broke out in the poor district, burning it to the ground. There was no other way to convince the poor to leave their homes.

It would take many years to shake this magnanimous and peaceful, but at the same time lazy and backward, people up out of the stupor of centuries.

Simple travelers like we were, just passing through Turkey, had it hard. The Turks of Asia Minor had no concept of tourism and looked with suspicion on all foreigners. There was an ordinance that required all strangers to be photographed and their movements tracked.

All newcomers were immediately photographed. We could spot a police station from a mile away because of the hoards of photographers surrounding it. Even as we traveled through the tiniest villages, we were immediately asked to identify ourselves, then taken to the police station, where our personal information was recorded and our photographs taken. No amount of begging could dissuade the Turkish officials from fulfilling their duty. Each interrogation meant a serious loss of time; even the photographs took long, and what's worse, we were forced to pay for them out of our own pockets every single time. After a few such stops, we learned that the best way to avoid long waits would be to carry dozens of photographs of ourselves at all times. If we stopped over in a small town for a short while only, one of us stood guard and alerted the other two whenever a policeman came in sight. Then, we would simply jump on our motorcycle and leave the screaming officer behind. After a few such run-ins, we were very ill disposed towards Kemal Ataturk and the entire line of Turkish sultans!

The quality of the road did not improve. It was equally horrendous for all 1,500 km of our Turkish travels. Although we had expected a slight change after crossing the mountains, we were disappointed yet again. Occasionally, we left the old military road to ride through farmland and stubble fields, where the going was significantly easier. When we traveled along rivers, we opted to go barefoot, because we were forced to get off the bike and push. There were very few bridges. We mostly found tie beams only; the body of nearly all of the bridges had been carried off a long time ago to be used for other purposes. Whenever we came to a river, we improvised, sometimes making use of combined bridges, which were entirely without railings and slowed our pace to a step-by-step ordeal. Every encounter with the railway required added effort on our part. The rails were, for the most part, so high, that we couldn't ride the motorcycle across, but we forced to lift it over instead. I hardly think I exaggerate when I insist that the roads between Sayhen, Kayseri, Ulukisla, Kirsehir, Ankara, and Constantinople had never seen a motorcycle or an automobile. My conjecture was supported by the astonishment of the locals, who formed enthusiastic crowds around our vehicle each time we stopped.

Ankara was spreading in all directions. There were some beautiful public buildings and statues to enhance the capital, which was home to 40,000 people and without running water or a fire station.

We had another "incident" 200 kilometers before riding into the capital. A number of spokes on the sidecar wheels had broken on the way, and after a while, we lost the wheel itself and could go no further. Detaching the sidecar from the motorcycle, which was still working properly, I loaded the bad wheel onto the bike, Mimmy got up behind me, and we headed for the capital. Our poor friend Bartha remained in the wasteland in the company of a broken sidecar and all our supplies. It took us four days to make it to Ankara and back and get the wheel fixed in the process.

We hurried back as fast as we could, because we were worried about our companion. He had little food and very few bullets; we sincerely hoped that nothing dreadful had happened to him in that lonely place.

As we approached the place where we had left Gyuszi, we saw him standing on the road and waving from afar. He was in very good spirits and seemed to have put on a bit of weight. "Let me show you something," he said, smiling furtively. He took us behind the hill and pointed out a small Turkish village, which had not been visible from the road. The village was comprised of tottering mud huts, but what we found to be even more fascinating was that it was inhabited entirely by women and children. The men had all gone off to build the railway. Our friend had spent four days in a village with forty Turkish women. As he told us later, the poor women had been at a loss trying to figure out how to please the distinguished "Magyar" guest who had come their way. As we reattached our sidecar and prepared to leave, we saw tears shining in the eyes of some women.

Most Turkish women were not very beautiful. They were just as old-fashioned and unkempt as were their men, and the pant-like clothing they wore was far from attractive, but then, they were primarily regarded as servants to their husbands. It was only in Constantinople that we saw modern-looking, attractive women, but even there, the truly beautiful ones were usually foreigners. There were many foreigners living in Constantinople: Greeks, Armenians, Jews, and Italians, as well as people belonging to nearly all the nations of Europe. However, we weren't fated to reach Constantinople without further hardships.

Upon passing Izmit, we found ourselves in a military zone, where the only permissible mode of transportation was the railroad. We were arrested in the village of Sapanca, and to prevent us from escaping, the police officer ordered four men to carry our motorcycle upstairs into the offices on the second floor.

Their attempts at lifting the motorbike amused and exasperated us to no end. The vehicle stayed put with one of the policemen perched on it until the train was ready to leave.

We reached Üsküdar by train, and then took a small boat across the channel to Constantinople and Europe.

The traffic in Constantinople, or, more precisely, Istanbul, took us off guard. Constantinople was somehow different from the rest of Turkey. Although far from clean, the city was nevertheless outfitted with all the amenities of a modern metropolis.

The coffeehouses, countless in number, were forever crowded. It was obvious that those who sat mildly by, sipping coffee, weren't very concerned with finding or holding down a job. But then how in the world did they make a living? The streets were also crowded; throngs of people filed along the narrow pavements. We had to be on a constant guard against swindlers and conmen, who were just as ubiquitous as they had been on the streets of Cairo or Alexandria.

On one of our walks, I spotted an old Turkish man stumbling after me, mumbling unintelligibly. When I turned around, I saw him pick up a ring off the street. He turned his head this way and that, pretending to seek the rightful owner. Becoming aware of my gaze, he immediately walked up to me and placed the ring in my hand, asking for baksheesh in a low voice. I took one look at the ring and realized it wasn't real gold, and the stone was fake as well. *"Istemem,"* I answered, indicating I didn't want it. *"Booyroom, booyroom,"* insisted the old man. It took a great deal of convincing to get rid of the old man, but his trick was admittedly a clever one. I am sure that many tourists were only too glad to pay a few piasters for the gold rings the old man "accidentally" picked up.

The beauties of Constantinople made up for the hardships we had suffered along the way. We had a much more difficult time leaving Turkey than we had had upon first crossing the border. There were so many different visas and documents necessary to enable us to leave the country that it took us days to collect all the necessary materials, pages of Turkish writing in our passports documenting our efforts.

We admired the beautiful Golden Horn Bay, wandered down the streets of the proud and distinguished Pera District, enjoyed the bazaar-like excitement of Galata and marveled at the mosques that filled the city. The Golden Horn Bay glowing with moonlight and the silhouettes of innumerable slender minarets combined to make an unforgettable sight. In the evening air, we perceived the sing-song voice of the muezzins, resounding over twilight streets, calling the people to evening prayers.

Turkey was beautiful... but only in Constantinople.

Balkans: the Back of Beyond

Our next stop was Bulgaria. Travelers arriving from Western or Northern Europe would most likely perceive Bulgaria differently and develop a host of opinions very distinct from ours. Our impressions, however, were heavily influenced by the conditions we had encountered in Africa and Asia Minor, and so we rejoiced at the tiniest indication that we were back in Europe.

We had no trouble with customs. Although our licenses had expired, we usually crossed borders in places where motorized traffic was unknown, and therefore, expiration dates seemed irrelevant to the accommodating local guards.

The low prices were a shock to us. Bulgaria was the poorest, if not the cheapest, country in Europe. Even Romanian, Serbian, and Greek prices were higher. A single Hungarian Forint was worth 700 Levas and was enough to provide us with room and board for days.

Bulgarian and Romanian roads varied in quality. Decent stretches alternated with more difficult terrain, where we were encumbered by mud and potholes. Although we tried to stay on the main roads, our progress remained relatively slow. At the same time, all we had to do was think back on the sands of Africa or the mountain roads of Turkey to become instantly satisfied with our lot in Bulgaria. We took a ferry across the Danube at Ruse into Romania. Before crossing, however, we enjoyed a satisfying meal in Restaurant Budapest, and even had ice cream at a local Hungarian-run sweetshop.

The Romanian customs officers in Giurgiu were more than accommodating. Although they went through all our bags at a feverish pace, they forgot about the motorcycle itself and failed to ask for our expired licenses. We were soon on our way, without having signed any documents or paid the usual deposit.

It was good to be among Hungarians again, although the many Hungarian signs, the Hungarian chatter and music around us was unusual. Unusual, but infinitely pleasing.

We couldn't complain about the Romanians. They were gracious and polite to us wherever we went, not only in the towns of Transylvania, but in Bucharest as well.

The best part of our stay in Romania, however, was the welcome we received from the Hungarians of Transylvania. We spent many lovely and spirited days in the Székely Lands of Eastern Transylvania, traveling on to Brassó, Marosvásárhely, Kolozsvár, Nagyvárad, Arad, and Temesvár, where we were able to appear only at a small portion of the official dinners and receptions held in our honor.

I suppose nobody would be surprised to hear that we returned to Budapest after our Transylvanian tour. We were so close to the Hungarian border that we couldn't resist revisiting our own capital. In the space of a few days, we visited the Automobile Club, briefly met with and embraced our relatives and, before anyone knew what had happened, were on our way to the Far East and to new continents altogether.

While in Hungary, we also parted from our faithful companion, Mimmy, who had stood by us through the best and the worst of times. With her frail body, it would have been unwise for her to risk the longer portion of our journey, when we ourselves were unaware of how long that journey would last.

Now there were only two of us, but not for long, because we soon picked up a young German shepherd that was still a pup but would grow up with us as we traveled across continents and most likely do us a service or two.

Our change of plans in Syria had cost us a few months, but we didn't regret our decision. The roundabout way had taken us through five new countries, and what's more, we knew we would be proud of our perseverance in Turkey forever.

As winter set in, we headed south until we had passed the last village of Hungarian speakers. We had met Hungarians in nearly every country we visited, and they had all given us a warm and friendly welcome. The Hungarian bartender in Tangiers, the carpenter in Tlemcen, the soldiers in the French Foreign Legion, the clockmaker in Oran, the soccer player in Algiers, and the waiter in Tunis had showed a great deal of joy at our coming, as had the Hungarian Jews of Palestine and the impoverished immigrant workers in Turkey. We wondered how long we would have to travel before we encountered our compatriots again.

As we traveled through Subotica, Belgrade, Nis, and Skopje, we were surprised at how warmly the Serbs welcomed us. It wasn't only the intelligent, urban Serbs who spoke well of Hungarians, but the backward Serbian peasants of the south held equally high opinions of our people. The Serbs were so kind and welcoming that we were ashamed. The roads, however, did not treat us with nearly as much kindness. Occasionally, we had the pleasure of traveling along newly constructed, quality roads; what's more, Serbian roads were generally better than those in the Bácska region of Hungary, but in many parts of the country, even the main roads were enough to wear out the toughest peasant boots.

The mud was our greatest enemy. Whenever a paved road ceased to be paved, we were forced to ride from pothole to mud-filled pothole. It would be hard to make up our minds, which was worse: sand, rocky mountain roads, or mud. Each posed a formidable challenge in its own time. Sometimes the mud was especially sticky, thick, and almost claylike. It soon covered both us and our motorcycle completely, without leaving a single square centimeter clean. We were forced to stop every few meters, get down off the bike, and push it out of the mud. Although we had a chain attached to the back wheel, it continued spinning madly without moving us forward. The engine puffed and wheezed; the wheels, like mini volcanoes, spewed mud in all directions. The space between the fenders and wheels soon filled with the soft, clay-like mud, which quickly hardened, completely disabling the vehicle. Scraping out the mud didn't help much, because we had hardly gone a few steps before our troubles began all over again.

The countryside past Nis reminded us more and more of Turkey. The villages, the mosques and minarets, the mixed people, all brought to mind the Turkish portion of our journey. The roads were also hauntingly reminiscent of Turkish roads, and upon entering the mountains of Macedonia, our feeling of déjà-vu was complete. The Macedonian hills were ugly, bald, and craggy; we felt as if a giant had picked up a handful of the Turkish mountains and distributed them in Macedonia just to spite us.

We crossed the border into Greece at Bitolj, but the landscape was slow to change. What did change was the security level, which plummeted as we continued in a barren landscape allegedly infested with Macedonian bandits. Macedonia wasn't, and never had been, a safe land.

It wasn't long before the legendary Macedonian bandits materialized before our eyes. We were high in the mountains, traveling near the town of Vodena. The sun was setting, and we were anxious to reach Vodena before dark. Suddenly, three men, armed with guns, appeared on the slope before us. One of them stood in the middle of the road, gesturing for us to stop. I automatically braked, but Gyuszi shouted, "Step on it! Now!" and I realized he was right. Gyuszi got hold of our gun, and I twisted the throttle. We drove straight for the man in the middle of the road, who jumped to the side to avoid the collision, screaming curses the whole time. We drove on as fast as we could for the next 3-4 kilometers. We don't know to this very day what those three armed men in the mountains wanted of us, but their guns, added to the near-darkness, the desolate countryside, and the knowledge that we were in Macedonia, more than satisfied our curiosity.

Greece seemed to be slightly more developed than the other countries of the Balkan Peninsula. A tangible sign of this slight advantage was the relative ease with which we were able to communicate with the locals in French. On the other hand, the country was overwhelmingly rural; the only truly urban settlement being Athens. Even Thessaloniki was nothing but a large overgrown village. It was inhabited by people of a distinctly small-town mentality.

In Greece, those who like mutton are in luck. We were served helpings of mutton for breakfast, lunch, and dinner. Restaurant menus revolved around mutton and its variation: cooked mutton, baked mutton, or mutton seasoned with paprika. The water tasted of iodine wherever we went, and when we turned to wine to drown out the taste of the water, we soon found that the Greeks spoiled their good wine by mulling it with the strangest spices.

Greeks showed especial ingenuity in money matters. Tearing a hundred-drachma bill in two produced two fifty-drachma bills, which could further be split into twenty-five drachma units. We even encountered seventy-five drachma bills, which were produced by nipping off a quarter of the hundred-drachma piece.

Winter in Greece was relegated to the mountains. Traveling along the steep mountain passes, we often found ourselves sliding backwards, and were forced to unload our packages, carry them ahead, and push our vehicle up the slope to catch up. After the mild, spring-like weather of the lowlands, we were buffeted by strong winds and blasts of snow, which soon produced a pervasive numbness in our limbs.

The inclement weather didn't prevent us from enjoying the magnificent beauty of the snow-clad hills through which we were traveling. Our efforts were repaid a thousandfold by the charms of nature, the white of the snow against the dark green of the mighty pines. Between Kozani and Larissa, we caught a glimpse of the snow-white peak of Mount Olympus, where the abode of the gods veritably swam amidst the rosy rays of the setting sun.

Athine, or Athens, was the only truly European city in the entire country. Its beauty shocked every visitor, and the rate of its development was promising. It seemed to grow bigger and more beautiful every day. The antique historical site had become a real metropolis, yet the Acropolis, which towered over the entire city, recalled the grandeur of its proud history.

Our honest love and admiration for beautiful Athens did not wane even after our run-in with the Greek police. I was forced to pay a 136 drachma fine for parking where I shouldn't have and for refusing to leave even after being asked to do so a number of times by the patient police. We were sentenced to pay the fine before we knew it and pay it we did, but the very next morning found us parked in the same spot, which had turned out to be a most convenient location.

We were forced to board a ship to continue our journey. There was no land route from Greece to India discounting the treacherous roads of Asia Minor, which we were in no hurry to retrace.

Egypt was therefore the destination of our choice. Once in Egypt, we planned to follow the Nile River as far up as we could and then cross into Arabia.

There were many ships to choose from. In order to save money, and because we were complete strangers in Greece, we opted for the cheapest method of crossing and purchased third-class tickets on a Greek vessel headed for Port Said.

To India

The seas were smooth and calm as we neared Egypt. Disembarking at Port Said, we found ourselves on African soil for the second time and citizens of a town we had visited only months before. Port Said is clearly visible on our world map as the place where our own paths crossed, the city we visited twice. Everything around us was familiar, and, to our delight, the Egyptians remembered us as well. Even the usual rush of porters, street-vendors, and would-be tour-guides gave us a good feeling, even though their enthusiastic onslaught almost cost us our motorcycle.

When our ship arrived in the harbor, it didn't approach the shore directly, so we were required to rent a small sailboat to carry us, the bike, and our luggage to shore. As soon as the sailboat brushed up against the shore, our motorcycle was surrounded by a crowd of 50-60 baksheesh-hungry Arabs, who immediately began pushing, pulling, shoving, and lifting the unfortunate vehicle in various directions. Some porters crouched under the motorcycle and attempted to lift it onto their backs. Although we shouted and gestured wildly for them to stop, our motorbike was soon up in the air, and, for a split second, we were convinced it was going to drop into the waters of the harbor. That very day, we traveled on to Cairo, and on the third day, we were well on our way south.

Had it not been for the ruthless heat, our journey into Southern Egypt would have been one of the most beautiful and enjoyable parts of our tour. We traveled along the same channels, on dusty, sandy, and occasionally damp roads, with nothing to stand in our way. It was spring in Egypt, and temperatures rose to 40 degrees C by ten in the morning. Because it was a national holiday, the villages were pleasantly decorated with colorful banners; we amused ourselves by imagining they had been placed there in our honor. If it hadn't been for the impoverished villages and thousands of aimless *fellahs* hanging about, we would have agreed that we had happened upon a country significantly more developed than Greece and the Balkans. The roads were decidedly better; the weather was gorgeous, and we were traveling under the brilliant blue dome of a cloudless sky.

The stretches of arable land surrounding the Nile grew thinner and thinner as we neared the southern reaches of the country. In the distance, we could make out the yellow of the desert sands; on our left, a mere kilometer or two from the river, we saw a couple of magnificent sandstone hills, the Jebel-Mokattam and the Jebel-Turah. Before reaching Hilvan, however, we were to get a taste of the desert sands.

We passed numerous Arab cemeteries. Wealthy Arabs built entire houses for their dead and moved in with their living families during certain holidays.

The cemeteries on the outskirts of Cairo comprised entire "cities of the dead," with whole streets of the typical flat-roofed houses. Occasionally, the tomb of a sheik, complete with towers and domes, would break the monotony of the streets of the dead. The graves of the humbler folk were marked by large stone tablets located in the courtyards of the houses.

The large, Arab cemeteries made us uneasy; we kept imagining that the entire population of the town had fled from an epidemic, leaving behind a deserted settlement. Occasionally, we thought about the unique difficulty of our undertaking: very few motorists had managed to make the long journey into Sudan. In the end, we were comforted by the knowledge that our compatriot, Pál Almássy, had traveled down the same route not so long ago, and that the members of the Court-Treatt Expedition had managed to make the long journey from Cape Town to Cairo. Their books proved more useful to us than the most eloquent of Arabian travelogues.

The railroad turned out to be another big help and continued to guide our steps until our arrival in Port Sudan. Another advantage was our motorcycle, which, considering the type of traveling we were doing, was infinitely superior to the automobile. We packed the supplies we could do without for a while onto the train and sent them ahead; then, arranging our food and water supplies on our significantly lighter motorcycle, we made excellent progress. Also, it was much easier to push or lift the lightened bike each time it became necessary.

We continued our journey at a good rate and in a very pleasant mood. There was never any lack of interesting sights; in fact, the view surrounding us grew more and more novel as we journeyed south. Had we traveled by boat or train, we would never have encountered the many remains of ancient culture that were at our disposal once we got on the motorbike. The step-pyramid of Sakkara, and numerous old temples and giant statues made our way more colorful. After two days of travel on roads varying in quality, we reached the city of Asyût. Two days later, we drove into El-Luxor (Luxor,) where we chose to make a longer rest stop after traveling the 700 kilometers from Cairo.

I won't go into great detail describing the countless historical sites and monuments we marveled at along the way. We visited Karnak, the ruins of Thebes, the Valley of the Kings, and were hardly able to tear ourselves away from the tomb of Tutankhamen, at the same time, we knew we must continue on.

The next stretch of our journey was a challenging one. We had a difficult time identifying the road along which we were to travel, so we found ourselves guides wherever we could. With the help of our guides, we somehow made our way to our next destination, meandering through a maze of tiny, godforsaken villages. Numerous channels crisscrossed our paths, and we were forced to disembark and facilitate our crossing with the help of spades and wooden boards.

Before we knew it, we were riding across the Nubian Desert. Leaving the Nile far behind us, we followed the train tracks for the most part.

Although the Nubian Desert was a travelers' bugbear, we found it to be one of the easier stretches of our journey. Of course, the tracks were a big help. The railway in the Nubian Desert did not resemble the Hungarian railways to which we had become accustomed. Because the soil was so soft, it had been impossible to construct a proper road-bed. The rails were simply laid across the ties; the occasional embankments were made of sand, and the desert sands further covered the ties, so that the sand-covered tracks turned out to be the best road in the country. As long as we stuck close to the tracks, we had nothing to fear, because a train regularly passed us every second day.

There were times, however, that we had no choice but to leave the tracks behind and submit to the difficulties of desert travel, which I have described before. It's enough to recall our experiences between Tripoli and Egypt or on the road to Palestine to form a pretty good idea of the agonizing pace at which we were able to travel.

The trip from Luxor to Aswân lasted three days, the Aswân-Wadi Halfa stretch another three. I would not enjoy repeating the latter.

Upon arriving in Wadi Halfa, we had reached Sudan. That was where the real desert began, the point at which we left the Nile behind, heading southeast across the Nubian Desert. As always, we stuck to the tracks, working our way from station to tiny station. The railroad workers at each station gave us exceedingly warm welcomes, always telephoning those at the next station, where we were expected to report to the next crew immediately upon arrival. We often enjoyed the companionship of guides and were provided with room and board, as well as food for the journey, miraculously entirely without charge.

Our desert travels lasted for nearly 600 kilometers. We encountered ten stations on our way, which were the only landmarks to break the monotony of the landscape. This was unsurpassed desert, not a soul in sight. Not even the hardiest caravans braved the huge distances of this particular desert, which was entirely without water, trees, and bushes. There wasn't so much as a blade of grass to be seen, only vast spaces of sand, arranged in thousands upon thousands of yellow-brown waves.

Some of our nights were spent under the stars. During the day, temperatures rose to 40-45 degrees C; at night, temperatures of 5-10 degrees C were common. The knowledge that we weren't even traveling in the warmest season somehow failed to cool us one bit. Around noon, we would halt, create

Sudanese desert sands

some semblance of shade under which to wait out the early afternoon hours. Night travel would have been impossible; there was just too much to pay attention to. If we were traveling along a railway embankment, we had to keep our eyes on the "road." If we strayed from the embankment, we were on constant guard against quicksand, which would cause us to lose precious hours.

Although it was best to stay near the tracks, we were occasionally forced to leave them behind. At one point, the railroad led up into a hilly, craggy region, where the sand which usually filled the space between the ties was scarce. The ties were too far apart for us to ride. Even when we did opt for the sand over the railroad, we kept a watchful eye on the tracks, making sure not to stray too far, and on the sand, which could hold innumerable unpleasant surprises.

After a while, we returned to the Nile, knowing we would soon leave it for good. We had our last glimpse of the river at the city of Berber, then Atbara. From Atbara, we traveled east, continuing along the railroad tracks for another difficult week before reaching a small harbor on the Red Sea: Port Sudan. The Atbara River had its source in Abyssinia; the way from Atbara to Port Sudan continued through the desert. Around the middle of the weeklong journey, we encountered hilly country. The distance to Port Sudan was merely 500 kilometers and wouldn't have taken us a week to traverse, even under the difficult desert circumstances had we not been forced to spend a day getting our motorcycle fixed at the railroad station in Haiya, on the way to the town of Kassala. As we neared the sea, the landscape began to change. We encountered sprawling fields of cotton peppered by numerous tiny villages as well as more and more travelers along the road.

In Port Sudan, we decided to board a small Arabian sailboat after discovering that there was no land route connecting Jidda with Aden. We planned to sail south along the Arabian coast until we reached a good caravan route leading south.

Everything went according to plan. It was good to rest on board the humble boat. The crew and the boat owner did their best to make us comfortable. While on board, we had nothing to fear, because the vessel had come recommended by a high-ranking British official in the Port Sudan government. Although we were sailing down an entirely unfamiliar body of water, we trusted that we would be taken ashore at the right time. The sea-voyage was very pleasant, taking us past the sandy shores of Hejaz and Asir at a comfortable pace. We landed in Yemen, not at a proper harbor, but near a small cluster of houses. Thankfully, we had stocked up on gasoline before leaving Sudan.

The road to Aden led us along a sandy caravan route. This stretch of road was wide and quite busy, and we made good progress. Our fellow travelers were Arabs, some on foot or horseback, but mostly riding donkeys and camels. The majority of them were headed north, towards Mecca. Some walked the entire way from Aden to the holy city.

These were real Arabs once again, resembling their brothers in Morocco and Tripoli much more closely than did the fellahs of Egypt. The men were proud and rode splendid horses.

Our faithful little dog was not very fond of Arabs or black Africans, for that matter. He seemed to be drawn to Europeans, as they were the only types of people he had previously seen. By the time we reached Aden, we had come up with a name for our dog: Hadji. The name, or title, rather, of Hadji, referred to those Muslim faithful who had made the pilgrimage to Mecca and, once there had fulfilled all of their religious obligations. The Arabs weren't too happy when they heard us calling a detested dog by that name.

We grew accustomed to Arabian food once again. *Ful,* essentially strips of meat fried in oil and seasoned with an unknown spice, became one of our staple foods; even Hadji enjoyed it. Another favorite was the ubiquitous *couscous,* which consisted of bean paste steamed in the company of a large quantity of vegetables.

In Aden, we had the opportunity to enjoy some of the Arabian traditions we had encountered before. We encountered snake charmers, fire eaters, and scores of scribes squatting in the street, conducting the correspondence of a nation. We also saw the misery in which a lot of people lived, the dirt and

Arab women in Aden

poverty that were a part of their daily lives. Many Arabs shared their homes with their animals; slabs of meat, often half-spoiled, hung covered with flies under a scorching sun. All of the food we encountered was covered with flies. Sick people and beggars lay in the street; many locals were blind or struggling with various forms of eye-disease. Women holding their small children in their laps didn't even attempt to shoo the flies from off the child's eyes. Amulets, special plants, pieces of iron, and animal furs, all believed to ward off illness, are cheap and ubiquitous. Walking through the marketplace, we entered one of the Arabian tents and sat down on a low divan. The tent was lined with colorful rugs; coffee was served in the mystical light, accompanied by the melancholy strains of an Arabian melody. Young female dancers moved gracefully to delight the traveler. After the coffee, we were offered orange juice in interesting small containers, accompanied by the popular almond- and coconut milk. *"Faddal, faddal,"* the Arabs cried in friendly voices, offering us a taste of all the delicacies. *"Bes, kattarheyrak,"* we answered, "enough, thank you very much."

Friendship was a life-giving force in Aden, which was one of the cruelest cities in the world. Only a tiny portion of the city, the most modern quarter, lay on the coast; the rest of the city was located 3-4 kilometers inland. Aden was under the auspices of the government of India. Many of its inhabitants were black Africans from nearby Somalia, Abyssinia, and Eritrea. There were very few Europeans.

It was in Aden that we saw camels hitched to a cart for the first time in our lives. Turbans also seemed more widespread; the Arabs wound colorful textiles around their heads and otherwise wore very light clothing, which usually consisted only of baggy, white pants. All attempts to create a few green spaces in Aden had failed. Aden was called "the devil's oven," and aptly so, as the entire city was surrounded by volcanic mountains and lava beds. The rocks drank in the sweltering heat during the day and retained it into the night, so that the unattractive town, with its dirty streets and tiny, flat-roofed houses, was never cool. All of Aden cooked, as in a cauldron, regardless of the season or the time of day. Europeans did not last long in the unbearable heat.

We were relieved to depart from Aden. As Hadhramaut was an impasse even to the most seasoned traveler, we crossed the Arabian Sea by ship only to reach the kingdom of our dreams, a country of a myriad distinct peoples and limitless contrasts: India.

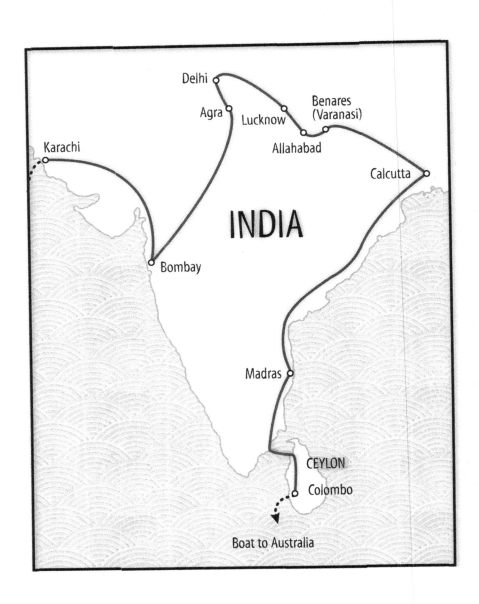

Delhi

Agra

Lucknow

Benares
(Varanasi)

Allahabad

Karachi

Calcutta

INDIA

Bombay

Madras

CEYLON

Colombo

Boat to Australia

The Secret Kingdom

India, and What We Found There

Before leading the reader onto a new continent, I would like to describe a few important circumstances related to our travels. As I have mentioned before, when undertaking a voyage as long and difficult as ours, there is more to consider than meets the eye. Enthusiasm and high spirits in themselves are not enough, even combined with a terrific motorcycle. Both the terrific motorcycle and the enthusiastic travelers are in need of fuel. The further one travels, the greater the amount and quality of supplies necessary. Valid passports and visas are an absolute must.

Regarding official matters, we hadn't run into any difficulties as far as India. Our passports had not expired, and we had obtained most of the necessary visas while still in Hungary, supplementing our collection with the remaining visas on our way. We did have a certain sum of money at our disposal, but as the journey stretched out more and more, we found it increasingly difficult to make do with what we had. Our lack of funds cost us many worried days and sleepless nights. We often wondered when and where we would be forced to stop, and whether we would then have enough money to return home.

Many of the countries we visited were rather difficult to enter, as the government discouraged tourism of all kinds. Nowhere was this tension more palpable than in the colonies. Every country had its problems, and in an age of economic uncertainty, those in power tended to be extra wary. For one, they were apprehensive of immigrant workers, whose arrival, in vast numbers, could make things much worse for the natives, many of whom were already unemployed. At the same time, and perhaps even more importantly, the powers controlling the colonies feared spies and an influx of ideas and worldviews that could radicalize local populations. To prevent trouble, they simply shut their gates, which would nevertheless open wide to the "Open, sesame!" of letters of credit and large accounts, not so wide to the bearers of letters of recommendation and not at all to the forlorn pleas of dubious private persons.

Somehow, we became the exception. Wherever we went, we encountered people with a deep respect for sportsmanship who mostly strove to make things easier for us. At the same time, we had to keep in mind that the only support we could count on was of the moral kind, and once we ran out of funds, we would find ourselves in an ignominious position: unable to continue, unable to turn back. We had to be prepared for whatever obstacles would arise.

The situation in India was especially difficult. One of the guiding principles of colonial politics was the preservation at all costs of aura of superiority surrounding the white colonizer. The British took great pains to preserve their prestige in the face of millions of Indian natives. Foreigners weren't allowed inside the country unless officials could be absolutely sure that the newcomers would in no way shed poor light on the English ruling class. Even British citizens had a difficult time obtaining permission to enter India. Unless the would-be settler had a tidy business lined up, unless he could prove that he would have no difficulty earning a living, he would never set eyes on India, even if he was the truest, bluest Englishman who ever trod the face of the earth. The only aspiring visitors exempt from the above categories were those in possession of large quantities of the British pound.

The colonists living in India would not allow their fellow Englishmen inside the country unless their economic status was a settled and comfortable one. In other countries we had visited, foreign consulates were often filled with citizens of the country they represented, come to apply for financial support in their time of need. British consulates were closed to such solicitors. Those who had difficulty attaining and preserving the prescribed level of financial security, those unable to achieve the lifestyle that British citizenship demanded were simply placed on the first ship headed to England. There were no poor Englishmen throughout the British colonies.

In India, the British felt it their task to prove to the locals the superiority of the white race. Everything the British did cried, "White men are wealthy!" and the miserable and often destitute Indians had no choice but to believe them.

Native Indians enjoyed low-cost living in their mighty homeland. Entire families subsisted on pennies; prices were astronomically lower than in Europe. Despite the standard of cheap living, foreigners visiting India couldn't but be shocked by the amount of money needed to support themselves.

Why was this? It was all a question of prestige. Europeans couldn't simply blend in with the Indian crowd. It was unimaginable that white men would buy anything but first class train or boat tickets. In fact, there were some train stations where the Indian employees refused to sell white men second-class tickets. White men weren't allowed to fill low-profile positions; then again, they could never have supported themselves on a native's salary. All Englishmen in India kept servants, down to the most insignificant orderly in the British Army. British men and women did not carry things. If an English-woman bought a bar of soap, she would immediately hand it to her servant.

There were no middle-class hotels or restaurants available. We encountered numerous Hindu or other Indian hotels, especially in larger cities; many of them were modern, clean, and in all ways satisfactory. Unfortunately, white men weren't allowed to stay in hotels for natives, and hapless white men willing to fly in the face of all social rules would very quickly find themselves visited by the British police with an uncanny interest in the financial status and travel interests of said hapless breaker of social conventions. Hotels "fit" for Europeans were of the five-star kind and charged properly exorbitant rates. In India, foreigners were judged according to the hotel in which they chose to stay. When in company, newcomers weren't asked to describe their occupation or reasons for coming to India. The first question was, inevitably, "Where are you staying?"

We were therefore stuck between the rock of paying ridiculous sums for unnecessary luxury and the hard place of being visited by the police. It didn't take long for us to realize that the more time we spent in this land of luxury hotels, lavish restaurants, scores of servants, and generous tips, the greater our chance that we would go broke before leaving India. The only choice we had was to live a seemingly luxurious life for as little as possible; this was the way to avoid eviction by the Brits!

Despite the strange difficulties we had run into, we were determined not to leave India earlier than planned and to make a special effort to see the unique and varied beauties of the Subcontinent. Roadside bungalows, small motels with convenient prices, and the support of a few friendly maharajas got us through the worst of our financial plight.

Our tour of India lasted months but was as comprehensive as a tour its length could be. After Karachi, we moved on to Bombay, then spent time in Agra, Delhi, Lahore, and then Lucknow, Allahabad, and Benares. Traveling on to Calcutta, we spent a few weeks in the famous harbor city and rode down the eastern shore of India to Madras. Our tour of India, which comprised 8,000 kilometers, was beautifully complemented by a charming jaunt to Ceylon, the "Pearl of the East."

Describing the myriad splendors of India on a few pages is hardly less difficult than the journey itself. India is immeasurably large; Indian life, although not as mysterious as Westerners would like to see it, was endlessly fascinating. Not a day passed without us learning a hundred new things and trying to preserve at least some of them on film. Monotony and boredom were strangers to us on the Indian portion of our journey. The sights, the life of the people, the countryside was like a pageant of novelty of which we couldn't get our fill, and we soon grew to love the Indian people, despite the darker sides of Indian life.

A world traveler crossing India sees much but not all there is to see. As there is more than meets the eye, even eyewitness descriptions by the keenest observer may turn out to be distanced from the truth of Indian life. This is a curse affecting all those who brave India. Numerous small insights helped us form a general understanding of the country, but deep meanings remained hidden. Those who think they can write objectively and transparently about India are gravely mistaken. It would take years, perhaps decades of studies and first-hand experience to grasp, in any real way, the many faces of India.

In my descriptions, I decided to stick to impressions, insights gathered over a relatively short period of time. Although my impressions may take readers far from the truth, I can honestly say that I traveled through India with open eyes and sincerely strove for objectivity in my writing.

Volumes have been written on India, and many more must be in the coming. The giant subcontinent can be divided into two parts: British India, comprising roughly three fifths of the territory and a cluster of independent states making up the remaining two fifths. Though both British India and the independent territories had ties to Britain, the ties of the official British section were tighter than those of the native-run states. The population of India, made up of people belonging to countless ethnic groups and religions and speaking a large number of different languages, could be considered a nation only from the political perspective.

The population of India was 320 million in 1920 and is 350 million today. 80 of the 350 million were citizens of the independent states. Hyderabad is the most populous of independent states, with 13 million inhabitants, but Rajputana and Mysore are close seconds and even Gwalior and Kashmir boast populations of more than three million.

Religion is a central part of Indian life; there is a clear Hindu majority of 230 million, followed by the Muslims, who count 80 million believers. There are 12 million Buddhist faithful, 10 million people practicing various Animistic religions, 5 million Christians, 4 millions Sikhs, and 2 million who place their faith in Jainism.

The Hindus, 230 million strong, could definitely rule the rest of their compatriots, were it not for the caste system, which puts them at a disadvantage in the face of their Muslim neighbors. Hindus are born into a caste, and, unless they convert out of their religion, remain members of that cast until the day they die. Castes have much to do with occupations; there are countless rungs on the social ladder, and those on higher rungs inevitably look down on people of lower castes. The highest castes are the Brahmin or priestly caste, the Kayasthas (writers), Khatris (soldiers), and Vayshas (producers). The four elite castes are followed by hundreds of smaller castes. The blacksmith, for example, is superior to the weaver, the shepherd to the miner.

The Hindus, an Aryan people, entered the territory of modern India sometime around 4,000 B.C. and settled along the shores of the Indus River. The Muslims derive their ancestry from the Persians and the Turks. When the Aryans settled in India, they encountered tribes of a primitive, socially unorganized people, whose religion centered on mystical elements. Their descendants are the Animists. Christian Indians were usually once Animist; Hindus and Muslims rarely part with their religion.

The situation the British found themselves in was far from simple. British India had been divided up into eight territories, each headed by a governor, but the governors were not to be envied. Difficulties developed when the natives demanded more rights and privileges and began claiming leadership positions.

At the same time, is this really a problem? India never could have become what it is today without the British, but must a country as mighty as India owe her colonizers a debt of gratitude forever? And must India repay this dubious debt with free labor? A country that boasts sons and daughters such as Rabindranath Tagore, the biologist Sir Jagadish Chandra Bose, the beloved prophet Mahatma Gandhi, the Muslim parliamentary spokesman Jinnah, the Brother Ali, Mohamed and Shaukat, leaders of Punjab and West India, Motilal Nehru, head of East India, Sarojini Naidu, feminist poet and speaker, or Patiala, the best-known of Indian maharajas, and scores of educated and enthusiastic young citizens, a country such as this cannot be oppressed for long.

The people themselves hate the British with such a fanatic hate that, were they not so heavily divided amongst themselves along religious and caste lines, and were they not so backward in a lot of ways, the map of India would undergo drastic changes.

This was the age of Mahatma Gandhi, who traveled from village to village and was greeted with overwhelming enthusiasm wherever he went. This physically insignificant man was the greatest of the Indian greats; millions trusted him, the modest man in his simple clothes, slippers, and uncovered head, to wrestle the British lion and emerge victorious. Gandhi walked miles on foot, bought only third-class train tickets or traveled in steerage when boarding a ship, but through his efforts, he amassed millions of pounds for a holy purpose. His followers were ready to make the final sacrifice.

"You sacrificed ten million people in the World War, and for no conceivable purpose," a high-ranking Hindu official once told me, "we are willing to sacrifice forty million for our freedom!"

Farming is the occupation of 240 million people. Indian agriculture is hopelessly backward and agricultural workers cling fanatically to the traditional methods, resisting change in all areas of farming. They use the same farming implements that were in use centuries ago. Most occupations were inherited; a son rarely departed from the path his father had walked before him.

As we grew to know the Indian people, we discovered that we had nothing to fear. I have never met gentler, humbler, and more generous human beings. As soon as they found out we were not British, they gave us a warm welcome. The British themselves hardly had to fear being mugged or murdered; white men were treated with respect wherever they went, and violent crime was virtually non-existent, unlike in civilized Europe. The police were an excellent institution; 70,000 British soldiers and an army of 200,000 Indians were enough to keep order in a country with a population of 350 million.

We had a very difficult time going through customs. Our motorcycle caused us the most trouble, and as we frantically ran from one office to another, we were haunted by uncomfortable moments with European customs. We did have it easier than the Indians though; the officials always dealt with us first, and specially appointed servants led us from one line to the next, pulling out chairs whenever we were forced to wait for longer. All the lavish courtesy did not prevent us from accumulating folders of material in a very short time. British bureaucrats, although much speedier than their Hungarian brothers, surpassed bureaucrats of all nations we had known and encountered in their pedantic precision. After collecting the proper number of references, we accumulated an equal number of signatures and paid a rather hefty deposit. The large deposit recalled our troubles in Palestine, and we wondered how long it would be before we saw our money again.

Indian currency was even more complicated than the British. The standard unit was the rupee. Each rupee consisted of 16 *annas*, which in turn were made up of 12 *pices*. One rupee was the equivalent of two Hungarian Pengő, therefore, a single anna amounted to 12 Hungarian Fillér.

Bombay was the first large Indian city we encountered. As we rode into town, population 1.5 million, we were dazed by the colorful multitudes filling the streets. The downtown region, with its wide, paved roads, gave us the decided feeling that we were heading down an avenue in Europe. On the other hand, there were very few Europeans in the crowd surrounding our motorcycle. The only white faces in sight were to be found gazing out of car windows. What was even more shocking than the lack of white Europeans was the sheer number of people that could fit onto a single street.

Hindus, Parsees, Afghans, Muslims, and various other natives we could not identify thronged from all sides. The most popular color seemed to be white. Parsees were easiest to recognize; they wore black, shiny hats with a sharp edge; others usually opted for small, round black hats or the well-known Indian turbans. Turban styles varied in color, size, and winding technique. Some men wore turbans perched on the tops of their heads, with a portion hanging off to the side. Others tied the turban in a bun; still others let it flow down their backs. Colors ranged from red to white to striped, but occasionally, we spotted turbans that were all colors at once. Children sported tiny hats embroidered in gold or silver. There were very few people on the street without any head-covering at all. Those without hats or turbans were bald except for a single lock of hair, which they let grow long and combed to the back. Men with long hair sometimes wore it in graceful buns. Still others were decked in the tall, white hats cooks or confectioners wear. The educated natives and all Europeans, including ourselves, wore tropical hats, otherwise known as pith helmets.

It was in India that we learned just how dangerous the tropical sun could be. Those who removed their hats for just a few moments could suffer severe heatstroke. It was best to keep heads covered at all times, even when the sky was overcast.

Those who wore coats usually belonged to the higher castes and opted for European-style coats. People of lower casts wore long, untucked shirts instead. Pants, as the West knows them, were replaced by baggy, white trousers that were gathered up around the ankles to allow the feet their freedom. The baggy skirt-pants, or *dhoti,* were very popular and always appropriate.

The poorest layers of society were the most scantily clad. Bare upper bodies were the norm for men, complemented with simple, white loincloths. Shoes and socks were rare, slippers and bare feet ubiquitous. Small children often went entirely naked discounting a bit of string around their waists.

Most European men wore shorts, including soldiers, policemen, tourists, even the elderly and the distinguished.

We saw very few native women. For some reason, the truly attractive ones all wore glasses and walked about in loose-fitting linen or silk clothing. Their skirts brushed the ground and were mainly hidden under layers of other textiles, which were twisted and draped about their bodies in various ways. Jewelry of all sorts was a necessity; women wore silver bangles on both their wrists and ankles in addition to necklaces, earrings, and nose rings. Most nose rings were large loops of bronze or silver; only the wealthiest women could afford precious stones to grace their noses.

Fashion in India was infinitely varied, but always loose to beat the heat, and colorful.

Bombay, commonly known as the "Gateway of India," was not the gateway to the rich past of the Subcontinent, but a window, rather, onto the colorful and mighty present. In Bombay, we perceived and marveled at the slow but persistent changes that were transforming India. A taxi carrying wealthy Europeans might park in front of a luxury hotel, but it was inevitably followed by a creaky wooden cart drawn by cows. Streetcars rumbled along streets crowded with rickshaws; beggar-like men, clad in the simplest baggy pants, kept so much knowledge in their heads that it could have filled libraries. Only a few kilometers separate the glitzy hotel and bank district from the temples of the Hindu triune god. A Hindu merchant, having traveled thousands of kilometers, may get off at the inconceivably busy Victoria Terminus railroad station and throw himself into the pulsating excitement of the stock market, only to emerge unscathed in the afternoon and immerse himself in religious meditation at the temple on nearby Elephanta Island.

Elephanta Island is covered with temples and ancient statues; only the necessity of buying entrance tickets reminds the visitor of the twentieth century. Stone images of Brahma the Creator, Vishnu the Preserver, and Shiva the Destroyer, alternate with symbolically carved facades, statues, and drawings. The artwork on Elephanta Island is entirely unintelligible to the white layperson. According to the Hindu faith, the human soul can become reincarnated in the shape of over eight million different animals. Vishnu himself is represented in the form of a fish, a turtle, a bear, or a lion; lesser gods appear in hundreds of animal forms.

After returning to Bombay, we had a hard time freeing ourselves of beggars. Hundreds upon hundreds of the poor surrounded us, many of them lame, blind, or hunchbacked. Some pointed to their open wounds, black with flies, others held up crippled limbs. Ugly, dark women urged their naked children to beg, and so after a while, we were unable to determine whether the beggar in front of us was a real beggar, or simply someone who had been taught to hold out his hand whenever he saw a white man pass.

We received another shock that very night. Walking through the elegant main streets with their brilliantly lit shop windows, we discovered rows of people lying side-by-side, even on top of each other, peacefully slumbering. Some had spread out dirty linens as sheets; others simply lay on the asphalt. Many covered their faces with newspaper to ward off the mosquitoes. They slept peacefully, despite the nightlife, which was just picking up around them.

Because it was February when we were in India, we didn't get a taste of real tropical heat until much later. February in India was reminiscent of May or early June in Hungary. Although the evenings were mild and warm, many of the Indians on the street were shivering. Some lit fires right on the street and warmed their trembling bodies. Even those gathering around the fires took care not to mix with the wrong castes. People with yellow dots on their foreheads avoided contact with red dot wearers; those marked with black stripes stayed away from blue circles. The color system was utterly incomprehensible to outsiders like us.

As the fires lit up on the elegant streets of Bombay, we experienced both

110

pity and secret envy towards the poor around us. They had no homes, no clothing to cover their bodies, but were also without worries. They lived from one day to the next. If one of them acquired a little money, he lived an idle life until it ran out, then started looking for a temporary job like carrying packages or other tasks in the harbor. A short period of work would be followed by another idle period of rest.

We took great care not to step on any bodies. Those we accidentally touched with our feet would mumble a few words in a submissive voice and move out of our way.

Passing through the repulsive red light district, where dirty houses lined equally dirty streets, we encountered Indian, Malaysian, black, Afghan, and Japanese women attempting to lure passers-by into their beds. They were scantily clad, and we wished for their sake and ours, that they had been fully dressed.

We ran into difficulties when trying to communicate with the natives. The only language of any use was English, which was pretty much ubiquitous and spoken by natives and colonizers alike. Throughout our travels, we had always sought to acquire a basic knowledge of the language of the country we were in, but in India, this noble pursuit proved altogether impracticable. We decided to focus on English instead.

Shop signs were spelled out in three languages at least: English, Mataro or Marathi, and Guajarati, which was mostly used by Parsees and other Muslims. Other forms of writing we recognized were Chinese and Sanskrit; Muslims often used Arabic, but the most widespread of native Indian languages was Hindustani.

It was enough to take a quick a look at Indian paper bills, which were inscribed in no less than ten languages, all of them with their own distinct writing systems. In this way, Indian money was far more polyglot than even the currency of the former Austro-Hungarian Monarchy.

Aside from languages, another problem was locating a suitable hotel. In the end, we gave up the hope of finding a moderately priced place. In Bombay, a hotel "fit" for Europeans cost at least ten rupees a day, which was an outrageous price, despite the fact that it included both room and board for a whole day and night. We would have preferred to rent a simple room somewhere and take care of our meals ourselves, but full service was included in the rental price of all hotel rooms.

In the end, we were forced to opt for a typical tourist hotel with its army of servants. The servants, called "boys," were everywhere, and they had the uncanny ability to guess what guests wanted even before the guests mouthed the words of a command. The most common word by far, and the walls seemed to resound with it, was "boy." If an English lady wished to light a cigarette, she'd cry, "Boy!" even if the box of matches were lying in front of her. The "boys" rushed to fulfill their mistress' bidding.

Everyone kept servants; wealthier homes employed fifteen to twenty. Servants outnumbered employees in the shops, banks, and offices. "Boys" belonging to prestigious homes were clad in elegant uniforms; hotel servants dressed in white with a wide red sash around their waists. All "boys" were barefoot and strictly observed the laws of the caste system even within their own servant society. Higher-ranking servants, for example, would refuse to do work they thought befitted servants of a lower rank. For example, a chauffeur would never carry his master's luggage inside; there was another "boy" available for that task. It seemed to us that servants higher up in the pecking order had their own servants, who, in turn, employed "boys" of their own.

The rooms were constructed with the unbearable heat in mind; balcony facing balcony, door facing door provided for life-saving drafts. Since we weren't in the hottest season yet, doors were constantly open to let the air circulate. In the summer, however, all openings were covered with reed mats, which were constantly watered by attentive "boys." Most rooms were outfitted with showers, and large ventilators lined the ceilings. Visitors not yet accustomed to the constantly moving air often suffered from headaches, but as air circulation was absolutely necessary, they soon learned to put up with its inconveniences.

Meals were royal. We often wondered how we managed to eat such large portions despite the sweltering heat. Most restaurants served a fusion of Indian and European cuisine. Indian food, by itself, was far from tasty. Some foods were so spicy that they became almost unsuitable for human consumption, even consumption by notably spice-loving Hungarians. Strong, pungent spices were added to every dish; even sweets included black pepper.

Every morning, a boy would scurry into our room with a cup of tea served to tide guests over until breakfast was ready. A bountiful breakfast was served in the hotel restaurant at nine every morning. This morning meal included egg dishes, roasted meat, tea and fruit, fish, butter, marmalade and coffee. *Tiffin*, a "light" midday meal consisting of four, five, sometimes six courses, was served promptly at noon, followed a few hours later by afternoon tea and a luxurious evening dinner.

Beef was mostly unavailable, aside from the menus of some European hotels. Hindus refused beef in much the same way as Muslims turned away from pork.

Alcoholic drinks were most commonly to be found at large hotels. Englishmen couldn't do without their daily whiskey or gin; most foreigners of other nationalities opted for beer, while natives rarely consumed alcohol. Bars and coffeehouses were unknown in India; whenever we felt like a drink, we were forced to visit one of the ever-expensive restaurants. Tea, served with every meal, was much more popular than coffee. Indian tea was the tastiest we had ever tried. It was definitely stronger than most other teas and had an irresistibly robust flavor. It didn't take us long to realize and enjoy the cooling advantages of a cup of hot tea. Iced drinks were relatively rare, as was ice cream and lemonade. Fruits were ubiquitous; at first, we enjoyed the limitless supply of bananas and pineapples but soon grew tired of them. Ordinary apples and pears counted as exotic fruits and were listed on the menus of the choicest hotels only.

We also had the opportunity to sample authentic Indian cuisine. Occasionally, a well-to-do Indian family would invite us to dinner, either in their home or at a restaurant reserved for natives. As we ate, the entire family would gather around us, many of them amused and curious. They proudly brought out national dish after national dish, and although we felt like we were sampling the jars at a spice shop, we politely played along and tried everything we were brought. Occasionally, we had the distinct impression that our hosts had added an extra helping of spices into our meals as a sign of limitless hospitality. We didn't dare ask if this was true, but we were all the more happy each time one of these spicy culinary adventures came to an end.

Very few Indians smoked, but betel-chewing was all the more popular. An Indian would take a betel leaf, smear it with a mystical red substance much like we spread bread, and, with movements reminiscent of a Hungarian peasant stuffing his pipe, would carefully and lovingly fold up the leaf and place it in his mouth. Then, they would chew rapidly and begin spitting out the red juice. All the walls of all the houses were covered with red fingerprints, where betel-chewers had wiped their hands. Red stains further dotted the private homes, streets, even the floors of streetcars. After two weeks, we stopped noticing the ubiquitous betel spots.

We had a hard time finding parking spots for our motorcycle. Garages were scarce in India, even in the city of Bombay, but, as we later found out, the natives had solved this problem as well with considerable flair. A car owner or motorist would simply employ a "boy" to guard his car. The boy was not allowed to leave the vehicle for a moment. If guarding it at night, he wasn't even permitted to sit down, lest he fall asleep. Even during the day, he could take a maximum of three steps away from the object of his guarding. A whole night of such surveillance cost an insignificant two to three annas. As I have mentioned, there were sixteen annas to a rupee, so we could safely say that a single anna was the smallest monetary unit in use in India. An anna was usually how much you gave a beggar on the street, however, attempts to give a waiter a single anna as a tip produced shock or disbelief.

Our lunches usually cost us three or four rupees; high prices such as these were common in "European" restaurants. The market was much cheaper; a pound of meat cost merely a quarter rupee, so a hotel cook could purchase twelve pounds of meat off the price of a single lunch. Import clothing was even more expensive, and the price of motorcycle gear astronomical. Recharging our batteries at a motorcycle shop would have cost us ten rupees had we not insisted doggedly on paying only five.

Vultures or worms?

Once in Bombay, we insisted on visiting the famous Parsee cemetery, the Tower of Silence. There was a total of 80,000 Parsees living in India, and more than half of them were Bombay residents. They were a proud and self-confident people, as they had every reason to be. Most Parsees were educated, influential, and wealthy and worked as judges, officials, or merchants. Milabar Hill, an area famed for its lush tropical gardens, was home to rows of luxurious Parsee villas, which neighbored the Tower of Silence, known far and wide for the infamous burial ceremonies it had witnessed.

As my good luck would have it, I made friends with an amiable young Parsee who brought me a typical pointed Parsee hat, with the help of which I was able to blend into the motley crowd hurrying to a traditional funeral. Strangers were strictly forbidden entry to take part in funeral ceremonies, but with the aid of my new hat, I went unnoticed in all the bustle.

Stepping through the cemetery gates, I found myself in a shady garden with five round towers entirely open to the sky. There were openings for corpses in the towers, located on steep stone embankments and shaped like triple circles. Each of the three circles was large enough to hold twenty to twenty-five corpses. Large circles were for men, the middle ones for women, and the tiniest circles were intended for the corpses of children. There were channels leading from each stone "bed" to the center of the circle, where a hole had been carved to let out the blood. Deep wells located at the side of the towers served as collection points for bones, which, once they had been stripped of all flesh, were swept into the sea.

I stood trembling, waiting for the ceremony to begin. The crowd processed slowly to a square plot paved with stone. Four people carried the corpse, which was covered with a single layer of white linen. Around me, I heard soft conversation and prayers. The men carrying the corpse opened one of the tower gates and stepped inside. At precisely this moment, hundreds upon hundreds of starved vultures left their perches on the nearby trees and towers and flocked to the tower next to which we were gathered.

As soon as the corpse had been placed on the stone embankment, we heard a single clap. It was impossible to see what was going on in the tower,

Vultures at the Parsee funeral, Bombay

and those around me continued praying. When we heard the second clap, I marveled at the strict discipline of the vultures. Although the corpse lay on the stone ledge, completely uncovered, the disgusting birds did not touch it until the corpse carriers appeared at the gate and clapped for the third time, quickly closing the gate behind them.

The third clap was the signal the vultures were waiting for. The air filled with their blood-curdling screams and cries as they threw themselves onto the corpse. I heard their sharp beaks knock against the bones and saw them fly off with their chunks of flesh. The crowd around me didn't seem the least bit perturbed by the sight of vultures vying over human flesh and began to drift off, murmuring quiet prayers the entire time.

"In a few hours, only the bones will remain," my Parsee friend explained. I fell into deep thought. The vultures were true professionals. I learned that there had been a time when the local vultures had not been enough to take care of all the dead. Because the plague was taking so many victims, the Parsees had been forced to send to Upper India for a few hundred more vultures.

"You must believe me when I say that the hideous burial scene I just witnessed would chill every European's blood," I said, turning to the young Parsee. He smiled scornfully and answered, "If you dig up any of your carefully buried dead, you'll see their bodies consumed by worms. Are your worms any better than our vultures?"

Hearing the question posed in such a way, I was at a loss for an answer, but I continue to be haunted by the sight of those towers.

In Bombay, we also learned about the famous Indian cult of animals. Despite rumors or writing to the contrary, Indians have profound respect for all living things, precisely because they can never be sure which of their ancestors has been reborn in the shape of an animal. Many animals wandered the village streets, unkempt, skinny. and uncared for, but the reason behind their desolation was poverty and not cruelty. How could the villagers be expected to feed their animals when they hardly had food for themselves? At the same time, Indians did their utmost to set up animal shelters, especially for old or weak cows and oxen.

White cows, the holy animals of India, filled the streets of both towns and villages. These cows made themselves at home in the busiest urban streets and felt just as comfortable lying in the grass next to a luxury hotel as they did roaming the dusty streets of remote villages. Nobody would drive them off; nobody even seemed to notice their presence. Although their tiny humps give them a humble aspect, most cows are savvy enough to know that they are off limits to men and automobiles alike. If a cow chooses to lie down in the middle of the street, pedestrians walk around it. Should the holy animal stray onto the road, the drivers of vehicles take special care not to inconvenience them in the slightest degree. Cows are allowed to dig around on trash heaps and can generally do what they please.

Pervasive hunger caused many animals to turn beggars. City bovines were mostly clean and relatively well fed and seemed to have mastered the mendicant arts. Standing in shop doorways, the patient cows would peer inside, blocking the entrance. Shopkeepers, anxious to allow customers in and out had no choice but to send a servant out with some greens, dried squash rinds, or sugarcane. Feeding the cows was the only way to get rid off them; any attempts to chase off the holy animals would have been greeted with firm resistance on the part of passers-by. After getting its fill, the cow simply walked to the next shop. Making its rounds every day, it was able to live a rather comfortable life.

Village cows, however, were in considerably more trouble. There were no shops in the villages; people were poor, without enough food for themselves and their families. Rural cows were often skin and bones and died quickly. Occasionally, to ward off gnawing hunger, they would enter the temples and lick scattered white flowers off the statues of the gods.

Beside cows, the streets were also home to myriads of stray dogs. Nobody killed dogs in India. I saw a poor creature whose hind legs had been cut off by

Cows on the streets of Calcutta

a passing cart, but nobody seemed to find it in his heart to put the wretched dog out of its misery. While passing through villages, we were forced to keep our own dog on the motorcycle to avoid contact with the hundreds upon hundreds of infected dogs, which were milling about. Many of the stray dogs no longer had hair and spent much of their day licking their bloody sores. The unfortunate creatures found their only nourishment in the trash heaps; many had rabies, others died of hunger.

The evening avenues of Bombay were filled with animals of an even more curious sort—automobiles, ranging from forty-year-old dilapidated wrecks to the newest Rolls Royces. The elegant cars held elegant travelers: Parsees with their pointed hats, enchanting Hindu women, proud maharajas, intricately dressed Afghans, Persians, and Muslims sporting fezes. Occasional cars filled with Englishmen or Americans rumbled past, even distinguished Chinese women, their hair held up with diamond pins, found it pleasant to take the air on Bombay's twilight streets. The elegant cars were mostly decorated with golden accents and banners and accompanied by "boys," two perched at the front, two at the back.

Englishmen were naturally superior to all the nations around them and felt responsible for retaining this image of superiority. I had the privilege of meeting white colonists of many nations during my world travels. They had one thing in common: I felt a strong aversion to them all. Middle or lower class Europeans and Americans living in Europe and America seemed a people distinct from the Europeans and Americans who had been forced by circumstance to settle in the colonies. Although stemming from the same social class, I doubt they would recognize one another. Most colonists, even those with a sincere longing for far-off lands, never truly grew to love their new homes and soon began to change in imperceptible ways. Once established, colonists were truly a breed of their own.

British superiority was manifest in all areas of life. The British placed great emphasis on luxury while striving to observe the customs of their nation. Although they had profound contempt for the natives, they never let it show. There was a particular brand of aloofness to which all Englishmen subscribed. They did not make friends with Indians, neither did they eat at the same table, and intermarriage was virtually nonexistent. Although the people they colonized bore no great love for them, nevertheless, the British inspired a certain respect wherever they went. To European eyes, the isolation and contempt of the British seemed overdone, nevertheless, they had their isolationist life-style to thank for their success as colonizers.

The French colonies had a different flavor altogether. French colonizers mingled with the natives, made friends with them, drank with them, and married their daughters. At the same time, bloody beatings were an everyday event. No colonists were as cruel as the French, who moved very quickly between congenial relations and the lash of the whip.

The Dutch were moralizing colonists, building school upon school to educate and elevate the newly conquered people. Dutch colonists on the whole were lazy and aimless on one hand, and infinitely humane on the other. Their humanity did much to improve native-colonist relations but often proved too counterproductive regarding the act of colonizing itself.

Half-bloods were the true pariahs of India, not welcome in either the native or the conquering culture. Although some mixed couples were of aristocratic origins on both sides, their children continued to be rejected by all layers of society. In Calcutta, we made the acquaintance of just such a mixed couple and were pleased to see their overwhelming joy and gratitude at securing our friendship and their continual striving to be seen with us in public.

Bombay was the first stop on our long journey through India. Our travel plans were comprehensive and included all the famous historical, cultural, and natural sights of the Subcontinent. The road to Delhi, our first destination, was 1,500 kilometers long. From Delhi, we hoped to travel another 1,700 kilometers to reach Calcutta.

The Western India Automobile Association provided us with both maps and good advice, but we found most Indian roads to be kind to the visiting stranger. It was strange to us that distance was measured in miles. As one mile is the equivalent of 1,609 meters, we found ourselves traveling longer to pass an equal number of road markers.

Our motorcycle was loaded to the gills. In India, we were forced to carry our bedding with us, because small hotels, sleeping cars, and bungalows did not provide any. The sidecar was brimming with luggage; I could hardly make out Gyuszi, and our dog Hadji was precariously perched on top of a mountain of bags. It was February, the most pleasant time of the year in India, and the roads were surprisingly excellent.

The road we followed most of the time was the famous Indian Grand Trunk Road, a wide, paved road flattened to perfection and dotted with precise road-markers and directions in English. We were to travel thousands of kilometers along these glorious strips of road. Roads throughout India were well constructed and easy to travel, excepting perhaps the Calcutta-Madras stretch in Southern India, where we did run into some problems. While the main roads were world-class, straying onto side-roads was less than advisable. A traveler bold enough to leave the main roads would very soon find thousands of unpleasant indications that he was actually traveling through the heart of Asia.

We grew accustomed to driving on the left side of the road as quickly as we had gotten used to the humility of the natives. Reflecting on this humility, we soon surmised the roots of the settlers' contempt. Europeans moving to the colonies achieved an immediate, quasi-aristocratic status. Upon arrival, they immediately found an army of servants anxious to do their bidding, and were treated with deference wherever they went. Of course, being treated like a king makes even the most insignificant of men think he is one, and the colonists' initial feelings of superiority developed very quickly into utter contempt for those who made their aristocratic way of life possible.

The roads were always open before us. Whenever we encountered carts driven by natives, we saw them try their utmost to allow us to pass through as soon as possible. Although the road was usually wide enough to allow traffic in two directions, the natives nevertheless continued to scurry out of our way as soon as they had spotted us. Occasionally, they would almost fall off the steep embankment in their efforts to reach the open fields and make way for our motorcycle. This happened every time, despite our vehement gestures to the contrary. After a few such encounters, we thought we might help the situation if we stopped our motorcycle altogether, but the Indians continued to drive their herds of cows and oxen off the road. We felt sorry for the Indians, especially when we saw how close some of them came to falling into the roadside ditches, carts and all, in their efforts to let us pass. We had a suspicion, however, that not all white men felt the same way.

Indians traveling by foot met us with the same degree of humility. There were plenty of cars and motorcycles in India, so the respect wasn't meant for the wondrous machines, but for the white men sitting on them. Many pedestrians would stop as we passed by, bow low, and greet us with hands held together, as if in prayer.

Indian roads proved to be just as integral to our experience of India as the beauties of its cities. The roads were incredibly busy, perhaps some of the busiest roads on earth. Most of the traffic, however, did not consist of automobiles, but was rather made of streams of carts and pedestrians. The cows hitched to the carts were much more wild and skittish than their meek masters. Occasionally we saw small Asian horses or oxen hitched to the carts, and, especially passing through central India, we encountered more and more lumbering elephants.

But the overwhelming majority of the Indian people traveled by foot. There was a wanderlust distinctly Indian and not relegated to any section of society. Even the poorest natives took to the roads as often as they could. Sites of pilgrimage, holy streams, and mountains dotted the Subcontinent, and made for excellent and inspiring destinations. At the times of year when work was scarce, entire families left their homes to visit friends and relatives. If there were no jobs to be had or if it was a bad year for farming, even greater crowds of Indians took to the roads.

Another distinct class of travelers was the pariah class, made up of those who had nothing to call their own. It was all one to them where they starved and where death graciously closed their eyes, and so many spent their entire lives walking the roads of India. These were the poorest and most pitiful people on the face of the earth. They had no claim on the material world. They did not own a bit of land or a small house even, many had no clothing aside from some rags tied around their waists and carried only two things: a rough walking stick and a small bowl for drinking. These people, without relatives, brothers, or sisters, without homelands even, for they had long forgotten the place of their birth, spent their entire lives walking thousands upon thousands of kilometers, sustained by the hope of receiving their portion of rice each day, without which they could not continue on.

We were unable to help them. As soon as we stopped the motorcycle, we were immediately surrounded by hundreds of the poor, pleading with us and stretching out their hands for alms. There is nobody in the world wealthy enough to feed these hungry millions. Our hearts failed us when we saw them in the distance, waiting respectfully as we drew near, only to crowd around us expectantly once we were close. When we threw away our old food cans, the poor travelers would sniff at them and fight over the remnants.

Well-to-do Indians traveled on carts. We met hundreds, perhaps thousands of carts along the roads, the clothing and features of the crowd changing as we left one region of the country for another. It was impossible to get bored. "I feel like we're at a never-ending circus," cried my companion. "Or at the movies, watching one film after another," I exclaimed.

Indian folk dress was colorful with infinite variety. Some carts were drawn by camels and crowded to full capacity, carrying as much as ten to fifteen people, of whom no two were alike. Some wore gigantic turbans on their heads; the glitter of their jewelry made our heads ache. I was inclined to change my mind and compare the scene to a lavish opera production instead. There were so many people dressed in such varied costumes that we began to suspect we were part of a holiday parade, yet this was a holiday parade that lasted for days, weeks, months, entire lifetimes. The arms and ankles of the women were heavy with bangles of copper and iron, their necks, noses, and ears weighed down by countless necklaces and hoops even as their fingers disappeared under clusters of cheap rings. Some little girls went completely naked except for a few hoops of silver or copper.

There were myriads of tiny villages in India, and we passed through a good number of them. At first sight, they were comprised solely of filthy, tumbledown mud huts, which seemed to lean against one another for support. Most of the huts were of sufficient size to house only three or four people, yet passing by, we spotted up to fifteen or twenty people in some of the huts. The feeling of claustrophobia was a result of the Indian custom of building inwards. The outside walls of family complexes were in bad shape, moldering even, but they surrounded a whole complex of small homes. Young people, once they married, simply added another section to the already existing family complex to house their own future families. Relatives and extended family had the custom of gathering in one home to spend time together, even if they all had their own, more spacious residences.

Although we discovered that the average Indian village wasn't nearly as dilapidated as one was inclined to think, we couldn't close our eyes to true misery around us. Countless families shared their tiny, filthy huts with animals, while the rice and cotton fields surrounding their pitiful villages were luxuriantly fertile.

Most villages were entirely without shops, and so it was impossible to buy anything, especially with money, which some villagers had no concept of. At the beginning of our Indian journey, we spent countless hours, stomachs growling, searching for bread in the Indian villages. Our efforts turned out to be in vain, partly because Indians did not eat bread. We had been able to purchase drinks, lemonade, soda water, even ice cream, in the remotest of Arab villages. In India, smaller towns were less well stocked than those of the Arabian beyond. For instance, there were millions of Indians who had never seen ice in their lives. We often amused ourselves by taking small slabs of ice out of our thermoses and giving it to the unsuspecting natives. The Indians would hold on to the ice for a brief second, then toss it away with a cry of pain as if they had been holding live coals, and proceed licking the wet spot on their palms. They were utterly amazed to see us lick the ice, then swallow it, or to witness how it melted in a glass of water. Perhaps the villagers thought us a breed of white fakir.

While on the subject of water, I must remark that good drinking water is very scarce in India. Drinking from village wells is the equivalent of flirting with death. Dreadful tropical diseases reared their ugly heads all over the country. Most villages did not even have proper wells; people simply made do with large, earthen cisterns at the edge of the village, cisterns that filled to the brim in the rainy season. In the dry season, however, the cisterns emptied of water, creeks dried out altogether, while rivers flowed, their water levels alarmingly low. In the unbearable heat, the water clouded over and was soon covered by a thick layer of scum, which stank to high heavens. The scummy water in the cisterns was used for bathing both animals and people, washing clothes, cooking, even drinking. Epidemics of the plague, cholera, and smallpox ravaged the country each summer, taking a toll of hundreds of thousands of lives all over India.

We soon learned to avoid drinking water altogether, whether in towns or in villages. Boiling or having our water boiled to disinfect it soon led us to discover the wonders of tea. In especially disease-infested regions, we resisted the temptations of tropical fruits even.

After leaving Bombay, we arrived in the town of Nasik. We had previously read in the papers that an epidemic of the small pox was devastating the population of the town and that it was advisable to steer clear of the entire region. Traveling around the town, however, would have taken far too long, so we decided just to drive through without stopping, hoping that we could evade the disease with speed.

As we neared Nasik, we saw carts piled high with baggage. The healthy were fleeing the town. The fields surrounding Nasik were crowded with their tents and makeshift huts and the roads filled with crowds of people traveling by cart or foot. Tying cloths before our mouths, we hurried through the town, which was entirely deserted except for the funeral processions and the moaning victims of the disease. Occasionally, we spotted a dead body on the street. Although Nasik was located next to one of the seven holy rivers, the Godavari, the bathing places were just as empty as the town itself.

We sighed with relief as we left the town behind us. The words "Go to Nasik!" have been a proverbial expression of anger with us ever since.

Even past Nasik, the road continued on as sturdy as ever. The foundations were strong; fresh layers of sand were applied regularly. Trees lined the wide roads of India, lush trees decked in broad green leaves, sometimes so numerous, that they seemed to form a living green tunnel above our heads.

Many-towered Hindu temples seemed almost to sprout on both sides. The buildings were chaotic at best and surrounded by holy stones that had been painted red, or by strange red statues of Hindu gods or other sacred symbols. The Hindu faithful often paused before these statues for the length of a prayer, pouring liquid over the foremost stones. Red was the color of holy objects and places. I read somewhere that an Indian railroad company had a difficult time preventing the milestones lining the rails from being stolen until someone had the ingenious idea of painting the stones red.

We traveled inwards, into the heart of India. Thanks to the Dak Bungalows, which took the place of hotels on certain regions of the country, we were never hard put trying to find a place to stay for the night. Thankfully, we were not forced to resort to our tents; anyhow, the thought of sleeping in a tent in a countryside full of unknown dangers wasn't the least bit tempting.

The numerous bungalows we slept in or passed by had been constructed by the government, local or national. The bungalows were outfitted with all the European amenities and came with garages. Bungalows popped up every thirty or forty kilometers and usually served European travelers or the native elite.

These comfortable lodgings were reminiscent of pleasant little villas, surrounded as they were by giant trees and enhanced by a lovely garden and courtyard. Smaller bungalows included a single suite, larger buildings could accommodate two to three suites. Each suite, in turn, was comprised of two bedrooms, a bathroom, and servants' quarters. Prices were set at one rupee per person and night, which made bungalows infinitely better deals than city hotels. We always saved money on the rural stretches of our Indian travels. There was no bedding to be had, of course, but the servants strove to make us as comfortable as possible, and some of them even proved to be excellent cooks.

Although servants did their best, we had trouble communicating to them in any language we understood what we wished to eat. Some of the bungalow cooks had mastered English cuisine, but we were forced to put up with outrageously spicy Indian cooking most of the time. Eggs, which have proven over and over again to be the only true international food, often came to our rescue. Whenever eggs were available, we had the freedom to make an egg dish that was friendly to our palates.

Obtaining eggs, however, was a different matter altogether. Facing an un-comprehending but helpful native, I would first try to describe what I wanted in all the languages at my disposal, then resort to charades. After a few fruit-less attempts, we found the best method was to draw a chicken with an egg next to it, but when our artistic or the natives' imaginative faculties proved too weak, Gyuszi and I would flap our arms and cackle frantically. This was usually the point at which the native left the room and triumphantly returned with an egg.

Whenever we passed through larger towns, we took care to stock up on canned food, which provided us with numerous tolerably tasty lunches and dinners. Although we grew accustomed to the ubiquitous taste of curry, a favorite of the local Brits, we never learned to enjoy the other, stronger In-dian spices.

We had trouble sleeping at night. In a small bungalow in the middle of no-where, kilometers from the nearest town and with very little knowledge of In-dia under our belts, we wondered whether we would be missed in the morning if somehow we disappeared during the night. Despite the oppressive heat, we kept our windows locked, our doors bolted behind a blockade of furniture. Our dog Hadji and a loaded revolver were indispensable parts of our sleeping gear. I now smile to think back on our thorough precautions, which had bordered on the paranoid.

In India, houses are specially constructed to enhance air circulation; doors and windows are perpetually open. An average room has five to six doors, which provide maximal draft when all are open. During our first nights in In-dia, we started at every noise, and noises there were many, both in rural bun-galows and city hotels. "Someone's coming this way," Gyuszi would exclaim in the middle of the night. He was a much lighter sleeper than I. Not a minute passed before we stood, revolver in one hand, flashlight in the other, ner-vously scanning our room. "Rats," I would answer, with a careless wave of the hand, which hid profound relief.

Rats were the omnipresent and scrupulously faithful inhabitants of all In-dian houses, especially bungalows. Indian rats, braver and more cheeky than their European counterparts, would veritably waltz along the floor of our room under Hadji's nose, accompanied by impudent hordes of mice. Hadji hated them with a fanatical passion and would pursue them so fiercely all night that we finally decided to station him outside our room, on top of our motorcycle.

While in bed, from the safety of layers of mosquito netting, we often cast curious glances at the strange worms and insects lining the walls of our room. Although dangerous spiders, even scorpions, were not uncommon, most of our nocturnal visitors were harmless. One of the most beloved

Dangerous reptiles in India

creatures of the night was a striped lizard known as the *chick-chock*. The *chick-chock* waged war on mosquitoes and flies of all sorts and was therefore much respected. *Tokis* were larger than *chick-chocks* and had distinct, deep voices. We soon grew accustomed to the presence of the most grotesque night creatures: whirring bugs, winged ants, and gigantic, lumbering frogs. At night in India, it was best to avoid looking, listening, and thinking and get right to sleeping.

Although we encountered and accommodated a series of grotesque creatures, we were unable to grow accustomed to snakes. India was crawling with them, and our dread of snakes only increased as we found out that the bite of most species was fatal. Naturally, we couldn't avoid meeting and even running over dozens of them each day, but if we saw a large snake slither onto the road in front of us, we often stopped at a safe distance and let it pass.

Cobras posed white men a lesser threat than they did the natives. Most Europeans wore shoes, or, in snake-infested parts, boots even, which served as excellent protection against fatal bites. Most snakes were not aggressive if left alone; at the same time, they perceived all movement as an attack. If someone stepped on them or so much as walked too close, the cobras would straighten up as quick as a flash and administer their deadly poison. Snakes weren't afraid to enter homes, even; on many occasions, we were forced to strike them dead in our very rooms. Even Hadji confronted and killed a snake once. Worried, we scanned his body for signs of a wound but found none.

We were reminded day in and day out that we were traveling in a strange country, far from human habitations and the possibility of medical help. A snakebite in such a situation was no laughing matter. Although we learned how to clean and cauterize a potential wound by burning it and then applying crystals bought from the natives, which stung upon contact, we were nevertheless aware that a snakebite would mean certain death. Carrying antidotes on us was not an option, because the types of poison were as numerous as the species of deadly snakes. The nearest doctors were usually hopelessly far, and so we quickly decided that our best weapons were extreme caution and our usual good luck. Thousands upon thousands of Indians die each year as a result of snakebites.

Our journey led us on under the brilliant blue dome of the Indian sky. Sometimes we didn't see a single European for days, but this didn't bother us in the slightest, as we had grown to love and trust the peaceful, amiable natives.

Upon passing through the borders of the independent states, we were greeted by border guards of sorts, clad in colorful uniforms and showing great interest in our travel documents. On one occasion, the guards held out a large, ragged book for us to sign. We didn't understand what they wanted us to write, but as they handed us a pencil, we couldn't turn them down. And so I wrote in Hungarian, *"Isten tartson meg jó egészségben,"* "God keep you in good health." The guards saluted and, after the necessary formalities, we were free to cross the border.

Where we would next obtain gasoline was our constant concern. It wasn't a good idea simply to proceed to the next large town and hope you would be able to replenish your fuel there. We always insisted on knowing for sure whether gasoline was available in the next town over. Occasionally, we had to stock up for longer stretches and, passing through smaller towns, encountered wildly fluctuating prices. A gallon of gasoline usually cost one rupee, but as we left the coastal regions, we found ourselves paying fourteen rupees for two gallons of fuel.

New Adventures, New Surprises

Our first Indian incident occurred somewhere between Gwalior and Agra. Wolves were common in Central India, often standing watch by the side of the road or on top of close-by hills, refusing to move even after hearing the rumbling of our engine. Indian wolves were somewhat smaller than their European counterparts and dangerous only in large groups, so, for the most part, we ignored them and continue on our way.

Shortly after passing the river Chambal, our motorcycle stopped. After realizing that one of our valves had gotten stuck, we decided to spend the night and to leave troubleshooting for the morning.

We set up our tent, completely covered with mosquito nets, in a nearby clearing and had soon prepared a tasty canned meal. By the time we lay down to sleep, the night was black as ink. After a few moments of silence, Hadji started barking and kept at it so long that I loaded our revolver and started scanning the surrounding area with a flashlight. Sure enough, a wolf was scurrying through a nearby clump of trees. It disappeared. Then we saw two more, and the shivers commenced running up and down our spines. "One of us had better keep watch," suggested Bartha. "Tie up the dog before one of these beasts gets it," I warned my companion, as Hadji seemed inclined to throw himself at the entire pack.

As time passed, our eyes remained open and watchful. By midnight, we were encircled by numerous pairs of eyes reflecting the rays of our flashlight. The wolves howled and Hadji howled back.

It didn't take us long to realize the dangers of the situation we had gotten ourselves into. We fired a few shots, hoping to kill some wolves and scare the rest away, but our stock of bullets was running low, and each time we successfully hit a wolf, three more seemed to take its place and edge closer and closer to our tent. It felt like only moments separated us from the general attack, which would surely end our lives, unless we managed to shimmy up the nearby trees before it was too late.

As we started running out of bullets, and as our flashlight began to flicker, we turned toward the campfire as our last escape. The trees were a ways off, but I managed to gather some firewood while Gyuszi did the work of an entire firing squad. Then, we poured gasoline on the twigs and branches, and the flames of our fire shot up into the inky sky. It was really the fire that saved us. The wolves backed down, and although they lingered in our general area, very few had the courage to approach the flames, and those we killed.

Needless to say, we didn't sleep a wink that night, but by the time the first rays of the morning sun lit the scene around us, we saw with profound relief that the coast was clear. We had left the local vultures and hyenas more than a dozen wolves.

Towards noon, our dog Hadji took off and barely missed joining his wolf cousins in the other world. Hadji often ran off during lunch to chase a passing monkey, squirrel, or other small animal. This time, we heard frightened screams and angry barking from a nearby field. Our playful dog had found a herd of goats and was wreaking havoc amidst the poor animals, chasing them in all directions, while the goatherds, convinced that a wolf had attacked their charges, grabbed their gnarled walking sticks and attempted to frighten Hadji. Imagine their surprise when we merely whistled and the "wolf" bounded over to us to take its place on our motorcycle!

Not long after, we passed through Gwalior where we encountered a real

Indian maharaja for the first time in our lives. After Gwalior, we seemed to pass through a tiny kingdom every day. Each of the myriads of independent kingdoms had its own capital. The first such kingdom we had crossed was Indore, then Dewas, finally, Gwalior.

Later, we passed through many more countries, each with its own maharaja, raja, nawab, or chief. The native rulers lived amidst unbelievable pomp and luxury.

There were a few hundred independent states in India, some small, others spanning large territories. Various princes ruled over the countless states; it was usually the Hindus among them who wore the titles of raja or maharaja.

Although under English influence, the maharajas of India ruled independently of colonial power. The wealthiest men on earth were to be found in their circles. Their fortunes, unlike that of American magnates, did not take the shape of factories, companies, and stocks, rather their wealth was in the land, and everything that came from the land, over which they held absolute power. Besides extensive territories, they also owned more tangible riches such as jewels, precious stones, and untold treasures locked away in their princely courts. Of course, not all maharajas were unendingly wealthy. Some were princes of modest means, others struggled with debts, but the great majority of local princes lived in luxury as splendid as the image of luxury conceived of by the most imaginative European minds.

We made the acquaintance of a number of Indian princes on our tour through the country. Many had received a Western education; nearly all spoke perfect English. Those who had studied at European universities often lived like Europeans themselves, others rejected the Western influence entirely and clung to their ancient Indian heritage.

Their palaces were astounding, often with beautiful marble halls furnished in both the European and the traditional Indian fashion.

The cities of the independent states were very different from those in English-run portions of the country. On the whole, purely Indian cities were more colorful, more surprising, more like Indore, which seemed to have been constructed solely to elicit wonder. Some of the larger independent cities boasted populations of 100,000 or more. Built in the Indian style, they did not imitate Europe but preserved, in stone, the true architectural heritage of India. A princely palace surrounded by colorfully dressed guards lorded it over the rest of the city. It all seemed like an exotic movie set. The streets were filled with people riding and pushing carts, balancing on camels and decorative elephants. We couldn't get our fill of the sights; each time a white man came in view, we felt like the place had been desecrated.

The Kingdom of Gwalior was the size of Holland and Denmark put together and was ruled over by the Scindia dynasty, whose white marble palace might have competed with the royal homes of the mighty of Europe. As we crossed the monumental city, we were greeted with curious glances, as there were no other Europeans in sight. We saw glass carriages pulled by white cows, and the columns holding up the palace roof were carved of a single rock. Inside the palace were rooms with mosaics of precious stones; miracle followed miracle.

The maharaja was an avid sportsman. The carpet in his office had taken generations to complete; today, it is the largest carpet in the world.

Besides a magnificent carpet, he also boasted interesting hobbies. For example, his passion for mechanics led him to fix his own car. The tables in his dining hall housed miniature trains on tracks, planned and executed by His Highness. The maharaja simply pushed a button or pulled a lever, and the tiny trains started up, taking the guests refreshments, main courses, even cigarettes. The "transports" stopped on command.

The maharaja of Gwalior, like many other Indian princes, was profoundly concerned with the well-being of his subjects. He was prime minister and headed the army as well. In his kingdom, reform followed reform; factories, schools, and hospitals sprang up alongside various clubs and societies for horse-racing. This wasn't the case in all of the independent states; many of the rulers simply collected taxes, amassed mind-boggling fortunes, and spent the rest of their lives trying to figure out ways to spend at least a small portion of their money.

Passing through Jaipur, Alwar, Burwan, and Benares, we made the acquaintance of all their maharajas only to see them again in Delhi, at the annual gathering of Indian leaders, where the affairs of the country were discussed and debated under the leadership of the governor-general of India. We further met the princes of Patiala, Kapurthala, Bikaner, Kashmir, and Nawaganar, Raja Mandi, the nawab of Bhawalpuri, and the rulers of Bhopal and Malerkotla, either in Delhi and Calcutta or in their respective kingdoms.

Indian princes were usually unapproachable, but Europeans were in a better position to begin with, and after collecting a letter of introduction or two, we were generally granted the desired audience. And how memorable each such encounter was!

Our first encounter with a real maharaja was not to be for long. He received us in a formal almost ritualistic manner, and then commenced to ask us a series of polite questions. Standing before our first maharaja, we expected one of the *One Thousand and One Nights* to descend on us. As we stood there conversing, His Highness clapped his hands, which elicited a response from an exceedingly humble servant who entered, bowed first to his prince then to us, and held out a jewel-studded ivory case. I began sweating profusely and whispered to Gyuszi Bartha, "Do you think this is a gift from the maharaja?" We hesitated, not knowing whether to take the case or leave it lying where it was. The servant then lifted up the lid and offered us cigarettes. I stopped sweating and starting profusely regretting my previous hesitation. Had I had the presence of mind to simply take up the case and thank the maharaja with a brilliant smile, nobody at court would have batted an eyelid, and today, I would be the proud owner of a fabulous treasure. Alas, no such opportunity presented itself ever again.

After the initial audience, those who found favor with the maharaja were invited to reside in his court for an indefinite length of time. In this way, we often had the honor of living at court.

Just what did such an invitation entail?

If so asked by the maharaja, we packed up our things and moved, motorcycle, dog, and all, into the prince's residence. Once established at court, we rarely saw the prince again until the moment of our departure. Upon arrival, we would be lead into the guesthouse, which was the equivalent of a fine modern hotel. In the guesthouse, we were allotted a luxurious suite of our own, outfitted with private bathrooms, telephones, electric lights, occasionally even typewriters and radios, exotic Eastern rugs, and excellent service. Lunch, dinner, and tea would be served in our rooms; the menu was varied and delicious.

Every morning, we were greeted by a whole line of servants headed by the primary servant, who politely inquired as to our intentions for the day. We had many options: bathing, strolling on the palace grounds, hunting, or riding in an automobile. If we were curious about our surroundings, there was always a friendly guide available to show us the important sights, lead us through the different wings of the palace, or else, we could undertake horseback riding or a game of tennis, and could even ask for a theatrical production or film, as well as female dancers who could be called in to entertain us. In fact, no request seemed unattainable; an army of servants surrounded us day and night, ready to do our bidding at the first indication.

Besides the quality of Indian hospitality, we were also struck by its longevity. Guests were never asked to leave and expected to stay as long as they desired. We encountered a young Hungarian painter at one of the royal courts. He had managed to paint a portrait of the prince and had been invited to stay on as court painter for as long as he liked. This young Budapest native had been a courtier for years, blissfully painting away, without showing the least intention of ever leaving his generous patron.

On the other side of the coin of hospitality lay the unbearable Indian heat. Despite our status as respected guests, not even the delicious food and luxurious beds of court could detain us once the temperature reached 30 to 40 degrees C at night. Too languid to enjoy the pleasures of court, we

Riding the elephants of the maharaja of Gwalior

decided to leave the maharaja and his fairy-tale treasures behind and head for cooler lands.

The unspeakable pomp of the royal courts dazzled us. There were households where the army of servants numbered five thousand; the maharaja's court was a complex of countless palaces, homes of varying sizes, and a series of stables. The garages themselves occupied a great deal of space, as some maharajas owned up to three or four hundred cars, including thirty or forty luxury automobiles used solely by the prince and his family. Occasionally, courts boasted not just a large outfit of guards, but an entire army, their own post offices, customs, even distinct currencies. The most powerful among the maharajas were constantly surrounded by the otherwise pompous Englishmen, who nevertheless clung to the mightiest potentates in the hopes of obtaining their favor, which in most cases could materialize in the form of a large fortune. Merchants and agents of various sorts lined the hallways, waiting for days on end for a chance to see the prince. They brought their wares with them and the hallways slowly filled with all imaginable goods under the sun. It was at one of the courts that I saw my first elephant agent, his brief-case brimming with photographs of elephants for sale. At 10,000 rupees each, the agent was bound to make a fortune, seeing as maharajas bought elephants by the dozen.

Automobiles in India were another luxury status symbol. The maharajas ordered the finest models from the foremost European and American facto-ries, and once in India, these choice vehicles were painted fantastic colors and lined with silver and gold. Nowhere in the world were there automobiles to match those of India. We saw cars decorated with flags or expensive weap-ons in intricate weapon holders, even covered all over the outside with tiny figures crafted of ivory. The insides even outdid the outsides, if that was pos-sible. Seats lined with expensive silk, animal skins and embroidery awaited the tired passenger in the company of finely clad drivers and servants. The most important additions to luxury cars, however, were the lamps affixed not just to the front and back, but to the sides of the vehicles as well. I once counted twenty-four lamps on a single car.

Leaving the shining courts of the maharajas for the roads and the people of India, we often encountered glaring contradictions. The pomp and circum-stance of the courts seemed all the more pompous and circumstantial when framed by the misery of millions. Precisely because the country was so popu-lous, work was incredibly cheap; people's entire lives, or rather, their life force and work could be bought for a few pence.

In many parts of India, human laborers took the place of domesticated ani-mals. We grew accustomed to the idea of "men of burden," unfortunate coo-lies who made their living drawing gigantic, laden carts along the streets of Madras, Trichinopoly, and various regions of Southern India. Coolies were common not only in the small towns but in large cities as well. The carts they pulled were piled high with sacks and crates, many of them used to transport the cotton crop. In the sweltering heat, sweat streamed down the naked bod-ies of these men of burden, two struggling in front to pull a load far too heavy even for two horses, while two pushed from behind. With drenched bodies and straining muscles they struggled on for a pittance of a few coins. Some coo-lies didn't even have a cart to pull; instead, they loaded whatever was to be carried on their heads, sometimes carrying beds, closets, sewing machines; a few coolies, when working together, could even manage a piano.

The tiny man-drawn cart known as the rickshaw was an epicenter of coolie labor. The rickshaws of Bombay and Calcutta were light affairs with tires, but those in the South were larger and heavier, constructed to hold two to three people. Riding a rickshaw from one end of town to the other was possible for a

The ever-popular Indian rickshaw

laughable sum; for a rupee or a rupee and a half, we could have rented a rickshaw, coolie and all, for an entire month.

Rickshaws often ventured outside city bounds. *Zemindars,* or traditional Indian landowners, often undertook long rickshaw voyages. Such long voyages required two or even three coolies, who would take turns pulling the vehicle while the other two ran alongside it, "gathering strength" for the next stretch. Litters were also widespread; four strong men, with their employer sitting in a small cabin perched on their shoulders, would plunge ahead at surprising speed. One such litter managed to make thirty-six kilometers in a little less than three hours.

Upon observing the hustle and bustle of Indian harbors, I noted the absence of pulleys and cranes in the unloading process, which was instead staffed by hundreds of coolies scurrying back and forth on narrow wooden planks separating the ships from the shore, carrying loads of coal, cotton, or other supplies. After every descent into the bowels of the ship, a coolie received a wooden peg, which could be cashed in at the end of the day for a minimal sum. The stronger the coolie was, the better his pay. There were three pegs to one two-hundredth of a rupee, so it was logical to prefer an army of coolies to an expensive system of pulleys and cranes.

At the time of our visit to Bombay, coolies earned, on average, a tenth of a rupee per day. That was approximately how much we paid a "boy" to watch our motorcycle for an entire night.

The simple workers got by on very little. Not having houses of their own, they slept outside. Their clothing consisted of a piece of linen, their daily food ration was a bowl of rice. We mustn't forget that tens of thousands of people died of starvation in India every year. Although the country has developed a lot since then, and the poor aren't nearly as exploited as they used to be, nevertheless, there are those who still rejoice upon receiving their handful of rice at the end of the day. Many others live on alms; in large cities, armies of beggars surround foreigners. Their misery repels. We see cripples of all types, some missing an arm, others a leg, still others must live with wizened or swollen limbs. Some suffer from hydrocephaly, leprosy, or various contagious diseases, or walk about with a limp, swollen bellies, hunched backs, or even pus-filled putrefied sores. There are professional beggars, who often maim themselves in order to look more pitiful; then, there are amateurs, who were simply taught to hold out their hands to each passing white man, and those hideously disfigured, true anatomical wonders.

White men, be they Americans or Europeans, must seem to these poor natives the very crown of creation. They see all white men as wealthy, presiding over a large income and armies of servants. Even bureaucrats, granted they had the good luck to be born white, are considered fortunate, wealthy men, magnates even in comparison to the natives who inevitably attain only the lowest ranks and significantly lower salaries. No poor white men must be seen in India, the English maintain. At larger offices, only one in ten employees is European. Starting salaries for native bureaucrats range from fifty to sixty rupees while white employees receive 300 to 400 rupees from the start, regardless of their level of education. Those in leading positions, those at the head of firms, chipping companies, etc. make astronomical sums; English merchants have nothing to complain of either.

I will never forget a conversation I had with a rickshaw coolie working for one of the hotels. In his broken English, he asked a myriad questions, rejoicing just to have the honor of talking to a white man. "Tell me, Sahib," he began, "in the country where you live, are there poor coolies like me to pull carts and carry loads?" I knew that by coolie he meant poor Indian workers, and there being none in Hungary, I shook my head. "Then who does the work in your country?" was his next question, and a logical one at that. They could not imagine that white men ever did physical work, especially of the backbreaking kind.

All servants, down to the simplest, passionately collected the compliments of their white clients. This custom might have stemmed from England; there were guest books placed in every shop and shopkeepers anxiously awaited the comments of their clients, who were expected to express their satisfaction with the purchase they had made. We were asked to record our compliments not just in hotel guest books, but in private books for the "boys" we hired to guard our motorcycle for the night or take Hadji for a walk.

While in Bengal, we spent a night under the stars. There were no bungalows to be had, so, instead of pitching our tent, we decided to spend the night in a half-made house by the side of the road. We had hardly managed to make ourselves comfortable when an Indian came to us and offered to fan us all night. We fell to thinking; it *was* very hot and a little fanning would have come in handy. Besides, we could think of no better way to live it up and feel like royalty for once in our lives, so we accepted.

Our trusty fanner attached a reed mat to the ceiling and a rope to the reed mat. The rope trailed out the window, and he took his place outside; it would have been unimaginable for him to share our room for the night. He tugged at the rope all night, providing us with a little air in the stifling heat. Exposing his naked body to innumerable insects and mosquitoes, he fanned on until the morning. He asked the usual wage of a tenth of a rupee and seemed very satisfied, especially after we wrote in his book to the effect that he was an excellent fanner. A previous inscription by an Englishman read that our fanner was the greatest talent at sewing on buttons in all of India.

Let's return to our voyage now, and continue our trek through India. Fascinating bits of country, ancient cities, and magnificent palaces lined our way. We spent days on end in the most renowned places, and so the months of March and April passed, and at the start of the hottest season, we found ourselves still in India. After passing through Agra and Delhi, we traveled on to Punjab, then to Calcutta and the East via Lahore. By the time the dreaded summer heat caught up with us in Bengal, we had left Lucknow, Kanpur, Allahabad and Benares behind.

Those who were able retreated into the mountains. Although the provincial capital was Simla, most wealthy Indians sought relief on the slopes of the Himalaya Mountains, that is, if they didn't have the means to travel to Europe. Ship tickets had to be purchased months in advance, and all the ships were full to overflowing. Most Englishmen traveled to England frequently; many owned companies in both countries, spending six months of the year in each. Those whose jobs forced them to stay nevertheless made every effort to send their families away to avoid the onslaught of the heat.

Englishmen were never happy to live in India. They were scornful of the very country that provided for them and for a significant portion of their compatriots. English babies were never born in India; would-be mothers traveled home in time for the child to be born on English soil, fearing that children born in India would be stigmatized for the rest of their lives.

Summer was from March to September; the big rains began in June and normally lasted four months. The heat was intense whether or not it was raining, but the hottest time of year was the dry season spanning March, April, May and June.

The roads we traveled took us through the lush vegetation peculiar to the tropics. In the rainy season, Bengal was a fertile land of widespread rainforests, exotic trees, and parasitic plants, twisted and snakelike. Occasionally, we drove through forests of bamboo and marveled at their exceptionally thick stalks. The various stalks, bending to the left and to the right, seemed to make up a giant, four-storied bouquet. In this region of the country, everything was built of bamboo. Black buffalo were hitched to carts made entirely of bamboo. Various tools, fences, wagons, and even houses had been constructed of this ubiquitous material. The roads were relatively empty. Most of the natives walked about armed with sticks of bamboo, axes with bamboo handles, and bows and arrows as protection against wild animals. Motorcycles must have been a rare sight, because the people were mortally scared; children hid, terrified, in thickets or climbed trees to escape.

Temperatures rose day by day. Thirty-five degrees centigrade counted as a mild day; temperatures of 40 degrees were much more common, but during the hottest hours each day, temperatures rose to 45 degrees C. Nights weren't much cooler at 30 degrees or 35 degrees C.

Traveling in such heat was far from enjoyable. Even discounting the hottest hours, during which even thinking about travel was impossible, we were often to be found on the road in forty-degree heat. When the temperature dropped to 35 degrees C, fast travel was pleasant as the currents of air created by our motorcycle managed to cool us, but at 40 degrees C, the rush of hot air only caused us to choke; the faster we went the more we choked. Every so often, we were assailed by puffs of hot vapor; it was very much like standing next to a sauna as the doors opened and closed. As in the desert, all the metal parts of our vehicle became firebrands, and we never ceased to wonder how our motorcycle managed to carry us forward despite the heat. Hadji was fading fast; the heat proved to be too much for him. Although we wrapped his head in linens to shield him from the sun, he refused to bark and showed no interest in his formerly beloved hunting sprees.

Cool drinks were out of the question; besides, hot tea was the best medicine against the heat. Even Hadji joined us in drinking tea, but passing through smaller towns, we had to make due with lukewarm beer. As the Ganges was nearby, we stayed close to the river and enjoyed the shadow of avenues of trees lining the road. Occasionally, the line of trees would cease, and we would be forced to continue on under the merciless rays of the tropical sun.

Millions upon millions of mosquitoes conspired to make our already un-bearable days even more unbearable. At night, we slept in the protection of our nets, but during the afternoon and in the twilight hours, whenever we stopped for a short rest, we were assailed by the pesky insects. We were con-stantly swatting at the mosquitoes, and whenever we stopped to adjust some-thing on our vehicle, we were stung raw in a matter of minutes, despite vehement efforts to keep the insects away. Mosquito bites were dangerous in that part of India, as many of the mosquitoes carried malaria. To avoid fevers, we started a daily regimen of quinine.

Once the sun set, the various towns and villages were wrapped in thick clouds of smoke. The thick, asphyxiating smoke impeded our progress. The locals built great big bonfires along the roads, in the courtyards of their houses, in city streets, and in their very homes. This was the only method they knew of protecting themselves against the bites of the myriads of in-fected mosquitoes.

The sweltering heat became somewhat easier to bear once we were in-stalled in the comfortable hotels of Calcutta. The stone walls, cold showers in every room, large fans pumping day and night and wet reed mats flapping in all of the window and door openings served to lower temperatures by a few crucial degrees. The streets were empty from one to four in the afternoon; ev-erybody stayed inside during the hottest hours of the day, bathing, sleeping, or pretending to. We felt sorry for the barefoot natives who were forced to switch from one foot to another, nearly hopping about on lava-like pavement. The soles of our shoes sank deep into the melting asphalt; the heat pene-trated to our feet. After a while, however, we grew accustomed to the heat, as we had grown accustomed to everything else about India.

It was in this inferno that we traveled the last 2,000 kilometers to Ceylon, the roads growing progressively worse. Our travel plans were to lead us through Bezwada, Madras, and Madurai on to the beautiful island of Ceylon. Once in Ceylon, we found ourselves in an incomparably more beautiful place than those we had passed, and, what's more, amidst milder weather condi-tions and traveling along excellent roads. South of Madras, we measured re-cord temperatures of 125 to 130 degrees F, or 52 to 55 degrees C. Temperatures routinely reached 40 degrees C by six in the morning and remained relentless until midnight.

Monuments and Wild Animals

As I have mentioned before, our apprehensions regarding the Indian natives ceased as soon as we had gotten to know this peaceful and generous people. Throughout our Indian voyage, we were never inconvenienced in the slightest

137

by the people of India. The same could not be said of the animals, however. We had been aware, even before our journey to the Subcontinent, that India was inhabited by much more than just mosquitoes, and that we needed to be prepared for all eventualities. I have already recounted our adventure with the harmless-seeming wolves, and not a day passed without a number of run-ins with snakes. Shortly after leaving Bombay, we met the first monkeys, troops of whom accompanied us on our way. We fell in love with the little creatures and stopped often to photograph them. Following our visit to Mhow, our ears were constantly filled with their racket. As our motorcycle roared along the road, hundreds of monkeys would run for cover and spring from the ground into the shelter of the avenue of trees. Most of the monkeys we encountered were of a smaller size, and although they bared their teeth at us rather viciously, we soon learned that they were harmless. It wasn't long before we got used to their omnipresence and weren't the least bit surprised to find them gathered, by the hundreds, in the courtyard of our bungalow or chattering away in the trees above our tent. There were monkeys in both the towns and the villages, living in rooftops, in gardens, on and around bridges. They were tame, for the most part, and occasionally allowed themselves to be caught. They did have one very negative trait, however. Monkeys were confirmed thieves, stealing anything and everything in sight, and so skilled, that the locals were forced to protect their valuables from them by affixing iron bars to their windows. Hadji, unlike his owners, was unable to grow accustomed to the monkeys. As their sworn enemy, he pursued them relentlessly, and if he caught one, we were hard put trying to free the poor creature.

Elephants were also common in Central India. Although we didn't encounter wild elephants until later, there were plenty of domesticated ones around, whose phenomenal strength was a great help in transportation, hunting, and carrying loads. Occasionally, one of these large gray creatures would settle next to our parked motorcycle to rest. Hadji, who guarded the bike with the utmost devotion, wouldn't take his eyes off of the suspicious-looking giants. The native owners of the elephants gazed on Hadji with the same distrust.

Flocks of birds accompanied us on our way. Frightened by the sound of our engine, colorful tropical birds of all shapes and sizes would take to their wings. We saw numerous wild peacocks, which resembled the peacocks we had seen in zoos and parks down to the least feather, only they had preserved their ability to fly. Eagles and vultures soared overhead unceasingly.

Here, I must make mention of the crows, who happened to be one of the most fascinating species of bird in India. Crows were excellent sanitation workers, cleaning the streets of cities, both large and small, of scraps of food, trash, and accumulated filth. Crows are to India what pigeons are to Venice; Indian streets would be unimaginable without them. We saw these sly and clever birds everywhere; if there wasn't enough trash to fill their nutritional needs, they often resorted to stealing. Squawking loudly, they made quick dives for anything and everything edible, sometimes going so far as to grab the meat an unwitting Indian carried on his head or food scraps off of hotel tables. However crows were not the largest and most dangerous animals we met in India.

Occasionally, we caught glimpses of large predators. During our nights under the stars, we were kept awake by the howling of jackals and hyenas, or the roars of tigers and leopards. Although we were surrounded by such big game, we had no opportunities to go hunting. Our primary aim was to travel around the world, and extended safaris could not be worked into our schedule or our budgets. Besides, large game was under governmental protection and could only be hunted for exorbitant prices.

Also, wild animals tended to seek shelter in the forests, mountains, and other deserted areas, and rarely ventured near the busy roads. The tigers sighted in villages were usually after domesticated animals rather than people. On the roads of Bengal, automobiles and carts sometimes came up against the dreaded tigers, yet human beings generally emerged from these encounters unharmed.

Tigers were hunted by beating, while hunters perched in trees or on elephants. Seeking game by foot was nearly impossible in the depths of the jungle, in the bush or among tall grasses. Successful tiger hunts required lots of experience, countless beaters, and precise techniques. The two of us, armed with our two rifles, never would have made it in the jungles of India. On the other hand, we never quite gave up hope that we would kill our own large game someday, however, this moment didn't come until we had left India.

Small game, however, we shot often. We carried with us two revolvers and another pair of guns, one an adaptation of a hunter's Mannlicher, and the other a common double-barreled shotgun. All four guns were loaded and ready throughout our journey across India. We used the Mannlicher to kill most of our small game in India as well as large game later on.

Bears, deer, and wild boars were the small game most common to India, and the species we focused our hunting efforts on, while we mainly kept our distance from bison and buffalo that could prove to be dangerous to inexperienced hunters such as ourselves. White leopards, red and black bears inhabited the Himalaya region. The largest animal we killed was a buck, the most dangerous, a wild cat. Although we sighted a tiger and a buffalo once, they fled from the sound of our motorcycle. When we were serious about hunting, we went about it at night, with the help of a flashlight technique that had proved successful. During the day, we successfully shot antelope, deer, gazelles, and various species of birds.

By this point in the book, it must have become apparent to all readers that I have neglected to describe the wondrous cities and marvelous sights in India, which are known the world over. Neither have I spent much time detailing Indian religion, and its sister, Indian art. Were I to undertake an account of all the wonders of India, my book would swell a hundredfold. Volumes could be written about the cultural treasures of Agra, Benares, Ajanta, Delhi, Ellora, Aurangabad, Amritsar, and Bhopal, to name only a few. There is so much to see and experience in India that it would be impossible to fit it all into a single volume and sinful, even, to attempt a summary without thorough knowledge of and insight into the land and its people.

Although I cannot pretend to draw an accurate picture of all the wonders of India, there are a few outstanding places that cannot be glossed over. With regards to the people inhabiting them, the cities of Lahore and Madras remain fixed in my mind as the opposite ends of a spectrum. Lahore is the capital of Punjab, a colorful and dynamic city inhabited by people belonging to various nationalities from the other side of the national border. On the other hand, in Lahore, as in Indore, I began to discover uncanny similarities in physical appearance between the Indian natives belonging to various higher castes, like that of the merchants and Hungarian peasants. Aside from the darker skin color, the large moustaches, faces, and demeanor of the Indian elite recalled, very strongly, some of the typical characteristics of the Hungarian peasant.

Madras was a typical South Indian town. Its population of half a million was incredibly diverse, comprised of Telugus, Tamils, and other South Indian groups, all of the Hindu persuasion. On the whole, their skin was much darker than that of other Indian peoples and led a much simpler lifestyle. Those of the lower castes went about entirely naked, discounting the ragged loincloths wrapped about their lower bodies. Instead of turbans, their heads were wrapped in red rags; at the same time, many went without a head covering altogether and wore their hair long, streaming about them, or twisted into a bun at the back of their heads. The women sported heavy necklaces of copper, silver, or gold, as well as bangles on both their wrists and their ankles. Nose rings seemed highly popular, as most women wore three or four at once, and a hole the size of a small coin in their ears was the place to hang earrings. Jewelry was a must; even women who went about in rags did so clanging with bangles.

While still in the South, we had a strange encounter. We had just left one of the small towns, when we spotted two large, curtained automobiles on the road in front of us. After stopping and waiting at a respectful distance, we saw a group of women alight. Dressed to the nines, they were escorted towards the empty fields lining the road by a number of armed guards. We couldn't make heads or tails of the incident for quite some time. The ladies, clad in aristocratic gowns and silk slippers, walked in circles on the dusty and uneven ground and marched back to the car after completing the desired number of orbits. It was only after they had driven off that we realized that the unfortunate captives were most likely the wives of a great prince, who, when they wished to walk along the barren stubble fields, had to do so outside town and with an armed escort. Only their guards and the birds overhead beheld their beauty.

Visitors to India are spiritually impressed by two cities. The treasures of these cities surpass all of the beauties of India, and the very name of India will never cease to conjure two other luminous names, that of Agra and of Benares.

Agra is the city of the Moguls. The world-renowned masterpieces found there serve the greater glory of Muslim art. Agra is home to the most beautiful building in India, and arguably, in the whole world: the Taj Mahal. This piece of marble poetry was built more than three hundred years ago by the lovelorn Muslim ruler of Northern India, the Shah Jehan, in tribute to the memory of his favorite wife, Mumtaz Mahal. Built of the whitest marble of Jaipur, its form, harmonies, and symmetries represent the epitome of Oriental architecture. The name of the architect remains unknown to this day. According to legend, Mumtaz Mahal, the pride and joy of the royal palace, died while giving birth to her fourteenth child. The shah wished to pay tribute to her memory by building a monument that was unlike any other. It is said that 20,000 men worked on the construction of the Taj Mahal for a period of twenty years until it was finished. Once the building was completed, the shah had the architect's arm cut off to prevent him from duplicating his masterpiece.

The Taj Mahal is exquisite from all directions. Located in the middle of a marvelous garden, it shines in the sun, as white as on the day it was completed. A pool of water, which tapers at its ends and is paved with white marble and lined by trees, lies between the palace and the gate. The building is so balanced and altogether harmonious that it exudes lightness and clarity despite its monumental size. A gigantic dome graces the middle portion of the building, while marble minarets towering at three stories each, guard its four corners. There is no photographer or poet in the world to capture the extent of the magnificence of Taj Mahal.

A marble stairway spans the space between the ground and the foundations of the building. Walking up the stairway allows one to revel in the peerless marble carvings. The walls are lined with a marble lace so intricate that we can peer through the crevices to the other side. There are large portions of the building, several meters across, carved out of a single block of stone.

The Taj Mahal is surprisingly small on the inside. Another staircase leads

The Taj Mahal in Agra

down into the crypt where the shah and his beloved wife are buried. Two empty graves, surrounded by astonishing marble carvings, cover the actual place of burial. The inner dome is lined with quotations from the Koran; although the individual letters are approximately ten meters tall, we felt like we were reading them from a book. The walls are further decorated with fantastic mosaics assembled out of various semi-precious stones such as jasper, carbuncles, onyx, sapphires, amethysts, turquoise, and malachite. The Taj Mahal draws tourists from the world over, while the Agra merchants make sure they don't leave empty-handed.

Anything and everything available in India is also available in the city of Agra. Five-star hotels alternate with elite shops; each shop is like a museum, bursting with treasures; stretches of magnificent silk, expensive textiles, both embroidered and woven, antique jewelry, soft carpets, marble statuettes, masterpieces by local goldsmiths, weapons, ancient books and manuscripts, and beautiful pictures catch the eye. Of course, nothing is for free. Even middling silk scarves cost 50 to 60 rupees a piece; ivory figurines sell for 20 to 30 rupees. Both the scarves and the figurines may take an artisan up to a month to prepare, so the high prices reflect not only the expensive materials but the intensive labor as well that goes into each and every one of these masterpieces. All of the wares in all the shops are kept under lock and key. Never had I seen so many locks in my life! There were locks on all the doors and gates, as well as on the doors of our hotel rooms. In the shops, most of the wares are locked away in cupboards, and the shopkeepers keep their money in iron chests, which they lock and unlock each time a purchase is made.

In Agra's Cecil Hotel, a crowd gathered each evening to listen to Hungarian music. Of all the European programs, the Hungarian came through best. Hungarian music, loud and clear, filled the evening air in India. We sighed when the announcer said, "Pontos idő hét óra tíz perc," "It is now ten minutes past seven." In India, it was past midnight.

Now let us move on to the other renowned Indian city, Benares, situated on the banks of the holy river Ganges. Benares is the religious capital of all the Hindu faithful, and appears as a thriving town in the most ancient literature of India. We must keep in mind, however, that it shifted its position along the river over the centuries and was razed by Muslim forces on countless occasions. Today, the Maharaja of Benares controls only the insignificant portion of the city located to the right of the river; the flowering part of town, with its industry and trade, is on British hands. The baths in Benares surpass other watering holes along the Ganges in much the same way as the Taj Mahal in Agra lords it over the other monuments of the Subcontinent. The River Ganges is wide, approximately as wide as the Danube in Budapest and carries sacred water, which the Hindu pilgrims believe can purify them. Palaces line the steeper bank—all of the maharajas of India have palaces in the holy city—while the lower bank is reserved for the purposes of ritual bathing. The various stretches of the strand all bear different names; Daswa Samedh Ghat, Mir Ghat, and Jalsain Ghat are the busiest, while Manikarnika Ghat is considered the holiest.

The bathers don't actually swim in the river. There are steps leading into the water as well as a number of raft-like structures to enable wading. Walking out at dawn, we saw hundreds of thousands of Hindus from all over India, fulfilling their religious obligations. The faithful come from all corners of the country, from the Himalayas to Ceylon, Punjab, and South India, Bengal, Tibet, and from all of the provinces with a Hindu population. The city is always overflowing with pilgrims, and although steam boats and the railroad have made pilgrimages much easier, most of the pilgrims avail themselves of carts, or otherwise ride horses, litters, or rickshaws. Some arrive on elephants, but thousands upon thousands are so poor that they must walk all the long way. A sea of Hindu believers threatens to engulf Benares and the holy river each and every day. They come in throngs, men, women, and children, young and old, walking barefoot in the sweltering heat of the day and the chill of night. When they rest by the wayside, the sight of their worn and bleeding feet induces passersby to give alms. Although many of the pilgrims must walk thousands of miles to Benares, they still reach the holy city of their dreams. Some make the pilgrimage following recovery from illness or hardships, others

Ritual bathing in the Ganges at Benares

choose this path to expiate their sins. They walk for months on end, sometimes an entire year, to wash themselves with a few drops of water from the
holy river.

Naturally, bathing in such crowds is neither aesthetic nor hygienic. The
visibly filthy water of the river is past physically cleansing anyone,

nevertheless, the pilgrims, their faces aglow with reverence, use small copper vessels to scoop the sacred water onto their tired bodies. Often times, a man covered with sores will be bathing right next to a child, neither do the pilgrims content themselves with bathing in the river, they also submerge beneath the waves and drink from the water.

In the hot season, Benares is a breeding ground for the most horrendous epidemics, yet the onslaught of pilgrims does not lessen. At the time of our visit, the grim reaper was present in the form of not just cholera, but smallpox and the bubonic plague.

Indian barber

Very few people bathe entirely naked. Most prefer to keep their "clothes" on, which usually consist of a single ragged loincloth. It's probably just as well, because after such a long journey, the rags most certainly need washing. Those finished bathing fill their vessels once more with the sacred water and pour it over temples, holy stones, and religious symbols throughout Benares.

Umbrellas and reed mats provide shade along the shore and in the water, both for bathers and for those simply washing their clothes. There are separate, closed spaces for women and aristocrats who wish to bathe unobserved.

The mild white cows mill about with the crowd of pilgrims. If the river is full, the shore is even busier, with hordes of shopkeepers, beggars, and fakirs. Barbers squat by their squatting clients to give them a shave. The poor buy flatbread made of rice, the wealthy eat *chapattis,* a type of Indian bread fried in fat. Besides the barbers, there are plenty of "beauticians" who trim nails, cut hair, apply makeup, especially the various caste symbols. There are tattoo artists, learned men to give advice, doctors and apothecaries, even surgeons, who perform operations, such as ear piercing, right on the riverbank. There are vendors who sell holy statues, shapeless stones, and wood for funeral pyres. Flower vendors are in the majority, as flowers are needed to decorate the countless statues and temples, from where they are grazed off by the sacred bovines.

Many Hindus, upon reaching an old age, move with their entire families to

Funeral pyre in Benares, on the bank of the Ganges River

Benares. Blessed is he who dies in Benares. Those fortunate enough to die in the holy city are then burned on funeral pyres, which can be seen to be smoking at various points along the Ganges. Those who die in Benares elude the chain of reincarnation and are no longer constrained to live another life in a different form.

Benares is also the city of temples. All of the wealthy faithful feel it a duty to build a temple. Even if it's no larger than a single room, the house of worship must still be topped with a decorative little tower. Today, there are 1,500 Hindu temples and 300 mosques in Benares. Holy stones as well as rough statues of Brahma, Vishnu, and Shiva, painted red, are kept in small niches.

The famous Durga Temple, otherwise known as the Temple of the Monkeys, is also located in Benares. Although the holy monkeys are free to roam all about the city, it is in the temple that they are provided with the rich foods befitting them. The temple is sacred to the wife of Shiva and is guarded by a ragged old man, who sits at the gate. Our tour guide warned us that the man at the gate was a learned holy man who understood the language of the birds. When we saw him, he was reading a manuscript written in Sanskrit, but as we drew near, he threw the book aside and began whistling in imitation of the birds. Afterwards, he held out his hands for baksheesh.

The most fascinating sight in Benares was the crowd of beggars or fakirs, otherwise known as yogis. They could be found by the hundreds all along the

A fakir relaxing on his far from comfortable bed

shore but especially in the vicinity of Daswa Samedh Ghat. Many of them were women, and the bodies of nearly all the fakirs were twisted and deformed in such fantastical ways that they could barely be called human. Some were ill, maimed, even dying, others covered with festering sores, which attracted hordes of flies. Wailing, begging, praying, and arguing, they often blocked our way; skin and bones old men, who could no longer walk but were forced to crawl about on all fours, had taken possession of the stairs.

Holy men, respected fakirs, were living witnesses of religious will, even fanaticism. There were fake fakirs as well, who tricked those around them into thinking they were doing strange and marvelous things, and did so not out of religious fervor, but in the hopes of receiving alms.

Yogis did not beg, yet the people gave them alms freely. Most of the yogis were naked and wore their hair and beards long. I saw fakirs who had sat in the same place without moving for years, their hair and beard swarming with worms. Another stood with his withered hand constantly outstretched, propped up by a stick to prevent it from falling. There were those who had clenched their fists for so long that their nails had grown through their palms; still others pierced their noses, ears, and tongues with needles, lay or walked over coals, or danced on shards of glass without sustaining wounds. There were fires burning all around, and some fakirs held their hands or feet over them for so long that the smell of burned flesh filled the air. Another fakir was eating his own hand; nothing but a bleeding stump remained where his fist had been, and he continued tearing his own flesh with his teeth. An old man, completely naked, would occasionally run through the crowd, shouting, while a younger man dug a hole in the ground and buried himself for a few hours. There were even yogis holding cobras, sustaining one poisonous bite after the other.

Passers-by greeted fakirs with polite nods of the head and handed them alms. Coins as alms were rare; even a single anna was worth something, so most visitors would buy an anna's worth of rice and, passing by the sacred yogis, fill their dishes with a handful of nourishment.

As our journey through India drew to an end, we began to doubt that we would ever come upon a country more able to satisfy our hungry eyes. Before leaving the Subcontinent however, we were forced to say a sad goodbye to our faithful dog Hadji, who had become an unwitting victim of the Indian summer heat. He had grown up on our motorcycle, our constant companion from Budapest to Madras. It was in India that he had reached adulthood and started being useful to us. It was also in India that we were forced to part from him. We felt, in a sense, like we were losing a brother. The dear animal had learned everything that a dog could know; he watched over us and the motorcycle, especially when we were forced to spend the night outdoors. His sense of smell had been so extraordinary that it helped him find our lost objects. He was also a dependable messenger between Gyuszi and myself.

People had offered to buy him for exorbitant prices. A rajah once made us an offer we could barely refuse; he would have been happy to purchase Hadji for 500 rupees. We couldn't part from our dog; we knew Hadji wouldn't survive the Indian climate or separation from us. How worried we had been in Calcutta, when he first showed signs of being ill. The intense heat had been too much for him, and he began growing weaker by the day. After spending four weeks at a veterinary school in an attempt to help Hadji recover, we felt he was strong enough to travel on with us to Madras, but as we neared our destination, he grew weaker and weaker, until we knew that the end was near. When he died—the heat had completely destroyed his lungs—we laid him to rest, teary-eyed, and swore we would never own another dog.

Ceylon: Pearl of the East

We spent a brief two weeks on the magnificent island of Ceylon. The milder climate of the island and the cool evening breezes were very much to our liking after the raging heat of India, and we gave ourselves plenty of time to enjoy the beauties of Colombo and the rest of the country.

Ceylon is rather small, no longer than 400 and no wider than 200 kilometers.

Two thirds of its population of four and a half million are natives, Sinhalese, the remaining one third is comprised of Tamils from South India, as well as Afghans, Persians, Chinese, Englishmen, and Dutchmen in small numbers.

After becoming acquainted with the capital, we traveled all over the island to enjoy its lush vegetation and tropical colors. Someone once told me that he had a much easier time imagining the Garden of Eden after he had caught a glimpse of Ceylon. And truly, Ceylon was a terrestrial paradise, the epitome of tropical beauty, as it was located on the seventh degree latitude and contained all the variety and natural pomp the tropics could offer. The land is forever green, rich, and fertile, lined by mystical mountains. The small island was to us like an enclosed garden, a modern garden at that, complete with excellent asphalt roads to accommodate the approximately 10,000 automobiles to be found on the island.

On the northern part of the island, a promontory reached towards a similar promontory extending from the Indian mainland. The space between them was filled with jagged reefs, whose very presence proved that the space had not always been there. In fact, this bit of land is called "The Bridge of Adam," and, according to legend, served as a bridge for the first man crossing from India into Ceylon. The first man was then followed by many men: the Portuguese in the sixteenth century, followed by the Dutch and the Englishmen, who ended by making Ceylon into a colony of the Crown.

The island climate is very healthy, the weather favorable and the sea a stabilizing force, in that sweltering heat is rare and cold unknown. During our visit, the country was not nearly as crowded as India had been, and standards of hygiene were high. A short journey through Ceylon was enough to acquaint the visitor with all the fruits of the tropics. Coffee-, tea-, and caoutchouc (rubber) plantations lined the roads; cocoa plants, sugarcane, rice, coconuts, hundreds of species of tropical fruit, even cinchona trees comprised the wealth of Ceylon.

History buffs couldn't but be thrilled to discover towns up to two thousands years old. The ruins of Anuradhapura haven't been completely excavated. This ancient town was built in the fifth century B.C. and is most likely the site of the oldest living tree in the world, the legendary fig tree under which Buddha himself sat. Another fascinating place was the temple in Kandy, which kept a curious relic: one of Buddha's teeth. We saw the tooth ourselves, and although it was too large and more likely the tooth of a crocodile rather than a man, we nodded at the story with conviction out of sheer politeness.

We spent most of our time on Colombo, among frequent rains. We suspected that the southwestern monsoon had begun blowing earlier that year.

Knowing that the mild winter of Australia would make up for our troubles amidst the vehement tropical storms, we forged ahead with gritty resolve.

Colombo was a very pleasant place, reminiscent of Port Said in the number of ships and tourists passing through each day. Clothing styles in Colombo were very different from what we had grown accustomed to in India. We saw very few women, and those we saw were clad in clean clothes, as were the men. Women wore skirts without exception, and these skirts were in reality not much more than long sheets wound round and round their waists. Many of the women had adopted European styles, but the Sinhalese especially insisted on wearing semicircular combs of sorts, ending in two points near the front of the head, so that their wearers seemed to be sporting tiny horns.

The houses were clean and in good shape, the roads excellent. There was never a beggar or stray cow in sight. The city was a veritable labyrinth of shady avenues, brooks, and tiny ponds. We saw palms trees wherever we looked, occasionally mingled with bread-fruit trees and bamboo groves.

There were many more rickshaws than cars, and the rickshaws of Colombo far outshone those of India. Their seats were covered in velvet and the vehicles themselves were meticulously clean. Surprisingly, each rickshaw had a small bell attached to it. We also saw Sinhalese carts drawn by cows or oxen, covered on all sides by reed mats, so that those riding in them remained a mystery.

There were plenty of wild animals on the island of Ceylon; bears, leopards, and wild boars were the most dangerous species. The Sinhalese, however, seemed proudest of their elephants. There were wild elephants living in various corners of the island, especially on the Eastern half, where a *kraal,* or elephant hunt, always made a splash. Domesticated elephants were loyal and obedient workers. We saw many such creatures throughout our travels. There were elephants carrying enormous loads, tearing out trees, building roads. Ceylon must be the sole country in the world where the roads are flattened by elephants pulling steamrollers.

One of the most popular products available in Colombo was the ebony elephant statue, which came in virtually all sizes. We learned that such statues brought their owners luck, but only as long as their trunks pointed upwards. The elephant statues whose trunks pointed upwards sold for more, and we decided this was rather ironic, seeing that it was the poorer customers who required greater luck.

Towards the end of our stay, the rain would come down at a set time every single day. A huge storm could brew in a matter of minutes and be gone just as quickly. The sun would then come out, shining brilliantly. There was never any mud, but the wetness clung to the air, making the climate extremely humid. Clothes and shoes, even when stored in closets, grew moldy very

Road construction on the island of Ceylon

quickly. The only way to ward off the mold was by leaving light bulbs burning everywhere: in closets, boxes, suitcases, radios, virtually all places where humidity was less than welcome.

Finally, I must mention the various species of poisonous snakes, which added a touch of fear and discomfort to our sojourn in Ceylon. Partly because we kept in the vicinity of Colombo, with its many doctors, and partly because they were ubiquitous, we soon grew used to the presence of these dangerous reptiles. We didn't even bat an eyelid after a while if a snake slithered out of our path just in time. Then again, we had to be on the watch for snakes of a strange kind, snakes that attacked people without any provocation. The most dangerous of them all was a snake that would wind itself into a tight coil, and lunge forward, like a spring let loose, in the direction of its victim. It was especially difficult to escape them, as they were swift and unpredictable. Other snakes dwelt in trees, waiting in silence to simply drop onto our heads as we passed by. Snake charmers were just as common in Ceylon as they had been in India. These brave people would carry the poisonous reptiles around in sacks or small baskets, often with their fangs intact. Then, the snake charmer would sit down, open their baskets, and begin playing on a recorder-like instrument. The snakes invariably slithered forth and drew themselves up, but the audience had nothing to fear, because they rarely left their trainers. Some of the snakes we saw were three to four meters long, and if one of them attempted to break loose, the charmer would place a large stone on its tail, thereby pinning it in place. The snakes would first begin nodding their heads side to side and would soon be swaying intensely in rhythm with the monotone music. Every performance ended with the inevitable rounds of the collection plate.

More dangerous encounters with snakes were not uncommon, as evidenced by our own frightening experiences. At this point in our travels, we were far from the self-assurance that later characterized us on our journey through the rainforests of Brazil. We were riding our motorcycle one day, marveling at the beauties of the landscape not far from Colombo, when a fine specimen of a snake suddenly appeared next to one of our wheels. We hadn't noticed it before, as it had been lying coiled up on the road, but by the time we did see the snake, it had flattened its head and taken up the position indicative of imminent attack. It must have been about four meters long, with a neck at least ten centimeters wide. Its head, approximately a meter above the ground, flashed towards my knee at lightning speed, but it missed, as we were traveling too fast. As the snake was a cobra, I asked Gyuszi to stop a little ways down the road, because I was eager to take a photograph. The snake sped towards us with such uncanny velocity, that I was forced to shoot at it, and the shooting having produced no result, we hopped back on the motorcycle and headed for safer ground.

It was during our stay in Colombo that a single table at the Bristol Hotel boasted six Hungarians. There was a single Hungarian at the Bristol. A prisoner of war in Russia, he had married and become the manager of the Bristol. Counting him, we were three, until the arrival of a Hungarian couple, who were being transferred by the company for which the husband worked from their plantation in Sumatra to a new site in West Africa. The sixth Hungarian, however, was to be pitied most.

He had also been a prisoner of war in Russia but was a lawyer by trade, a lawyer who had never dreamt he would one day own a caoutchouc (rubber) plantation on the island of Borneo. He had worked hard to receive this admirable and enviable position. As the manager of a plantation, he was allowed a year of vacation in Europe after every four years of work in the colonies.

Travel expenses to and from Europe were complimentary. He had boarded a ship for Europe with his Russian wife, three small children, and Malaysian servant. The children were very young; they had been born in the middle of the jungle, and that is where they had learned to walk and to talk, amidst a thousand dangers, which threatened not only them but their parents as well. Their first encounter with civilization was on board the ocean liner, and their eyes sparkled with the novelty of electric lights, groups of white people, shiny clothes, a cacophony of different languages. Upon first tasting ice cream, they spit it out in astonishment, the little Tarzans that they were. Although they had managed to avoid the thousand dangers of the jungle, one of the small boys became ill on the ship. He had contracted dysentery upon his first contact with civilization. His father had been forced to disembark with him in Colombo. Despite the efforts of the Colombo doctors, the small boy died in the hospital. By this time, the other Hungarian couple were on their way to Africa, so only four sad Hungarians remained to see the little boy settled in his final resting place, in the cemetery of Colombo, beneath the palm trees of Ceylon.

The city grew lively each night; the very streets glowed with excitement. Rickshaws and cars, peopled by elegant people in evening dresses, bustled to and fro. Strains of guitar music and jazz filled the evening air, and the heat of life would burn steadily through the lukewarm equatorial night.

A gigantic ocean liner soon swallowed our own motorcycle as we left Asia, the immeasurable, the mighty, and the holy, and set out for our fourth continent.

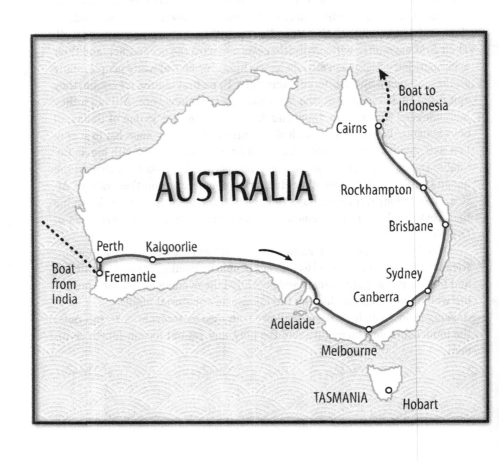

AUSTRALIA

Boat to
Indonesia

Cairns

Rockhampton

Brisbane

Perth   Kalgoorlie

Boat
from
India

Fremantle

Sydney

Canberra

Adelaide

Melbourne

TASMANIA   Hobart

The Roads of White Australia

No Savages, No Kangaroos

A new, virtually unknown world lay at our feet. Although we could glibly repeat the population of Australia, describe its climate, geography, and recite the names of its important cities like a couple of schoolchildren, we hadn't the faintest clue about what traveling across it would be like.

Our ship journey from Colombo to a harbor in Western Australia took ten whole days, which gave us plenty of time to reflect that we were soon to be as far as it was humanly possible from our homeland. Rethinking our past experiences, we looked forward with anticipation to the travels ahead.

Sitting on that ship, we were quite content with ourselves. Although we had been on the road for a little less than a year, we had crossed twenty-three countries on three different continents. We had every reason to hope that we would achieve what we had set out to do. To make things even more pleasant, our nagging financial worries had finally ceased. Although we had no wealthy patron and had not struck it rich while in India, we came to realize that, with a little resourcefulness, we could become entirely self-sufficient. After all, necessity is the mother of invention. While we still had money, the idea of earning our way through the years and the continents had struck as preposterous, but as we neared the end of our rope, we realized that it could be done. The passage to Australia having swallowed up the remainder of our savings, we were free to think of creative ways to replenish our funds.

Actually, we had begun to reflect while still in India. Our knowledge of the English language was rather rudimentary and we felt anything but undaunted and resourceful, but we did have a hidden treasure, a secret weapon of sorts in the form of a myriad of photographs documenting our voyage. To top it all off, I developed an itch to write, a sort of anti writer's cramp, and so I began seriously documenting our voyage. I sent out numerous articles, aimed at journals in India and Hungary, Australia, Japan, and the United States. The British, German, and French newspapers we tried all turned us down. Although an article or two would appear, sometimes accompanied by a few photos, we rarely, if ever, saw money in return. The little we got was far from enough.

"Why don't we try selling the wealthy Indians something?" my friend asked. We began assembling albums of our photographs; some held only thirty to forty, others as much as a hundred. The photographs we labeled in English and the albums bore our personal signatures. Once we had a few albums for sale, we made every effort to gain an audience with a maharaja, either via letters of recommendation or under the pretext of wanting his autograph. As soon as we were in the presence of the royal personages, we would invariably take out our albums, which almost always elicited surprise and pleased compliments. Not satisfied with empty words, we would insist that the beautiful album was for sale and were rarely refused. Numerous Indian princes, British clubs, companies, even individual Englishmen were happy to purchase a set of our photographs. Of course, we couldn't set the prices very high, not wanting to risk being stuck with the albums ourselves. We had spent a considerable sum on the albums, and often found ourselves standing in front of maharajas of legendary wealth who could have paid any price. However, royalty rarely bothered with questions of money. We were usually issued our payment by the secretaries, who were never as generous as the position of their masters might have allowed. Nevertheless, we sold quite a few albums, thereby earning our passage to Australia and making sure we weren't entirely without resources once we reached our fourth continent.

There were two factors that helped our progress. The first was the extent of the road that lay behind us, which increased every day, progressively drawing more and more of the world's attention to our undertaking. Many newspapers published stories and pictures of us; the interest of the world in our travels grew considerably. Many people were pleased by the efforts of two Hungarian students and were willing to help us in concrete ways. Large companies, for example, weren't long in realizing that by financially supporting our travels, they had hit upon an exciting way to popularize their own products. In a short time, we were well stocked in gasoline, oil, motorcycle parts and tires, and all for free. From that point on, we always got our bike repaired for free and even our hotel costs dropped significantly. Occasionally, clothing merchants who had purchased our albums would supply us with a few new outfits; larger companies provided us with suits in order to be able to say that we had chosen them for our clothing needs.

The other factor that aided us in our travels was our refusal of all luxury. We lived very simply and tried to save as much money as we could. We opted ' for tents over hotels many times, and when there were no bungalows to be had, we sought out the cheapest lodgings in a nearby town. We also often cooked our own meals, eating out of cans even to avoid the high prices in hotel restaurants. As for amusements, we only went out when a generous host paid for our evening.

With the help of generous support and our own frugality, we were able to achieve considerable results. At the same time, we always made sure to purchase souvenirs at every point in our travels and send them home to Budapest. We were anticipating the time we would be back in Hungary, free to reminisce about our travels with the aid of the countless souvenirs we had bought along the way. The badges we received from various Automobile Clubs were our pride and joy; we collected five such badges in India alone. Another part of our collection that made us happy was a set of at least twenty signed photos of Indian princes with whom we had become acquainted along the way. We collected the numerous newspaper articles covering our journey in a separate album. This album came to prove not only the extent of interest people showed in our undertaking but also contained a number of very positive writings about Hungary and kept tangible record of the places we'd been.

We had also been blessed with good health along the way; we partly had our own cautious natures to thank that we had not contracted any grave illnesses. Aside from a few repairs, our motorcycle had held out splendidly and had shown its mettle on the toughest roads and in the most merciless heat. As time passed, Gyuszi and I also became first-rate mechanics and drivers. Although we did overturn twice, all four of us, people, dog, and motorcycle, came out unscathed. Our single collision was with a cow. The poor beast unwittingly came onto the road just as we were passing and was duly injured. The two of us were not hurt, but Hadji did a flying act and landed quite a few meters ahead of us on the road. Not accustomed to flying, he took his wrath out on the poor innocent cow.

In sum, then, we had no reason to complain as we sat on the ship to Australia. Once we reached Australia, since it was the furthest point from Hungary, we could imagine we were heading home. The fatigue, our struggles, and inconveniences seemed insignificant in the light of all that we had seen and learned.

Our next plan was to publish a short volume detailing our travels. We hoped that it would sell in higher numbers than the albums had. The book, planned to include thirty to forty pages of travel descriptions, was slated to appear in English first. An English passenger on the ship helped us gather our thoughts, and we were counting on the Australian editors for help regarding grammar niceties.

Although we were hopeful, we were also very much aware that our undertaking was a daring one. After all, we were soon to land on an immense continent with a population of only six million. We wondered if there would be a market for our books, or if our sole pleasure would be in kangaroos and other wild things.

We crossed the Equator for the first time in our lives. The sailors celebrated each crossing by splashing the passengers and each other with buckets of water, a custom reminiscent of Easter in Hungary.

The way from Ceylon to Australia was longer than the sea route connecting Europe and the United States. We were to sail 6,000 kilometers before reaching the western shores of Australia. We disembarked at the first port we hit, namely Fremantle. We had heard so much about the beauties of the country from Australian passengers that our appetites for novelty were whetted to the extreme.

We tried not to expect much; after all, white civilization had reached Australia only one hundred years back. It was in 1829 that the first white settlers landed on the new continent under the leadership of Captain Fremantle. One hundred years was not much in the life of a country and a people, yet it had been enough for the British to kill off the natives. Only 50,000 aborigines remained, and they lived, for the most part, in the interior of the continent. It was rumored that some of them were unaware even of the existence of white man. We found this highly likely, because the continent was immense and filled with many unexplored tracts.

The settlers didn't have much to boast of regarding their origins. The first shipments had consisted of convicts, the dregs of British society. At the same time, criminals mingled with heroic Irish patriots, who had been assigned the same fate of exile. The presence of the Irish improved the image of the first settlers. The word "criminal," however, remains taboo in the eyes of many Australians. A favorite saying they use among themselves is, "You're talking! And your ancestors wore chains!" And they are absolutely right. The names carved into the walls of Australia's prisons are the very names of today's Australian elite. An onslaught of speculators and gold miners followed the advent of the prisoners, all of them of dubious origins. The people who didn't come were the people the country most needed: hard-working farmers.

After our ship had landed, we were subjected to thorough medical examinations to prevent us from carrying tropical diseases into a healthy country. The encounter with the doctors was followed by a thorough examination on the part of the police, who were anxious for the details of everyone's travel plans. Although the country was open to immigration or whites, it was closed to all people of color; the Chinese, Japanese, Arabs, and Indians were unwanted guests. Even Europeans were only allowed to enter if they had at least forty pounds of capital to prevent them from running into hardships at the beginning of their stay. No 40 pounds, no landing.

Gyuszi and I were considerably worried about this rule, seeing as we had only seventy pounds between the two of us. Fortunately, the police appreciated our bold travel ventures and, counting the value of our motorcycle, concluded that we had the required eighty pounds at our disposal.

Finally, we were free to carry our luggage on land. I repeat, we, ourselves, carried our own luggage. The sight of white men working was mind-boggling to us after our sojourn in India. Burly Europeans carried stuffed bags, and to our astonishment, our fellow passengers considered it natural that they would carry their own suitcases and boxes on shore. The good life was over. There wasn't a single colored man in sight.

Later on, we did encounter a few aborigines, especially in the northern regions of the country, and most people won't believe me when I say that white Australians were just as astonished to see them, as Hungarians would have been had they walked down one of the avenues of Budapest.

The aborigines of Australia were stuck on a very low level of civilization. They had no past and no traditions and resembled African natives to a great extent, only their skin was a shade lighter. They enjoyed greasing and painting their skin and roamed the wilds of Australia naked, their bodies decorated with scars. These nomadic natives ate insects and worms, showing a special fondness for ants and earthworms. They also consumed snakes, but cannibalism was slowly dying out.

As soon as we set foot on Australian soil, we were bombarded with questions by a crowd of Australian journalists. It really was a pleasant surprise. They took photo after photo of us, and we knew that the story of the Hungarian motorists would soon spread throughout the land.

We were at the forefront of attention throughout our Australian stay, and this attention, I am happy to say, brought us monetary rewards. Leaving the harbor of Fremantle, we headed straight for nearby Perth, the capital of Western Australia. In Perth we received a warm welcome; people cheered each time we appeared in the street. Two distinguished oil companies hurried to our aid, and by this point in time, Gyuszi and I were savvy enough to turn their spirit of competition to our benefit.

Thinking back on our time in Australia never fails to make me happy. The Australians, an excitable and enthusiastic people, soon grew to like us, and we them, despite the strange customs that had first made us wary of the country. We drew enthusiastic crowds in every city we visited. Generally we would make our entrance and head straight for the post office, where hordes of automobile drivers and bikers would gather to welcome us, along with countless journalists and civilian spectators. We joined various clubs as honorary members, received countless free theater tickets and invitations and made lots of new friends. We hardly spent any of our own money, because those we encountered on the way made sure our physical needs were met;

they showed their approval of our undertaking in the form of canned food and medicine, and most hotels asked for only a signed photograph in payment. It often happened that innkeepers in the most backwater little villages insisted on letting us board for free.

Our first task was to look for the right kind of clothing. Although we were well stocked in clothes for the tropics, we were not prepared for winter in Australia, however mild. In fact, the winter felt like spring, and it rained rather often until we reached the desert. As the climate changed, so did our outfits. We generally kept a set of traveling clothes and a set of city clothes, accompanied by the necessary underclothing and shoes. Ours was a minimalist's wardrobe; in fact, we didn't own topcoats until we reached Australia.

Our plus fours induced a great deal of merriment wherever we went. At first, we decided to stick it out and wear our trusty plus fours despite the annoying custom Australians had of laughing out loud upon seeing anything unusual, but we gave up after two days of being laughed at by simple and sophisticated folk alike. Cars would stop in the middle of the street, their passengers lolling about with mirth. In an attempt to preserve our last remnant of dignity, we bought a pair of pants each and decided to save our plus fours for more understanding peoples.

Australian laughter at everything unusual was an ingrained quality of the people, who knew very little about the rest of the world and showed minimal interest in what went on outside their continent. For them it was simply impossible to imagine a country better or more beautiful than Australia, and they weren't ashamed to air their views in front of visitors. According to Australian parochialists, Melbourne and Sydney both counted as the busiest cities in the world, at least a dozen towns claimed to have the most pleasant climate in the world, others insisted they lived at the feet of the most beautiful mountain in the world or enjoyed the proximity of the largest harbor, most prestigious university, and so on. Although Australians insisted on drawing sweeping comparisons between the beauties of their country and the rest of the world, they knew very little about the rest of the world. They had no idea of the population of Paris or Berlin and couldn't name, for the life of them, the capital of Switzerland, Holland, or Argentina. Neither did they speak a single foreign language; of course, they were exposed to very little besides English. If one of the cinemas screened a newscast with a few sentences of French or German, the entire movie theater would erupt with the laughter of the audience, who could not control their mirth upon hearing the incomprehensible jabber.

One time, I cautiously remarked that New South Wales was the province with the best roads in Australia. In the next day's paper, I was quoted to have remarked that the roads of New South Wales, which were in fact few and far from ideal, were the best roads in the entire world.

As I have mentioned before, the population of Australia at the time of our visit was six million, and this number had not increased despite an average of a hundred thousand new immigrants each year. New immigrants had plenty of opportunities to make money and did not tremble for their existence, nevertheless, the number of people leaving the continent each year pretty much matched the number of immigrants. Australia had trouble loving newcomers, and newcomers never quite got used to Australia. Maybe it was the pride and arrogance of the people or the conformity of Australian life, or perhaps the countless strange customs that induced immigrants to become emigrants as soon as they had collected a bit of capital.

There was an incredible sameness about Australia. People and their knowledge of the world were the same; the mayor was no different from merchants or laborers. People wore the same kind of clothing, lived in identical houses, and kept the same traditions. Flipping through my journal, I find the initials S.O.S.O. next to every single Australian town we visited, as well as each hotel we stayed at and every meal we enjoyed. S.O.S.O. stands for "same old same old" and is an apt expression of the monotony of all aspects of Australian life. Any two houses, whether a few meters or 10,000 kilometers apart, looked identical and were furnished in much the same way. This sameness extended to the way hotel workers made beds and the size and shape of the eating utensils we were given. To top it all off, there was a uniform, weather-related greeting in use everywhere. Whether I walked into a shop to buy cigarettes, or visited the barber, the newspaper vendor, or ordered breakfast at a restaurant, my "Good morning," would inevitably be followed by "Very nice morning today, isn't it?"

Lunch was called dinner and dinner, tea. Tea was served with every meal, regardless of the time of day. Even if we ordered a simple bowl of soup, it would come accompanied by a slice of bread and butter and tea. Without exception Australian cuisine left much to be wished for and little to be hoped for. It was the same old same old everywhere we went.

There seemed to be two types of soup in Australia, which, when accompanied by some form of meat and garnish and a serving of pudding, made up a typical Australian meal. The portions were the same everywhere we went, regardless of the capacity of the person about to consume them. We had to say thank you after every single dish, but the waiter insisted on saying thank you himself.

Mealtimes, even in private homes, were announced by the sound of a bell. When visiting a restaurant, we weren't allowed to sit where we wished but were instead seated according to a set order. Every chair at a table had to be occupied before the waiters were willing to seat someone at an empty table. If there was a single chair left at a table and large party walked in, the single chair had to be filled by a single person, and the rest of the company was given a new table. Once we walked into a restaurant with ten free tables, and the waiters insisted on seating one of us at a nearly full table, while the other sat alone. Other times, the two of us might be sitting at a table, and a person would walk in alone. Instead of choosing one of the ten or twelve empty tables, he'd head straight for ours.

The welfare system in Australia was admirable. People lived well and had few financial worries, yet not many of them realized that the greatest obstacle to further economic development was their refusal to allow cheap labor, even in the form of colored immigrants, to enter the country. Immigrants did come, but they were of the wrong kind. British immigrants preferred jobs in the industry, and vast stretches of arable land went untended. Australia, a country meant for agriculture, was leaning more and more towards industry, and this prejudice did not bode well for the people. Work costs were so high that raw materials often had to be taken abroad to be processed. This is how it happened that the famous Australian wool was exported to England, while Australians made their clothing out of British linen. Because wages were so high, work was scarce, and unemployment rates increasing.

Those who did have jobs, however, made lots of money. Minimal wages were universally recognized and the preset sums strictly enforced. This meant that workers could not be employed for less than four pounds and forty shillings a week; employers who offered their workers less very quickly found themselves without a work force. Would-be employees preferred unemployment to lower than minimum wages. Officials, engineers, architects, namely, non-physical laborers of all kinds earned up to eight pounds a week. The best paying job, however, was to be sought in the most unusual of places.

A Hungarian immigrant friend of ours, the youngest son of a Calvinist preacher, had found just such a job and was dressing well and in all ways, living the high life. He earned his bread through physical labor, as a shoreman. By carrying chests and sacks at the harbor eight hours each day, he managed to make twelve pounds a week. Day-to-day living was cheap, especially in comparison to the wages people earned. Room and board in a decent flat cost a pound and a half per week; two pounds a week bought you a very comfortable lifestyle. Thus, wage earners had over half their wages left after their bare necessities had been paid for.

Besides high wages, Australians also enjoyed other benefits, such as all manners of insurance. Even the unemployed were able to live decently with help from the state; everyone had access to medical treatment and hospital care, and elderly Australians lived out the rest of their days in quiet comfort.

The state also made the education of children a priority. There were no tuition fees; schooling didn't cost the parents a single penny, as textbooks, notebooks and writing utensils were all provided by the government. In places where there was no independent school, the state would assign a teacher to every ten children, and in places where children were few, parents received ten pounds a year to hire tutors. Out in the Australian wilds, where the spaces between houses were immense and schools far away, school buses provided by the state carried children to and from school. We often saw children riding to school on horseback, but even this was unnecessary, because those living on isolated farms could opt for an education by correspondence. Even the stamps were paid for by the government. In Western Australia alone, 3,000 children and their families had chosen this form of education and regularly sent out completed assignments and tests to receive them corrected in the company of further schoolwork.

Servants were rare, even in wealthy families. Keeping servants was not traditional on Australian land, and besides, servants' rights far outnumbered their responsibilities. Domestics made two to three pounds a week, in addition to the costs of their room and board, which generally amounted to 50-70 pence. Washerwomen, for example, held a respectable position in society and went about elegantly dressed. They earned three pounds a week. Household worries always belonged to the women. Men took their wages home and received only a bit of pocket money from their wives, while the rest of the money was at the women's disposal.

11,000 Kilometers Around Australia

While in Australia, we traveled through six different states or provinces. Speeding along unknown roads in an unknown country, we made our way across West Australia, then South Australia, and Victoria. From Victoria, we proceeded to Tasmania and up north, into New South Wales and Queensland. Fremantle, Perth, Adelaide, Melbourne, Hobart, Sydney, and Brisbane were the largest cities we hit on our 11,000 kilometer trek through the giant continent.

It was a journey of many long weary months. We never would have thought that the roads would be as bad as they were in a country inhabited by white men who drove automobiles. Then again, four of the six million inhabitants of Australia lived in the large cities, and the remaining two million, scattered throughout the vast continent, were not eager to take up the costs of a high quality infrastructure spanning nearly uninhabited regions. The transcontinental railroad was dependable and all of the large cities were accessible by sea. We imagined that very few people had taken the time to cross this hundred-year young country.

By a twist of fate, the very beginning of our Australian stretch proved to be the most difficult, but as we progressed along the seemingly endless roads, we found our task to be easier and easier. We also had great luck with the weather; it was neither too cold nor too rainy. We enjoyed mild, spring-like weather for the most part, not experiencing tropical heat until we reached Queensland towards the end of our trip.

The asphalt road disappeared after the first sixteen kilometers of our journey. As we left Swan River, where we stopped to marvel at the famous black swans, we found ourselves riding along a tractless expanse. A dirt road would continue for a stretch, then give way abruptly to wheel ruts, which were the only indication of the direction in which we were supposed to be traveling. The further we got from Perth, the fewer the villages, the people, even the animals. The distance between Perth and our next stop, Adelaide, was 2,700 kilometers. This stretch happened to be one of the most deserted parts of our journey.

Once we left the tiny town of Kalgoorlie, we found ourselves in the middle of a barren wasteland. Traveling across the wasteland, which hid some world famous goldfields, we reached a very interesting small town by the name of Coolgardie. Thirty years before, the name of Coolgardie had been known the world over on account of its goldmines. There wasn't a soul in sight; it felt like an epidemic of the bubonic plague had killed off the entire population. Coolgardie was a ghost town. There was grass sprouting in the streets, and although the houses were intact on the outside, they were emptied of all furniture and entirely deserted on the inside. Although some buildings were labeled as banks or shops of various kinds, they proved to be just as empty as the private homes. Coolgardie was a town without townspeople; even the rats had fled its cellars. After the gold ran out, people soon found that it was impossible to make a living on the dry, waterless, infertile land. There was nothing to be done; the citizens of Coolgardie moved out.

We could still make out the famous water-pipes. In the hey-day of the town, these pipes had brought drinking water to Coolgardians from 600 kilometers away, much like the water system connecting Kalgoorlie with its water source. Water was the gold miners' most precious commodity, and they had paid in gold to have it brought to them. The townspeople of Coolgardie had guarded the water pipes with more devotion than their goldmines. The land around Coolgardie showed signs of having been dug up and turned over and over.

In the year 1886, the entire continent of Australia had produced a mere eight kilograms of pure gold. The record year had been 1903, with an amount

Goldmine in Kalgoorlie, Western Australia

of 64,000 kilograms. Ever since 1903, there had been a decline in gold mining, so that the year before we arrived, mighty Australia had managed only
12,000 kilograms. Of course, pure gold was not to be found lying around; it
had to be won from the rock, as it is done today, and separating gold from
dross was a very expensive procedure best done by large companies. Quartz,
sandstone, and granite were the types of stone with the most traces of gold.

Elevator-like devices bustled up and down the mineshafts, bringing stones to the surface. The rest of the mining process was accomplished above ground, in large plants.

As we got further from civilization, we encountered tin houses by the sides of the road, the beginnings of new settlements. After leaving Norseman behind, we were hard put trying to locate the road itself. We soon reached the arid regions, where sheep farmers were forced to collect every precious drop of the annual scanty rainfall, which amounted to a single or maximum two rainstorms, if they wished to prevent the death of their entire flocks. The first covered wagons that had traversed the groves of eucalyptus trees had left the ruts, which, when retraced by hundreds of successive wagons, had produced the transcontinental road. Forests were scarce, trees precious, especially if they were in a position to be transported.

Two renowned species of tree had made it to this wasteland from Western Australia, the *jarrah* and the *karri,* both excellent for building. Despite scanty rainfall, trees tended to reach heights of fifteen to twenty meters, but since trees were so scarce, they customarily served as fire wood rather than building material. The simplest way to fell them was to set fire to their trunks and allow nature to take its course. As soon as the lower part of a tree's trunk had burned, the tree fell of its own accord. We passed through numerous burning forests on our way but were never in danger, as the trees were few and far between. The only times we were inconvenienced were when burning trees fell across our path and hindered our progress. At such times, it often cost us a great deal of effort before we were clear of the burning woods. In rainier regions of Australia, these same trees reached heights of 120 meters; the province of Western Australia exported half a million cubic meters of wood for a total of two million English pounds each year.

We sometimes rode for hundreds of kilometers without encountering a single soul. Of course, we had to take care to replenish our food and water supplies before such long deserted stretches. Occasionally, we were forced to carry as much as 100 to 150 liters of gasoline on us. We bought the gasoline in wooden chests; each chest contained two metal containers with four gallons of gasoline to every container. Thus, a wooden chest held 32 liters of gasoline, and we were often forced to carry three such chests on our already crowded sidecar.

Animals were almost as scarce as people. Birds, however, were in abundance. As we drove along, groups of hundreds of large, colorful birds would take off into the air. There were many parrots and cockatoos, as well as birds of paradise and an Australian specialty, the kookaburra.

The kookaburra was famous for two reasons. First, it was able to imitate human laughter, so much so, that it often fooled us into thinking there were humans around. We might be struggling along an especially difficult stretch of road when we'd suddenly hear the laughter of the kookaburra, as if it had found our situation exceptionally funny. We usually informed the bird that we would proceed regardless of what he thought, and then we'd plunge on with gritty resolve.

The kookaburra's second claim to fame was its ability to kill snakes and promptly consume them, or at least, taste their flesh. This is why kookaburras were beloved and protected birds throughout Australia.

Kangaroos were also important creatures in the eyes of the Australians. There are very few kangaroos today as a result of heavy hunting in the past. On our journey, we saw mostly wallabies, which are smaller versions of kangaroos. Emus were more common; their quick feet often saved them from the hunter's gun. We also saw many different species of aquatic birds: cranes, pelicans, and the ever-delicious wild turkey. Shooting a wild turkey always meant a tasty lunch.

After a while, we grew accustomed to our loneliness in the bush of Western Australia. We led a nomadic lifestyle, driving anywhere between 150 and 200 kilometers a day. Large fields appropriate for sheep grazing lined the road to the left and to the right. Many of the plots of land were fenced in. There were gates on the fences, and we were often obliged to drive through them as we drove from one field to another, taking care to close each gate behind us. The ubiquitous sheep were the only living things in sight. Otherwise, we spotted a number of sheep-shearing stations, which were spaced a day's journey apart. There were always tin containers filled with water at these stations, so we were able to replenish our supplies, but people were nowhere to be found; they only came out at sheep-shearing time.

Exciting Days in the Wilds

After leaving Balladonia, a large sheep-ranch complete with actual homes, we turned our motorcycle in the direction of Eucla, the next small settlement more than 540 kilometers away. The stretch between Balladonia and Eucla was the most deserted bit of country we had encountered, and it was precisely there, in the middle of nowhere, that we met our doom. Sometime towards the evening, we heard a loud crack, and after a quick examination of our vehicle, we concluded that we were stuck. The gearwheel on our dynamo had gotten jammed, causing the controls gearwheel to lose three of its cogs. No mechanic in the world could help us; our only option was to replace the gearwheel.

But where were we going to get a new gearwheel? Perth and Adelaide were our only options, but both cities were hundreds of kilometers away. It was a sticky situation. The nearest town was Balladonia, itself two hundred kilometers away. The distance to Eucla was 340 km, the distance to the railroad line 250 km, even the sea was 220 km off. We still had plenty of food and even if we ran out, shooting small game was always an option, but our water supplies were running low. We had water for three, maybe four days, and 200 kilometers was far too long to be walked on foot. Our only hope was that a traveler or perhaps a caravan would pass by within a few days. At the same time, we were aware that we might have to wait for two weeks before anyone came.

Gyuszi and I tried to look at the bright side of things, but inside, we were scared to death. This was the worst calamity yet, and we thought almost fondly of the wolves around our campfire in India, finding even them preferable to the oppressive silence surrounding us.

We pitched our tents. There was plenty of firewood to be had, and we spent the night sitting up next to a blazing fire. Neither of us could sleep. The next day also passed in grim silence. We didn't hear so much as an airplane pass overhead, and figured they probably followed different routes. We hardly touched our water.

The second night passed, peppered with the chilling howls of jackals and hyenas. On the third day, we decided to wait until morning and then set out for Balladonia. We hoped to walk the 200 kilometers in three days, but what if our strength failed us?

The hours felt like days, and we grew more and more discouraged with the passage of time. To make things worse, we had hardly any water left, and the little we had, we were forced to save for our trek to Balladonia. The feeling we had then we had never had before and will most likely never have again. As the evening fell, we composed our letters of farewell and placed them in bottles, as if we'd been at sea, to protect them from the elements and from the ruthlessness of the vultures.

Shortly after having done all this, we heard what seemed to us to be heavenly sounds! As we ran in the direction of the voices, we became more and more convinced that they were real and not simply a feverish dream. Our joy upon encountering a large caravan cannot be put into words! We were safe. There was a huge cart, loaded with bales of wool and pulled by sixteen camels. Two men sat on board on their way to Balladonia. Finally, we had plenty of water. Hitching our motorcycle to the cart, we joined the men, who were only too glad of company, and spent four slow but pleasant days journeying to Balladonia.

Balladonia, as we came to discover, was virtually a tiny kingdom. It was a giant homestead completely isolated from civilization, but a homestead where we were able to rent rooms and a bathroom, end enjoy a radio, a piano,

The cotton caravan that saved our lives

electric lights, plumbing, and even a tennis court. From Balladonia, we sent a telegraph to Perth detailing our situation. The new gearwheel arrived a few days later, and our host sent someone in a car to fetch it for us. After six days of rest, we were ready to be on our way.

During our four days with the caravan and six days at the homestead, we hadn't encountered a single soul either from the direction of Perth or of Adelaide.

We were truly touched and eternally grateful for the fine hospitality our host had shown us. In its warmth and unselfishness, it reminded us of the best of Hungarian hospitality. Although we were somewhat behind schedule, we were grateful for the few days of quiet rest we had enjoyed. The owners of the homestead also owned a sheep ranch the size of a county. The hundreds of thousands of acres of arid land would have made shoddy farming ground, but the twenty thousand sheep inhabiting it were a source of a considerable income, especially if they managed to survive. The ranchers, both of them Scotsmen, had been living in Australia since their youth.

During our six days in Balladonia, we became acquainted with the sheep growing trade. The sheep lived on giant stretches of land surrounded by wire fences. Not even the ranchers knew the precise number of sheep they owned; there were no shepherds to care for them, so they roamed the land all year, feeding and breeding. At sheep shearing time, three or four horsemen would ride out to collect our woolly friends. These horsemen weren't so much in charge of the sheep as they were responsible for the upkeep of the fences. Sheep farmers regularly counted twenty acres per sheep, so the amount of land necessary for the raising of hundreds of thousands, even a million sheep, boggled the mind. Southern Australia, with its heavier rainfall, was a low-risk area for raising sheep, but Western Australia itself was home to eight million sheep the year we traveled through.

Sheep farming was a booming business. Each sheep was worth ten dollars, and produced ten dollars of profit every single year: five in wool and five in lambs. In good years, profits were enormous. Unfortunately, truly good years were rare. If the rainwater that had been collected was not enough, the sheep all died. They also died if the weather was too hot for the grass to grow properly, and even the thorny bushes dried out. In such years, sheep died of both hunger and of thirst.

The sheep walked about in small groups. There were many dangers lurking about even discounting the heat. Poisonous plants, epidemics, storms, and wild dogs decimated the flocks.

The Merino wool produced in Australia is world famous, and sheep ranchers do their utmost to improve its quantity and quality. At an exposition in Melbourne, we saw, with our own eyes, a thoroughbred sheep unable to move for all the wool it had grown, sold for 5,000 British pounds.

Sheep farmers sought to protect their sheep against wild dogs, or dingos, with traps and through other means. The government supported the hunting of dingos, offering two pounds per pelt. We did our best to cross paths with a few dingos ourselves and landed a considerable reward.

Most farmers owed the government a debt of gratitude. Rabbits were especially numerous and multiplied at mind-boggling rates. In the dry season, they would ruin entire pastures by eating all the edible plants and chewing away at the bark of trees. Whole forests were destroyed in this way. After laying waste to the wastelands, rabbits would head west to the grain fields. To protect the grain crop from devastation by these rabbits, the government constructed a double layered, densely woven wire fence over six thousand kilometers long.

Once on our way, we made 1,000 kilometers in five days, and the 2,700 kilometers stretch to Adelaide thus took us twelve days to traverse, discounting our stay in Balladonia. Our progress was slowed by the sandy bits of road. When traveling by forests, thick roots that had overgrown the road itself jutted out of the ground and blocked our way. Sometimes, the tough roots would rise 8-10 centimeters above ground, and our poor motorcycle heaved and groaned as we were jolted along on the uneven ground. In places where there were no trees, rocks made our going plenty difficult. And so on forest roads,

Fighting the mud in Southern Australia

we yearned for rocky roads, and rocky roads made us think fondly of rooting around in the forest. I can't make up my mind to this day as to which was more unpleasant!

Western Australia, and indeed, all of Australia was aptly named "The Land of Opportunity." It was a wealthy region of the world, with many resources and few people to take advantage of them. The extent of Australian progress was limited only by Australian economic policy; possibilities seemed endless.

The roads were gradually improving throughout the provinces, but the only true quality roads were located in and around the large cities. As we made our way to the east, the parched, arid land was crisscrossed more and more often by small rivers and streams. Instead of the excessive heat, the flooding of these rivers and streams became our biggest problem. Occasionally, the entire road ahead of us, at least as far as the eye could see, was entirely under water. At such times, one of us was forced to walk in front of the motorcycle with a stick to size up the depth of the water. The wet countryside was also more populous. We encountered numerous settlements, homesteads, villages, and even small towns. New South Wales was the most beautiful province in all of Australia with its expansive rivers, forest-clad hills, and flowery valleys. There were no bridges over the rivers, but ferry services were regular and dependable. We made twenty ferry crossings on the way from Sydney to Brisbane. The camels of Western Australia were substituted by horses in large numbers. Horses were a common sight both on the roads and around the farm. Twelve to sixteen horses pulled giant carts, while eight horses were generally required to plow a field. Large containers of milk, completely unguarded, lined the country roads waiting to be picked up by passing milk trucks.

Australians were a friendly people and especially so whenever we began enthusiastically praising their country. The ode to Australia is a must for any would-be visitor. We learned the importance of Australia worship the hard way. Standing in front of a crowd of children, we were asked to repeat all we had said regarding the beauties of Australia. Bored with the idea of parroting ourselves, we decided to answer questions. When the children asked whether we'd ever visited a country better than theirs, we only answered, "Could be." This was really too much for the young patriots, and our daring response was followed by such a volley of stones that we barely escaped.

Simple farmers weren't always as enthusiastic and hospitable towards guests as our Balladonian Scottish hosts had been. Most homesteaders refused to speak with us, and if we asked them if they might put us up for the night, more often than not they would simply slam the door in our faces, shouting, "This is no hotel." We couldn't decide if their distrust was based on experience or if they were simply uneducated and xenophobic. Although we had trouble securing a bed, the farmers did not let us go hungry. There were slaughtered sheep available at every farm; all we had to do was walk up and cut away as much meat as we needed.

Adelaide, Melbourne, Sydney, Brisbane, and Rockhampton were some of the larger cities we visited. They were all filled with car traffic; horse-drawn carts were rare in urban settings. Streets were arranged according to a wheel and spokes pattern, that is, all roads led to and radiated from the city center. Melbourne and Sydney were rather cosmopolitan; we even spotted a few skyscrapers, which stood out all the more when considering the relatively small size of both cities. The downtown area in both cases was surrounded by extensive suburbs comprised of kilometer upon kilometer of small but friendly wooden family homes. The homes were all constructed in the same fashion, even their yards resembled one another. Australians returning from work often walked up to the neighbor's front door by mistake and wondered that their keys didn't fit the lock.

In Sydney alone, there were 200,000 automobiles and 50,000 motorcycles. Traffic police skillfully directed the onslaught of vehicles; at night, their white clothing reflected the brightness of the headlights. There were some movie theaters with underground parking for 300 cars. The cities grew virtually empty at six in the evening, with everyone hurrying home, but filled up just as quickly an hour later as people anticipating a night out gathered in the downtown. Finally, the city would grow quiet again around 11 p.m., and by midnight, the silence enveloping the sleeping city was palpable.

On our Australian journey, we also passed through the city of Canberra, chosen capital of Australia, a city that was under heavy construction. When we passed through, numerous streets and public buildings were ready for use, including the sizeable but puritan, one-story parliament. The citizens of Canberra, like their compatriots in other towns, insisted that theirs was both the healthiest city in the world and the city with the most beautiful sunset. Despite these laudable characteristics, Canberra was slow in growing. Speculation had driven price of land so high that few people were anxious to move to the slowly evolving capital.

Letters we sent from Queensland took six weeks to make it to Hungary. We had indeed come far from home. Although we availed ourselves of the general delivery service throughout our correspondence and had let family and friends know in advance where to send their letters, it didn't make much sense to wait three months for a response.

Before visiting Australia, we'd had no concept of the British Sunday, and once there, we were especially astonished by the nature of Australian holidays. Those who could went hiking or took various field trips; the cities were entirely deserted. There wasn't a drink or a meal to be had for miles, even the movies were closed and sports events nonexistent. In some towns, even golf and tennis were prohibited on Sundays. Thus, people were generally bored to death, and a sign Gyuszi and I spotted on the billboard of a large church really drove the point home. The sign said, "If you're bored, come on in."

Unemployment was slowly starting to take its toll. In Sydney especially, unthinking Australians often resorted to theft and armed assault to make a living. The crime rate was high; most crimes occurred in deserted parts of the city and in parks. My friend Bartha was mugged in just such a park; with the barrel of a revolver against his ribs, he hardly had to be told to stick up his hands and allow his attackers to search his pockets. Needless to say, the thief, whoever he was, didn't gain much by mugging Gyuszi.

Alcoholism was another pressing problem. Australians, on the whole, consumed vast amounts of alcohol even though bars and saloons were open only a couple hours each day. These bars and saloons, after closing their official front entrance, nevertheless kept a back door open for thirsty customers. Beer and whiskey were the most popular drinks, and we were offered them constantly. Alcohol was the social drink par excellence. Whenever two people met, they would exchange the mandatory remarks about the fine weather and then one of them would inevitably exclaim, "Let's have a drink!"

There was no Hungarian consulate in Australia, so we were worried at first when we had to renew our passports. This obstacle was nothing for veteran world travels like us. We simply visited the Swedish consul, who was very obliging, renewing our passports under the pretext of having represented our country at one time. Although that time was before the First World War and the country he had represented, namely the Austro-Hungarian Monarchy, no longer existed, the broad-minded and geographically far from knowledgeable Australians let it pass.

Towards the end of our Australian journey, we drove straight into a tropical Queensland spring. We took out our shorts and pith helmets and left the forest-clad hills for the company of tall palms. As we made our way towards Queensland, we encountered more and more plantations, vast orchards of banana trees, followed by sugarcane, cacti, pineapples, and our old friends, the poisonous snakes, which were just as deadly as their mates in India or Ceylon. Shortly before reaching Brisbane, we killed three snakes in the close vicinity of our tent. There were many more aborigines in the tropical regions, and we learned a lot about their famous traditional weapon, the boomerang.

Boomerangs are flat with a sharp edge and carved out of hardwood in the shape of a parabola. Aborigine hunters are so skilled with boomerangs that they are able to throw them off at considerable speed and expect them to return, unless they hit a man or a beast along the way. Once I saw a man work a boomerang so skillfully that it flew off and around a small house, returning precisely to the hand that had thrown it.

Our journey led us to the sea. The seashore was an excellent place for travel, so we decided to stick close to it for as long as we could even though we were unable to go swimming in the tempting quiet waters because of the sharks. Sharks often swam out into the shallow water, and not only on deserted beaches, but in the most crowded spots in the midst of bathing season. The sharks attacked and killed many people each year, even though the smaller bathing places were surrounded by a wire mesh and large resorts employed guards stationed atop specially built shark-watching towers. Whenever the shark guards rang their warning bells, tens of thousands of bathers rushed towards the shore, crushing one another and screaming at the top of their lungs.

There were Hungarians to be found even in Australia. In fact, Australo-Hungarians made up quite a crowd in comparison with those we encountered in India: the single Hungarian in Colombo, the three Hungarians: a shoemaker, a pianist and a jazz drummer in Calcutta, and the Hungarian official at a German company in Bombay. Aside from these lone specimens, in Delhi we'd made the acquaintance of a Hungarian merchant tycoon from London.

There were approximately fifty Hungarian families living in Sydney. They were laborers or artisans for the most part; many of them had emigrated from Ankara upon discovering that they wouldn't be able to make a living in

Turkey. Although they lived well in Australia, they never quite got used to the idea of Australia as home. One of the Hungarians we met was an engineer, the other a veterinarian, a young man but skilled at what he did. He was already a lecturer at the university and was highly respected and admired. There were no Hungarian confectioners, however, which really was a shame because Australians loved sweets and Australian sweets were atrocious.

In Melbourne, we were invited to dinner. Our host was quite an extraordinary man in the guise of an ordinary British traveler. In a nutshell, this man had pretensions to the throne of Hungary and insisted that he was the sole rightful heir to the crown. He traced his lineage back to Prince Géza, or to his wife rather, who was mother to the first king of Hungary, King István or St. Stephen. Our host's father had left Hungary when he was still young and later became a subject of the Queen, spending the rest of his life in India, in the service of the British army. Upon retiring, he and his family had moved to Australia, where they had been living for the past twenty years. When he died, the sole survivor of his family was Gyula von Benke, our host. Our dinner invitation was signed Gyula Baron von Benke. I have an article about him from a local newspaper. In the article, "Baron" von Benke is described as a staunch advocate of British democracy who prefers citizenship in democratic Australia to "the dubious advantages of kingship in a strange land." Although our good baron didn't speak a word of Hungarian, we soon found out that Bishop Mikes had visited him at one time and that he would accept the responsibilities of King of Hungary only after he had amassed a fortune large enough to start a sizeable propaganda campaign.

Four weeks after our memorable dinner, we received a letter from our erstwhile host. He had been promoted. The letter was signed: Count Gyula von Benke. We figured if he got so high up in the pecking order so quickly, well, it wouldn't be long before he truly was crowned King of Hungary.

Another compatriot we met was a dance teacher in Perth. Yet another fellow Hungarian we met in Brisbane had been living in Queensland for fifty years, and he was therefore a true pioneer.

It was in the northernmost part of Queensland that we bade white Australia farewell to return to a continent of colored people. Our memories of Australia are fond ones of fascinating experiences and warm welcomes. Our travelogues, published in English, had been a huge success Down Under, so we were able to enjoy the comforts of financial security for some time. And so we left Australia behind and said goodbye to a land where we had seen neither kangaroos nor savages.

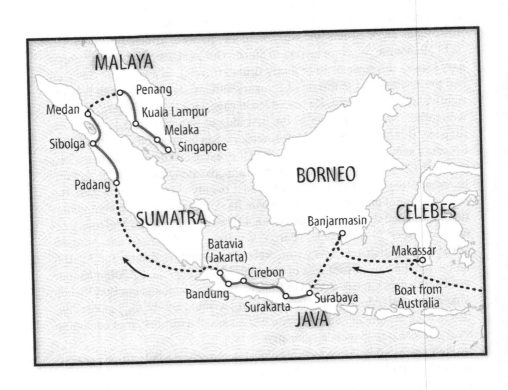

MALAYA

Penang

Medan

Kuala Lampur

Sibolga

Melaka

Singapore

Padang

SUMATRA

BORNEO

CELEBES

Banjarmasin

Makassar

Batavia
(Jakarta)

Cirebon

Bandung

Surabaya

Boat from
Australia

Surakarta

JAVA

The Ancient Lands of Malaysia

Equatorial Islands

It was smooth sailing on the calm ocean waters between Australia and Asia. Had it not been for the endless stretches of water surrounding the ship, it would have felt like we were standing on dry land.

The land in which we arrived was a colorful one. Although our English had improved by leaps and bounds during our Australian stay, we had come to a country whose language was entirely strange to our ears. I must confess, however, that out of all the languages we spoke, English proved to be by far the most useful on our world travels. It didn't take us long to realize that English would be as useful to us in the Dutch East Indies and the Malaysian Peninsula as it would prove later, as we traversed Siam, China, and Japan. I would also like to take this opportunity to reveal the best method for mastering a foreign tongue. Constantly on the road, we hardly had time to learn the variety of new languages we encountered from textbooks or dictionaries. However, we took care to learn a few basic expressions and fundamental vocabulary that would enable us to communicate with the natives. In our notebooks, we assembled small dictionaries consisting of a few dozen foreign words, the core vocabulary of each new language. It didn't take us more than a few days to have these words by heart, and they usually proved to be sufficient for the duration of our stay. Traveling through Southeast Asia, we realized the impossibility of learning Malay, Chinese, Thai, or Japanese in the few months we had at our disposal, so we decided to concentrate our efforts on English instead. We took every opportunity to converse in English and read all the English-language newspapers we could lay our hands on. The best place to learn English, however, was at the movies. There were plenty of American films available for our viewing pleasure, and I speak from experience when I say that they proved to be by far the best way to master the English language. The radio was also helpful as we perfected our pronunciation as radio announcers in both England and the United States were carefully selected and represented the finest English.

After leaving Australia, we arrived in Dutch colonies, where we soon learned that the Dutch language wasn't nearly as widespread as one might have surmised. Englishmen made sure those they colonized spoke good English; the French were willing to compromise and usually ended up with a Creole of sorts. Dutchmen, however, insisted on learning the language of the natives. Malay was the official tongue in the Dutch East Indies. All Dutch colonists spoke Malay, while only an insignificant portion of the native population had mastered Dutch.

We passed through Celebes and Borneo, but as our motorcycle remained on the ocean liner, we had to content ourselves with the short visits to the mainland that our ship's travel schedule allowed. We had enough time, however, to acquaint ourselves with the harbor cities of Makassar and Banjarmasin. The only way we could have visited the interior of the islands of Celebes and Borneo would have been by joining an organized expedition. Riding a motorcycle inland was out of the question. Thus, we first rode out on our motorcycle in Java, where the city of Surabaya became the starting point for our Southeast Asian adventures.

Many of the large equatorial islands such as Java or Sumatra were the epitome of the white colonist success story. The economic situation and general condition were such that white colonizers had nothing to lose and everything to gain by settling on these paradisiacal islands. The gates of immigration were closed however, and strictly guarded. Only tourists were welcome. Holland guarded the borders hawkishly; not even Dutch settlers were allowed unless they had signed a contract back in Europe or owned a lucrative business.

Java, truly paradise on earth, hardly welcomed us with open arms. We had to pay a large deposit covering our persons and the motorcycle and were forced to wait until leaving the country before we could reclaim our money. During our stay in Java, we were under constant surveillance.

The Island of Java is one of the cluster of Greater Sunda Islands, which lie between Asia and Australia and is comprised of the islands of Java, Madura, Bali, and Sumatra. The archipelago of many islands was officially known as the Dutch East Indies and ruled by little Holland, where the wealth and profits flowed. Java alone counted forty million inhabitants, while the population of Holland didn't exceed a hundred thousand.

The natives of the archipelago were ethnically Polynesians, Malaysians, and Papuans. The Malaysians were not a uniform people, however, rather they were comprised of various tribes, who were as different from one another as are the French and the Germans. What is more, the intermingling of various different peoples had been going on for centuries; Hindus and Arabs, Indians, Japanese, and Chinese had all contributed to the face of modern Malaysia. The Hindus had gone so far as to found empires on the islands of Java and Sumatra, but in the end, they assimilated into the native population. The most influential foreigners were the Chinese, yet their influence was felt mainly in the commercial sphere. Real power, political power, was in European hands.

The inhabitants of Java, Madura, and Bali had had extensive contact with civilization, while the most primitive peoples remained the Dayaks of Borneo, the Toraja of Celebes, and certain tribes on the island of Sumatra. The Batak and Minangkabu people of Sumatra led an agriculture-based lifestyle similar to that of the Javanese, while the Papua New Guineans were wholly nomadic.

There had been few visitors to Java around the turn of the century, but in less than thirty years, white men had discovered the wondrous beauty of the island and were coming by the hundreds of thousands each year to experience this tropical island paradise. Those who had the good fortune of visiting Java wished to pass on their knowledge, and indeed, more travelogues have been written about Java in the past few years than about any other place on earth. We ourselves had read so much about this place, that reaching Java was a bit like visiting a dear and familiar place. Our sense of novelty was significantly weakened.

Java was the heart and soul of the entire archipelago. A producer's paradise, it was also home to fertile plantations of rice, sugarcane, tea, coffee, tobacco, and caoutchouc.

We visited every city on the thousand-kilometer long island, traveling more than 2,500 kilometers along the island and zigzagging between its shores. This highly enjoyable journey from Surabaya to Batavia took us several weeks.

The town of Surabaya was an astonishing and novel sight. Set in a lush tropical setting and embraced by sweltering Oriental air, Surabaya was inhabited by a colorful people reminiscent of those we had met in India. There was a vast difference between Java and India, however. Java was much cleaner, most likely because there was no real poverty on the island. Life was slow-paced and laid-back on the whole; Malaysians contented themselves with having their daily bread and didn't worry about the next day or the next. In fact, Malaysians were a lazy people, and it wasn't long before Dutch colonists adapted to this new lifestyle.

On a purely human level, this was right and natural, but looking at it from the point of view of the colonists, the Dutch were bad politicians. Financially, they sucked all the life out of this fertile region, but at the same time, they strove to educate and elevate the natives to their standards of living. The mixing of peoples was common; we had never seen so many half-bloods in our entire lives. By allowing the natives to rise to their level, the Dutch were unwittingly enabling educated dissent. Malaysians did not like to work and had little respect for the Dutch. In fact, they never even learned the language of their colonizers as the Dutch made every effort to master Malay.

Tandyung Perak was the name of a harbor; an electric train route connected the harbor to the actual city. Surabaya was an important commercial center specializing mainly in the production of sugar. 20,000 of its population of 200,000 were of European descent. Downtown was an incredibly busy place. The paved roads were continually crowded with taxis; fares were cheap, and Europeans rode cabs everywhere. Those who owned cars also employed drivers; this was all very different from the practice in Australia. Malaysians were skilled drivers, yet they somehow did not feel that the rules of the road were binding. The police directing traffic generally sported parasols tied to their backs to shield them from the rays of the sun and generally came down on the laissez faire side of things.

White men lived in supreme comfort. There were no cramped quarters housing numerous families; each family lived in its own private and very tidy stone house. An army of servants anxious to meet their every need filled the homes of the colonists; men returning home from work could expect a line of cool and exquisite drinks freshly concocted for their pleasure. Pajamas were the norm, both indoors and outside.

Besides taxis, *soudas* were the most popular mode of travel. A *souda* is a small, two-wheeled cart drawn by a single horse. There is space for a driver and one passenger per *souda*. There were no taximeters; passengers generally paid 50 Dutch cents a ride. A ride in a *souda* cost exactly half as much.

The cities of Java all resembled one another. Distances were so small that they prevented the development of distinct cultural systems and lifestyles. What we saw in Surabaya, we invariably reencountered in Batavia. In general, Javanese cities could be divided into two main groups with reference to malaria; there were hilltop towns and flatland towns. Malaria was a very widespread disease; most natives had it at one point in their lives, but colonists were not immune either to the ravages of the disease. The rainy season was especially dangerous, because it was at these times of the year that mosquitoes flourished, especially in the flatlands and close to the sea. Nobody ever recovered from malaria, rather, those who had contracted it experienced alternate relatively symptom-free and symptom-filled periods. Surabaya, Semarang, and Cirebon especially were hotbeds for malaria, but not even the capital Batavia was free from the disease. Quinine was the best antidote. Cinchona trees, out of whose bark quinine was extracted, grew all over Java, and so there was plenty of quinine available to everyone. In fact, it was passed out completely free at schools, the post office, and pharmacies.

We had no choice but to grow accustomed to the bitter taste of the medication and knew better than to disregard the good advice offered us every step

Javanese landscape near Buitenzorg, dominated by the volcanic peak of Salak

of the way. For example, each time we arrived at a hotel, we scanned the mos-
quito-crowded walls to assess the ratio of malaria infected mosquitoes to
those free of the disease. Mosquitoes infected with malaria, as we soon
learned, held their bodies at an acute angle to the wall while the bodies of
healthy specimens were parallel to the wall. We generally found there to be
just as many infected mosquitoes as there were healthy ones, but when visiting towns in the hilly regions, we were pleased to discover that all mosquitoes
lining the walls did so in a strictly parallel fashion.

Mosquito netting, however, was an absolute necessity wherever we went.
The *klambu* was the most important part of every room; without a klambu,
sleep was both dangerous and impossible. Dense nets surrounded the bed on
all four sides. We were surprised to discover that blankets were unknown on
the island of Java. Not only did the Javanese not use comforters, they didn't
even use thin sheets to cover their bodies at night. Hotel rooms followed the
Javanese tradition of bare beds.

"And what in the world is this for?" we asked ourselves upon spotting two
cylindrical, sausage-like cushions next to the traditional pillows lying on our
beds. We laid the sausages aside and only after a few days and a few glimpses
into other hotel rooms did we realize that the sausage cushions were meant
purely for comfort. Some people slept with the cushions between their legs,
others placed them under their feet or behind their backs to obtain the ideal
sleeping position. We soon grew so accustomed to the strange cushions and
lack of covers that we found it strange and utterly unacceptable when greeted
by a traditional hotel room.

There were few tall buildings even in the city. Most of the houses consisted of a single floor, or a ground floor and first floor at the very most. What the cities lacked in tall buildings, they made up for in shops. There was a number of stores run by the natives, but these seemed insignificant next to the countless Chinese stores and *tokos*. The part of town inhabited by Europeans was comprised entirely of villas. We felt like we were in Holland; small, modern houses surrounded by tidy gardens lined the streets, and what's more, each and every house was unique and unlike the one before. There was a verandah built onto every house, and these verandas were lit by lamps with the most colorful lampshades. Even hotel rooms had their own verandahs.

It didn't take us long to find Chinatown. There were many Chinese living on Java; most of them had never seen China, but were born, lived, and died on the island. Most of them spoke better Malaysian than they did Chinese, but ethnic Chinese managed to preserve their writing system and traditional clothing, so they were very easy to spot.

It was rumored that there were no pure Dutch on the entire island of Java. In Malaysia, half-bloods counted as Europeans; this phenomenon would have been entirely unimaginable in India. Half-bloods on Java looked down on the natives, wore European clothes, and strove to keep their knowledge of Malaysian a secret. Although the Dutch had been living in Malaysia for centuries, they had not managed to win the respect and admiration of the natives. The colonists were wealthy, lived well, and kept many servants, yet they were not "high class" in the way the British in India had been. As labor was cheap on the colonies and natives numerous, Dutch colonists, even the few who came, had difficulty finding positions in bureaucracy or trade. Waves of unrest among the Malaysians were common and directed at their colonizers. Dutch girls wore their hair in long braids, as they did at home, and remained loyal to the "ancient" Dutch vehicle of transportation, the bicycle.

Half-blood girls were all the more beautiful. They had excellent figures, fiery dark eyes, and pleasant tan skin. Yet their every wish was to be whiter. They kept special diets, visited quacks of all kinds, and shielded their faces from the rays of the sun, all in an effort to obtain lighter skin.

While in Java, we had to do as the Javanese do, which was neither difficult nor unpleasant. There was a private bathroom attached to every hotel room, and the Javanese generally took two baths a day. We also had to change our white linens at least twice a day, but neither bathing nor putting on a fresh change of clothes posed insurmountable challenges. Although Javanese tailors produced a full outfit in a mere four hours, we weren't in need of too many outfits seeing as our dirty clothing was washed and pressed each night and lay neatly folded next to our beds each morning.

Javanese roads were incredible. Leaving Surabaya, we soon found our-

Terraced rice paddies on Java

selves whizzing along on broad, paved roads. This same paved road ran on for all 2,500 kilometers of our island journey. The only bumpy stretches occurred in places where the asphalt had melted in the heat. These mild discomforts were dwarfed by the lush natural beauty of Java.

Leaving Surabaya, we rode on through fields of sugarcane stretching as far as the eye could see. Sometimes, the sugarcane plants by the side of the road reached the height of four meters. Leaving the sweet fields behind, we continued on through fields of rice. There wasn't a square inch of unculti-vated land in all of Java. Growing rice, for example, required extensive water-covered flatlands. As there were no suitable natural plateaus in the hilly re-gions of Java, rice fields had to be carved out through centuries of back-break-ing labor. Javanese farmers had reached the mountaintops, cut out the forests and carved out huge steps on the hillsides to accommodate the rice planta-tions. We saw such giant steps wherever we looked, and each step was a field of rice, ready to be submerged. A system of channels brought water to the rice fields. Some of these channels consisted of giant concrete pipes that crossed bridges, other times the water supplies trickled to their destination along underground paths.

After a while, the expansive rice fields gave way to caoutchouc planta-tions. Caoutchouc trees, neatly numbered, stood side by side, their barks slit each morning to allow a milky white substance, raw rubber, to flow out into specially prepared cups or into coconut shells tied to the tree for that very purpose. The coconut shells and cups were emptied in larger containers, where the rubber milk was allowed to thicken. Then, the raw rubber was pressed into large, pancake-like formations or else rectangular blocks in the

Harvesting rice on Java

plantation workshops and shipped to factories throughout Europe and the United States.

Tea and coffee flourished on plantations the size of entire counties, especially those located in the mountainous regions where the climate was significantly milder. We often stopped to enjoy some bananas or other delicious tropical fruits growing by the road. Pineapples, planted one by one and located close to the ground were easy to harvest, while our yearned-for coconuts mostly stayed out of reach.

The road led us up and down, and the climate changed constantly depending on the elevation. Sometimes we ascended 1,000 or even 1,500 meters in a matter of fifteen minutes; truly flat land was rare in Java. Well-constructed serpentine roads led us to the heights; sudden changes in temperature caused us to sweat and shiver alternately. The Automobile Club of Java had done an excellent job marking the roads and indicating directions. It was nearly impossible to get lost. Even the length of our upward climb was marked, along with the degree of the incline, and there was gasoline available in even the tiniest villages.

On the whole, Javanese villages were superior to their European counterparts. The first village we encountered, Bangil, was inhabited by 16,000 natives and 100 Europeans. Everyone lived in tidy, well-constructed homes; there were plenty of shops and public buildings and schools were in excellent condition. We even saw a post office and a hospital. There were hotels in nearly every village, or at least a cluster of bungalows reminiscent of our quarters in India, but on Java, these special guesthouses were called *passangrahans*. Needless to say, these neat *passangrahans* were populated by insects, large, winged ants, lizards, frogs, and even Javanese cats famously lacking their tails. Cats on Java weren't tail-less because of human cruelty, rather, they were born with no more than a bob of a tail. Our worst enemy wherever we went was the omnipresent mosquito. We'll take three lizards over one mosquito under the *klambu* any day!

Java was an incredibly rich land! The natives grew rice, which was exported in massive quantities, while Europeans tried their luck at producing sugar, coffee, tea, tobacco, rubber, valuable bark of cinchona used for making quinine, indigo, cocoa, and a variety of fruits and spices. But this was not all. There were plenty of minerals waiting to be discovered and exploited: gold, diamonds, and silver alongside carbon and iron ore. There were plenty of trees for lumber, and pearl fishing was equally widespread. Cotton grew well in the Javanese climate; cow-, sheep-, and snakeskins were also popular export goods.

There was plenty to do on Java. There must have been almost two hundred sugar factories scattered about the island; 40,000 kilograms of tea were exported each year. Land was not for sale; large companies were forced to rent it from the natives or from the government.

The climate was the main force that shaped Javanese life. Although located very near the Equator, the island of Java, by virtue of being an island, was not afflicted by the sweltering heat we had experienced in other places. The monsoon winds, when blowing from the southeast, caused a six-month dry spell, while the northern monsoon inevitably brought rains. We had arrived in the middle of the rainy season, yet it was far from unpleasant. We knew precisely when the rain would start each day. It invariably came sometime in the afternoon, and, depending on which part of the island you were traveling through, it was relatively easy to calculate when the rain would hit. The afternoon rains were punctual to the minute, arriving amidst bursts of thunder and lightning. Immense amounts of water would fall within a few minutes, and the best thing to do was to get under a roof as soon as possible. Those accustomed to the daily monsoon rains had a comical way of preparing for them. Instead of looking up at the sky and scanning it for tell-tale clouds, they would simply look at their watches. When the moment came, regardless of whether or not there was a single cloud visible in the sky, savvy natives would run inside, shut their doors and windows, or don heavy raincoats if they were out on the street. The deluge would come inevitably, but as all roads were paved, mud was virtually unknown. Instead, clouds of steam would rise from the overheated asphalt, which dried completely in just a few hours as soon as the tropical sun had reestablished full sway over that part of the island.

The lowlands and coastlands were the hottest parts of the island. Although temperatures rarely rose above 36 degrees C, the humidity made it feel like much more. Temperatures weren't much cooler at night, so if we wanted to sleep well, we generally opted for lodgings in hilltop towns.

We reached the cities of Djokjakarta and Surakarta, or Solo, without any grave difficulties. Both lay rather inland, and both were imperial centers. Although there was a number of independent sultanates throughout Java, the unfortunate sultans lacked many things, most notably, independence. They generally owned large palaces, and huge walls surrounded the *Kraton,* yet a subtle poverty prevailed. The palace was a little shabby, the pomp was a little shabby, even the gift we received from the sultan, a box of cigarettes manufactured in Egypt, was pitiful. The hundred cigarettes in the box were worth fifty Budapest cigarettes.

All the towns were equally busy; those living on the outskirts of town would set out for the city center early in the morning. Although taxis kept to the downtown areas, private cars filled the streets of both the center and the periphery. Occasionally, a *souda* would make its slow way along the road, but the number of pedestrians exceeded that of automobiles and *soudas* altogether. Every single person on the street was holding an umbrella or a leaf from a banana tree, which proved to be much more effective in warding off rain. Porters carried their loads on long poles laid across their shoulders; because the often heavy loads hung from their shoulders like a balance and bobbed up and down on the light bamboo poles, porters were forced to walk quickly and in keeping with the rhythm of the swaying bamboo to lighten their loads as much as possible. Some people carried enough wares to fill a small shop on their backs; others made use of the strong bamboo poles to transport heavy chests, even furniture. We often saw so-called "flying restaurants," in other words, large quantities of food carried around on bamboo poles by street vendors. These vendors would walk along the streets, sometimes trying their luck on the country roads, and settle down to prepare a quick meal each time they discovered a willing customer. On one side of the balance hung a tiny stove, suitable for preparing meals on the go; the other side was for the necessary utensils and ingredients: pots and pans, vegetables, spices, live fowl, fuel, and beverages. To top it all off, most flying restaurant owners added a tiny stool or two for the convenience of their guests. There were larger flying restaurants with an entire team of coolies carrying the food and supplies. The owners of such lucrative businesses simply walked behind the poor coolies and told them what to do.

Javanese "flying restaurant"

Women carried bundles on their heads or in large shawls slung over their shoulders and brushing against their sides. These shawls were tied around their necks for support. The most common "bundle" women carried were children, who rode in the shawls as naturally as anything else the mother might have carried.

As we made our way inland, we grew more and more accustomed to life on Java. Travel was expensive; prices, especially those of European hotels and shops, were high. A moderately-priced European hotel cost 8-10 Dutch Florins per person per night, but this price covered not only a comfortable room and excellent service, but also luxury bathing and fine dining. For those who did not have 8-10 Florins to spare, there were plenty of native-run hotels to choose from. Europeans often resorted to Chinese hotels, where rooms were cheap and dining costs low and separate from the rental fees.

Every Javanese meal was a royal meal. "Rice or potatoes, please?" was inevitably the first question we were asked at every meal. If we asked for rice, we would receive an authentic Javanese meal, potatoes meant European dining. One delicious course would follow another, especially if we ordered the famous Dutch-Indian *reistafel*. Rice, cooked simply in water, stood in large white mounds on the table; servants generally brought out the rest of the food. The line of servants bearing one amazing dish after another made us feel like royalty. Curry dishes were followed by cold cuts, various types of meat

187

and fish, and eggs. Each servant brought a different tasty delicacy, and we would take a little from each dish and arrange it all around the rice on our plates. Of course, plenty of experience was needed to make good choices at lunch, seeing as the unsuspecting tourist never quite knew when the line of dishes would cease. Sometimes, we would fill our plates with food from the first few dishes, not realizing that there were delicacies beyond our wildest dream to come. On such occasions, we would simply ask a servant to take our hastily filled dish away and start all over.

In many restaurants, the only food available was traditional Javanese cuisine. I still have in my keeping a Javanese menu from a restaurant in Surabaya. This menu lists all the traditional Javanese meals with detailed explanations as to what they consist of. This menu was a great help to us as we got to know the finest of Javanese cuisine. One of our especial favorites was *nasik goreng,* or rice cooked in butter and mixed with small bits of meat, eggs, and fish. *Bami,* actually a Chinese dish, was prepared in the same way as *nasik goreng,* only noodles were substituted for the rice. Rice was to the Javanese what bread is to us. Some foods had even more exotic names: *tyhing thingtyim* and *kwiehwahietyhie* and would take too long to describe.

Our travel time was restricted to mornings because of the heavy monsoon rain that hit each afternoon. Traveling mornings only, we soon reached the seaside towns of Semarang, then Cirebon. To reach them, we had to cross a momentous volcanic mountain range. There are a hundred active volcanoes on the island of Java, and while there, we managed to climb quite a few of the smoky monsters. Expansive rice fields lined the feet of the volcanoes; their slopes were a jumble of lush tropical vegetation. Bromo was the largest of volcanoes; its sulphurous breath could be felt for 30 kilometers.

Djokjakarta was perhaps the most traditional of all Javanese cities. It was there that we saw the most beautiful batik work and enjoyed the art of the most talented male and female dancers.

We also saw many architectural wonders throughout the island. The overwhelming majority of the Javanese was Muslim, although small Hindu and Buddhist minorities did live on the island. Nevertheless, the most beautiful monuments belonged to the minority. We saw one gorgeous Buddha statue after another along the roads, even in the seemingly deserted tropical forests. The most beautiful temple we encountered was the one at Boroboedoer, near Djokjakarta.

The largest and loveliest Buddhist monument on the island of Java was the mighty temple at Boroboedoer. It seemed like a mountain that had sprouted from the earth. Built to encircle a round hill, the temple was empty on the inside and consisted mainly of impressive stairways and lofts housing various reliefs, niches, and statues. Each side of the building measured 180 meters

Ancient Hindu temple, Boroboedoer, Java

and the length of the statue-lined meandering corridors added up to more than three kilometers. The temple was built in the ninth century but buried by the islanders to protect it from invading Muslims. According to legend, the temple lay hidden underground for three entire centuries.

Although we spent a whole day walking through and admiring the temple at Boroboedoer, we felt we had seen only a small portion of all the beauties it had to offer.

Upon reaching the city of Garoet, we went on an expedition to one of the largest volcanoes on Java, the nearby Tangkoreban Prahoe. The volcano's name aptly reflected its outward appearance. In English, Tangkoreban Prahoe means "upside-down boat." In the year 1772, forty villages were destroyed as a result of an eruption. We rode our motorcycle all the way to the top; the crater lay 2,000 meters above sea level.

The journey along the shore brought sweltering heat, the danger of malaria and the promise of encounters with wild animals.

There was plenty of game on Java, but few animals besides snakes ventured onto the busy roads. There were plenty of snakes, however; we ended up killing quite a few of them along the way. The rivers were filled with crocodiles; we shot one, in fact, when it came too close to our camp on the shore. These were our only encounters with dangerous animals throughout our stay on the island of Java. Monkeys seemed to be ubiquitous, especially sweet little ones of the white, Javanese kind. This species was to be found only on the island; all attempts to export it failed. Orangutans and tigers were to be found only on the island of Sumatra, elephants on Borneo and Sumatra. The

Javanese bamboo bridge, near Bandjarnegara

rhinoceros, however, was very much a Javanese resident, only it managed to hide so well from human hunters, that it rarely was caught.

Despite the large number of automobiles and bicycles whizzing along Javanese roads, we still managed to attract quite a bit of the natives' attention. Whenever we stopped, it didn't take long for a large crowd of curious spectators to encircle us completely. Poor Hadji was no longer with us, and we were not able to leave our motorcycle unattended, as Malaysians had a predilection for the goods of others and didn't find us forbidding enough to give up all hopes of taking our Harley. Occasionally, cars left unattended overnight were found the next morning missing all four tires. As our shouting wasn't enough to keep the skirt-wearing crowds, men and women alike, away from our motorcycle, we were obliged to cover the vehicle with a large white tarp to dampen the curiosity of the onlookers. Malaysians did not wear pants, but opted for *sarongs* instead. *Sarongs* were skirt-like outfits sewn of colorfully dyed linen, worn by men and women, old and young alike. The natives were masters of the batik technique, preparing the paints and the patterns themselves. The precision and unique quality of their art exceeded by far anything a textile factory could produce.

We later returned to the mountains to spend time in the healthiest and most attractive city of Java, Bandung.

Bandung is located 800 meters above sea-level, and was a beloved resort for Europeans seeking to beat the heat. Each hotel was headed by a *mandur,* an arch-servant of sorts who oversaw the work of countless *jangasses,* the Javanese equivalents of the "boys" of India. It didn't take us long to adopt the lovely Javanese custom of taking a nap between the hours of two and four each afternoon. Afternoon naps were the norm on Java, and those who refused to catch forty winks at the allotted time were considered highly odd. Besides discovering the beneficial quality of afternoon naps, we also soon discovered that it was best to wash our own socks and handkerchiefs, seeing as laundry workers were paid by the piece; it cost just as much to clean ten handkerchiefs as it did to wash ten shirts or ten pajamas.

Batavia was our last stop on the island of Java. We headed for the sea via Buitenzorg, where we visited the famous botanical gardens. The lushness of the foliage would have stunned us had we seen it outside of Java, but as the entire island was a singular botanical garden offering natural wonder and novelties every single day, the numerous species of beautiful trees and handsome orchids had no staying power, except maybe for the gorgeous Victoria Regia. After passing through a few *kampongs,* or native villages, we arrived, suffocating with heat and wilting in traffic, amidst the old houses of Batavia. Once in Batavia, we made our way as quickly as possible to Weltevreden, the somewhat airier European district, where we reflected on our Javanese journey while relaxing in a comfortable hotel.

Java truly was a land of contradictions. Women stood doing their laundry in the Molenvliet channel, in the very heart of the metropolis, while all natives, young and old, immersed themselves in the waters of the same channel to be purified as automobiles whizzed past them at considerable speeds. Malaysian women used stones to grind rice into flour in the villages, even as their husbands worked shifts in state-of-the-art sugar factories. Fertile farmland alternated with tractless jungles, peaceful villages slumbered under the auspices of smoking volcanoes. Although the lowlands were filled with all the dangers and discomforts of a tropical zone, excellent roads, modern buses, and punctual trains made it easy to escape into the cooler mountainous regions.

We had visited Bali as well towards the beginning of our Javanese journey. So much had been written about Bali, that the famous, topless female dancers must be known the world over. There were so many tourists on Bali that the peaceful lifestyle of the indigenous Hindu population was slowly coming to an end. Bali has become a center of tourism, and just as the peasants of Mezőkövesd will continue to don their traditional Hungarian outfits for the benefit of tourists, centuries from now, the Balinese will still be stripping half naked to delight the eyes of foreigners.

Leaving Java, we made our way to the island of Sumatra, an island whose uninhabited and uncivilized wildness was more than welcome after the modernity, comforts, and exaggerated safety of Java. Although we were advised against this trip countless times, we wouldn't have missed Sumatra for the world, especially when we were so very close.

Jungles, Wild Beasts, Savages

Fifty years before, all of Sumatra had been an impenetrable, forbidding, and tractless wild. Few, if any, white men ventured onto this island until the 1890s, when an engineer by the name of Yzerman headed an expedition whose goal was to traverse the jungles and swamps of Sumatra and reach the eastern shore despite the menace of unfriendly natives. A number of the members of the expedition paid with their lives for their boldness.

At the time of our visit, Sumatra was much changed, but it still counted as an island waiting to be explored and conquered. Only parts of the island were populated, while large portions of Sumatra were covered by dense rainforests in which no man had ever set foot. A traveler on Sumatra never knew what to expect on his trek through the wild. There was a single road on Sumatra, connecting the cities of Padang and Medan. It was this road we were hoping to find and follow.

Although the island of Sumatra was much larger than Java, it had a population of a mere five million as opposed to the forty million of Java. Most of the people living on Sumatra had been transferred there from Javanese plantations.

To get an idea of the immensity of Sumatra, it's enough to keep in mind that the island is 1,700 kilometers long and 400 kilometers wide at its widest. The road we traveled stretched on for 1,500 kilometers.

Many different tribes inhabited the island of Sumatra. The people of the Lampong and Lebong tribes formed agriculture-based communities; the primitive Redjang tribe was fierce and warlike while the Orang-Ulu and Orang-Lubu, were peaceful people. The Minangkabu were the only purely Malaysian tribe; furthermore, they were the only natives who did not buy and sell wives, but rather made women into the heads of families, enjoying ownership of both their land and their children.

Another notable group was the Batak people, living on the shore of Lake Toba. Cannibalism was dying out all over the island, and contact with white settlers influenced native life in a decisive manner. Tribes living near the sea had seen white men arrive on ships and lived amidst them, while those Sumatrans hidden deep in the jungle were more or less unaware of the advent of European settlers. There were regions, especially in the central and eastern parts of the island, surrounded by dense forests on every side, that have remained a terra incognita to white man, despite the occasional boats, which ventured, along the rivers, into the heart of these unknown regions.

Our long journey across Sumatra began in the city of Padang, population 50,000, the largest city in Western Sumatra. This city, where we hoped to stock up on the supplies we would need, was graced by an enchanting harbor constructed around a bay, which jutted deep into the side of a mountain. Padang was not very different from Javanese towns with its orderly business district and countless automobiles; only the native district seemed somewhat smaller.

While in Padang, we purchased plenty of gasoline, ammunition, and food for our journey. Leaving Padang, we continued on for some time across cultivated land. Of course, Sumatra was not Java, and there was much more land, especially of the uncultivated kind. Villages were fewer and further in between. We saw no motorcycles on the Sumatran roads, so our vehicle caused a commotion every time we drove through a village of wondering natives.

The entire Plateau of Padang was populated by members of the Minangkabu tribe. After passing through Padang Padjan, we found ourselves traveling on the high surface of the plateau. The road wasn't nearly as good as Javanese roads; it was a gravel road with plenty of potholes and loose stones, but considering we were on Sumatra, we decided to be satisfied with the conditions at hand. Sumatran volcanoes belched forth smoke or hid behind clouds, as had the volcanoes on Java.

The homes of the Minangkabu were a memorable sight. These houses were built mostly of wood, high above the ground; the concave arches of each roof ended in long, upward curves where the eaves were. Even the most primitive huts were artfully carved. Some houses boasted more than one roof, each supporting plenty of decorative curves. The various roofs were compactly built up against each other. Each extra roof meant a married child, who continued living with his parents even after founding a family of his own.

Fort de Kock was the first actual town we encountered, at an elevation of roughly one thousand meters. We enjoyed the mosquito-free freshness of the mountain air, and, despite our proximity to the Equator, did not feel the least bit hot. Sumatra, like Java, was a hotbed of malaria, so caution remained of the essence. From our vantage point at Fort de Kock, we could clearly make out the peaks of the Ophir, Merapi, and Singgalang volcanoes.

The road leading out of Fort de Kock was a mountain road. We managed to break our motorcycle's chassis while crossing the railroad tracks that had followed us that far, so we were forced to proceed with caution until we reached a place where we could get it welded together again.

Real Sumatra was still to come. The landscape around us grew more and more uncivilized; occasionally, we would spot a Minangkabu woman in a colorful dress and head covering or cross a poor little village, but for the most part, signs of civilization grew fewer and fewer until we reached the rainforests, where they ceased altogether.

Although we had seen jungles in Bengal and on Java, we did not know what the word jungle meant until our encounter with the unparalleled forests

Sumatran rainforest

on Sumatra. It didn't take us long to get used to the jungle, which we encountered at first in spots that took merely a few hours to cross, then longer
stretches, through which we traveled for days without seeing more civilization than a lone plantation. Even while traveling through forests where there

wasn't a fellow human for a hundred kilometers, we were able to travel along fine paved roads.

I get butterflies in my stomach just thinking back on the natural, almost naïve way in which we traveled across these mysterious, frightening forests. In reference to travelers' qualms, I have the following interesting observation to make. Whenever we knew a dangerous stretch was coming up, we got mildly worried. On our way there, we would continue worrying about the danger and about how it could be avoided. As soon as we arrived at said dangerous place, our worries would cease, and we would travel on, calm and fearless. Once the danger was past, we generally began worrying about what could have happened and wondering how we could have been so careless as to ignore the warnings of people far more sensible and knowledgeable than ourselves.

This is precisely what happened as we made our way across the rainforests of Sumatra. Once there, we rode through the dense jungle with the nonchalance of royalty.

Rainforests are imposing, even frightening, in their unique majesty. The narrow road we traveled was hemmed in on both sides by dense walls of vegetation. There is no orator who could rightfully describe its majesty, no writer's pen gracious enough for the task, no camera artful enough to capture the beauty of the rainforests.

At the very edge of the road began the wide swathe of rainforest; the foliage was dense and dark, and the exhalation of the forest cool. This coolness of the forest only enhanced its other beauties. Tree giants, interspersed with smaller trees of average stature, reached towards the sky. Their long, straight trunks, covered with a bundle of intricately knotted vines, seemed to lose themselves in space. Under the tree giants grew a line of smaller, thickset trees, and below them was a dense thicket of ferns, palms, gigantic leaves, grass as tall as a man, and impenetrable bushes. The entire rainforest, from the crowns of the highest trees to the fronds of the smallest palms was bound tightly, wound round and round by parasitic plants of all kinds; sarmentose tendrils, runners and trailers hung from the height of a few stories. The forest was "walled" off by just such plants on both sides of the road, and it would have been impossible to take a single step into the impenetrable green without a hatchet. Even the animals of the rainforest used the same, well-trodden paths; only the elephant was capable of creating a new path through the dense vegetation.

It was impossible to get lost. Although the rainforest stretched for hundreds of miles on both sides of the roads, there was no way in. We could only marvel at the Herculean labors it must have taken to cut a usable road into all this wildness. The forests lined not only the plains but the steepest mountainsides as well, so that our only glimpse of their shady interiors came when we followed the line of a small brook with our eyes. Although there were large rivers trailing through the forests, the trees and other vegetation grew so close to the bank that it would have been nearly impossible to leave the boat. The images that passed before our eyes and the quiet that framed them were both majestic; we found the huffing and puffing of our motorcycle engine to be almost sacrilegious. Hundreds upon hundreds of orchids bloomed along the trees and in the thickets, and the movement of the indigenous animals was harmonious rather than jarring.

We kept our guns loaded and within reach. After a few days of travel through the rainforest, we began to long for an encounter with big game. At first, we found the presence of wild animals to be unusual, and the sound of our engine usually drowned out the sounds of the forest. Whenever we stopped, however, we began to pick out the voices of the animals. The tropical rainforests of Sumatra were home to big game such as the rhinoceros, tiger, leopard, elephant, tapir, wild buffalo, and the wild boar. The orangutan, from the Malaysian *orang-utan*, or forest-man, was a further inhabitant of the rainforests. We were often surprised to hear the roar of a tiger from nearby, accompanied by the trumpeting of an elephant. It didn't take long before we were able to tell the animals apart by the sound of their voices. Thousands of monkeys leapt from tree to tree in the surrounding forest, doing their utmost to escape from our droning engine. In fact, we had nothing to fear in the way of wild animals as long as our engine was making its usual sounds. Occasionally, a panther or a tiger would leap out onto the road in front of us, but it generally disappeared in the forest on the other side before we even had time to raise our guns.

The natives were most afraid of the tiger, even though the predators of the rainforests weren't nearly as dangerous as people made them out to be. Most large game had eyes only for small game, for other animals. As long as there was plenty of prey in the forests, tigers rarely ventured into human villages. Occasionally, a tiger might appear on a plantation and stroll in a leisurely manner amongst the frightened coolies without so much as touching them. Only very hungry tigers, or wounded tigers seeking revenge, or tigers that felt threatened and acted out of self-defense ever attacked people.

While in Padang, we heard a couple of fascinating stories. A tigress, the mother of cubs, had attacked two people just outside the city limits. The natives were horribly afraid of tigers, while respecting them in a profound way. For example, when talking about large predators, Malaysians often used the title "sir." Most people refrained from ever calling a tiger by its name and stuck to the safer "He."

It was also on the Padang plateau that a carload of tourists was attacked

Crocodiles on the tropical riverbank

by wild elephants. Elephants are very sensitive to sound, so they were the only animals we had to be wary of even while riding our motorcycle. When the elephants attacked the automobile, the passengers leapt from their seats and sought refuge in the neighboring trees. The elephants then proceeded to play with the car, rolling it round and round until it was nothing but a heap of crushed steel.

Another animal deserving of caution was the snake. There were numerous poison species of this disgusting reptile hidden about the rainforest. We usually hit a snake per day as we traveled along the road. Monkeys screaming as they scurried from tree to tree was another indication that there was a snake nearby. Snakes dropping from trees onto the heads of their unsuspecting victims were only some of the dangers we faced; passing next to rivers, we were especially wary of lurking crocodiles.

Besides the monkeys, troops of the most varied birds were our constant companions. These birds were generally exorbitantly colorful and sported amazing plumage. In the hours before and following dawn, the sound of their voices drowned out even the most resounding roars emerging from the jungle.

There were plenty of other dangers lurking in the forest, and most newcomers were advised against striking out on their own without a thorough knowledge of the tropical world. Swampy bits of ground, marshes and morasses lay hidden throughout the length of the forest and often captured a stray scientist or two. Poisonous gasses bubbling up out of the swampy regions posed an additional threat. Tiny worms and parasites would become

197

An obelisk marks the Equator on the island of Sumatra

lodged in our skin, even under our clothes, making our skin itch so unbearably that we would have to stop often to remove the intruders from our bodies.

Natives walked about the forests entirely naked. They generally carried wooden sticks sharpened to an edge, with the purpose of scratching parasites off their bodies. The only protection they had against larger animals was a stick, or, in some tribes, blow-pipes for discharging poison arrows capable of killing even the largest game.

Passing through the villages, we saw that the natives lived out their lives in the proximity of animals. Houses were built on poles and stood high above the ground. People locked their homes for the night and kept domesticated animals behind fences four to five meters high. These fences were built of bamboo, and mostly protected bovines, which were an especial favorite in tiger circles. In fact, tigers preferred the meat of most domestic animals to human flesh.

Giant butterflies, sparkling with many different colors, flew overhead. With their wings outspread, they were each the size of a plate. Eagles circled up above, and vultures waited patiently for their prey.

THE ANCIENT LANDS OF MALAYSIA

We crossed the Equator shortly after passing through the village of Bandjol. At the time, I thought Sumatra was the only place we could cross the imaginary black line on a motorcycle. We duplicated the feat much later, while traveling through Ecuador. We found it very strange that our shadows disappeared at noon; under the vertical rays of the sun, our entire bodies cast no more shade than the pith helmets on our heads. It was our second time crossing the Equator, but the first time we had done it by land. It being February, we went, in one split second, from summer into winter. There was a stone column to mark this place of primary geographical significance, and the hut of a native stood right next to the column. Although he lived next to the column his entire life, I doubt anybody could have convinced him of its importance.

The climate remained unchanged. As long as we stayed close to sea level, it was terribly hot, but while traveling through the mountains at heights of a thousand, fifteen hundred, even two thousand meters, we found ourselves shivering in the cool evening air. There was no rainy season on Sumatra; it could rain any month of the year. It never got much hotter than 36 to 38 degrees C, and these average temperatures held regardless of the season.

Traveling on, we passed through another series of villages and reached the sea near Sibolga. In Sibolga we experienced just how high the prices on Sumatra had been driven. This is not to say that we had lived for free on Java, but our living costs on Sumatra exceeded all expectations. It cost us 20 Dutch Florins to purchase lodgings and food at a very humble, small-town hotel. We had to pay extra for the garage and for the food to be brought to our rooms. A day in Sibolga cost us approximately 50 Hungarian Pengő.

From Sibolga, we reached the stretch of road famous for giving travelers a bad case of seasickness. The serpentine road meandered up the steep slopes of a mountain, twisting and turning so often that we grew dizzy attempting to follow it to the top. Although the distance traveled was no more than 38 miles, we encountered more than 1,500 sharp curves along the way. The road, as far as we could tell, had been built on an amazing amount of cheap labor, but the twists and turns we encountered every step of the way forced us to keep our eyes off the island-speckled sea and dramatic gorges graced with waterfalls and on the road in front of our noses.

It didn't take long for us to reach another plateau, namely, the Toba Highlands. Once we had passed the town of Taratung, we knew we were on Batak territory. Although German missionaries had been working with the Batak natives for quite some time, they remained a very primitive and backward people. There was a mission school and a hospital for lepers, both located in Taratung. Those who allowed themselves to be baptized received a Dutch Florin and a change of clothes. Some natives stuck to their old ways despite this

199

attractive offer while others had themselves baptized twice in an attempt to make the most of the generosity of the missionaries. Not long before our travels, the Batak people had been a cannibalistic nation. Although they had mostly given up their old ways, we were convinced that should we stray off the beaten path, we would encounter a few isolated villages where human flesh was still very much a part of the Batak menu. Most Bataks were peasants and grew rice crops. They also raised pigs, which were an unusual sight to our eyes that had become used to Muslim Malaysia. 125,000 of the 500,000 Bataks were Muslim, another 100,000 were Christian; the rest had remained pagan.

Upon reaching magnificent Lake Toba, we passed through countless Batak villages, where we received a variety of welcomes. Villagers who had seen white men and motorcycles tended to crowd about us in curious throngs. The inhabitants of more remote villages, however, generally flashed their angry eyes at us, shouted at every attempt to photograph them and ran into their homes, firmly bolting the door behind them. Children were especially scared of the motorcycle and ran in various directions each time we came in sight. Others would start crying or screaming, still others would hide behind trees or climb up into the protective embrace of their branches. In some villages, we would encounter a group of angry villagers gesturing frantically for us to leave their territory. At moments like this, we usually availed ourselves of our guns, which they recognized by sight. A few warning shots, and even the angriest villagers would run back to their homes as fast as their legs could carry them.

"Look, it's your mother-in-law," the two of us would joke each time we spotted a Batak woman. Batak women were ugly in a legendary manner. They were naked to the waist, wrinkled and dirty, and constantly chewing betel. The disgusting yellow fluid left two visible lines at the corners of their mouths and down their chins, in the direction it usually flowed. According to Batak custom, the teeth of young girls were filed almost to the level of their gums. This way, Batak women gave the impression of toothless hags.

We mused sorrowfully on our poor luck with women. Arabian woman, for example, had been beautiful with their delicate features, deep, fiery eyes, and fine figures, but alas, they had insisted on wrapping themselves in white sheets so that only their eyes were visible. Batak women, who were almost nauseating in their ugliness, boldly went about in their birthday suits.

Pigs were just as ugly as the women; we simply called them "Batak pigs." They had long, sharp, funny-looking noses and were entirely black, very skinny, and covered with bristles. Remarking that there were no dogs in the village, we soon learned that the Bataks loved dogs so much that they ate them. Any dog unfortunate enough to be caught by a hungry Batak was quickly roasted.

Sumatran Batak woman

Occasionally, we saw women wearing clothes, which were invariably long shirts, dark blue in color, with similarly blue, bundle-like headdresses to match. Children, of course, walked about entirely naked.

Lake Toba was a picturesque spot. Not so long ago, foreigners unwise enough to approach the holy lake had paid for their hastiness with their lives. Today, there's a hotel on its shores. The lake is nothing but a large crater, approximately 90 kilometers in diameter. The Island of Samosir, shaped much like the lake itself, graces the center of this body of water lined by high mountains, some of them functioning volcanoes. The steep volcanic mountains slope to the very edge of the clear, blue water, which, at its deepest, reaches 500 meters.

We spent the night in a tent by the shore of the lake. This solution was cheaper and infinitely more pleasant than spending the night in the dubious hotel of a dirty village. As we weren't able to purchase any food from the Bataks, we resorted to our canned goods. Canned dinners weren't too bad, provided they didn't occur too often. Thanks to the canning industry, we could sit in the middle of Sumatran nowhere enjoying a menu of bacon, French liver paste, California fruits, and washing it all down with delicious Ceylon tea.

A night spent in the open was not without its dangers. Wild animals, men, and snakes could all prove harmful. Whenever we felt our position to be especially perilous, we built a large fire. The large fire did not always have a large flame, however, so more often than not, we would take turns watching, gun in hand, as the other slept. Many mornings, we woke to find that both of us, watcher and watched, had fallen asleep and slept on comfortably as a group of curious natives sat around and looked on. One time, Gyuszi and I fell asleep on the motorcycle; we slumbered through a jungle night, with me perched on the driver's seat and Gyuszi comfortably snoozing in the sidecar.

Batak houses far surpassed those of the Minangkabu; Batak homes were constructed of wood and bamboo and carved in fantastic and intricate shapes. Roofs were built with large eaves to protect the inhabitants both from heavy rains and from the rays of the tropical sun.

As we traveled on, the jungle revealed to us some further treasures in the form of flesh-eating plants and flowers and giant spiders that occasionally caught monkeys in their webs. Some days passed without our encountering a single human soul. We generally traveled at night, however, when hunting was better. If an animal crossed the road in front of us, or if we merely stopped our motorcycle but left the headlights on, we saw the light reflected in the flashing eyes of the nocturnal animals. Our hunting was unusual in that we never quite knew what we were shooting at, seeing as we didn't have the necessary experience to be able to tell wild beasts by the way their eyes reflected the light. The animals themselves were hidden of course, sometimes in the tall grass, other times in the thicket, so that all we saw of them were their flashing eyes. We generally aimed between the eyes; and the combination of patience and a high quality rifle usually brought results. Shooting at an especially large, brilliant pair of eyes, we were often convinced we were going to down a tiger, only to realize moments later that we had killed a small bird or an innocent gazelle.

Of course, a hunter's luck could turn any moment. It was on the island of Sumatra that we shot the largest beast that ever fell victim to our hunting prowess: a tiger! And we shot him with a rifle, too! The truth be told, we weren't expecting such large game as we neared the body of our victim, and were surprised and shocked upon seeing the tiger's stripes through the foliage. We ran back to our vehicle as fast as our legs could carry us. After all, what if the tiger was still alive? What if it was merely wounded and getting ready to pounce? Once we were sitting on the motorcycle, we drove closer and shone the lights on him. Then, cautiously leaving the vehicle, we made our gunned way to the animal. Sure enough, it was a tiger, and a dead one. The bullet had

Batak houses on Sumatra

entered its head from relatively close range. We were filled with inexpressible pride and joy; after all, we were no longer mere world travelers, but Sumatran tiger-hunters.

We had the tiger skinned the very next day. The skin dried in the sun, but we had no time to curry it. Upon reaching Medan, we had it cut into further parts and made into seat covers for our sidecar, where the skin of the tiger we had killed in Sumatra graced our vehicle for years. The natives were almost as happy as we were upon learning we had killed the tiger that had been ravaging their flocks for a long time.

We also saw fellow hunters among the natives. These men went about entirely naked, armed with blow-pipes and giant bows and poison arrows. They

The first and only tiger we killed, in Sumatra

only hunted during the day, but were courageous enough to leave the confines of the road. Whenever a group of hunters saw us, the otherwise bold men would scurry off into the vegetation. Of course, it was understandable; they had never seen a motorcycle.

Before reaching Medan, we encountered our first orangutans. It was raining so hard that we were forced to stop and cover our vehicle and ourselves with tarps. A bit further down the road, we saw a giant figure of a man snapping twigs. Where there was one man, there were bound to be more, we reasoned, so we started our engine in the hopes of avoiding an encounter with suspicious looking people in an entirely deserted place. As we whizzed past the "man," we found him not to be a man at all, but a well-grown monkey specimen. We stepped on the gas pedal and were only relieved when there was quite a lot of distance between us and the orangutan.

The first fork in the road came after the town of Pematang Siantar. Here, we headed toward the famous Brastagi resort and the fertile Plains of Deli in an effort to reach Medan, our final destination.

The landscape was changing fast. We learned quite a bit about the natives, including the methods they used to rid themselves of evil spirits. Now, we were used to the natives showing us a degree of respect. We weren't always sure whether it was out of fear or respect, but natives traveling along the road tended to step aside and let us pass. On our way to Medan, however, we encountered an entirely new phenomenon. Not only would natives refuse to let us pass, they would actually place themselves squarely in the way of our motorcycle and refuse to budge despite our honking and shouting. Not knowing what to do next and suspecting a ruse of some kind, we drove on, straight at the resolute man and would have hit him had he not jumped to the side at the very last moment. As this nearly-hit-and-run scene repeated itself a number of times, we were sure there was a reasonable explanation of the strange behavior of the natives. In Medan, we found out that the men standing in our way had simply been attempting to drive demons from their bodies. These people believed that their bodies were inhabited by evil spirits, which had to be purged, and so they would stand in the middle of the road and wait for any fast vehicle, be it an automobile or a motorcycle, to approach at full speed, waiting for the very last moment to jump to the side and thereby save their lives. The demons living inside them, however, were believed to be much slower, and so they were hit and run over by passing vehicles as the bodies of the people they had inhabited lived on. Of course, natives had a way of ridding themselves of evil spirits even before the advent of the motorcycle, and we often saw them sprint toward the shores of a deep river or the edge of a cliff, only to pull back at the very end. With the demon drowned or crushed to death in the abyss, the natives would return home with peaceful smiles.

The countryside grew more and more populous as we made our way to Medan; plantations spread on all sides where the rainforests had been. There were giant cultivated tracts of land in the vicinity of Medan, and the natives were braver, cleaner, and more intelligent. Out in the rice fields, we saw village women threshing rice with their bare hands. Most of the workers were positioned under a protective awning to protect them from the rays of the sun. These workers no longer hid when the motorcycle passed by but ran out onto the road to greet us. What's more, they were neither naked nor wearing sarongs, rather, pants of various kinds seemed to be the norm. Some men wore European-style pants, other sported colorful pajama pants.

The rice fields were followed by vast forests of caoutchouc trees. The plantations were in European hands; hard-working natives scurried back and forth among the carefully numbered trees. Still further on, we encountered plantations of tea. It was not uncommon to find tea growing side by side with coffee and caoutchouc. There was nothing but the green of ripening tea all around; harvest had begun on some of the plantations. Hundreds of coolies were gathered to collect the leaves in large sacks, which were then loaded onto trucks waiting along the road. The tea leaves were transported to tea factories, where they were dried and packaged.

The plantations were normally interspersed with villages, which in turn were surrounded by rice fields, orchards, or coconut trees, which were planted and cared for by the natives. We saw men plowing the fields; hitched to their plows were the *karbau*, lazy buffalo whose task was to draw the simple wooden implements along the muddy rice fields.

Arriving in Brastagi, we realized that Brastagi was to Sumatra what Darjeeling was to India and Tosari to Java. Brastagi was a splendid mountain resort at more than 1,600 meters above sea-level. Only two hours from Medan, it offered a mild, spring-like respite to us and to those Sumatrans who had the means of escaping the sweltering tropical heat of the lowlands. The city of Brastagi was hemmed in by two picturesque volcanoes, the peaks of Sibajak and Sinabung.

One of the last impressions we have of Sumatra is the sight of endless tobacco plantations stretching throughout the Deli region and into Medan. Tobacco was the most important of Sumatran products; in fact, Sumatran cigarettes were known worldwide. The monotony of the fields was broken only by large drying stations. Each field was surrounded by four to five rows of trees planted side by side. These trees, with their large leaves and dense foliage, provided not only excellent wood for building but also served to protect the tobacco from men, animals, and the dust of the road. Some fields were allowed to lie fallow; the earth needed its repose after all. The tropical rainforests reclaimed the fallow ground within two years, but the fields were let alone for a period of up to five or six years. Everything grew very fast near the Equator. Ten-year-old trees in Sumatra looked like forty-year-old tree giants in Hungary, and all manner of trees, bushes, and trailers managed to reconquer the fallow lands, so that a small deforestation campaign was required before the fields could be used again.

It was on the road between Brastagi and Medan that we lived through our last dangerous Sumatran adventure. Traveling along the slope of a mountain, we found ourselves amidst a formidable tropical storm. As the rain was pouring from the rent clouds, we were forced to stop and wait for the storm to recede. After a short while, we began to worry that the heavy rains would wash us and our motorcycle down the side of the mountain, so, to be on the safe side, we secured our vehicle to some large trees nearby with the help of ropes we carried. Just half an hour after casting our lot and the lot of our motorcycle with wayside trees, we heard inordinate rumbling coming from approximately one hundred meters down the road. The forest soil was virtually billowing along the road. We were in the middle of a landslide. Water, soil, stones, entire hillsides, and uprooted trees tumbled onto the road in front of us. It was impossible to continue on. We spent the night wedged in this far-from-comfortable place and managed to clear the road sufficiently the next morning to allow us to pass and continue our journey to Medan.

Medan is the capital of Eastern Sumatra, a modern small town with a population of 20,000. Its harbor, by the name of Belawan Deli, lies at a distance of twenty kilometers from the city proper. We made a rest stop in Medan, and during our few days there, we discovered that it was an important center for the European plantation owners, who gathered every second Sunday for fun and games, in an effort to let off steam after two weeks of head-scratching and back-breaking labor. The city therefore glowed with life twice a month. Drinks and money flowed equally swiftly in the European hotels. Many young Europeans earned excellent wages, which they spent on alcohol for lack of better amusement. White women were about as rare as black swans, but money there was in vast quantities! A note to the ladies...

Medan was the only city in the Dutch Indies that boasted rickshaws. Tiny, native-owned shops were wedged between the pompous residences of the plantation owners. The signs in many of the shop windows brought a smile to our lips. Pious natives who had allowed themselves to be baptized for one Dutch Florin received proper German Christian names, and so shop owners, their names spelled out in bold, colorful letters in their shop windows, boasted such incongruities as Johann Tunjungkabumikortewa or Karl Sukebamiworakabumota.

We finally had our chance to go swimming in the ocean, which turned out to be a joyless experience thanks to the *gvallis*, or plate-sized gelatinous sea creatures, notable for the acid they released upon contact. This acid, when it came in contact with our own bodies, caused a painful, burning sensation reminiscent of the sting of nettles, which refused to go away until the next morning. Gyuszi and I both have our *gvalli* memories.

We met fellow Hungarians in Medan. There were few Hungarians in the Dutch Indies, as Hungarian artisans or laborers stood no chance against cheap native labor. In fact, the trickle of immigrants from Hungary had dried up altogether. The fortunate Hungarians we encountered had arrived in earlier, more favorable times. Others settled only temporarily.

Here I must take note of the Javanese Hungarian doctors. Those specialists who had been brave enough to undertake work on the tropics at the request of the Dutch government had received their reward. Hungarian doctors had not only made progress in their fields and attained widespread renown, they had also amassed what amounted to small fortunes. And of course, they brought honor to their homeland, which was no trivial consideration. It was no joke for eight to ten Hungarian doctors to rise a head above the thousands of doctors on Java. Not that Dutch doctors were much competition. Nevertheless, Hungarian doctors were trusted throughout Java, as I myself found out. While traveling through a small town, we were told there was a Hungarian doctor living there who would most likely be delighted at a visit from his compatriots. We paid this doctor a visit only to find that he didn't speak a word of Hungarian. The young man was terribly embarrassed. No wonder, because he wasn't Hungarian at all, but an Austrian from Vienna who had told his Javanese fellows that he was Hungarian in order to gain their confidence.

We did find authentic Hungarian doctors in Djokjakarta, Semarang, and Batavia, even in Padang, on the island of Sumatra. We will treasure the memory of the pleasant hours spent together forever. While on the island of Java, we spent the Christmas holiday with a compatriot of ours, who, after creating an Old World atmosphere, began recounting his difficulties in adjusting to the unexpected challenges men of his profession faced on the colonies. He explained that he had been forced to set aside Hungarian medical ethics in order to better serve his patients, who were, for the most part, wealthy Chinese with a distinctly different image of the ideal doctor. As it turned out, to the average Chinese patient, the doctor wasn't simply a medical professional, but a lawyer and general counselor.

Temperatures "dropped" to 35 degrees C by the time we sat down to our Christmas dinner, but we hadn't been at it for long before our host was called for. The servant announced the arrival of a native in desperate need of an injection of some sort. Although the patient in question couldn't name his illness and would not let himself be examined, nevertheless, he insisted that the injection, and only the injection, would heal him, as it had healed his brother. He did get his shot in the end, but only God and our doctor friend will ever know what was in it. Anyhow, it was certainly neutral, if not helpful, and our new friend earned ten florins for his efforts. If he had charged less or hesitated to administer the shot, the patient would simply have gone on to the next doctor.

Ten minutes later, the phone rang, and duty in the form of a rickshaw called our pajama clad doctor friend away for yet another half hour. Upon his return, he graciously explained that a wealthy Chinese businessman had fought with his wife and called the doctor to set things right. The doctor showed up at their door, listened, soothed, gave advice, and earned another twenty Florins. He had even had time to get us a present on his way back, a cooling thermos, a very practical present on the island of Java.

One of our fellow guests was another Hungarian medical man, renowned professional and official dentist to the sultan and his court. His was an enviable position; the sultan's two hundred wives and countless young princes depended on his services daily.

There were Hungarian families in most of the larger towns we visited. They remained good Hungarians despite the distance from their motherland and strove hard to keep traditional Hungarian households. A Hungarian woman doctor, responsible for setting up a children's clinic in one of the Javanese towns, plantation owners and administrators, the high-ranking Dutch-Hungarian statesman in Bandung whose brother owned a hotel in Batavia were only a few of the Hungarians we met on our Javanese journey. Böske Bodor and her band made beautiful music at the Grand Hotel in Semarang, while a talented young Hungarian was engaged in mapping the unknown territories of immense Sumatra. Another Hungarian of a more clandestine nature spent only parts of the year on Sumatra, capturing wild animals, which he later smuggled out of the country and sold to large zoos abroad. Finally, there were Hungarian plantation-owners on Sumatra, who ran their own extensive farms.

We met our last Sumatran compatriot in Medan. He was a respected chemist and traveled constantly from one sugar factory to the next. With so much experience behind him, he was able to fill us in on the fascinating and little-known details of plantation life. His home, furnished luxuriously, was his castle, and his bachelor's life was made comfortable by an army of servants and a number of fine automobiles. When we remarked that he hardly needed all those cars, seeing as the companies he worked for provided him with vehicles for free, he was quick to respond that a man of his rank and financial position was expected to keep cars, whether he needed them or not. He had been living on Sumatra for seven years when we met him and earned a stellar 2,500 Hungarian Pengős a month. A bit of a bohemian, but kindly, as bohemians tend to be, our host explained to us that those who earned beginner's wages worked hardest on the island. As people rose in rank, they worked less and less and earned exponentially more. He himself worked very little, top leaders were paid astronomical sums for doing nothing.

Administrators' positions on a plantation were some of the best jobs to be had. These administrators were overseers of sorts, earning a regular, impressive salary and a fixed percentage of the profits. Of course, overseers didn't always have it easy. Some coolies were difficult to handle, but order and discipline were to be kept at all costs. Occasionally, coolies would resort to violence in an effort to wreak vengeance for a minor offense. Administrators had to be scrupulous and quick, making sure that the punishment never outweighed the crime. We heard of one coolie who killed his administrator's young wife after being unfairly fined two Florins.

Plantation administrators were also responsible for protecting the farm animals against various wild beasts that might stray onto the farm. Occasionally, coolies would disappear without a trace, and one plantation owner was surprised by a tiger on his own verandah while enjoying an afternoon nap. This happened to a Hungarian farmer, and before he or his servants had come to, the tiger had disappeared, carrying the master's prize German shepherd.

Both plantation owners and their employees were dear to the hearts of merchants. Europeans rarely had to pay for what they bought; they had unlimited credit for the most part and were constantly being asked whether they would like to pay by cash or check. Checks could be cashed any time.

We left Sumatra on board a small ship and headed back to the Asian continent we had left so long ago, arriving soon on the Malay Peninsula, which might more aptly be called the Chinese Peninsula.

The Most Beautiful Park in Creation

This was a country like no other we had seen! Rainforests lined the two sides of the road, dark, green, virgin forests in which no man had set foot. The forests teemed with life, innumerable wild beasts that had never seen a human being lived out their lives in its green depths. Our eyes gorged themselves on the incredible sights, and, growing sated, refused to attribute all of this incredible beauty to nature. It felt to us like we were traveling through the set of a multi-million dollar movie for which the producer had striven to gather giant trees, palms, trailing vines, thousands of monkeys swinging on said vines, and a forest more impenetrable than our wildest dreams.

A road ran through this primeval wilderness. To our right and to our left lay hundreds of kilometers of mysterious lush vegetation, and yet, we had the great fortune of traveling along some of the best roads we had encountered, smooth paved road of asphalt and bitumen, straight as the flight of an arrow, without the smallest bump or hindrance. All divergences were marked with clear precision, bridges, bends, and inclines dotted with columns of white stone or lined with a safety fence. What extraordinary countryside and what an extraordinary road! Despite the occasional snake wending its way along the road and despite the cries of the wild beasts resounding throughout, our impression was that we were traveling through an extraordinarily well kept garden watered by the same faithful gardeners who kept the endless stretches of road clean and free of stumbling blocks. We seemed to be traveling through a beautifully arranged park, the greatest park that could be imagined, planted and kept by the Creator and by nature: virgin rainforest.

There were a thousand kilometers between Penang and Singapore, and although the scenery changed dramatically as we progressed, the quality of the roads remained the same. As the day passed, our joy and satisfaction that we had chosen the right direction increased.

The real dilemma had begun once we had reached mainland Asia. Standing in the middle of the Malaysian Peninsula, we couldn't make up our minds whether to head north or south. A brief ferry ride would take us from Penang to the mainland, but where would we go from there?

Malaya, otherwise known as the Malaysian Peninsula, was made up of two parts: the Straits Settlements, which were in British hands and the various Malaysian states. The Malaysian states belonged to two further groups: the Federation of Malaysia, comprised of states such as Perak, Selangor, Negri

Sembilan, and Pahang, all of them under rather strict British surveillance and influence. Although native-born sultans ruled these various states, these sultans were always accompanied by British "advisers." The non-confederate Malaysian States, such as Kedah, Perlis, Kelantan, Trengganu, and Johor were ruled in much the same way.

The Straits Settlements were most important to the British from a colonial, economic, and strategic point of view and were therefore naturally named crown colonies. Penang and the small states across from it: Wellesley, Dindings, Melaka, and Singapore therefore did not have the option of joining either the confederate or the non-confederate Malaysian states. The above states were all located on the southern end of the very long and narrow peninsula. The northern part of the peninsula belonged to Siam, and, still further north, in an intimate embrace with Malaysia, lay Burma.

Our confusion was complete. We took the opportunity to stop at the Penang railway station and mull over our options. The Penang station was the most fascinating of its kind. The station building was of the highest order and outfitted with everything necessary: ticket-windows, waiting-rooms, buffets and restaurants, restrooms, newspaper stands, and street vendors were all in their proper places; the only thing missing was the railroad itself. There were motorboats however, intended to carry the passengers from the station buildings to the rails themselves and back again.

We made good use of the large maps available at the station. Our goal being Siam, one option was to head due north until we hit the border. The problem was that there were no roads to speak of in Siam; the only way to get to Bangkok was by sea or via the railroad. If we chose the sea or railroad route, we would miss nearly all of British Malaya, as well as Singapore. Heading south, however, would mean retracing our steps once we reached Singapore and riding our bike back to Penang or taking a ship straight to Bangkok. Throwing our hands up in confusion, we headed south, and were very grateful we did.

Our beautiful journey south and the many fascinating sights along the way only served to reinforce our decision. Fifty to sixty years ago, the entire peninsula had been a mystery, as little as seventy years ago, there wasn't a single white man among its inhabitants. The tiger, elephant, rhinoceros, and buffalo had lorded it over the intractable jungle wilds. Then came the caoutchouc plantations, a veritable death sentence passed on the rainforests. The various indigenous tribes had since been subjugated by outsiders both white and Chinese, who managed to make great fortunes on the fertile lands of the peninsula. The advent of civilization, however, was slow and arduous. Even in the western portion of the island, the part that was best-known and most civilized, vast stretches of land were still swathed in rainforests. The indigenous tribes who dwelt in the jungles had managed to preserve their primitive way of life. The Semang people, woolly-haired and Negroid in features, dwelt in tree-houses, wore clothing made of leaves, and wielded blowguns. The Sakei people, lighter skinned and originally stemming from Indo-China, led a very similar life. Two more groups completed the spectrum of indigenous tribes: members of the Jakun tribe, who were the pirates of Malaysia and the Muslim Sam-Sam, who traced their origins to Siam.

The Malaysians here were mostly of Minangkabu origin, had come from Sumatra, and preserved their ancient customs. Women ruled this strictly matriarchal society. Indian and Chinese immigrants had arrived much later than the Minangkabu. Malaysians, Chinese, and Europeans comprised the ruling class in a population of roughly one million.

Although we were far from China itself, we had plenty of opportunities to become acquainted with the Chinese people and their customs. Chinese men were either merchants or plantation owners. There were Chinese signs in every town; fancy, colorful Chinese palaces regularly stood on the outskirts of larger towns and settlements. Most of the rickshaws in town were Chinese-run, as the Chinese tended to be either very wealthy or destitute. Wealthy Chinese wore European-style clothes or white linen pants, while Chinese commoners, men and women alike, opted for black canvas. Chinese women were the most comfortably clad of the world's female population: their baggy pants reached just below their knees and were compliemented by a capacious blouse of the same fabric and wooden clogs, which created a deafening clatter on the paved streets.

The people of Malaysia bore the English yoke well. English politicians had solved the independence issue once and for all. Indigenous Malaysians were well aware that they would not be able to rule the large number of Chinese immigrants who had settled on their peninsula, and so they opted for British rule instead in all of their confederate and non-confederate states, with or without the agreement of their sultans. The Chinese were also satisfied with their popular, educational, and economic superiority and dependent on the British to keep order and the well-oiled machinery of the economy running.

We reached Singapore after a thousand-kilometer journey along the Malay Peninsula. Although I had read numerous travelogues as a child and had excelled in school, this country was entirely unknown to me. I knew very little of Malaysia before actually traveling across it, and I feel that I was rivaled in my geographic ignorance by many of my compatriots. Or perhaps I am mistaken. Do we, Hungarians, know the first thing about the magnificent city of Kuala Lumpur, the capital of the state of Selangor, population 100,000? Have we the faintest idea of the beauty of its public buildings, palaces, and modern hotels? Do my fellow Hungarians have any idea that transportation in Kuala

Lumpur excelled by far that of Budapest and that the economy of this great city flourished despite the proximity of the endless rainforests? Neither I, nor many living Hungarians, had heard of the lovely towns of Ipoh, Taiping, Seremban, or Johore Baharu, where Gyula and I were greeted in cordial ceremony by the members of the newest Automobile Clubs.

The quality roads made Malaysia into an automobile paradise. Even the tiniest villages, home to no more than twenty to thirty families, housed large parking lots specially intended for buses. Over a dozen taxi drivers awaited their passengers, who, for the most part, weren't tourists, but poor coolies on their way home after a hard day's work. Coolies had no use for money, as Mother Nature satisfied their immediate needs, and so the wages they did receive went towards amusement, including long, expensive taxi rides. In some parts of Western Malaya, the tree-dwelling Sakei and Semang people left their trees and joined their Chinese and Malaysian brothers in the taxis. In other parts of the state, members of such tree-dwelling tribes were mortally afraid of everything new and strange, especially of the loud noises our motorcycle made. We encountered people who led very primitive lifestyles. Clad in dirty rags, they most resembled the Tamils near Madras, India, who had the same dark skin and bounteous hair.

Automobile promenades were popular in all urban settings, especially in lovely Penang. And what a sight they were! The Chinese enjoy lights anyway, but the citizens of Penang showed their appreciation for glitz by carrying chairs and benches onto the street and perching on them for hours on end, just watching the traffic flow by. The cars were generally filled with Chinese men and women in fancy clothing. The women seemed to have donned all of their jewelry at once, and as the cars inched their way along the promenade, hot on each other's heels, the diamond-wrapped and pearl-clad women leant out into the cool night air, showing off their glamour to the amused lookers-on.

We passed through a number of the lovely towns mentioned above: Taiping, then Ipoh, and Kuala Lumpur, paying visits to two native sultans on our way. These sultans were surrounded by a certain shabby pomp much inferior to the opulence of the Indian princes. We wouldn't have stayed in their courts for long even if they had asked is to, which they did not.

The world of the plantations held much more fascination in our eyes. Before a plantation could be established, however, a relatively large plot of land first needed to be cleared of rainforest. The death of a rainforest generally meant the birth of a new plantation, and on our journey, we had the opportunity to witness the different stages of such a birth. Each time a swathe of rainforest disappears, the clearing must begin from the inside. Workers make their difficult way into the forest, and, once they have arrived at some distance, they turn back and retrace their steps, creating a road back to civilization by clearing the "path" they had followed in. Once the way is clear, it's time to chop down the trees that are in the way of the would-be-plantation. Tropical trees are generally very wide at their base, and so it's easiest to chop away about a meter above ground, where the trunk reaches its more slender dimensions. Work progressed much faster when coolies sawed away into a whole row of trees, taking care to always saw on the same side, then, by felling the last trees in the line, they produced an admirable domino effect among the wounded tropical giants. The stumps usually stayed put for a long time; only after becoming completely dry were they burned to the ground to make way for the caoutchouc trees. Caoutchouc trees were planted in straight lines and hemmed in by irrigation canals. All bushes, thickets, and weeds of all sorts were removed from the vicinity of the precious caoutchouc trees and various species of short, mat-like plants were planted to prevent jungle vegetation from reclaiming its proper habitat.

Plantations were cut into numerous small slices by the roads leading from one end of the establishment to the other. Other necessary elements of plantation life were the coolies' huts, which often formed entire villages, and the elegant homes of the plantation owners, administrative workers, and European officials. Finally, no plantation was complete without the press- and smoke-house.

A single caoutchouc tree usually produced about a tea-cup's worth of milky substance each day, but natives also collected liquid rubber from trees in the wild and used hand-held presses to form this lower quality product into the acceptable shape. Caoutchouc trees were beautiful, not very large, and somewhat reminiscent of our poplars. Of course, as the number of plantations grew, rubber sold for less and less, and the profits, which, for the pioneering plantation owners were astronomical, decreased drastically. Although many of the plantations we saw were Chinese-owned, we saw entire caoutchouc forests belonging to the Dunlop firm on the Malay Peninsula. We'd seen the plantations belonging to Goodyear back in Sumatra.

The caoutchouc plantations alternated with large swathes of jungle and forests of coconut trees. The palm trees were usually planted and tended by natives, and although the rows of trees were straight, the individual trees rejected the strict order imposed upon them and twisted this way and that, sometimes bowing to the ground, sometimes twisting wildly in the direction of the sky. Some palms grew taller than the tallest trees of the jungle, others were so earth-bound that a man could gather coconuts standing on the ground. We had our fill of coconuts in Malaysia!

The people of the peninsula made two million pounds a year exporting coconuts even though vast quantities of coconuts were consumed before they

Caoutchouc tree on a plantation

even left the country. Coconut milk, harvested when the nut itself was green, is an excellent and refreshing drink. The flesh of the coconut is also edible and its shell very useful for making a variety of kitchen utensils, including pots and containers of all sorts. Raw rubber, more often than not, was stored in coconut containers. Coconut trees require very little care, grow of their own accord, and produce fruit by their sixth year. Each tree produces an average of fifty to a hundred coconuts per year, but these are no European nuts; Malaysian coconuts are the size of large cantaloupes. Their husks are ideal for making ropes but also burn well. Few people are aware that coconut shells, because of their absorptive qualities, are used to make gas masks. The white flesh of the coconut, its most precious part, is dried in the sun. This product is called *copra*, which is further used to make coconut oil, soap, or margarine, but it also makes for excellent fodder and fertilizer.

Palm trees grow so tall that harvesting coconuts can be a real challenge. There are people who specialize in coconut-gathering and travel from village

You have to climb high for coconuts

to village. Others work with trained monkeys. The monkey, tied to a long rope to prevent its escape, sidles up the palm tree quick as a wink, and, perched on top, sorts the ripe nuts from the unripe. The ripe nuts it twists and turns until their stems break and the nuts fall to the ground. Passing through the state of Johore alone, we must have seen millions and millions of palm trees.

Besides rubber and coconuts, pineapples comprised another primary Malaysian crop. Back in 1910, all of Malaysia had been covered in jungles. Just two decades after, it was peppered with plantations. Nevertheless, large swathes of virgin rainforest remained. The country was sparsely populated and backward. We passed jungles which were being cut down, in other places, we saw nothing but burning stumps, thickets, and grass. A little further on the large stumps alternated with caoutchouc saplings. In yet other parts of the peninsula, ripe pineapples smiled up at us from the ground. The pineapples were duly made into preserves; the whole pineapple industry was in the hands of the Chinese.

"Stop already, let's have a pineapple," my friend Gyuszi would occasionally shout. While in Malaya, we had more delicious fruit than we knew what to do with. On Java, Sumatra, but most especially in Malaya, we familiarized ourselves with all the delicious fruits the tropics had to offer. We were bored to death of bananas, so were the native children, who, on the other hand, had probably never had an apple. Pineapples were very much to our liking; coconuts were a little high up and therefore, sour, as old Aesop's grapes, but Gyuszi insisted on tasting everything. He plucked, observed, smelled and tasted everything in sight, but only if he saw a monkey eat it before him. After all, what was a good enough for a monkey…

There was variety to please even the most experienced connoisseur. What we found to be rather entertaining was that in the home of the banana, nobody knew what a "banana" was. The banana was known in these parts as a *pisang*, and nobody seemed aware that a *pisang* by any other name would taste as

Yes, we have bananas today

sweet. Oranges were equally widespread, but our new favorite was the papaya, which unfortunately grew on trees, but was nevertheless sweet and reminiscent of cantaloupes. Another interesting fruit was the *nangka* or *duryan,* which grew on narrow stems from the trunk of the tree. A favorite among natives, the *nangka* sent most Europeans running with its pungent ordor and lingering aftertaste. Mangos and *mangistans* were also delicious, but then who could list the magnificent tropical fruits unknown in our parts, whose taste and savor exceeds that of most of our fruits.

As we traveled on, the road was still lined with trees. Would-be firewood was usually burned on the spot rather than carted away. Who needed all this wood anyway? Gyuszi and I were often forced to make our way across burning forests, as the only road led through them, and we didn't want to waste weeks of our time waiting for the fires to die out.

217

Magnificent tropical fruits

Malaysia, besides being rich in plantations, was also home to innumerable mines, especially in the vicinity of Ipoh, where zinc and tin were produced in large quantities. There were all types of mines, panners worked alongside multi-million dollar machinery. The workers, from the panners in the streams to the coolies running the machinery, were all Chinese.

Traffic seemed to increase once we had passed Kuala Lumpur. As there was no railroad, everybody was forced to take to the splendid modern roads, mostly in not-so-splendid, rickety old cars. We were stuck behind a large, lumbering truck for quite some time, and, to our consternation, encountered the bloody, mangled body of a snake, then a dog. At this point, we hurriedly passed the truck, afraid the next road kill would be an unfortunate native.

Two hundred and fifty kilometers before Singapore, we reached the city of Melaka. This old city, originally founded by Portuguese colonists, lay on the fetid seashore and was comprised of stone houses lining narrow streets, no shade and the merciless rays of an uncompromising sun. Aside from a few descendants of the Portuguese, the town was inhabited by Chinese families. Melaka was home to the world-famous bamboo walking stick, however, this was a nicety we could do without.

An eight-hundred-meter long pier connected Johore Baharu, the seat of the sultan of Johore, with the island of Singapore. The pier was a full twenty meters wide, wide enough for a road and a set of railroad tracks. Twenty-five kilometers later and at the other end of the island, we rode into Singapore.

Out of the 420,000 people living in Singapore, 320,000 were Chinese, 60,000 Malaysian, 30,000 Indian, and only a few thousand European. The city reflected these proportions; it was distinctly Chinese for the most part. The streets were paved but without sidewalks, and very dirty. We reached Singapore after an exhilarating Malaysian journey, and were one of the very few people who arrived in this great international sea-port via land. The city was extremely busy, teeming with automobiles, buses, streetcars, and rickshaws. The European district was lined with palaces, shops, and fancy hotels. Music flowed from the hotel restaurants, where world travelers sat side-by side exchanging stories and downing one drink after the next. The streets were filled with noisy Chinese throngs.

An "imported" Indian policeman of sorts was making feeble attempts at directing traffic. This curious man did not move his hands. Attached to his back were two wooden signs, one saying "stop," the other, "go," and it was by pulling a bit of string attached to these signs that he created, for himself, an illusion of order.

While walking the colorful streets of Singapore, we were surprised to discover that the Chinese did not dry their wash on clothes lines or even wires, like all the other nations of the earth. Instead, they stuck their pants, shirts, and underclothes on long poles and hung them out their windows. Many such flags waved from the windows of each Chinese family.

Singapore, and, indeed, all of Malaya, was the most expensive part of the world. Local currency was strong; a single Straits dollar was worth three Hungarian Pengő. A single night at our very mediocre hotel cost ten Straits dollars. It seemed to us that costs had been growing throughout the Asian portion of our journey. Java, we had thought, must be the most expensive place in the world, but we soon found prices on Sumatra to exceed those on Java, then came Penang, which we perceived to be astronomically expensive until we reached Singapore. We often wondered how much higher the prices could possibly go. Then again, we were in fine shape as long as our Chinese friends continued to show interest in us and in our undertaking. Of course, we turned their vanity to our advantage. Everyone who had purchased a copy of our book was allowed to record his name in a fancy anti-guestbook of sorts we had assembled for the occasion. This was balm for the Chinese soul, and many would have been outright insulted had they not had a chance to record their names in our lovely book.

A hundred ships sailed in and out of the Singapore harbor on any given day. Most of the seven thousand Singaporean rickshaws stood on the shore, their owners anxiously waiting for a customer, who might be from practically any country in the world. There was an overwhelming number of British and American tourists; many of them were going tiger-hunting in Malaya. These fierce tiger-hunters were, more often than not, simple American businessmen. But then, for a handsome price, anyone could become a fierce hunter in Malaya…

"Winged" Singaporean policeman

There were whole tiger-hunting businesses that took care of everything for a certain fixed sum. Customers were properly dressed and provided with the necessary weapons, transported to the jungle and placed in a very comfortable tree-house. Then, with the help of some raw meat, usually from an animal it had killed a short while ago, the tiger was lured within shooting distance. Up in the tree-house, a Malaysian hunter would aim, and the American businessman would pull the trigger. Just in case he still managed to miss, a professional hunter perched in the next tree-house would make sure to fire at the same time and finish off the unsuspecting tiger. Of course, our heroic businessman would then return to America and tell tall tales of his harrowing adventures hunting tigers in Malaysia. The tiger skin as well as an original movie of the various stages of the hunt, were generally included in the thousand dollars.

We met only two Hungarians in Singapore: a vagabond pianist and a ladies' hairdresser. The hair-dresser was quite a character! He had spent only a month learning the trade before coming out to Singapore to try his luck. Our hapless beautician admitted to giving the worst hair-cuts in all of Singapore and generally avoided encounters with people whose hair he had "dressed." At one point, he made such a mess of a little girl's hair that her father beat him up. To make matters worse, he spoke no language but Hungarian. Nevertheless, he pursued his dream with great tenacity, landing jobs at new salons each time he was sacked. We figured if he had the chance to practice a couple more months, he'd end up mastering the trade, which, in Singapore, provided a man with an excellent living. His one worry was that one of the women he'd unwittingly stripped of her crowning glory would have him arrested before he achieved his dream.

Leaving Singapore, we also left behind the lands of the Malaysians: Java, Sumatra, and Malaya, where we had enjoyed pleasant roads and accumulated a wealth of interesting experiences. Those familiar with the first-rate asphalt, marble, granite, and laterite roads of Malaysia will certainly agree when I grant Malaysia, along with India and Ceylon, the title of "The Happy Cycling Grounds of Asia."

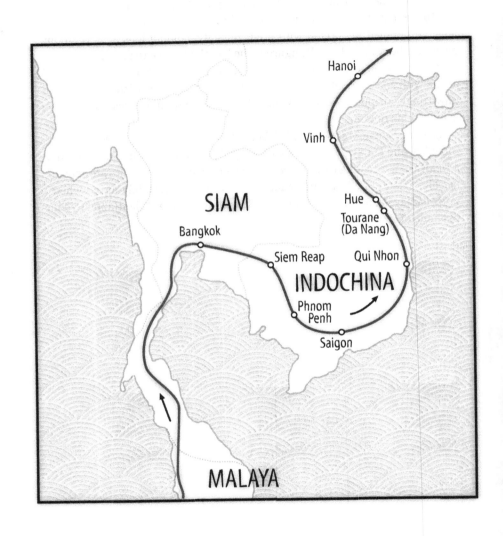

Siam and Indochina

Home of the White Elephant

Our Siamese journey began with a sore disappointment. While exploring the attractions of Krung-Thep, or Bangkok, we happened upon the white elephants. As white elephants are considered holy in these parts, they mostly get away with eating large quantities of food and not doing a whit of work all their days. Even visitors were expected to feed the saintly creatures; "After all, it's tradition," the guard told us, while handing over a few sprigs of sugar cane in return for a handsome tip.

Our bubble burst as soon as we spotted the famous creatures. The white elephants were not white! And no amount of imagination could make them so. Granted, they were somewhat lighter than your average elephant, but only somewhat. Certain specimens even sported lights spots on their hides, but far from being white, these spots were pink or straw-blonde.

We were traveling north, but instead of the weather growing cooler, it essentially got warmer as we journeyed deeper and deeper into spring and then hot summer. Siam was interesting and independent, but it was missing something essential to all bikers: roads. We struggled long and hard to make our way through the tractless wilds of Siam. I don't think anybody had tried a similar feat before us. The railroad was splendid and modern and in the hands of the wealthiest and most influential men of the country, mostly the princes of the land. These same people governed the country and were technically responsible for the roads, but they weren't about to sacrifice a portion of the income to improve the infrastructure of a country crisscrossed by myriads of water-ways, which were the traditional avenues of transportation. Land travel was virtually unknown in Siam.

We stuck to the dams separating rice fields and rode them, at snail's pace, past unknown lands and people. Occasionally, we were forced to leave the relative comfort of the dams for muddy rice fields. Hiring guides at every major juncture, we made our way from village to village, towed by water buffalo through the muddiest portions of the trip. *Nota bene:* unless you insist on exploring the somewhat more civilized northern portion of Siam, it's best to stick to Bangkok and vicinity. There really isn't much to see outside of

Gorgeous temples in Bangkok

Bangkok, or Krung Thep, but the capital is uniquely Siamese and more than worth visiting.

Bangkok, with a population of 800,000, was an infinitely varied and fascinating place with good roads leading both through the town and to nearby towns in the region. We saw a good number of automobiles in town but no motorcycles whatsoever. Our bike was duly surrounded by throngs of curious natives wherever we went. There was a grand total of 5,000 cars in all of Siam, which was a very small number considering the size of the country and the veritable car-worship of its neighbors.

Magnificent palaces, many-turreted temples, original Siamese art and customs, and eccentric dancing were some of the highlights of our Siamese journey. Not a minute passed by but it brought something new and exciting. Holidays abounded, and each holiday brought its own set of colorful festivities. A visitor might spend weeks in Siam without once feeling bored.

Siam is a part of Indochina. This giant peninsula between India and China has been a bone of contention for various peoples for many years. European colonists made their own dash for the meaty bone in the sixteenth century, since which time Indochina consists of three parts. The French ruled the eastern portion of the peninsula, known as French Indochina. The British lion swallowed up the western territories: Burma and Malaya, while the centrally located kingdom of Siam preserved its proud independence.

The Chao Phraya, or Me Nam River, has its source in the mountains of the north and brings life-giving water to most of the country. Krung Thep was established on the banks of the Chao Phraya; both the capital and the entire country are "water-based." Bangkok is not an old city; it was founded in 1765 after the destruction of the original capital, Ajuthia, in the Burmese war. The city is a vast network of channels and waterways; all parts are eminently accessible by water and by land. Hundreds of thousands of people live in houseboats on the channel, and *klongs,* as they are locally known, have come to replace traditional streets. Once on the water, we observed not just tranquil houseboats but a myriad of forms of channel-life. Boats came and went, "street"-vendors strove to get rid of their wares, entire shops, restaurants, even hotels floated peacefully along. Occasionally, parts of a channel would get so crowded with buyers and sellers that entire water-markets were born. Some boats had been stuck in the same place for years, others, like the water-taxis, for instance, were much more agile and would take you from one end of town to the other for a few coins.

Tourism was on the rise, as evidenced by the number of large cruise ships landing in the Krung Thep harbor each day. The king of Siam, realizing the economic potential in tourism, had recently turned one of his many palaces into a posh hotel by the name of Phya Tai. Not only was Phya Tai a luxurious establishment, clients also had the satisfaction of knowing they were spending the night in a royal palace.

In the squares, on the streets, and throughout the city parks, the form of entertainment par excellence was the puppet theater, a popular establishment in the Punch and Judy vein. Hundreds upon hundreds of natives thronged about each puppet stand and enjoyed the various performances immensely. We ourselves also preferred the puppet theater to the classical Siamese theater, where the movements of the performers, like those of traditional dancers, were classical and unique, but also highly repetitious and therefore soon tiring.

The inner courtyard of the Ministry of Defense was populated by white elephants, the outer courtyard crowded with decrepit canons from Germany and the Austro-Hungarian Monarchy. They hadn't been there for long, and the story of how they got there is an interesting one. Evidently, an influential Hungarian businessman had managed to convince the Siamese government that important public buildings were best graced by canons captured in combat and proceeded to sell the gullible officials a whole shipload of worthless military rubbish. The old canons proudly grace Bangkok's public places to this day.

It didn't take us long to grow to love the Siamese. They were an intelligent, skilled, and hospitable people. Their one character flaw, one we had observed

The Wat Arun, or porcelain tower, in Bangkok, Siam

with many other nations, was that they thought a little too much of themselves. They were somewhat light-headed, had a great love of bets and duels, and an inclination towards the fine arts.

We marveled at the colorful turrets all over town and at the beauty of the *wats*, or temples. Porcelain seemed to be quite the popular form of decoration. The Siamese imported entire shiploads of broken china, vases, ceramic dishes, and used the colorful shards to decorate the roofs and the towers of their temples, from their bases to the highest heights. When the sun shone on any such tower, it lit up in a splendid, kaleidoscopic way. The most beautiful of the towers, in our eyes, was the famous porcelain tower, the Wat Arun. Wat Arun was only one of more than 300 temples and palaces situated all over Krung Thep. To truly appreciate the architectural prowess of this glorious people, visitors would have to examine each and every one of these master-pieces, but most especially the Pantheon, home to the ashes of kings of old, the Wat Phra Kao, or Temple of the Diamond Buddha, and the numerous demon figures standing guard outside of these temples. Everything we saw was blissfully free of outside influence; the monumental proportions, intri-cacy, rich gilding, and sheer, riotous color were extraordinary. Statues of Buddha in gold, silver, bronze, wood, and enamel surrounded us.

Siamese architecture deserves the "Indochinese" epithet. The temples, at their most basic, are built in a Chinese style, but the tall, slender pagodas, called both *praprangs* and *pracheddis* are reminiscent of the Hindu and Bud-dhist architecture of India. The Siamese have managed to combine these two disparate styles into a unique single style. They borrowed the weighty roofs from the Chinese, but created something new in their use of columns and ce-ramic decoration. The usual heavy ornamentation of Hindu temples is miss-ing, resulting in holy places with a much more tranquil atmosphere.

The women of Bangkok were highly modern, mostly sporting short hair. There were more page-boy haircuts among Siamese women than in any coun-try of Europe. At first we were amazed that this relatively revolutionary Euro-pean fashion had made it so far east and so fast but soon realized that Siamese women had been wearing their hair short much longer than their Eu-ropean counterparts. During the Burmese war, it is said, Siamese women fought like men on the battlefield, and once the war was over, the "weaker sex" who had fought as valiantly as the men were granted the privilege of wearing their hair short.

The Siamese language proved to be an insurmountable obstacle. As the en-tire writing system was foreign, we stood completely helpless in the face of their indecipherable script. Languages with their own distinct alphabets are always hardest to learn. To make things worse, very few Siamese spoke for-eign languages, although we did get by fairly well with English.

Out of a population of ten million Siamese, we encountered a single compa-triot. This fellow Hungarian had been working as a leading official in a German firm in Krung Thep for some years. I believe the delight of our encounter was mutual, as he most likely hadn't heard a word of his mother tongue in years.

After saying our good-byes to our newfound friend, we headed off into the pathless countryside. Rice fields, channels and rivers alternated in rapid

Short-haired Siamese women

succession. Although the distance to the border with Indochina was a mere 240 kilometers, it took us eight whole days to get there. We struggled on as best we could, by boat or ferry, manpower, but most often, with the help of the water buffalo. Of course, we kept handing out rewards to the helpful Siamese; in the end, the amount of baksheesh it cost us to get to the border would have bought us two plane tickets in the same direction.

Yet we had the satisfaction of having arrived at the border by land. Not far from the border, we were engulfed in a sea of mud and were forced to scrape the sticky clay off our motorbike wheels every few steps. After a while, the situation got so bad that we removed our fenders and let our wheels, chains and all, spin helplessly in the quagmire.

The rice fields of Siam, much like their Sumatran counterparts, were a wonder to behold. Each plot of land was family owned and the master of the house watched over the tender rice shoots with eagle eyes, anxious to protect them from the ravage of flocks of hungry birds. He did this with the help of an intricate network of string arranged in a web-like manner, with all the strands running together at one edge of the field, as at a telephone station. The farmer sat on a high platform of bamboo built up at the edge of the field, the end of each strand in his hands. The strings were all attached to wooden levers, which, in turn, were decked with ribbons and scraps of fabric. Whenever a bird landed in the field, the farmer would pull the right string, causing the ribbons and rags to flutter and frighten the intruder away. Sometimes, whole flocks of birds attacked his field, but the Siamese farmer would simply commence tugging at all the strings at one time. The farmer or a member of his family generally sat on the bamboo platform day and night; there was always someone present to chase off the birds. Who says the Siamese don't work? They spend half the year shooing feathery intruders. We couldn't but

At the Siamese border

wonder what the farmer would have done had his plot of land been ten times the size of the current one!

We followed the tracks of buffalo-drawn carts across water and mud to finally arrive at the last Siamese village, whose name, Aranja, sounded almost Hungarian to our ears. The Siamese portion of our journey had tired us immensely. At night, we had enjoyed the company of hoards of mosquitoes and reptiles; it was a wonder and our good fortune that we reached the border of French Indochina at all. I think we had the relatively dry weather to thank. Anyhow, we left Siam reflecting on how good it would be to return. Siam was truly a land of possibilities, and although life was still difficult, there was a great future in store for spirited Europeans, especially of the engineer variety.

French Indochina: A Hunter's Paradise

"Halloo! Anybody there? Halloooooo!" "Nobody? *Où sont les douaniers?* We have no time to waste!" Gyuszi and I shouted at the desolate border station, which consisted of a single decrepit wooden hut. Someone was supposed to be checking our passports, going through our belongings, exacting fees and producing stacks of paperwork. And, to our consternation, there was absolutely nobody in sight. Unlike other border stations, this particular tiny outpost between Siam and French Indochina did things its own way. After dutifully waiting a half an hour, we decided to push on into Indochina.

Our high hopes with regard to the quality of the roads were dashed for the moment, and we made our way, Sisyphus-like, through the sea of mud that separated us from the village of Sisophon.

Once in Sisophon, we were delighted to discover the beginnings of a road. Did I say *a* road? There were, in reality, two roads, and for some mysterious reason, they both led to Saigon. When we tried to ask the villagers' advice on which road to take, they simply smiled and nodded, but were of no perceivable help. It seemed the direction our travels were to take was strictly up to us. We were determined to visit Angkor, so the northern road seemed the more logical choice, and once decided, we stuck to our decision despite a French sign clearly stating that the road was impassible. Even an impassible road was better than no road, and Heaven knows, Gyuszi and I had had our share of roadlessness.

The northern road, helpfully labeled as impassible, was, in reality, not so bad. The rainy season had not come, although it was April already. The rains were late that year. The heat, however, more than made up for it. We were up around the fourteenth degree latitude, and we were still so far from the mild spring of more northern lands.

Our road was . . . a road. Occasional large puddles and quagmires made the road "impassible," at least according to French standards. Since the land was flat, we had an easy time avoiding the mud. The road was even paved, for the most part, and we reached exhilarating speeds on the newfound smooth surface.

The monotony of the landscape around us was oppressive. There was nothing to see and not a soul in sight. The rice had been harvested a while ago, and what remained was a barren waste stretching to the horizon on both sides. There was very little shade; trees were few and far between. The houses we saw, almost as rarely as the trees, looked like cages. Their most important element seemed to be the fence. Some houses were completely open, almost transparent, but the fences around them were two- even three-fold. The huts were covered with thatch roofs, and their inhabitants seemed to be in hiding.

We were still in the state of Cambodge. Most of the country is flat and watered by the Mekong river, which has its source in the Himalayas. The Mekong is one of the largest rivers in Asia. When it rains, it spills over and covers hundreds of kilometers of land, fertilizing it with a thick layer of silt. There are wild animals everywhere; we enjoyed a fine hunt ourselves in the close vicinity of the temples at Angkor.

On our way to Angkor Wat, we stopped at the village of Siem Reap, which

Angkor Wat, Cambodia

was a mere six kilometers from the famous ruins. Once at the ruins, we spent an entire day in wonder. Angkor Wat was witness to the artistic prowess, fine taste, and unique conception of the people of Cambodge. The temple at Angkor deserves world fame. It would have taken us weeks to explore and observe every beautiful detail. The old city comprised more than six hundred architectural gems. The artistry of these great monuments spoke eloquently of the glorious past of the Khmer people, who live in such poverty and backwardness today. Angkor Wat had flourished from the ninth century into the fifteenth and lay forgotten and jungle-engulfed until the French colonists rediscovered its splendors in the twentieth century.

It would be impossible for me to describe all that I saw: the stately walls, the gates and galleries, the park and ancient city of Angkor Thom, the numerous noteworthy temples. I have neither the time nor the strength for such a task. Or should I write only of the fifty-one towers of the Bayon Temple and the eleven thousand men and animals peopling its reliefs? Perhaps I should begin with a description of the famous twelfth century temple at Angkor Wat, which is undoubtedly one of the architectural masterpieces of the world. Our day in Angkor Wat will forever be remembered as one of our personal thousand and one nights. Only the religious ideals of India and Brahmin mythology could have given the Khmer people the talent and strength to raise such masterpieces and decorate them so lavishly.

Leaving Angkor, we sped along perfect roads, smooth, stone structures pleasing both to motorcycle and riders. As distances were not very great and the roads remained excellent, we soon reached Phnom Penh. Arriving on the banks of the Mekong River, we were forced to wait for the ferry to take us across the vast stretch of water. The roads persisted in their excellence, and we managed to cross the border with Cochin China the very next day. That same day, we rode into Saigon, the "Paris of the Orient."

Cochin China was a colony, while the other four states: Cambodge, Annam, Tonkin, and Laos were French protectorates. The Mekong meets the sea not far from Saigon, and the river is so large that it includes 2,400 kilometers of waterways.

French Indochina was mostly populated by Annamites, a people of Chinese origin who moved south around the time of Christ. Thirteen of the sixteen million inhabitants of French Indochina called themselves Annamites. Their language, religion, traditions, and Chinese-derived writing system all served as clear proof of their origins. Those of Khmer ancestry, approximately two million in number, lived mostly in the Cambodge (Cambodia) region, along with roughly half a million Chinese immigrants, Indians, a few thousand Europeans and, in the most isolated parts of the country, primitive native tribes. An example of such a tribe were the *moï* people, an entirely nomadic and unclad community of skilled archers, who used their poison-tipped arrows to hunt both animals and human beings. Their excellent body-build, general good health and pleasant tans made us want to throw away all the trappings of modern civilization and run into the embrace of Mother Nature.

Traveling through Cochin China, we not only enjoyed even better roads but also had many opportunities of getting to know the local Annamites. The Annamites wore only black and white; other colors were rare and women often painted their teeth black to match their clothing.

Once in Saigon, we felt like we were back in Europe. The whole city was very French, and the European influence was palpable wherever we went. We heard almost nothing but French in the hotels and shops, as well as on the streets, which were surprisingly clean and orderly. The natives were humble and obedient; their French colonizers cruel. Saigon was a heady mix of traditional Mandarin culture and French creativity and joie de vivre. The night life, the crowded, musical cafes and the countless clubs and bars seemed strange to us after our long travels. There were some restaurants where even the waiters were French. The French colonists weren't nearly as guarded and dignified in their behavior as Englishmen usually were in their own colonies. Life in the French colonies was somehow more direct and true, even though the natives weren't treated nearly as well. We took time to enjoy the delights of French cuisine, and had we not known that we were precisely 13,500 kilometers from Marseille, we might even have forgotten about the tropical heat. Although eating and drinking played important roles in our daily life, we sought out other sources of amusement. Saigon, like Paris, had its own hidden delights, including the countless opium dens. There was a monopoly on opium and a visible sign labeled R.F. over the entrance to every den. Once inside, we found none of the glamour we had expected; opium dens, for the most part, were dirty, crowded, and oppressive. The customers were as dirty and repulsive as the establishment, and we were glad to get a whiff of fresh air upon leaving.

One of the advantages of Saigon was the bon-system, which gave European visitors almost unlimited freedom. The concept behind the system was that any European, regardless of where he was from and whither he was headed, was given unlimited credit in all the hotels of the city. All he had to do was sign a slip of paper, and he could have whatever he desired. We spent days at a hotel without once having to open our wallets. The hotel employees brought our food and cigarettes, cleaned our clothes, posted our letters, and paid our fares, all on the hotel's money. The system was very satisfactory, and we were asked to pay everything in one sum at the end. Pleasantly enough, bons had a funny tendency of getting lost.

The rickshaws in Saigon were named *pous-pouses,* and we often saw impatient Frenchmen using their walking sticks to urge sweating coolies to a faster trot. American sailors, after leaving their army ships, very quickly picked up this habit from the French. They had other, more rambunctious habits I would rather not talk about. Suffice it to say that they always had money and energy for a night on the town, and after a night of revels, the faithful coolie, instead of being compensated for his services, was often simply thrown into the sea.

Although there were only five thousand Frenchmen out of a population of 150,000, their presence transformed life in Saigon. We spent enough time in Saigon to form an idea of the next long section of our journey along the so-called "Mandarin Road," 2,500 kilometers long, stretching from China to Siam. The road was actually a renovated and widened version of the original ancient Chinese road. The distance between Hanoi, the capital of Tonkin, and Saigon was 1,730 kilometers, and the road connecting the two cut through some of the best-known hunting grounds of the region.

Cochin China and its neighbor, Annam, were home to entire herds of game. It was enough to travel a mere thirty kilometers from Saigon to arrive in prime elephant hunting grounds. Bien-hoa, Baria, and Bao-lieu further south were home to large game. Besides elephants, tigers, leopards, wild cats, and wild boar were common throughout Cochin China. There were plenty of wild cattle and wild buffalo, although the Annamites and Laotians had succeeded

French Indochina: hunters' paradise

in domesticating large numbers of the latter. Those who preferred to hunt small game were hardly disappointed by the fine specimens of deer, rabbits, pheasants, partridges, wild turkeys and cocks, pelicans, and marabou storks.

We didn't even have to make an effort to go after the game. It was enough to cruise along the road or take a walk in a secluded patch of forest, and the game veritably leapt in front of your gun. Our guns were loaded and ready from the first moments of our journey. In the time we spent in Cochin China and Annam, we killed more game than in all the other countries we visited combined.

There were groups of Annamites rebelling against the French government, but their efforts met with little success. They merely managed to make traveling somewhat more complicated. The Annamites had an undue fondness for money. These multiple-god-fearing people were willing to sell anything for a few piasters: rice, bananas, coconuts, animals, household deities, wife, and daughters. Most of them were ready to stab your enemy in the stomach for a few coins.

Not far from the Annamite border, a mere one hundred kilometers from Saigon, in the town of Trang-Bom, we enjoyed the hospitality of the only Hungarian family in Indochina. The men, two brothers, had been living there for twenty years; one of them was married to a Hungarian woman. They had read about us in the papers and, not having seen Hungarians in twenty years, they all piled into a car and sped to Saigon to catch us at our hotel. It was there that they invited us to spend a few days in their home, and seeing as we were headed their direction anyway, we accepted the invitation.

The brothers both worked for a French lumber company, and their home stood in a clearing in the middle of the rainforest. We saw by their example that it's possible to grow used to and even to love this kind of life, the unending jungles all around, unexpected animal visitors on the porch, and shotguns as life-companions.

The house itself was outfitted with all the modern amenities, even luxuries. Everything a cultured human being could wish for was contained in that jungle home, from a radio and piano, to running water, electricity, an icebox, large library, even a pool-table. Leaving the well-equipped house, however, there was no telling what danger the hapless adventurer would face: tigers, elephants, poison snakes, parasites, and unfriendly natives were only some of the obstacles to the full enjoyment of the tropical paradise.

Not far from the house lay a stretch of wood ominously called "The Forest of Death." All attempts to clear it had failed; nobody who entered the wood ever came out alive. Whole teams of natives had died in the various attempts, until our compatriots finally shed light on the forest's baleful secret. They used ropes to mark their path into the woods, and it was thanks to these clear markings that they made it out alive once they discovered the source of the danger. Poisonous swamp gases had caused the deaths of so many natives, but the work of cutting down the forest progressed quickly enough after that, with the help of gas-masks, of course.

It was in the company of our newfound friends that we discovered the joys of big-game hunting. Local hunters, that is, real hunters, scorned the type of hunting we had seen on Sumatra. They would never have responded to an ad and sat perched on a tree while the hapless tiger neared the carefully placed bait. These hunters preferred the excitement of the night-hunt, the dangers of an expedition along the narrow trails marked out by lumberjacks.

We had the opportunity to partake of such a hunt twice. We headed into the forest in the company of two coolies, who could not be trusted with weapons, and the two Hungarian brothers. Jungles are frightening enough by day, but we found the forest by night to be no less than petrifying. The only reason we joined the brothers on their trek was because they were known in the entire region as the best hunters.

Walking along the narrow path, we had to take care to fend off the hanging branches and trailers. There were small lights attached to our heads; these we used to locate the shining eyes of the wild animals. The woods were never silent for long; the occasional quiet spell was always interrupted by roars, trumpeting, and growls of some kind. The coolies trembled with fear. They were always seeing things and whispered together continually. Then again, they had some cause to be afraid, as we ourselves soon began spotting pairs of eyes looking at us from various directions. Only the most experienced huntsmen could tell the type of animal by the size and shape of its eyes at night. At one point, I fired my gun at a fluorescent insect. Gyuszi managed to shoot an owl. We grew more and more scared with every shot, just as our sense that we were being watched became stronger. Finally, we managed to hit a few deer. "No shoot now!" the coolies warned us at one point. We crouched in silence as the coolies scrambled up a nearby tree. It didn't take long for us to figure out the reason for their disappearance: a herd of six lumbering elephants crossed the path in front of us and made their dignified exit into depths of the rainforest on the other side. We learned that elephants are the most dangerous game. When wounded, they're implacable and don't give up until they have taken revenge. They're capable of knocking a tree down, hunter and all, in order to get at him, or if the tree is too big, they'll stand there for days, making all escape impossible. We had not counted on elephants and had left the appropriate guns at home, but the sight of the small herd catapulted our compatriots into a state of excitement, and they began enthusiastically planning our elephant hunt the next day.

The following day, we were no longer able to locate the elephants, although we cut and hacked our way fifteen kilometers into the jungle. Needless to say, such excursions kept novice hunters like us on our toes. For one, we had to be on a constant lookout for snakes. Our second day brought more success than the first: two leopards versus deer and assorted small game. One of the brothers and I actually killed one of the leopards, but we later determined that both our hits, taken separately, would have been fatal. We were on our way home when the sight of a pair of shining eyes stopped us in our tracks. The older brother, first in line, broke the heavy silence by firing the initial shot. Then we waited, but nothing happened. We approached the spot where we figured the animal would be, our loaded guns in our hands. To our great joy, we found we had shot a tiger. It was an average-sized animal of great beauty. The bullet had entered its head precisely between its eyes. "I've been hunting His Majesty for quite a while now," one of the brothers said. "He's caused me and my bison a lot of grief." Gyuszi and I remembered the bison returning home night after night, covered in battle scars. Some had been so severely wounded that their flesh had hung in threads. They had to be sewn up to prevent them from bleeding to death.

While in Trang-Bom, we heard that the French official living next door to our compatriots shot a large tiger on the path running by his house. It didn't take long for the dust to settle; such incidents were relatively common. Then our host told us the case of his other neighbor, a tippling Englishman, who once left his house thoroughly inebriated and made a valiant attempt to walk home. He didn't get far and was found lying in the yard in the morning. He had most probably tripped and fallen and slept there until daybreak. When they found him, he was snoring contentedly, surrounded on all sides by large tiger paw prints. More likely than not, it was his drunkenness that had saved him. Most of the community believed that the drunken Englishman, reeking of brandy, had repelled a tiger of refined tastes.

Although we were tempted to stay, and even implored to stay, and make further use of the Hungarian household, Hungarian atmosphere and cuisine, as well as the finest French champagne, we heard the call of the Mandarin Road and knew we had to obey.

Leaving Trang-Bom, we sped along at a good rate; there were no obstacles in our way. There were excellent concrete bridges over most rivers; where there was no bridge, there was sure to be a ferryman waiting night and day to speed us across on his engine-powered ferry.

We fondly remembered the elder of the brothers, nicknamed "the devil" by locals, who had attempted and failed to murder him five times. It was a combination of skill, physical strength, presence of mind, and sheer luck that had kept him alive for so long, and after five failed attempts, the natives gave up trying and looked up at him with a combination of fear and awe.

We traveled a thousand kilometers in a mere three days. These speedy kilometers were followed by a bumpier stretch, where we took turns driving for twenty-five hours straight and made four hundred kilometers in that time. We were in a hurry to avoid the rainy season and were therefore forced to prematurely abandon our newfound hobby of hunting. If we did shoot something, it was usually wild fowl, which made for excellent lunches. Although the heat abated as we made our way north, the rays of the sun continued to beat down mercilessly, so much so that we were forced to wear our pith helmets even in the shade if we were to avoid fatal sunstroke.

On our way to the border, we stopped by Qui-nhon, Quang-ngai, Tourane, and Hue, finally passing through Vinh and Thanh-hoa into Tonkin. Even the smallest towns boast French-style comforts, and so our memories of Indochina are amongst the most interesting and pleasant.

We passed through numerous villages inhabited by people who had never seen a motorcycle. Despite the unfamiliarity, nobody was afraid of our bike. Instead, the villagers crowded around us, old and young, faces smiling, mouths open in excited laughter. We were pretty sure they had no idea of what the motorcycle was capable, how far we had come, and how far we were to go. This part of Indochina was populated by the usual Annamites and various other primitive tribes. We did not have to travel to Laos to see members of

Annamite village on the Chinese border

the tree-dwelling Bahnar, Sedand, and Rongao tribes or to encounter fair numbers of the *moï* people.

There must have been a fierce battle raging between the tribes and the formidable wild animals ranging free all over Indochina. The poisons the natives used killed quickly, and their experience and courage made up for the lack of shotguns. There was a special, not altogether simple method for killing elephants. A daredevil hunter, poison knife in hand, would creep up on an elephant and poke one of its legs. The angry animal, in an effort to crush the impostor, would raise its huge foot and bring it down, not on the skillful hunter, who'd roll to the side in the meantime, but straight into the poison knife. The poison acts quickly; the elephant collapses, unable to pursue its assailant because of the knife stuck in its foot.

Hue, capital to the region of Annam, was the most exotic location we visited, home to the emperor of Annam, magnificent palaces, royal burial places, and splendid pagodas, all in an attractive European frame. Later on, traveling through Peking and other large cities of China, we remembered the colorful Mandarins dressed in their glorious, ancient garb, set like jewels in a pendant of tradition, already an extinct breed in China, but very much alive in Hue.

The further north we traveled, the blacker the traditional costume of the Annamites became. Black clothes were the norm in town and country. Baggy pants and the ever-popular straw hats completed the outfits; the hats either ended in sharp little points or resembled upside-down washbowls.

Rice was still the main agricultural product of the region. We rode across many irrigated fields, watered according to the Egyptian model. All the traditional modes of irrigation were there, including bicycle-run water wheels.

To indulge our newfound love of hunting, we often traveled at night. Most of the animals we shot around daybreak, and we did our best to take advantage of the dawn hours. For reasons of practicality, we sought out mostly edible game, which could then be traded in town for a bed and service at the hotel of our choice. Occasionally, we'd hunt from our motorcycle, taking care to affix movable searchlights to the front and to suppress the sound of the engine as much as possible. If the searchlight fell on a wild animal, only in the rarest of cases did it manage to escape. We'd slow our pace or come to a halt, and the person sitting in the sidecar would fire immediately. At night, we hunted along the road. It's danger enough to enter an unknown stretch of rainforest by day, but at night, a few steps, and you're lost forever. We never managed to kill anything larger than a deer, except for a small leopard Gyuszi shot by daylight. We spent two hours waiting in vain for its mother to appear.

Once in Tonkin, the rainforests disappeared, and our hunting was relegated to ducks and waterfowl. Nevertheless, our guns were useful for more than sport reasons. We always had them conspicuous and ready; our revolvers we wore on our clothes. There was widespread animosity in Tonkin against all white men, regardless of whether they belonged to the hated French or the incomprehensible Hungarian race. Natives posed a much greater threat to white visitors than the fiercest of jungle tigers.

Rains were more common, temperatures fell, and by the time we reached Hanoi, we were past the twentieth degree latitude. The excellent road to the capital of Tonkin and the primary city of all of Indochina, Hanoi, wound its way through plantations of caoutchouc, rice, beans, coffee, and tea. Hanoi, situated in the proximity of the Black and Red Rivers, served as an excellent European-style rest stop, complete with an opera house of its own. We took some time to recover our strength after our trek through Indochina. Haiphong, the harbor belonging to Tonkin, lies twenty kilometers inland. We rented a *sampan* and sailed along the beautiful river, feasting our eyes on the myriad species of waterfowl.

"The way to China is an impasse," everyone told us. Not only was the road difficult, but entering China, for a white man, was the equivalent of tempting God.

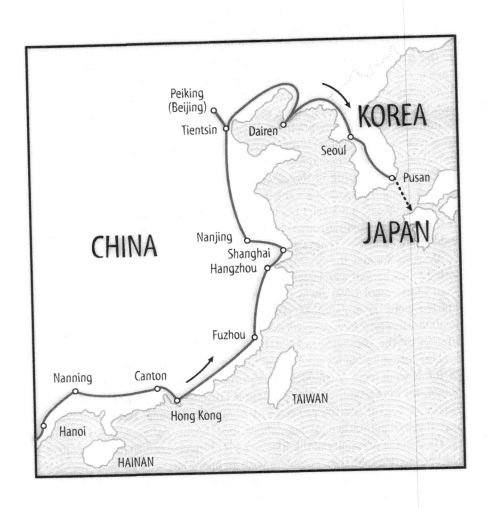

Extreme Orient

The Horrors of the Yellow Kingdom

Our first destination, upon leaving Hai-phong, was Lao-cai, a border settlement between Tonkin and China. Hai-cai was located all of 300 kilometers from Hanoi, nevertheless, we made up our minds to be extremely cautious as we set out. We packed most of our belongings, leaving only the bare necessities, and shipped them ahead of us, to Hong Kong. Although our motorcycle was considerably lighter after this operation, it wasn't only the quality of the roads we had to fear. We could count on being attacked and robbed at any point along the way. Loaded guns and plenty of ammunition were imperative if we were to assure our safety.

Despite the careful preparations, we ended up changing our travel plans at the very last minute, when we discovered that we wouldn't have to take the roundabout way through Yunnan Province; instead, although the road was not marked, we could enter the Guangxi Province directly, if we left Indochina via Lang Son. From Lang Son, we hoped to proceed through Taiping, Nanning and Wuzhou into Canton. This road promised to be a great deal shorter than the first alternative.

We opted for the second, shorter route. The road from Hanoi to Lang Son was only 156 kilometers. We arrived at our destination in the space of a morning. Traveling twenty more kilometers along Dong Dang, we finally reached the border and had disappeared down the highways and byways of China by noon. The road in China was strangely reminiscent of its Siamese counterpart; in other words, it played hide-and-seek with the unfortunate traveler. Wide, well-constructed stretches alternated with simple dirt roads. There was no rain; had it rained, we would have found it impossible to proceed. We weren't stopped at the border, nobody looked at our papers; truth be told, there wasn't even a simple wooden hut to mark boundary, as there had been in Indochina. The railroad ended abruptly at Dong Dang; we surmised that very few people had made the journey north into China.

It didn't take long for us to find the numerous warnings of danger in China confirmed. Our trial by fire came the very first day. It was an encounter to be reckoned with, one that could have cost us the success of our undertaking, even our lives. The danger materialized in the form of a group of Chinese men blocking our way somewhere between Longzhou, the first Chinese village from the border, and our destination of Taiping.

"Don't stop; drive on," Gyuszi called out, but seeing as some of the men were armed, I wasn't too anxious to try a dubious escape on the rough road. We soon found ourselves surrounded, first by five or six, then a dozen, finally approximately forty men. We gave them blank looks. We had no idea who they were and what they wanted from us. For all we knew, they might have been soldiers, policemen, or border guards, possibly deserters from the war between the provinces, or simply a band of robbers with little regard for our right to life and property. Their clothing was motley, but then again, simple soldiers rarely wore uniforms. They usually went barefoot and sported a range of different guns. Needless to say, we couldn't understand a word of what they were saying. They made us get off the motorcycle and began looking over the machine. They were evidently attracted by the shiny medals, and as we looked at them more closely, their faces appeared less and less bloodthirsty. The main idea was to keep cool and be on guard.

"Let's talk to them," Gyuszi said, and he began speaking in heavily accented French, making faces as he went. Although the men were entertained, it was obvious they couldn't understand a word he was saying.

"Who speaks English?" I asked them but got no answer. As they didn't understand a single language we tried, we decided to stick with Hungarian. They all laughed at the seeming nonsense we were talking and at the gestures we made. Although they hadn't touched anything on our motorbike, they refused to let us get back on. They never had to take us to their leader, because their leader came to us. He addressed us in Chinese and began talking rapidly.

"Seya, seya, " we repeated the only word we knew, indicating that we were poor wanderers, world travelers of sorts. In the meantime, we pointed to ourselves to help them make the connection. We showed them our things, including the photographs, which they passed around with great interest. It was at this point that I was divinely inspired to show them the article that had appeared about us in the Saigon Chinese paper. The leader took the article and read it aloud. We crossed our fingers that the journalist had written nothing negative. Next, we started passing out photographs and postcards; almost everyone got a small memento. When we had won our "hosts" over, we tried to explain that we were headed for Canton, where we hoped to earn money to continue our journey. Our explanations were followed by a long caucus, during which both Gyuszi and I began sweating profusely. No wonder; we felt our lives might very well be at stake.

"Money, money," the leader shouted, suddenly turning to us. His request did not take us by surprise. We quickly took out our wallets, which held only a few piasters each, explaining that the "money" was in Canton, and these coins were all we had. Placing all of our coins in the leader's hands, we stood and waited. He was evidently perplexed as to what to do next. Fortunately, the rest of our money was safe in the form of British traveler's checks.

The encounter ended as the members of the band unpacked and searched all our belongings. They divided our clothes among themselves, and the leader laid hold of our shotguns and ammunition, but they didn't touch what was most important: our checks, writings, passports, and books. We also got to keep our camera, film, and gasoline stores. The last thing they took was a few cans of food, but they left most of our supplies intact. Finally, the leader gestured that we were free to go.

We breathed a sigh of relief, but it suddenly occurred to us that they might be waiting for us to get back on the motorcycle so that they could shoot us from behind. I started the engine, smiled and waved at the men one last time, and we were on our way. We took off as fast as we could, traveling in a zigzag line to avoid being shot. We had escaped and were on our way to Taiping.

We felt the loss of the two guns most sorely. "Good, old tiger-hunting gun, and Mannlicher, who would have thought you'd end up the property of Chinese bandits!" Fortunately, our revolvers had remained in our pockets. We planned to replace our shotguns once we reached Hong Kong or Canton.

To this day, I have no idea who the men we met on the road could have been: a border patrol? Outlaws? We'll never know, but we can't be too thankful that they let us go in the end, instead of taking us captive, as Chinese bandits were known to do. Then, they might have taken us to the consulate or other officials and demanded a ransom. There were plenty of foreigners, especially missionaries, on the roads of China in these chaotic years. If the ransom didn't arrive, the prisoners were killed. And who would have thought to ransom us in the no-man's land between Longzhou and Taiping?

We remember our journey through China as one of the most chaotic and unsure parts of our travels. On the constant lookout for bandits, we could never be sure when we would be attacked next. Neither did we know where we would wind up by the end of the day and whether there was any more road in the direction we were headed. Even if we managed to make ourselves understood, asking for directions was useless, as nobody seemed to know the first thing about the roads. Nobody used the roads, especially now because of the volatile political situation; most people traveled by railroad, ship, or river barges. When traveling through a new town, you could never be sure who the leader was and whether the old inhabitants were alive. There were no telephones, no telegraphs, no communication. The merchants and missionaries, who had served as messengers in earlier, more peaceful days, were too scared to leave home. The railroad itself was sparse; many trains did not travel according to schedule because of the civil wars and ranging bandits.

We struggled on along the outrageous roads, anxious to at least keep abreast of the rain. If the rainy season had found us still in the south, God knows if we would ever have rejoined civilization.

It didn't take us long to perfect our survival skills particular to China. If we wanted to spend the night but were unable to find lodgings, it was best to pitch our tents out in nature, as far as possible from the villagers. We took turns watching at night. The goal was not to let a single stranger near us. If we ever stopped during the day, we still had to take care to keep away from the crowds. An interested passerby or two were all right, but when people began forming a circle around us, we quickly revved the engine and were on our way. Armed and money-hungry bandits weren't the only thing we had to fear; the greater threat was the unspeakable naïveté of the simple people. Those who lived in isolated inland villages, and there must have been millions upon millions of them, had never seen either a motorbike or a white man. These people lived under almost animal conditions; they did not have a concept of Europe or of Asia and had no idea that there were people in the world who led very different lives from theirs. Their life was a daily struggle for survival, a war on starvation. When the opportunity arose to make their lives just a little bit easier, the Chinese villagers did not hesitate to rob and even kill passersby. When they saw something strange and new, their first move was to make a part of it their own.

I made a note of an interesting similarity between the two most dissimilar people on earth, the Americans and the Chinese. They both had a passion for collecting mementos. Both the Americans and the Chinese we met filled their homes with souvenirs of all sorts: towels from hotels, a bit of wood or metal from an interesting machine, a glass or eating utensils from a far-off restaurant, an ashtray from off a ship, and a myriad of other knick-knacks, the taking of which did not exactly qualify as stealing. Of course, the Chinese considered many more items to be souvenirs than did the Americans, simply because so many things were unknown in China. This passion for mementos posed a real threat to our motorcycle. A friend of mine in Hong Kong related the following anecdote. There was a French airplane flying from Indochina into Hong Kong. Due to engine trouble, it had to land on Chinese soil, near a tiny village in the middle of nowhere. The villagers saw the plane land and duly surrounded it. They had never seen an airplane up close, and the hundreds of curious villagers began touching and stroking the strange machine. After a few minutes, a few brave villagers climbed onto the wings and were soon surrounded by dozens of their fellows. Like ants they swarmed onto the plane. Then, it occurred to one of the climbers that he should secure a souvenir of some kind, and he was soon seen toting something from the cabin. Then, a second villager pried a piece off the cockpit. It didn't take long before the entire airplane was cut, beaten, and pried apart. Everyone who managed to get hold of a souvenir ran home happy; those who were still in the village came running to get their share of the spoils. Despite all efforts to the contrary on the part of the desperate pilot, within two hours of his landing, there was no plane to be found anywhere. He hadn't even managed to save his personal belongings, writings, and most vital gadgetry.

As I have mentioned in an earlier chapter, we usually didn't realize the extent of the danger we were in until it was past. Today, I tremble to think back on our trip through China, and I doubt I would undertake it again. We were no less than reckless, only our luck was greater than our recklessness as we managed to make it through the Yellow Kingdom alive.

China had always been unsafe but was especially so at the time of our travels. The whole country was in an uproar, sunk into chaos so profound that even the natives had trouble making sense of it all in the summer of 1930. Not only was the "official" civil war between North and South raging, but there was unrest and turmoil within the provinces themselves. There were innumerable armies led by a variety of self-proclaimed leaders, whose aims were varied, but, under all appearance, strangely similar. The primitive masses of China had no principles; their sole goal was to get by. Many people signed on as mercenaries in return for some scanty pay and the promise of a share in the booty. It goes without saying that such mercenary troops were far from trustworthy; generals had to take care to outbid their rivals, otherwise, they could very easily find themselves without an army. The generals fought for a number of reasons: principles, patriotism, fanaticism, or sheer business. In case of a victory, the conquerors could count on tribute money, new territories and significant booty. Finally, regardless of how the battle turned out, mercenaries had perfected looting and exploitation to an art and always came out of a battle better off than they had been going in.

We tried our best to keep away not only from the front, but all military zones and gathering places. Even more than the soldiers, we had the Chinese bandits to fear, whose numbers had risen sharply as a result of the chaotic political situation. Chinese soldiers were forever on the run, and there were plenty of band leaders to round them up into groups of hundreds, even thousands. These bands of outlaws would then scour the countryside robbing, murdering, pillaging, capturing foreigners, driving off all live animals and generally procuring whatever they could lay their hands on.

There were such bandits all over China, and the locals were entirely without protection. The central Chinese provinces of Honan, Hubei, Hunan, Jiangxi were especially troubled. In the province of Jiangxi, bandits attacked the locals until the banner of Communism. Communists from all the neighboring provinces began flooding Jiangxi. I still have a newspaper report of the damages in that province alone: 37,000 houses destroyed, 87,000 people killed, $214,000 stolen. Thousands of refugees flooded the urban area as people's lives and property were only safe in large cities. Foreign-run seaports were the most popular places of asylum. We had most of our news by word of mouth, but nobody was ever able to tell us particulars. Most of the white missionaries fled to Hong Kong or Shanghai while they still could. There were entire counties run by bandit governments.

The "lawful" war continued to rage, but newspapers in the North and those in the South differed greatly in their reports. Chiang Kai-shek was the most powerful military figure in the south, and his charisma did his country a great deal of good.

In our eyes, the Chinese infighting was nowhere as serious as a European war. Weapons were primitive, military training virtually nonexistent. When the soldiers marched through the cities, there were no two dressed alike or carrying uniform equipment. Most of the guns were from the nineteenth century, and a portion of the army was made up of ten- to twelve-year-old kids whom we saw struggling under their heavy loads. There was no discipline to speak of; the rag-tag armies marched barefoot, carrying their umbrellas to ward off the rain. Rainy days were automatic truce days in China. The Chinese had an abhorrence of rain so strong that whenever it rained hard, all work ceased. Officials skipped work, children stayed home from school, all shops were closed for lack of customers, and if someone did have to leave home, he wouldn't walk a foot without his gigantic mushroom of an umbrella towering over him. In times of war, it was impossible to hold both a gun and an umbrella, so soldiers hung on to their umbrellas and waited patiently for the rain to stop falling.

The state of many of the villages we passed was saddening. If we saw that the houses were empty, the huts still smoking, the pigs and chickens gone from the yards, we knew that a band of robbers had passed through. The smoking homes were an indication of how long ago the band had passed through; the inhabitants showed us which way they had gone.

It was a terrible feeling to travel through a country in such upheaval, along rocky dirt roads. Sometimes, we traveled for long stretches following a pair of tire-tracks or were left to our own devices: a compass and a poor map. The map was in Chinese; we couldn't even read the names of the towns we were passing through, but we had marked the general directions we intended to take, and, whenever possible, asked locals to read the names out to us and point us in the right direction.

The first portion of our trip took us from Nanning to Wuzhou. Nanning was the first large city we encountered in China, and it had everything a modern city needed. Passing through Nanning and other sizeable towns, we concluded that the Chinese weren't as backward as we had initially perceived them to be. Guangzhou, or Canton, the unofficial capital of South China, was a real, fully-developed metropolis with a population of 800,000. There were precious few white men to be found; the Chinese had built up the entire city themselves. Eight- to ten- storied hotels and trams all added to the modern effect, yet Canton remained distinctly Chinese.

Chinese cities, in general, were so varied that visitors couldn't turn the street corner without being taken by surprise. The best way to describe China and the Chinese is "too much." There was too much of everything, especially people. The five hundred and fifty million inhabitants of the kingdom filled everything: village and city streets, shops, trains, and ships. Many lived out their lives on barges or houseboats. Those living in the cities weren't nearly as destitute as the villagers we had encountered. South China, in general, was far wealthier than the northern provinces. Business was booming, trade expanding. Merchants sat shirtless in their tiny shops. There were plenty of customers to be had. The Chinese were excellent merchants and had mastered all the different branches of the business. They had a virtual monopoly over the trade of the Far East.

After a few walks through the city, we noted that there were very few shop signs on the street. Instead, we saw numerous painted flags, hanging side-by-side with the clothes on sale. Written on the flags were the types of merchandise being sold as well as current prices. These flag "signposts" also served as theater billboards, ship travel schedules, and menus. Music was another important element of business. The wealthier a shop, the larger and more deafening the brass band in front of it, stationed there to attract guests and drown out the calls of neighboring shops. Sheer volume, and not melody, was of the essence. Stepping into an average shop, we were amazed by the number of shopkeepers and other personnel. Even the tiniest, hole-in-the-wall places boasted at least three employees, while larger shops were home to dozens of workers. One reason for the surplus of shop workers might have been cheap labor, while the main reason was the so-called partnership system. With the exception of those working in the newest, most modern stores, most Chinese shop assistants, sales clerks, and errand boys did not receive wages, that is to say, that instead of picking up their wages at the end of each week, they left their money with their employers and invested it in the shop instead. From that moment on, they were considered co-partners. Although the workers did not receive regular wages, their room and board was taken care of, so in reality, they had very little need of money. Their wages went toward advancing the shop, and, of course, their part in the profit depended on how much they had "invested." It was amusing to watch how closely these various partners watched one another; there was little trust lost between them. Whenever the cash register opened with a customary ping, three co-workers would rush to the scene and watch with eagle eyes how much money was being taken out and how much money was put in.

There were two points in a day when it was useless to enter any shop as a customer, and these were eleven in the morning and five in the afternoon, official mealtimes. Although the shop door remained open, the passerby could clearly make out a large table placed at the center of the shop and all the workers, bearded old men and youngsters, seated around it, enjoying a communal meal. If you entered the shop at such a time, you were either ignored or politely, but firmly informed that it was mealtime and you were to return later.

The Chinese had no rivals in business. They were skillful and calculating, unpretentious and very hard-working. Business went on, despite the chaos wreaked by civil war, bandits, and bloody insurrection. The age-old Chinese trade companies were known the world over for their integrity. Few of their transactions were actually recorded, there were no stamped receipts or signed contracts; the spoken word was binding and worth more than all the writings in the world.

Shop life was colorful and bustling from morning until night. People haggled on the streets, but this happened in secret, under the cover of their long sleeves. Customer and shopkeeper would touch hands and use their fingers to spell out how much they were willing to spend or how much they were asking for a given item. A single finger stood for 10, 100 or 1,000, while a bent index finger represented 9, 99 or 999. The thumb and pinkie simultaneously stretched out meant 6, 66, etc. It was easy enough to shop like the Chinese, even if you didn't know the numbers in their language.

The attractions of Canton and Nanjing, in our eyes, far surpassed those of Hong Kong and even Shanghai. While the latter showed a heavy Western influence, the former were almost purely Chinese, with one European for every hundred thousand natives. Impressive wide boulevards crisscrossed a veritable sea of buildings. Back in Hungary, our image of China had been shaped by the movies. When we thought of Chinese life, we pictured tiny, narrow alleys, women with maimed feet and men sporting long braids. Instead, we saw entire palaces of concrete, large buses, attractive shops, streetcars, and telephones. We saw our share of tiny alleys trod by even tinier footed women and men in braids, but large cities were more European than Chinese. Or rather, they were bizarre mixtures of the ancient and the new. Some large stores were so dark and dirty inside that we were afraid to enter, and the streets were brimming with a varied and very real Chinese crowd, a constant reminder that we were, in fact, in China.

The streets of Canton following a violent confrontation

The island of Shameen served as the European quarter in Canton. It was inhabited by Japanese and Germans, the Germans having been deported from Europe after the war. The tiny island was licensed to the Europeans; it was, by far, the best place for a white man to live. The island was surrounded by a network of wire fences; quiet and peaceful inside, it was well guarded by French and English police and ruled by French and English governing bodies. Two bridges connected Shameen with the mainland; soldiers were on constant duty beside the iron gates leading to the bridges. These were closed at nine in the evening, and no Chinese persons were allowed to enter, unless they bore a pass of some kind. Canons and machine-gun nests surrounded the island, and the wire fences could be turned into high voltage barriers anytime. Shameen was impregnable, as evidenced by the failed attempt, two years before, on the part of Chinese troops to capture the island. In the end, though, who knew what the future would bring? Europeans did well to be on their guard throughout China.

Armed rebellion and small-scale revolution were common in Canton. We often witnessed such scenes ourselves, heard the gun sallies, and saw the bodies on the street.

Wherever there was a body of water, a river or the sea in China, we discovered entire floating cities. Thousands of barges of all sizes covered the surface of the water. They were forever docked side by side, forming large clusters, even streets, of barges, boats, and ships. The floating cities had their own restaurants, shops, storehouses, and markets. Merchants made their way from market to market much as they would have done on land. The houseboats were home to entire families, who spent their whole lives on the

The "floating city" at Canton

water, cooking and cleaning, fishing and trading. Small children, like galley slaves, were chained to large metal balls to prevent them from falling into the water. Approximately one fifth of the entire population of the city lived in the floating part. Many people were born, lived out their lives, and died on the water, without once having set foot on land.

Whether we were traveling by motorbike, walking through the fields, or exploring the floating city, we concluded that in China it was the women who did the lion's share of the work. Chinese women, as a result of the heavy labor they performed day in and day out, had large and developed muscles, occasionally surpassing those of their husbands. Working in the fields and rowing the barges was the responsibility of women, who might hoe the fields from morning until evening or row the heavy barges with small children tied to their backs or hanging from their sides.

Reaching Canton, we had completed a thousand kilometers of our journey through chaotic China without experiencing any major setbacks or difficulties. Once in Canton, we began making plans for the next stretch of the trip, the portion that would take us to Hong Kong and Macau. We insisted on visiting these two cities, yet knew they were inaccessible by motorbike. For the stretch between Canton and Hong Kong, we had two options: a ship or the railroad. After all, the Chinese considered a land road superfluous when there

250

was both an excellent railway and a superb waterway serving their travel needs. Besides, there were so many tiny rivers and channels between us and Hong Kong, that we opted for a small boat, which was to carry us 200 kilometers up slow-paced Chu-Kiang River. As true-blue bikers, we were less than excited to take a sailing trip, but these 200 kilometers on the Chu-Kiang gave us an understanding of life on the waterways so vital to the Chinese.

Our small boat was romantic in a distinctly Chinese way. A wire fence separated first and second class from steerage. The officers on watch sported revolvers; we even spotted a machine gun up near where the captain was stationed. These wooden boats, many of them hundreds of years old, filled the waterways of China. They were passed on from father to son, and the use to which they were put always depended on the current owner. It wasn't unusual for a peaceful fishing boat to turn into a savage pirate ship.

There was a small watchtower built up on the bow of the boat, complete with cannons and portholes. All the cabins were outfitted with lamps and matches to light them, because in the case of a river battle, attackers always made sure the electricity went first, creating panic in its wake.

The countless barges, or *junks,* as locals called them, made for a very picturesque view everywhere along the river. Painted on the bow of each junk was a large pair of eyes. According to popular beliefs, boats, like people, needed the power of sight and eyes to see with. Most of the junks were outfitted with sails, which were, in themselves, a curious sight. Brown in color and sewn together out of hundreds of shreds of cloth, they were, for the most part, more hole than sailing surface.

On our way up the Chu-Kiang, we passed by a few British patrol-boats and large clunky steam boats, veritable Noah's Arks, which made so much noise in passing that they managed to drown out the shouting of the Chinese crowds on board. Our captain was most concerned with the pirates' barges. They sprang up unpredictably, like mushrooms, and although up to a hundred such boats were captured weekly, there were usually a hundred new fishing-boats-turned-pirate-ships to ensure that the noble business would continue. Sometimes, pirates ventured very near Hong Kong and attacked and captured everything from fishing boats to motorboats to large passenger ships. A ship might be sailing peacefully along and suddenly find itself surrounded by hundreds of tiny boats and barges filled with people with large iron hooks. The pirates would then proceed using these hooks to secure their hold on the ship, and, looking very much like a group of determined monkeys, they would skillfully leap on board. Once the pirates were on board, the captain, crew and passengers could say goodbye to all their cargo, belongings, everything that could be moved. If anyone resisted, the crew and passengers could be killed and the ship burned. Even the largest passenger ships rarely managed to break out of the ring of smaller vessels.

The river pirates had another time-tested ruse, namely, to buy proper tickets and pose as passengers. Then, at the appointed time, they would pull out their weapons, overrun and loot the ship and steer it in the direction their own barges lay.

Our own boat trip on the Chu-Kiang was quiet and peaceful, not counting a single exciting incident when we found ourselves surrounded by more barges than usual, and the captain ordered the sailors to increase the boat's speed to the maximum. "All passengers to their cabins," he commanded, and we had no choice but to seek refuge in our cabins, peeking out the windows nevertheless to see what was going on. We sat there for hours, watching and listening, but were no wiser than when we began. We couldn't even determine whether the captain's warning had been a false alarm or whether we were truly in danger. Our boat managed to evade the ring that had been forming around it; we sailed past a small American cruiser, and as we put more distance between us and the presumed pirates, we heard something very like gunshots.

Most of the ships carried the favorite food of the Chinese, pigs, as their main cargo. The live animals were "packaged" in a rather unique way. First, the animals were placed in egg shaped bamboo cages, which were further woven until the animals were completely trapped. The pigs were rolled, tossed, and stacked while in their bamboo cocoons. The advantage of this method was that the pigs took up very little space, a small boat could carry up to eight or ten, furthermore, they could be stacked four high or carried on porters' backs. Despite the hustle and bustle, the live animals reached their destination unhurt. Our boat carried approximately one thousand pigs, its belly sinking deep into the water. Gyuszi was sure we were going to sink. The Chinese passengers on board slept on top of the pigs. We figured they had delectable dreams of roast pork.

Pigs were the favorite domesticated animals of the Chinese. Chinese pigs were much better behaved than their Hungarian counterparts; instead of running around and making awful noises, they would quietly lie on the porch for hours and even walk in and out of the house, in perfect harmony with their owners. These pigs also looked different from European porkers; they resembled Sumatran pigs with their comical, long bodies and sagging bellies that brushed the ground. Dogs were the second favorite companion of every Chinese business and family. There was no shop or home without at least one, the most popular breeds being the tiny, delicate Pekinese and bear-shaped, wolf-headed chow-chows.

Although it was somewhat out of our way, we took a ship to Macao to see this fascinating city of Portuguese origin. The European influence was very

Chinese pigs in transport

palpable in the houses, inhabitants, and waving flags, but aside from the successful gambling industry, there really wasn't too much to see in Macao. Of all the people in the world, I think it is the Chinese who have the greatest passion for gambling, and Macao was their capital city in this respect. The games went on everywhere, from tiny, insignificant hovels to grand palaces. Whatever was forbidden in the other cities of China was permissible in Macao: lotteries, betting, cards, roulette, opium. The so-called "Fan-Tan" houses were brilliantly lit up at night, but Macao, the "Monte-Carlo of the East" was shabby and nothing to write home about. The tables in the casinos were usually surrounded by a ragged mob, and although gains and losses were calculated in small, worthless copper and silver coins, guests weren't even allowed to sit at the tables, which were reserved for the casino staff. Those wishing to gamble would be offered seats in the surrounding balconies and asked to place their bets in tiny baskets, which they would then let down on a piece of string. The most popular game was also the most primitive. Someone would throw a handful of copper bits on the table, which would then be sorted according to some simple mathematical rule. Winning numbers would then be called out based on what was left over after the sorting. Opium, both for sale and ready to be smoked, was intensely popular and entirely legal in Macao. Most people didn't think more of smoking opium than of puffing at a cigarette.

And now for the rest of our Chinese journey! The second half of our trip through China was just as uncertain as the first, but the mud on the roads grew gradually less, and the quality of roads brushed on good in a few instances. Our stay in China might be divided into two categories: travels and city life. In most of the countries we had visited, travel outside the cities and through a varied, rural landscape had proven to be the more fascinating, while in China, the excitement of the large cities was a welcome relief from the monotony of the tiny, isolated villages.

Our experiences post-Hong Kong were just as unforgettable as our journey from Indochina to Hong Kong had been. We passed through rice fields, across irrigation canals, and traced tracks left by bison-drawn carts. Wading through dust and mud respectively, we were often forced to hire help in its animal or human form to ensure our progress on the rough terrain. To our good fortune, we hardly had to travel more than an hour or two from one village to the next; what's more, the workers in the surrounding fields were always happy to lend a hand in return for a few copper coins, which, in the eyes of China's poor, were small fortunes. We never encountered a single automobile or motorcycle. If the roads were clear, rickshaws were the most popular mode of transportation. Wealthy Chinese had themselves carried around in litters.

We sent our luggage ahead into Shanghai and on into Tientsin. This was the best way to ensure the safety of our belongings and to significantly lighten our load. Even the widest dirt roads were full of potholes; rivers and canals gave us the most trouble as bridges were few and far between.

Staying close to the sea, we passed through the provinces of Kwangtung and Fukien, stopping to rest in the famous harbor cities of Swatow and Amoy, which proved to be amazingly busy centers of trade. While in the cities, we always felt perfectly at ease; our troubles began when we left the urban boundaries and found ourselves in the middle of the countryside, without anybody who could give us directions, left completely to our own devices.

The road to Shanghai was more than 2,000 kilometers long. Upon reaching Fuzhou, we headed west instead of following our previous prevalent direction: north. After 300 kilometers, we turned in the northerly direction once again. Once in Hangzhou, we discovered, to our great delight, the railroad that would lead us straight to Shanghai.

Most of the rivers we encountered, we crossed on barges, haggling for reasonable transport fees at the outset. For example, if the ferryman asked for twenty dollars, we knew he'd be perfectly satisfied with a dollar or two, although it did take a bit of convincing with a firm and confident demeanor before he would agree to take us across. We had to be on our guard the whole time we were on the river, not allowing more than two or three strangers on the barge or the slightest deviation from the planned route.

One time, our oarsmen rowed us halfway across the river and suddenly

The Chinese district in Shanghai

stopped. There were three of them. They simply laid down their oars and held out their hands, indicating that they were expecting us to pay them right then and there. We had agreed back on the bank on a fare of two dollars. We had always paid upon arrival and found it strange that they were asking for their money in the middle of the river. "All right," we thought to ourselves, "if we don't trust you, how can we expect you to trust us," and we gave them the money, thinking that would solve the problem. They still refused to move; their voices grew louder and more insistent. I grew angry myself and half shouted, half gestured "Row us to the shore immediately; we'll talk once we're there." Gyuszi and I smiled to ourselves. We were veteran travelers after all, and what were three Chinamen to us? But the rowers still refused to budge, insisting that if we didn't give them more money, we weren't going anywhere. In the meantime, we had begun drifting downriver. I grew worried that the water would carry us past a village, where the rest of the band might be waiting. Our rowers had gone on strike.

"All right, if you won't row, give us the oars, and we will row ourselves," I said, reaching for the implements. The three men would not hand the oars over; one even grabbed Gyuszi by the arm and held out his hand once again for more money. Before they could realize what was happening, I punched one in the jaw so hard he fell down. The other two had little time to react, because Gyuszi and I pulled out and pointed our revolvers at them.

Now this was something they had not expected. The three men got down on their knees and began crying and begging for their lives. They thought we'd shoot them for sure. Gyuszi and I suppressed a smile. Although they were crooks, we hadn't the slightest intention of shooting them. If we hadn't had those revolvers on hand, they might have pulled out their knives and attacked us, which would have been unhealthy in the highest degree.

"Let's get out of here," I shouted at them. No Chinese ferryman had ever rowed as fast as those three. Once we reached the other side, I had them carry us back upstream as punishment, and even got our two dollars back, in an attempt to preserve our fellow white men's trampled dignity.

Not only were European lives and fortunes in danger, native Chinese were also in constant dread of what the future might bring. They never knew when their village might be looted. Wealthy landowners trembled in anticipation of the day they would be divested of their fortunes and become penniless wanderers. That is why their houses looked more like small forts, which they surrounded with towers and ramparts, complete with an armed guard, and even a cannon or two. The tried and true way of preserving large fortunes was to make them as mobile as possible, to sell everything that could be sold for money, and then move into the relative safety of one of the large harbor cities. Life under the protection of foreign flags and a European navy was the safest after all.

The last stretch of our journey through China wasn't a bit safer than our previous travels had been, but we had amassed so much experience and even a small Chinese vocabulary that we were no longer as lost as when we had set out. The distance from Shanghai to Tientsin was only 1,200 kilometers, and we mostly followed the railroad tracks.

During the few days we spent in Nanjing, the unofficial capital of the Southern Chinese, we had the honor of an audience with General Chiang Kai-shek himself. Shortly afterwards, we crossed the mighty river Yangtze. The Yangtze flows from its source in Tibet for almost 6,000 kilometers, and, besides being endlessly fascinating, it also proved to be a great obstacle to the two of us. After two days of traveling, we reached the famous Imperial Canal and arrived in Tientsin after a smooth ride of two days' duration.

On the way, we spent most of our nights in nature. We always selected the isolated spots and attempted to stay far away from the villages. Even so, one of us was always on guard, gun in hand, and our motorcycle stood ready to take off at a moment's notice. We felt the loss of our faithful dog especially keenly during our nights in China. By day, we took care to pass by all passersby at the highest permissible speed but stopped in larger towns for gasoline, food, and water, which we no longer had to carry ourselves. Wild animals spared us. Not counting our first day in China, the rest of our trip was happily bandit-free. Sometimes, we reflected that the many warnings we had heard had been sensationalistic and distorted, but in reality, I think we were very lucky. I don't know to this day what we would have done had our motorbike broken down in rural China. We would have been in grave danger.

A street in Peking

As I have mentioned before, the essence of China was to be found in the urban and not in the rural settings. We spent many nights in Chinese hotels and ate Chinese food, which was far from bad. Kitchen hygiene was certainly not one of the Chinese virtues, but for the most part, a traditional Chinese lunch or dinner was very much in line with European tastes. The only problem was we never quite knew what we were eating, which is probably just as well, because our experiences in the traditional markets had revealed that dogs and cats were prime delicacies in China. In village markets, I often saw especially delicious kittens sold separately. Old tomcats probably sold cheap. Snakes were also favorite commodities, usually sold live in woven baskets and baked or fried as you might bake or fry fish. Soup made out of the nest of a certain species of bird was also tasty. The strangest thing about Chinese dining was that the food was served on plates, rather than in bowls and on platters. Meat came cut up in small bits and pieces and already mixed with the rice or noodles, so that we never quite knew what was on our plates. Some species of insect, when roasted, also made for popular snacks and were sold by the sackful. We soon got used to chopsticks and didn't much miss European eating utensils. Another big favorite was roast pig, especially tantalizing when prepared in the Chinese way. The red, crispy meat, sliced in a variety of shapes and sizes, was available on every street corner.

It was generally impossible to tell Chinese restaurants from private homes, both from the outside and even inside. Every group of guests was assigned a separate room, where numerous courses would be served in slow and luxurious succession. People didn't eat continuously, but stopped to

A Chinese pagoda

drink and chat between courses. The most popular drink was green tea without sugar, served regardless of what food you had ordered.

Occasionally, lunch or dinner guests would strike up a game of Mah-Yong, a form of dominos. Walking down the street on a Chinese evening, you could hear the clicking of the dice through every open window. We played along and ate along, trying swallow's nest soup, fish and snakes, bamboo delicacies, piquant sauces, and old eggs. These eggs were allowed to stand for years before they were opened. They were black in color, didn't smell particularly foul, but the taste I would leave to the Chinese.

Whenever we ate at a European hotel, we were served a meal fit for kings, much more luxurious than anything we had ever encountered. Seemingly endless feasts consisting of up to twenty, even twenty-five courses, were to be had for minimal sums. We never got past the sixth or seventh course, despite being culinary veterans after years of travel. China was one of the cheapest countries of the world. Currency was constantly losing its value, but its buying-power stayed the same. Three feasts a day and lodgings for the night cost no more than a single American dollar. While in the cities, we felt very distant from the bloody battles raging in the countryside. Not even the sight of wounded soldiers disturbed civilian nerves. Rumor had it that there were no wounded in the Chinese army, which had neither money, time, nor equipment for dealing with sickly warriors. Those wounded inevitably died. Although bandits were forever on the prowl in the country and just outside the city boundaries, city dwellers lived on in peaceful ignorance of the dangers of the world about them.

Visitors to China had to be on their toes when it came to changing money. There were paper bills, copper and silver coins in all shapes and sizes, and the thousands of money-lenders lorded it over gullible foreigners. Country people didn't trust paper bills, so they generally clanked and rang their way through the streets, carrying handfuls of coins in textile scrolls and stockings. The luggage of a typical Chinese traveler consisted mostly of large quantities of coins. Currency differed from province to province, even from one large town to the next. In Canton, we encountered a silver twenty-cent coin, which was the equivalent of thirty-six copper pennies. Instead of ten cents, we were obliged to count out eighteen copper coins. Coins were forever being sifted in large pans; we were in China after all, and counterfeiting money was rampant. Chinese merchants therefore had a great deal of calculating to do, which they never would have managed without the abacus. Had it not been for the abacus, all of Chinese trade would have shut down. Even educated Chinese were completely dependant on the abacus for their addition, subtraction, multiplication, and division needs.

The value of the Chinese dollar depended on where it had been issued. The whole monetary system was infinitely complicated by the concept of *tael*, which was a form of theoretical money. Although tael didn't actually exist, its value changed from day to day. Then there was "big money" and "small money," paper bills and change respectively, which were worth very different sums even if the number value stamped on them happened to be the same. Paper money was always the more valuable, and this brought with it humorous consequences. Prices were given both in coins and bills. Occasionally, I'd buy something for ten cents, hand over a paper dollar bill, which was worth a hundred only to receive one hundred and ten cents in coins, because coins were, by their nature, worth less. If the price of the item in question was worth more than a dollar in small money, and we handed over a paper dollar, we always got change. If, on the other hand, something cost a dollar in big money, we'd have to hand over more than a dollar's worth of coins. Consider the following mind-boggling possibility:

The "Marble Ship" in the Summer Palace

what if the price of something was given in big money, but we paid in small money and, as change, were given a mixture of coins and bills!

Chinese cities were colorful and lively by day and brightly lit at night, pulsing with life and busy with trade. The U.S. and various European countries all looked to China as the ideal market. Everything could be sold in China, even products nobody would ever think of buying in any other country. Even the smallest countries strove for their share in the Chinese market and established consulates wherever possible. We were unable to discover either Hungarian products or a Hungarian consulate.

The streets were crowded and noisy far into the night. Rickshaws and coolies, street vendors of various sorts filled the streets to overflowing; smells were overwhelming. Shopping streets were flooded with light; those of Shanghai, Canton and Hong Kong would have stood their own next to the brightest streets of Paris, even New York. The palaces, hotels, restaurants, and theaters were lined with lights, making the night as bright as day. "Sing Song" girls, elegantly clad, would scuttle from one restaurant to the next. Gambling was a passion, and passions ran high. Everyone was very much alive, everyone was gambling and everyone was losing money rapidly. Whatever your wages, it was impossible to save money in the casinos of Shanghai.

We took an excursion from Tientsin to Peking. The road between the two cities was the only consciously constructed road in China, all 120 kilometers of it. In reality, it wasn't much more than a high earth embankment, perilous both to the automobiles and the motorcycles for which it was intended. Carts and other non-motor vehicles were banned from the road and struggled on foot after torturous foot in the mire, when they hardly would have damaged

Speeding is forbidden in China!

the earth "highway." It took us four days to secure permits to use the Tien-tsin-Peking road. The last ten kilometers of the road were paved; overjoyed, we picked up speed, when, alas, we were greeted by a gigantic hump! The Chinese, in their wisdom, had reasoned that a new road should not be spoiled by speeding motor vehicles. To prevent anyone from enjoying the ten kilometers of paved road in China, they built up a small but firm mound every hundred meters with the intention of sending transgressors flying. Cars crept across the mounds at a snail's pace; we actually had to get off at each such landmark and lift our motorcycle over, its frame was so low. Nobody ever got a ticket for speeding along this road!

The beautiful city of Peking made up for all the trouble we'd had getting there. Eckener, the commander of the Zeppelin, had called the aerial view of Peking the most beautiful sight in the world, and we were distinctly happy we had gone out of our way to see this lovely city, its broad, regular avenues and boulevards all intersecting at perfect right angles and massive houses hiding beneath a lush canopy of trees. Peking is entirely one-of-a-kind and not to be missed by any traveler to the Orient. It most resembled a comfortable, sprawling country town with its myriad small houses and expansive, low-roofed palaces. The paved road ran parallel with the old one "made" of mud; cars and litters traveled side by side.

It was in Peking that we realized the greatness of the Chinese people and how advanced their civilization had been when our European cultures were just being born. We spent a long time between its four-layered walls in an effort to visit at least a small portion of its hundreds upon hundreds of wonders. We strolled through the "Tartar City" and "Imperial City," familiarized ourselves with the "Chinese City" and were thoroughly enchanted by the beauties of the "Forbidden City." The monumental walls, the centuries-old palaces, the thousand-year-old temples and historical sites, the parks with their lotus-covered ponds, the many-storied pagodas and mysterious imperial burial places were all open to our inquiring eyes and hearts. Whatever was beautiful, great, and perfect in China was to be found within the walls of Peking. The schools of Peking were the best in the country, its arts and crafts the best developed, its monuments the most impressive. We'd heard that the most hard-working police were also stationed in Peking. This I witnessed with my own eyes when a policeman, who had formerly been directing traffic, suddenly left his post and walked up to a coolie who had just broken a rule of transportation, undid his belt, whipped the unfortunate man and went back to his post, where he calmly resumed his previous occupation.

We visited all the famous artisans, marveled at intricate carvings, embroidery, and jewelry. We could have bought ivory and wood carvings, silks, carpets, and silver for next to nothing. Although the artisans worked with the most primitive tools, their products were of the highest order. Then again, a European mademoiselle might have thought twice between wearing one of the elegant jade necklaces had she seen the workshop in which it had been crafted. We took our pick of china, both new and old. Unable to resist the temptation to stock up on these artistic masterpieces, we promised ourselves we would send our new purchases ahead of us, to Hungary.

In our free time, we made sure to visit the Chinese cinemas and theaters. They were not to be missed, but one visit turned out to be more than enough. At the movies, we found a pulpit of sorts, where a man stood, declaiming the plot of the movie in a sing-song voice. If a male actor appeared on the screen, the worthy "commentator" sang in a male voice; when Greta Garbo came on, he made a feeble attempt at imitating her. The theaters were full of Chinese stars, but as it was very hot, a small, half-naked, and very dirty little boy followed the female lead around with a hand-held fan. The public ate and drank their fill; the orchestra drowned out what the audience had not, so much so, that the performance was entirely inaudible even to those sitting in the front row. The coolies' bare feet dangled above the stage; the director and stage hands squatted in one corner of the stage, smoking cigarettes. The background swayed perilously at every gesture. One of the flute players, tired of sitting, suddenly got up and commenced walking up and down the stage in order to stretch his legs. The actors didn't seem the least disturbed.

The Great Wall of China

The police forbade photos everywhere we went, but, in return for a few pennies, they were willing to disregard the very rules they were there to uphold. We took the bumpy road back to Tientsin, cursing the Chinese emperors the whole way. To the left and right of the embankment, we spotted a line of simple wooden coffins. The Chinese poor placed their dead in thick wooden coffins, carried them outside the city boundaries and simply left them by the side of the road. On our way back into Tientsin, we saw whole columns of such coffins to our left and to our right. Wealthy Chinese could afford expensive funerals, complete with masks, music, banners, all sorts of finery, huge crowds of people, and hundreds of wailing women.

Before leaving China, we visited the Great Wall, the Ming burial places, and left Tientsin with the intention of tracing the line of the huge bay into Manchuria, Korea, and Japan.

We had spent a mere four months in China, but these were four months to remember. We had gotten a glimpse into the everyday lives of the Chinese people and a taste of the bitterness of their fate. Even if they didn't have it in themselves to awaken our pity, we felt sorry, in spite of ourselves, for this people with their glorious past, who were so sorely exploited by the enemy. Foreigners ruled their largest, most beautiful and most important cities. For every trade transaction, the Chinese were obliged to pay heavy tolls to their foreign conquerors. Countries were growing rich off trade with China, while millions of Chinese were on the verge of starvation. Foreign navies guarded their harbors. Had it ever occurred to any of these high and mighty powers that China belonged to the Chinese? All the harbor cities were split into

The Temple of Heaven in Peking

zones; each foreign power was supreme lord on its own territory. Was it just that the city of Tientsin belonged to no less than seven different foreign powers, and that the miserable rickshaw-pulling coolies needed seven different permits to enter the streets of their own city? Woe unto him if he wandered into the wrong district without the proper permit issued by one of the seven "protectors" of China.

China was home to four hundred million people, four hundred million who had no dignity, no political or economic independence. Chaos ruled, and there was nobody to lead the people out of chaos. What a power China could be if its people woke up and worked together. The Chinese are good workers, lively and quick to learn, if only somebody took the trouble to teach them! They need a railroad, infrastructure, good domestic security, telegrams, telephones, radios, electricity, machines to work their fertile lands. The Chinese have great creative power; skyscrapers have sprung up overnight, replacing clusters of wooden huts. It is impossible to conquer China; Chinese history is a chronicle of those who have tried and failed. All sorts of foreign powers and would-be conquerors have invaded the land, but China has preserved its distinct Chinese character. As for the conquerors, they were conquered and became more Chinese than the Chinese. Those four hundred million people swallowed foreign cultures whole. There are still Chinese who respect and know their heritage, worship in the ways of their ancestors, and haven't changed their traditional clothes for modern fashions or turned their hearts inside out to fit into some temporary scheme. These Chinese will win out in the end, both over their irresponsible, prodigal countrymen and the strangers they respect but cannot love. Traditional Chinese would die for their country and are only waiting for the leader who will unite them all, trample inequality, abolish civil war, and restore order. Who knows, a single outside attacker might do more to unite the Chinese than a leader from among their own people. This awakening, were it to happen, is not to be feared. The Chinese have no designs to conquer other countries, but they have the potential to enrich the world and play a vital role in the fate of humanity.

These were some of the thoughts on our minds as we left the Yellow Kingdom, feeling both happiness and relief to escape from the chaos and instability of today and take with us memories of the glories of yesterday and hopes for a better future for this great land.

"I sincerely hope we'll manage to make some money in Japan," my friend Gyuszi said, reflecting on our four financially draining months in China. The torturous roads and city living had depleted our resources drastically. To make matters worse, the expensive ship journey to America was still ahead of us, and it seemed more than doubtful that we could scrape together enough money to make the crossing. The future seemed bleak, both ours and that of the Chinese, but there was no turning back.

While still in China, we often met Hungarians. We hadn't had much contact with the Hungarian missionaries in inner China, but we knew of thirty to forty of our countrymen in Shanghai, eight in Tientsin, a single Hungarian in Canton and a famous Hungarian businessman living in Hong Kong, whose chain of stores had spread throughout East Asia. Although the earthquake in Japan had cut back his profits, he and his sons were holding out for better times in this far-off place. Some of the Hungarians we met had been prisoners of war under the Russians, and after regaining their freedom, decided to try their luck in the Far East. Many had married Russian women but strove hard to preserve their Hungarian heritage. There were doctors, lawyers, merchants, hotel workers, musicians, engineers, and architects among them. While in Peking, we spent a few luxurious and restful days in the mandarin palace of the city's only Hungarian, who also happened to head a large American business. The editor of the English newspaper in Canton also had a Hungarian last name. We looked him up and discovered that his father had emigrated to the US, and while he himself spoke no Hungarian and hadn't seen a single Hungarian since he was a child, he was proud of his Hungarian origins.

The Hungarians in China generally lived under very good conditions. Had they been physical laborers, they never would have made it in China because of the overwhelming competition, but good craftsmen, businessmen, and anyone with a knowledge of languages and a measure of creativity had a future in China. Our Hungarian friends all agreed that they disliked the Chinese, who, in their eyes, were poor and ugly. China is a great and wealthy country, they insisted, and life could be beautiful—if it weren't for the Chinese.

Manchuria, Chosen, and Japan

"One Chinese man is worth more than a single Japanese, but a hundred Japanese amount to much more than a hundred Chinese," says the Chinese proverb in reference to the Chinese tendency toward infighting and disunity. In China, it's every man for himself, and even if some men agree on a common end, the means to that end will prove radically different. In Japan, people work for the same end using the selfsame tools to build a common future. Japan is undeniably a strong nation, and its strength stems from a strong sense of national unity. The four larger islands, which constitute the lion's share of the territory of Japan, are not much larger than historical Hungary and far too small for a population of seventy million. To make matters worse, the population of Japan grows by one million every year, so the first priority on the political agenda has been territorial expansion. This process began in 1905, when Japan took over Korea, or Chosen, population twenty-two million, then Manchuria, and finally set up the Man-Chou-Kuo province in Northern China. These maneuvers increased the territory of Japan fivefold, and the population of greater Japan increased by approximately fifty-five million. Japan showed and still shows no inclination towards contentment, and who knows what the future might bring?

We didn't see much of Manchuria, outside the Kwantung Peninsula and the city of Dairen (Dalian). Most of the population of Dairen and neighboring Ryojun (Port Arthur) was Japanese. Traveling the world by motorcycle, we realized that we rarely crossed a political border to find ourselves suddenly immersed in a completely different civilization. Instead, by the time we reached the new country, we were already familiar with its people, who naturally populated not only their motherland but neighboring territories as well, and had grown familiar with their customs and picked up a few words of their language. This had been the case with the Arab, Indian, Malaysian, and Chinese cultures, and we were experiencing the same cultural gradations with regard to the Japanese. Although Japan proper was still far away, the Japanese were everywhere.

Dairen was a very attractive town, a busy seaport on the coast of Manchuria. Our next stop was Port Arthur, connected to Dairen by an asphalt road a mere 48 kilometers long. Forty-eight kilometers of bikers' paradise! The name of Port Arthur lit up Japanese eyes with pride. The street names in that town were all reminders of a recent and glorious past: Nogi, Togo, Yamagata, Oyama. Once in Port Arthur, we visited the famous Northern Forts, the site of the tunnel battles, and Hill Number 203, whose claim to fame was the bloody bayonet battle fought thereon.

We traveled a triangular route along the Laodong Peninsula, along the

Beating the tumble-down bridges of Manchuria

Manchurian railway, touching upon the city of Mukden, where we turned south and headed towards the Korean border. Memories of endless green grain fields, the hospitality of the Russians and Hungarians in Mukden, and the pleasures of Dairen soon blurred, as did rumors of Korean Communists and Chinese bandits on the prowl in the mountains of Ann-Tunn. The roads and people of Korea claim precedence over all other memories.

We traveled a thousand kilometers along the Korean Peninsula to reach the part closest to Japan. The horrors of our journey, which led through Heijo, Keijo, Jinsen, Taiden, Taikyu, and Pusan, lasted two whole weeks. We hadn't even left the cities before being confronted with the scarcity of cars and general ignorance of the quality and direction of the roads. Nobody had traveled large distances in Korea on a motor vehicle; everyone we asked preferred the train. As there were no road maps to be had, we depended on some old Japanese ones, which we strove very hard to decipher with little success. Even if we did see a road sign, we were utterly mystified by the Chinese characters painted on it and were forced to wait until a helpful local willing to read it out to us passed by.

The road we had hoped to take did, in fact, exist, but we had picked a very bad time for our Korean tour, as the country had sustained severe floods just a few weeks before. Bridges and entire hillsides had been washed away; seas of mud and silt impeded our progress. Miserable kilometer after kilometer tried our bodies and our souls; we were like two wretched coolies, working from morning till night. Passing through towns, we always stocked up on various logs and boards, which we then used to build impromptu bridges, sometimes

It's all Greek to us!

working for hours at a single site. In other spots, we repaired the roads we were to travel or carried our vehicle over ditches and treacherous pits. Shallow rivers we simply waded across, but upon encountering a deeper body of water, we had to row our motorbike over to the other shore, piece by piece. Whenever possible, we hired men and animals to aid our progress. There were long stretches where the road was so narrow that the sidecar would have floated in air had a hired man not held up its wheel, meter after miserable meter. The pleasures of the journey multiplied as temperatures rose to 40 degrees C.

Railway bridges proved to be exciting in their own right. Worn out and at our wits' end, if the river was very deep, we often disregarded all warnings to the contrary and attempted to cross it by the railway bridge. We'd watch and wait for moments on end, our ears plastered to the rails, making sure there was no train headed our way. Then, we would cautiously proceed to push our motorcycle across, balancing on the bare rails, laying down the boards we had purchased to ease our path and prevent laying down our lives instead. We generally trembled the whole way, fearing that a train would show up when we were halfway across, bringing with it a hefty fine or death. At one such perilous crossing, we barely had time to push our motorbike aside at the foot of the bridge before the express train streamed past us, leaving us pale in the face and weak in the knees. "Never again," we swore to ourselves, but a few

The Nondaimon Gate, Seoul, Korea

hours later, we were perched atop our next railway bridge, cursing the Korean governor and the Japanese emperor all the way.

The helpful ways of the people of Korea were astounding. They did their best to aid our progress and never haggled over their wages. Sometimes, they refused to accept a single penny in payment. Entire villages of forty to fifty capable men would set their work aside and push, shove, and carry our motorbike into the next town or village. Occasionally, we took the motorbike apart and hung the pieces from poles, which groups of men shouldered and carried forward. Our biggest difficulty lay in making ourselves understood. The simple people had no idea how to handle such a large machine; Gyuszi and I had to show each and every one where to place his hands, how to lift the machine and place it back on the ground, how to move ahead. Occasionally, one of the men would slip, cry out, and let go of the vehicle. If one let go, they all let go, and the motorbike tumbled to the ground.

By the time we had reached our destination of Pusan, we were all of ten kilograms lighter. That was how much weight we had lost since Shanghai! Nevertheless, we had the satisfaction of knowing that we had crossed Korea on a motorcycle.

We had grown to love the helpful and hospitable people of Korea. They were different from both the Chinese and the Japanese and infinitely more lovable. Koreans were also surprisingly clean; both men and women wore sparkling white shirts ironed to perfection. Nobody went around in dirty or ragged clothes. Maybe there is something to the theories that Hungarians and Koreans are related. The pleated skirts, uncovered heads, and pretty little vests worn by the women of Korea called to mind our prettiest Hungarian country

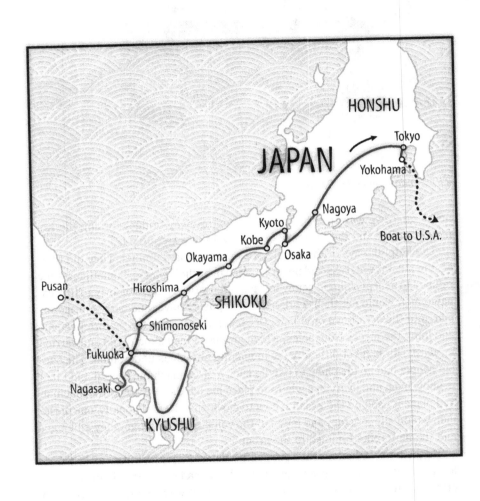

women. Their towns, which consisted of wooden dwellings and stone-paved streets reminded us of the Balkans, even Turkey, in all but their extreme cleanliness. Men wore long shorts of sorts, which they secured around their ankles.

Korean fate also hauntingly recalled Hungarian fate. They, like us, were an agriculture-based nation with a war-ridden past. The relationship between Korea and Japan paralleled the ties that had bound Hungary to Austria before the War. No true Korean approved.

A small boat carried us from the Korean peninsula onto the Japanese island of Kyushu, where we landed in the town of Fukuoka. It didn't take us long to realize that we had left Korea far behind. Not that the Japanese were rude or inhospitable. On the contrary, they were infinitely polite, and bowed to us and smiled at us continually, doing their utmost to ingratiate themselves. For the Koreans, all this had come from the heart, while Japanese love of visitors was calculated to please. Those visitors who spent only a few days in Japan would visit some of the large cities, make a few new friends and leave for home with stories to tell of the warm hearts and thoughtful ways of the Japanese.

We spent three months in Japan, visiting all of its famous sites. During these three months, our contact with other Europeans was minimal. We stayed at Japanese hotels, ate Japanese food, and sought out Japanese amusements. Not only was life in the big cities an open book to us, but we also went out of our way to visit rural places, tiny villages where no white man had yet set foot. We grew acquainted with the Japanese, and our knowledge of them was deeper than that of a visitor who spent no more than a few days in the select social circles of the largest cities.

The Japanese, at the bottom of their hearts, were not fond of strangers, but they did their best to hide this fact from visitors. All Japanese strove to make a good impression on foreigners in the hopes that stories of Japanese courtesy and hospitality would travel far and wide. And they did.

The people of Japan cultivated thoughtfulness as an art. The country had been locked away from the rest of the world up until roughly a hundred years ago. It was in 1854 that the first foreign ships were allowed to land in Japanese harbors, and many more years had to pass before Japan became a free country. The transition was extraordinary. The Japanese suddenly discovered the merits of other cultures and took to borrowing and adapting the best of what the rest of the world had to offer. They quickly discovered that commercials and propaganda held limitless possibilities.

My personal feeling was that the sudden social and economic shift that had come upon the Japanese went to their heads. This is the only reasonable explanation for Japanese daring-do in the face of the Russian superpower.

Each military success was followed by a heady rush of national pride. The Japanese people seemed to me the proudest and most confident people on earth; at the same time, they went out of their way to make themselves liked and admired.

Our wanderings through Japan were a succession of surprises, large and small. There were many strange and new customs to get used to; some annoying, others laughable, still others breathtaking. It didn't take us long to discover that not only did the Japanese dislike strangers, we could safely say they hated them, regardless of the nation to which they belonged. With their admirable self-control, however, the Japanese managed to hide their xenophobia beneath a kind and polite demeanor. Nobody left Japan with anything but the highest praise for the ways of the Japanese.

We lived the good life in Japan. All the newspapers were aware of and interested in our presence and traced our travels for the duration of the three months we were there. There were lots of papers in Japan; the press was wealthy, healthy, and widespread, and played a vital role in the daily life of the people. Newspapers founded and supported charitable organizations, gave people good advice; in fact, large newspaper offices were lined with cubicle after cubicle of employees, anxious to help trusting citizens in all their needs. Japanese citizens made travel plans, ran businesses, and gave large-scale dinner-parties all with the help of the newspapers. All the receptions to which we were invited had been planned by the press. Every time we arrived in a new city or town, there was a convoy of cars and motorcycles waiting for us at the city limit. Their first task was to escort us to the representatives of the press and the curious public. Next, we would be installed at a hotel, often given a car to use, and given a tour of local sites of interest. Our tour guide was, more often than not, a leading figure in the press, and he made sure we missed nothing that was worth visiting. Banquets, parties, and invitations followed, and once we were ready to move on, the same convoy would regroup and escort us out of the town and often into the next city.

When our visit to Japan seemed too much like an endless series of cocktail parties, we often ran off on our own to catch a nap or enjoy "civilian" life. Even our free time was divided between the various theaters, cinemas, restaurants, and teahouses to which our enthusiastic hosts veritably carried us. It was undeniably pleasant to immerse ourselves in a sea of smiling faces, but a little voice in the back of my mind told me that all this love and welcome was fake, worse than fake, it was two-faced. Our hosts knew very well that I was in touch with a number of newspapers and magazines and were therefore anxious that their country should come off well in the eyes of Western readers.

Aside from the disingenuous quality of Japanese hospitality, we were constantly under the impression that we were being observed. Every step we

Japanese pagoda near Nara

took was noted by watchful eyes, and I feel I am right in saying that every Japanese citizen doubled as a bit of a Japanese spy. Japanese officials kept asking us whether we had visited Russia, where we had been and where we were headed.

Once they had a detailed idea of our proceedings, they let the police in the next town know that we would be coming. This system worked so well that we never arrived in a new town without the local police knowing everything about us. We also noticed, to our astonishment, that whenever we came within sight of a new town, the first Japanese man or woman who saw us quickly ran to the nearest phone to notify the police of our arrival. After all this, we were no longer surprised when hotel owners, restauranteurs, and shopkeepers all over town, people we had never seen, knew not only our names, but where we were from and where we were headed.

Often upon our arrival to a new hotel, we'd barely had time to change before the police paid us a friendly visit. They were polite, not pushy at all, but their questions were many and thorough. We always got a map of the town we happened to be in, with all the places where taking photos was not allowed clearly marked. Forts, military and naval bases, some factories and airports were not camera material. Whenever we neared one of the more important forts, we'd suddenly find ourselves in the company of a tour guide, very polite but impossible to get rid of. Sometimes, as on the beautiful island of Miyajima, we got fed up with our escorts. The mountains of Miyajama were laced with fortifications, and in the valley lay one of the most popular excursion destinations in all of Japan. We feasted our eyes on a series of gorgeous parks, promenades, the ever blue sea, and our faithful tour guide, who insisted on spending the entire day in our company. He very enthusiastically pointed out the finest of all there was to see, but in the meantime, he kept a close eye on all our movements as well as those of our camera. We stopped by a restaurant for lunch and he trotted in behind us, but would not accept either a drink nor the cigarettes we offered. "We'd like to go bathing in the sea. Are you coming with us?" we asked later that afternoon. *"Arigato,* thank you, but no. I'll just wait for you on the shore." "Don't tire yourself; we'll be in the water a long time," we explained, hoping to finally rid ourselves of his company. Next, we took off our clothes and our chaperone immediately offered to watch them for us. He spent the whole afternoon squatting on the shore, the sun beating down on him mercilessly, even as Gyuszi and I splashed around in the cool water or sunbathed on a sizeable barge.

Not even in the tiniest village hotels were we immune from these detectives, whose polite excuse was always, "How can I help you? Please let me know." My friend Gyuszi, in his slyness, came up with a fool-proof method to get rid of our unwanted companions. He began sending them on errands: for cigarettes, for English papers, for beer. The most delectably difficult errand of all proved to be for milk. There was virtually no milk available in the smallest Japanese villages. Gyuszi would therefore explain how much he loved and needed milk, how he simply couldn't do without milk. Our man would then be gone for hours, scouring the village for a glass of milk to prove his willingness to serve. The milk-method stood us in good stead throughout our Japanese journey.

The island of Kyushu was the first we visited. The originally well-constructed, paved roads were in a deplorable state due to neglect. The Japanese railroad, however, was amazing, with a dense network of rails, comfortable cars, and short travel-times. It's no wonder that nobody paid the roads much attention; most people opted for the train over the automobile. Once we had reached the southern portion of the island, we spent days on end in lovely Unzen Park, a unique volcanic national park enhanced by natural hot water springs and geysers as well as herds of tame deer that fed at visitors' hands.

If I were to sum up my impressions of Japan, I could do it in two words: "mild disappointment." Japanese propaganda had made the country out to be such a land of indescribable exoticism and wonder that it would have been impossible to fulfill raised expectations. Disappointment was inevitable and most visitors seeking out this "land of charm and color" rarely got past the charm and color.

Japan's heady rise from insignificant cultural backwater to global superpower meant that it was practically head to head with the most developed countries of the West. The Japanese, however, believed they had already surpassed the U.S. and most of Europe, and this attitude of self-congratulation seeped into their schoolbooks and newspapers. Journalists reflected on the possible consequences of a future war against the United States. The Japanese were convinced they were citizens of the best-developed and strongest nation on earth. Although great advances had been made, the masses remained distinctly Asian. In the modern cities, everybody, down to the simplest coolie, was literate and read the papers, which were published in vast quantities and installed in every shop, office, and private home. Japanese journals were hardly insignificant; the Osaka Mainichi, for example, sold two million copies.

Leaving the larger, modern cities behind, we discovered life in the small, isolated villages of Japan Asia still reigned supreme. Rural life was primitive to the utmost; long, plain shirts took the place of silken kimonos. Children went entirely naked, men almost; women didn't cover their breasts. Villagers gave us fearful, suspicious glances; most of them had never seen a white man in his life.

Life in the large cities was modern but without a distinctly Japanese flavor. The so-called modernity of Japan consisted of aggressively and all-too-swiftly transplanted foreign elements, which had nothing to do with traditional Japan. Modern technology, literature, music, and art had preserved nothing of old Japan. The colorful traditional clothes, the great love of nature, the simplicity of domestic life, respect for others and for one's ancestors, in other words, the greatest things about Japan, were not the results of modernization. It was infinitely more pleasing to behold a young mother in a silk kimono, carrying her child on her back than young Japanese girls in tacky uniforms, bent over their typewriters.

Our visit to Kyushu was followed by trips to the islands of Shikoku and Honshu, the latter being the largest of the Japanese islands. The islands, in fact, the whole country of Japan, was one of the most beautiful parts of the world. Our way was enhanced by gorgeous panoramas of great natural beauty, mountains and valleys, tender green rice fields, pine forests, brilliant snow-capped peaks. Countless mountain streams, having their source in the highest heights, tumbled into the valleys filling their air with a steady gurgle and light mist. Thousands upon thousands of shrines, memorial columns, and small pagodas stood ensconced in the shady woods. Suddenly reaching the sea, we were greeted with a smattering of jewel-like small green islands on a blue surface of mirror-like smoothness.

We passed through Shimonoseki, Hiroshima and Okayama, explored larger cities such as Kobe, Osaka, and Kyoto, finally spending a restful couple of days in Nara and Nagoya. These were the first Japanese cities where we met a few fellow Hungarians. Most of them, like the Hungarians living in China, had been prisoners of war under the Russians. We could tell trade was booming by the sheer number of lucrative businesses and palace-like office buildings. The only truly good road in Japan lay between Kobe and Osaka. It was a wide, modern asphalt road with the single disadvantage of being no more than thirty kilometers long.

The cities, for the most part, were far from beautiful. Small towns consisted of a single main street, which branched into countless narrow alleyways. Side-streets were too narrow to allow two cars to pass at once; there were no sidewalks to speak of and any cart drivers brave enough to risk trying to pass through had to put up with constantly brushing up against the wooden walls of the houses. Like in China, the streets were full to overflowing with people walking or riding bicycles. Cyclists, but especially pedestrians, made a huge mess of every street. Pedestrians lorded it over those riding in vehicles, walked in the middle of the road when they so preferred, and generally showed very little interest in our motorcycle despite the resounding honking, shouting, even screaming that we waged against them. The general consensus seemed to be that pedestrians had just as much right to the road as did those sitting in motorcycles or automobiles. If we met a pedestrian head on, he might be prevailed upon to get out of our way, but whenever we were headed the same direction, they simply refused to budge to the left or to the right. Not being blessed with the sublime patience of the Japanese, I occasionally allowed our front wheel to gently bump the legs of an especially slow pedestrian. The most I could get out of him was a quick glance over his shoulder. He would then flash a polite smile and continue on his way.

We had opportunities to sample Japanese patience on the open road as well. One time, we were riding along a narrow country road behind a car with its single driver. Suddenly, the car stopped in its tracks, and we were forced to brake ourselves. Glancing past the vehicle in front of us, we discovered a loaded cart standing crosswise in the middle of the road, with the horses grazing in a nearby field, the driver nowhere in sight. It was impossible to

The giant Buddha statue at Kobe

drive off the embankment to pass the cart, and as moving it off to the side by ourselves was equally preposterous, we were forced to stop and wait. The driver of the car in front of us gave a few calm shouts, but, after getting no answer, settled down to a cigarette. It took half an hour for the cart owner to appear. In any other country but Japan, he would have been beaten or at least severely chastised for foolishly leaving his cart smack in everybody's way. Had he parked the cart at the edge of the road, we might have been able to pass through. Granted, traffic was light on that stretch of road, but he should have expected something to pass by in the space of half an hour. But what happened in Japan, the land of infinite patience and courtesy? As soon as the cart driver appeared, the man got out of the car in front of us, walked up to him and bowed several times. Then they struck up a conversation peppered with polite head ducks, somewhat along the following lines. "Would it please you, esteemed brother, to pull your cart to the side with the help of your horses, as I am in a great hurry?" asked the car driver. "Welcome, my esteemed friend, I will grant your noble request immediately," answered the carter and walked off in the direction of his horses. It took a full ten minutes for him to hitch the animals before the cart and drag it off to the side of the road. "May the heavens repay you for your kindness, respected sir, and grant you and your children a long life," answered our man, bowing many times in quick succession, "I thank you for the kindness you have shown your unworthy brother." "With all my heart, oh sir, and I assure you that if I have the great good fortune of crossing your path again, I will be more than happy to pull my cart aside a second time." Following this soulful conversation, the two men bowed for the last time, and we were finally able to continue on our way.

During our entire Japanese journey, whether passing through large cities or small country villages, we never once saw two Japanese so much as quarrel. Scolding and loud disputes were unknown in Japan. The gravest conflicts were solved amidst polite smiles and bows.

We found their constant bowing to be rather comical. The handshake was unknown among the Japanese, so polite greetings took the form of bows instead. Each encounter looked and sounded much the same. Two people might meet, one would bow deeply and say something banal and polite, then his partner would do the same. Straightening up, they would begin the whole process all over again. Whoever was older was allowed to stop bowing first, but problems arose when those meeting were so similar in age that they couldn't tell whose right it was to cut the ceremony short. In such an event, there was simply no limit to the number of bows made, which occasionally repeated themselves fifty, even sixty, times. Once, two such champions of politeness stood blocking traffic in one of the typically narrow Japanese alleys. A policeman appeared out of nowhere, took them by the arm and conducted them to the sidewalk, where he left them at their game, but not before politely bowing himself. Whenever we left a party of people behind and were forced to say good bye to more than one, the pattern of "bow and let bow" became so intricate that we stopped keeping track and began bowing in a revolving fashion to everyone.

We spent a longer period of time in the cities of Tokyo and Yokohama. Although a recent earthquake had laid both cities to waste, Japanese initiative and willpower had rebuilt them so that there were no signs of the destruction at our passing through. Daring skyscrapers reached for the heights among countless tiny homes, life was cosmopolitan, the boulevards were broad, well-lit and brimming with cars. Tradition and fear of earthquakes limited the height of buildings, so that the houses lining Tokyo's main street, Ginza, were rather short and squat. Smaller buildings were made of stone, larger

The theater strip in Kobe, Japan

buildings of steel and concrete. The magnificent public buildings, picturesque Japanese theaters, gigantic stores, luxury hotels, and a bustling population of five million all helped make Tokyo deserving of its capital role. This figure of five million was misleading as we found out. The actual city of Tokyo counted no more than two million, but all towns and villages within fifty kilometers of the capital counted as suburbs of Tokyo, resulting in a gross population of five million.

In the streets, chaos reigned supreme. Automobiles mingled with bikes in a heroic effort to avoid running over hapless pedestrians. Motor vehicles generally drove around placid pedestrians, who had every intention of proceeding, undisturbed, right down the middle of the street. Each family owned a bike or two; bikes were the most popular form of transportation by far, serving not only the transportation of persons but of large packages as well. There must have been millions upon millions of these handy vehicles carrying the lion's share of the loads of Japan. Some cyclists went so far as to carry beds, closets and large chests on their bikes. Nobody observed traffic rules. Cars and other vehicles swept along both sides of the streets; at night, people were constantly making wrong turns by the non-existent light of the traffic lights. We found it strange to have to drive on the left side of the road; this was a rule we hadn't encountered for a long time.

The imperial palace was built on one of the hills in Tokyo. Although we weren't able to catch a glimpse of the Japanese emperor, we did enjoy an audience with and receive an autograph from the soon-to-be-murdered prime minister, Hamaguchi. The emperor rarely left the palace; when he did, hundreds

The Todaiji Gong at Nara

of thousands stood on attendance, anxious to gaze upon his majestic face. When the emperor was abroad, drivers were obliged to prop up their front wheels to prevent them from taking off too suddenly. What's more, heavy curtains were drawn across all the first story windows of all the houses to keep mere mortals from gazing on the emperor from above.

While in the capital, we stayed at the most luxurious hotel of all, the Hotel Imperial. In small towns, we usually opted for authentic Japanese hotels, in an effort to both save money and gather more authentic Japanese experiences. We hadn't been in Japan for more than a day or two before we found ourselves obliged to keep the custom of taking off our shoes in the gateway of any building we were about to enter. This custom continued to inconvenience us during our entire Japanese stay, and we had to take special care to keep our socks hole-free. Once we had taken off our shoes, we were given wooden slippers and could enter into the first corridor. If, however, we had ambitions of entering one of the rooms, we were forced to leave even the wooden clunkers behind and had to proceed in stocking feet. Everything was amazingly clean. The wooden floors of the various corridors and hall-ways shone like mirrors; rooms were "carpeted" with reed mats. There was no furniture to speak of. The furnishings of a typical room included a low table with pillows for sitting, a couple of pictures and decorative statues, and a rack-like structure for hanging our clothes. There were no doors to speak of. The walls were constructed of thin wooden frames covered with a material of vellum-like consistency that could be pushed to the left and right, thereby providing us with enough space to exit one room and enter the next.

Upon arrival to a new place, we were always led to the baths. The Japanese were a very clean people, bathing at least once a day, mostly in the evening. Special occasions and arriving from a journey also warranted a bath, as did visiting a restaurant, theater, or other cultural establishment. Gyuszi and I enjoy baths, but we did find the occasional three or four dunks a day to be excessive. Then again, at least we were making up for bad hygiene in China!

In hotel baths in the city or public baths in the country, we were surprised to find female bath attendants in the all-male section. These ladies served us, washed our backs, and did their best to make bathing a pleasant experience. In some womens' baths, male attendants took up the role of the ladies. Despite these strange circumstances, the Japanese were not immoral. Public bathing was a traditional ritual; the baths for the Japanese were like our clubs or cafes, a place to meet, enjoy ourselves, and talk politics. The presence of members of the opposite sex only made the experience more pleasant and heightened the conversation.

The Japanese were not shocked by the naked body. People walked up and down the hallways of hotels in short pants and little else without raising a single eyebrow. When the weather was hot, hotel guests opted for near-nakedness in their rooms; men could even entertain female visitors or hotel staff thus scantily clad. In small villages, shopkeepers went nearly naked, and, if there was no separate bathroom in their home, families simply carried their large wooden tubs onto the street, where men and women bathed together, naked, entirely oblivious to those passing by.

But let's return to the hotels! Once we had finished taking our bath, we were given comfortable breezy kimonos to wear and were allowed to return to our room, where we made ourselves comfortable on the ground. It wasn't long before a young girl would enter bringing green tea and cigarettes. After providing us with these essentials, she's take a seat on the ground and watch us carefully, anxious to guess our wishes before they were spoken aloud. As we weren't able to talk to each other, we simply smiled.

A few minutes might pass in quiet when we would suddenly notice the walls being slid back and Japanese faces appearing all around us. They rarely hesitated to enter our room and make themselves comfortable at our side. It

Japanese hotel room

was especially in small towns that news of us spread like wildfire; we were motorists, strangers, exotic Hungarians, and everyone wanted to see us. People would appear by the dozens, fill our room and sit staring at us, not speaking, just smiling, for quite some time. After satisfying their curiosity, they would leave as suddenly as they had come, making room for new visitors. Our room became a thoroughfare, and we soon tired of being the center of attention. Guszi then had a brilliant idea. He grabbed my arm and led me to the next room, then, through the walls, to the next. We made our way through the maze of sliding walls, taking a peek in every room we were able to enter. After all, we were just as anxious to satisfy our curiosity as our hosts were.

We were obliged to take our slippers off before entering not only private homes, but theaters, cinemas, restaurants, and temples as well. The difficulty always lay in trying to locate our own footwear in the mound of shoes and slippers that generally stood at the entrance to every building.

While in Japan, we received countless dinner invitations, even from some of the most illustrious families of the country. Most of the time, we were invited to meet our hosts at fine public restaurants, but the occasional dinner at a private home was a special treat. Wealthy Japanese families always kept up a room or two in their homes furnished in a European fashion with the purpose of making the occasional European guest feel at home. We ate our way through countless lunches and dinners in a traditional Japanese setting, seated around a small circular table set with plates and chopsticks. Whenever we sat down to a table with chopsticks, we saw in our hosts' eyes the expectation that we would make fools of ourselves and the readiness to stifle a smile or a chuckle. In this regard, they were sorely disappointed. We had

Japanese waitresses in the restaurant yard, Nagoya

acquired the skill of eating with chopsticks while in China and elegantly picked at individual grains of rice to show off our skills.

Japanese cuisine was much worse than what we'd encountered in China. We found some of what we were served to be inedible. At one home, we were presented with "delicious pastries" made in our honor. The delicacies looked like dumplings, weighed at least half a kilogram and tasted atrocious. "Outstanding!" we cried, madly scanning the table and its precincts for a discreet avenue of disposal. Most of the meals we had involved the traditional *sukiyaki* dish, which required a special table of its own with a hole in the middle for the fire. Various tidbits of meat and fish would then be fried right there in front of us. The meat and fish were mingled with vegetables and placed in a large bowl from which they had to be retrieved with the aid of our chopsticks. Once we had such a tidbit firmly in our grasp, we were obliged to dip it in raw egg yolk and a disgusting spicy sauce that managed to ruin whatever the yolk left untouched. While picking away at this choice delicacy, we were forever making polite remarks intended to boost the moral of the unfortunate cook who had brought it all into being.

There were only waitresses in Japan, no waiters. These waitresses did more than serve the food; they sat down at our tables and politely waited throughout the meal. They ate and drank nothing and would not accept a tip but were there to make sure our beer was poured out and our sake glasses always full. *Sake* was a Japanese vodka of sorts, drunk warm, and the waitresses were paid after every glass their guests drank. All parties, however small, were given their own room in Japanese restaurants, as they had been in China. Only in the big cities did we come across European-style restaurants furnished and run in the Western manner.

According to Japanese belief, women existed for the purpose of serving men. The first time we visited a Japanese family in their home, we were given ample evidence of this. Our host happily led us up to the gates of his palatial residence just outside the city. The lady of the house came to the gate, and our host introduced her simply as "My wife." As soon as he had said those words, this elegant lady, clad in silk and jewels, knelt before us and touched her forehead to the ground. Gyuszi and I were profoundly embarrassed. Not knowing what to do next, we took a quick look around and knelt before the lady, touching our heads to the floor as she had done. Our greeting was greeted in turn by a melodious chuckle. We burst out laughing ourselves, and the amused husband explained that men never knelt to women. It was the task of the womenfolk to make obeisance to men as an expression of their respect. Although Japan was changing, wives greeted their husbands as they returned from their offices and shops in the very same manner.

The existence of the Hungarian-Japanese Society in Tokyo came as a pleasant surprise, as was our presence in Tokyo to the enthusiastic patron and president of the Society, the refined aristocrat Sumioka Tomoyoshi. Mr. Tomoyoshi was a great Hungarophile who studied Hungarian in his spare time, believed in the Turanian Theory according to which the Hungarian language was related to languages of the Far East, and supported the entire organization, including the publication of the magazine *Dai Do*, or *The Way*, at his own expense. Although the society was small, nothing but a grain of sand in a desert, its president received a prodigious number of letters from Hungary each month. Sumioka Tomoyoshi was delighted to meet not one, but two, Hungarians, especially as the society didn't have a single Hungarian member. He immediately asked me to translate some of the letters he'd had from Hungary into German. Once I had done so, he realized that they were of secondary importance, mostly polite requests from Hungarian travelers, stamp collectors, congratulatory notes and other harmless but heartening documents. As we already knew of a Hungarian man who was living in Tokyo, we invited him to accompany us on one of our visits to the society. From then on, our compatriot, who had been a prisoner of war under the Russians and currently worked as a butcher, became a regular guest at events sponsored by the society. As it turned out, the society hadn't been aware of his presence just as he'd had no idea there was such a thing as a Hungarian-Japanese Society, even though he had been living in Tokyo for years. There was also a Hungarian tailor living in Tokyo, one of about four or five Hungarians in all of Japan.

284

Dinner at Sumioka Tomoyoshi, President of the Turanese Society in Tokyo

Foreigners had a difficult time making a living in Japan and generally relied heavily upon each other. I doubt that our Hungarian friend ever made clothing for Japanese customers.

The price of living in Japan was also rather high. A single yen was worth fifty American cents, but its buying power was very low. Most things cost about three times as much as they had in neighboring China. A room in a decent hotel cost 10-15 yen per night, and we generally paid 2-3 yen for a meal, which would have added up to roughly twenty yen a day. We actually ended up spending much less, because while still in Korea, I'd written a letter to the Hotel Society of Japan, which had then been forwarded to hundreds of establishments all over the country. In the first Japanese city we came to, we found hundreds of invitations waiting for us from various hotels promising discounts of twenty, twenty-five, even fifty percent, while still other hotels offered to let us stay for free. Japan was one of the most expensive countries we visited, but only for foreigners. The Japanese themselves held material goods in little regard. They had few possessions, no furniture, and bought clothing cheap. An average bureaucrat earned no more than 50-60 yen per month.

My overarching impression, then, was one of wealth and not poverty. Restaurants, clubs, and theaters were full to overflowing; the brightly lit streets were home to joyous and carefree people. The strands of Osaka were charming. Thousands of colorful paper lamps hung suspended above the water and reflected in its waves. People sat in floating teahouses, where they were served by lovely geishas who smiled, danced, and poured drinks. Osaka was the capital of industry and trade and reminded us both of Venice and of

Bangkok with its myriad rivers and canals. We had heard wondrous tales of the monumental factories of Japan, which turned out to be a disappointment, rather small and workshop-like. Large products were almost always imported: rails, railroad cars, construction beams, and the gorgeous ships running in and out of the harbors all bore the inscription "Made in U.S.A." or "Made in Canada." Japanese brands were nothing but skillful imitations of Western products, matching their American or European prototypes down to the shape, size, and color. We were hard put to discover signs of original Japanese talent. Although the Japanese made use of all the latest technical advancements, they weren't able to use the machines and raw material they had in ways as inventive as an American or a European. I was present at the launching of a new type of submarine, which did little more than sink like a rock on its maiden voyage. Japanese diligence and enthusiasm made up for lack of expertise. Although the submarine and warships were simply being tested and not actually launched in battle, the experiment cost the country two large ships and countless lives.

We continued our way north toward the island of Hokkaido, stopping many times along the way in an effort not to miss any of the important attractions of Japan. The roads started out poor and remained poor throughout. Pitifully narrow roads connected even the largest cities; traffic was virtually nonexistent. It was a shame, because the landscape was indescribably beautiful and unique in the world and would have provided anybody brave enough to travel by motor vehicle with ample pleasure. Instead, people opted for carts and bicycles or simply traveled by foot among the suffocating dust clouds of high summer. We bumped along the rough roads of Japan and had very little energy left to enjoy the view. The countryside was heavily populated, so that we hardly left one village behind without already finding ourselves at a short distance from the next. The villages, and the villages only, were inundated by mud. Although it hadn't rained for days, the villagers poured bucket after bucket of water in front of their homes in an effort to beat the dust. We did derive some grim pleasure from splashing the most obstinate pedestrians with mud.

By the time we neared Hokkaido, we had learned quite a few Japanese words and were using them regularly. A polite *sayonara* at the end of a pleasant encounter meant much more to them than the fanciest English greeting, and asking *ikuradeska* instead of "how much?" always resulted in better deals at the market. The Japanese, on the whole, experienced extreme difficulty trying to master foreign languages and, unless they were absolutely secure in their knowledge, they rarely had the courage to speak up in a foreign tongue. Those who did attempt to communicate with us in English did so laboriously and sweated profusely in the process.

Japanese geishas

The Japanese were also awful at mental math. My high school teacher in Hungary had once told me that the Japanese, even the simplest among them, had a special talent for numbers and could perform complicated calculation in the wink of an eye. I found the opposite to be true. Shopkeepers and bureaucrats used small calculators for even the simplest calculations. For example, if I bought something that cost 25 sen and paid one yen, the person at the counter would inevitably resort to his trusty counting machine to calculate that I'd be getting 75 sen back. Once at the post office, I bought eight different stamps, and quickly adding the figures up in my head, I placed the correct change on the counter. I then proceeded to wait for three or four minutes as the postal worker laboriously calculated the grand total on his abacus. Discovering that I had placed the precise amount on the counter before him, his eyes opened in wonder and he looked at me as if I had been a demigod.

All the villages we visited were outfitted with electric lights, and we stopped to explore every site proclaimed worth the exploring. After a while, one temple starting looking mighty similar to the next; the schools, public buildings, and plaques all began to blur before our weary eyes, but we were led by enthusiastic guides from one site to the next, so we were obliged to make a careful study of everything they felt might fascinate us. If there happened to be a four-story building in the village, it certainly counted as one of the tourist attractions, and we weren't allowed to continue on our way without climbing to the top of the house and admiring the fine view that lay before us. Sometimes, our self-proclaimed tour guides took us on excursions. On one such excursion, we rode out of town in a dilapidated Ford and traveled for four hours before arriving in a plain. When we got out, our companions explained that this plain had been the site of a great battle back in … that had resulted in a glorious Japanese victory. After receiving this rousing bit of information, we jolted our four-hour way back to the village.

In places where it wasn't forbidden, taking photos was almost mandatory. Whenever we met an important public figure of sorts, a policeman, let's say, or a mayor, he would strike up a pose next to our camera and refuse to depart until we had taken his picture. As soon as the photograph was ready, they brought along their wives, children, and all their relatives, and we were forced to take pictures of them, too. In the end, they all wanted to be in our book; they knew very well that we were assembling a picture chronicle of our journeys. After taking various family portraits, we were instructed to take photos of all the public buildings in addition to aerial shots of the entire village from the rooftops of the public buildings. Rather than hurt their feelings, which we couldn't have afforded to do in any case, we decided to play along, and made hundreds upon hundreds of snapshots of everything of interest to them. Our hosts were happy and so were we, especially after we figured out that we didn't actually have to put film in our camera to make it seem like we were actively recording everything we had seen.

At one point on our journey, we found a small town barricaded against our arrival. As we neared the city limit, we were greeted by a number of men in kimonos, who escorted us into town, not to a reception this time, but straight to the police station. There was nobody around who could understand us or read what was written on our passports, so they locked us up in a room by ourselves, where we listened to three hours of anxious phone calls as our captors did their utmost to round up a competent interpreter. When the interpreter arrived, we gave a detailed explanation of who we were and also gave vent to our severe discontent at being forcibly detained. Our explanation and raging was followed by a long discussion between the policemen and the interpreter. Finally, our English liaison turned to us and said, "The police only wanted to be of service to you. Please state your needs." I doubt the interpreter gave an honest rendering of what we said next.

The Japanese people were avid travelers. Constantly on the move, they were very anxious to discover all the hidden beauties of their country and spent all their free time engaged in this noble pursuit. There were accurate maps, signs, and plaques everywhere to aid the process of self-discovery, and Japanese tourists showed a profound and enthusiastic interest in anything having to do with the history of their country. Cheap train routes made inland travel highly affordable.

It was at a train station that I was witness to the second scene which, in my mind, was the epitome of Japanese courtesy. The train stood at the platform, ready to depart within a few minutes. A well-to-do Japanese man stood surrounded by eight or ten of his relatives who had come to see him off. He commenced saying good-bye, politely bowing to each in turn. By the time he got to the third person, the last passengers had jumped on board and the train rolled past the platform amid a cacophony of shouts and whistles. Our worthy traveler, his baggage already loaded, ticket in hand, continued bowing to his relatives even as the train he had hoped to catch rolled away from behind him. His train must have arrived to the next station by the time he finished bowing to his relatives, but he never so much as batted an eyelid. After all it would have been highly impolite to jump on that train before saying a proper good-bye to all the good people who had accompanied him to the station.

Our journey back to Yokohama led us along the coast. The miraculous blue surface of the inner sea shone upon us as we progressed along the dreadful roads. Granted, they were paved, but the manner in which they were paved was astounding! Pothole after pothole, mound after puddle, we made our miserable way to our last stop in Japan, the city of Yokohama.

We spent our last few days in the company of acquaintances we had made, taking a few days off to revisit Tokyo by electric train. Even our third class seats were soft and comfortable, complete with a range of pillows. The Japanese did their utmost to accustom the people to European-style seats. Most Japanese found sitting in chairs or other types of upright seat tiring; they much preferred to make themselves comfortable on the ground, where they could sit for hours with their legs folded under them. On the trains and streetcars, we saw countless Japanese attempting to sit in the traditional fashion, even though the seats were modern and state-of-the-art, especially those in offices, which were outfitted with inflatable rubber cushions just to make sitting on them that much more comfortable.

The Japanese also disliked European clothing, but they knew in the back of their minds that their traditional garb was disappearing fast, as were the Chinese characters from their writing. Children were forced to wear Western clothing; school uniforms were prescribed and mandatory. Everyone entering an office building or a large store was expected to wear Western clothes; only women had the privilege of preserving their luxurious silk robes. In fact, very few Japanese women opted for European clothing. Traditional outfits for women were charming and graceful; the robe-like kimonos men wore, however, were far from beautiful, revealing both their legs and the clumsy wooden slippers they wore. Those men who retained their traditional clothing also sported typical straw hats, which only heightened the comical effect. And now it remains only to picture a fully dressed Japanese man balancing on the ever-popular bicycle!

Men and children, those most affected by the clothing reform, hated their new attire and, after returning from school or from work, exchanged it for kimonos in the privacy of their own homes. The evening streets of Japan billowed with kimonos and little else, and the clattering of the wooden clogs drowned out all other sounds.

In the harbor at Yokohama, we located and boarded the colossal ship Tatsuta Maru, which was to take us far away not only from Japan, but from all of Asia, and possibly, for good. Many of our newfound Japanese friends came to see us off, some traveling from as far us Tokyo and Kyoto to say good-bye. Whole columns of cars and motorcycles escorted us to the shore, and this was a good-bye we will never forget. All the vehicles were decorated with Hungarian flags, and there was one giant red-white-and-green banner waving in the sea breeze as we set off. This was the way the Japanese said good-bye to two penniless Hungarian students. As our ship departed the bay, we lost sight of the individual people, then the large flag, the harbor, the city of Yokohama and, finally, the snow-capped peak of sacred Mount Fuji. *Sayonara, sayonara, Nippon!*

On board the Japanese ship, we felt like we were still back in Japan, with the sole difference that we were no longer obliged to sleep on the floor but were provided with excellent and comfortable Western beds. Our pillows were stuffed with down, not rice, and as we lay down to sleep that first night, we were keenly aware that we were headed towards the New World, on our way to America!

Our stay in Japan had been very pleasant; not only had we received the warmest greeting on our entire voyage, but our travel books had sold so well that we had managed to make the three hundred dollars we needed to cover our fares to America. I don't know to this day what we would have done had the Japanese not bought up our books as enthusiastically as they had. The large number of motorcycles in Japan had also been to our advantage, in that it had helped popularize us and our undertaking. Of course, the two of us on our faithful Harley were a walking commercial, which Japanese motorcycle companies would have been fools not to make use of, and we anticipated some kind of reward once we reached America.

Our memories of Japan are almost all pleasant. We grew to like the Japanese, even if we never could love them. They had also done their best to please us, doing their utmost to mask their intense dislike of strangers. They were clever and knew all about propaganda and popularity but very little about how to incite true admiration and love. It's strange that I should be writing this when the months we spent in Japan were among the pleasantest

Japanese friends gather aboard the Tatsuta Maru to bid us farewell

of our trip, but I never could force my heart. I may have been mistaken and un-just, but I never could grow to love the Japanese.

Leaving Japan, we reflected that we hadn't met a single like-minded world-traveler throughout all our Asian journeys. By world travelers, I don't mean wealthy tourists who travel the globe for their pleasure, but those daring, re-sourceful young men we had encountered in hordes in Europe, especially the Mediterranean, so that, at one time, globetrotting had seemed to us an international industry.

Many countries shrugged off "knights errant" like us; we really belonged to a class of our own but were a mixed crowd in general, consisting of stu-dents, waiters, doctors, and the unemployed. It wasn't love of sportsmanship that drove us on; our goal was to travel and make enough money to travel some more. The best way to make money was by keeping up a regular corre-spondence with various journals and newspapers, which would then publish our brief reports, earning us the money to go just a few more miles.

Some traveled by foot, others on horseback or by automobile. Others rode unicycles, pushed baby strollers, kicked soccer balls around the world, or rowed a boat on dry land. Still others invented all sorts of complicated devices to record the distance they had traveled. One Hungarian boy traveled the world with a fake moving pictures camera, while a young Dutchman insisted on pushing his travel partner around the world on a wheelbarrow. It goes

Our bike takes a well-deserved break in the bowels of the oceanliner.

without saying that both the Hungarian boy and the Dutchman rode trains from one town to the next, putting on their walking shoes and gear only when they appeared in public and made every effort to raise money for the next stretch of their trip. I once met a Frenchman who had been traveling around the world for two years without once leaving the Paris city limit. Another Frenchman, proposing to walk around the world, ended up riding the train second class from town to town, taking a taxi from the station to an elegant hotel, where he would put on his "boy scout" clothes and gigantic backpack and head out to sell "authentic" postcards and first-hand reports of his travels. Once he finished in that particular town, he put on his suit, called a taxi, and took the train to the next town over.

One especially resourceful German man claimed to be walking around the world, and, using the connections he developed as a result of his daring mission, kept getting discount tickets on all the Italian railways.

There must have been hundreds upon hundreds of world travelers out there. The Germans started it all, but were soon followed by Hungarians, Dutchmen, Italians, and daring sons of the Baltic states. There were so many of us that most governments and newspapers, even the general public, disapproved. People stopped buying postcards and authentic reports, and many self-made globetrotters suddenly found themselves out of business. Most of them never made it out of Europe anyway, or, even if they did, they rarely got past North Africa and the Middle East. We never met the likes of them in Asia, Australia, China, and Japan. I remember the disbelief and mischievous twinkle in people's eyes when we first set out and told them of our plans. Many of them didn't believe we'd ever achieve what we'd set out to do. There were so many phonies out there that we chose not to use their most popular motto, "Round the World" in any language, whether it was spelled "Rund um die Welt," "Giro del Mondo," "Vuelta al Mundo" or "Autour du Monde." These few words would have done us more harm than good. Instead, we made up our minds to dress professionally, act confidently, carry a few letters of recommendation from powerful people as well as enough money to get by until we made some more. Our number one recommendation, however, turned out to be the incredible miles behind us, the distance we had already come.

And so we left the immense continent of Asia, where we had seen and learned so much. It was in Asia that we had discovered for ourselves the kind of life lived by the colonized on their own land, a life both of great color and of destitution. We, Europeans, really have no right to complain when faced with the poverty of millions upon millions of Arabs, Black Africans, Malaysians, Indians, and Chinese, who make up a good portion of the population of our world. If we were to divide up all the nations of this world into two large groups, one for the wealthy and one for the impoverished, very few, if any, European countries would have the right to sit down at the table of the poor.

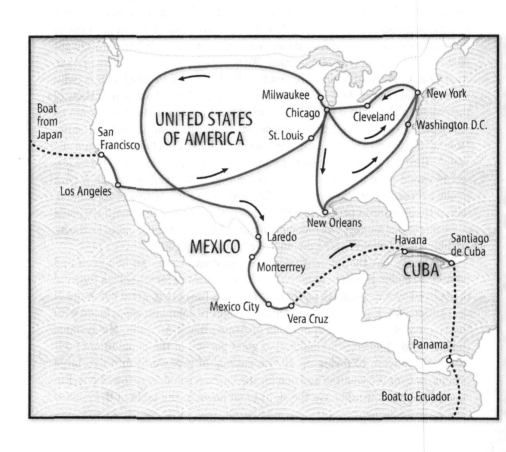

Boat
from
Japan

San
Francisco

Los Angeles

UNITED STATES
OF AMERICA

Milwaukee
Chicago
St. Louis

Cleveland

New York

Washington D.C.

New Orleans

MEXICO   Laredo

Monterrrey

Mexico City   Vera Cruz

Havana   Santiago
de Cuba

CUBA

Panama

Boat to Ecuador

The New World

Evergreen California

Hawaii. The volcanic mountains appeared at a distance after eight grueling days of travel. As our ship was to stop over in Hawaii for the space of twenty-four hours, Honolulu was to be our first impression of the United States of America. Honolulu, the capital of Hawaii, featured smooth concrete roads lined by gorgeous palm trees. The trees grew naturally; the roads were an American privilege. As a sizeable portion of the indigenous population had died out, large groups of Japanese had moved in to revive the failing work force. Not only was Honolulu charming, but so was the entire island of Oahu, along with the neighboring islands. It seemed quite natural that American millionaires held Hawaii in high regard and often made it the object of their excursions. The shores of California were only four days off by ship, and Honolulu's coasts were lined with luxury hotels to satisfy the most elegant tastes. Hotel prices, however, weren't cut out for our budget. The cheapest room at the Royal Hawaii Hotel cost $25 a night.

Live and extinct volcanoes, the grotesque beauties of the island, the palaces of ancient Hawaiian kings and princes, the near-miraculous natural beauty, and the air of mystery shrouding the islands all added to the attractions of Hawaii. When the sun set, guitar players tuned their instruments and black-haired, bewitching Hawaiian women danced the Hula to the strains of the melancholy music. Everyone, from the American flapper to the Australian farmer, found the lush, tropical heat of Hawaiian nights irresistible. How fine it would have been to stay there forever, but the continent was waiting.

We set sail for California, arriving four days later in San Francisco. Our first sight of the American continent was a picturesque image of the Golden Gate Bridge and the daring skyscrapers of the city of San Francisco. We were well aware that entering the United States was difficult business and sat through our medical examinations and meeting with the border guard with worried expression. Simply getting a visa was no child's play, however, Gyuszi and I had bought our permits to America while back in Australia. Visa in hand, we still were unsure whether we would be allowed to enter the country. We were all the more worried because our money was running low; the

ocean journey from Japan had drained our resources considerably. If we'd been required to pay the usual deposit of $500 per new arrival, we never would have set foot in America.

What saved us in the end was that we were Europeans arriving from the direction of Asia. The other factor in our easy entry into the country was the American love of sport. Once we had explained who we were and what we had set out to do, we were immediately swept past the border guards, officials, and other formalities, given a permit to stay in the United States for not six but twelve months, and, before we knew it, we found ourselves on American soil. Our encounter with the customs official was brief but memorable. He explained that unless we were prepared to pay a large deposit covering our motorcycle, we'd have to pay the proper customs fees. Then, looking at our motorbike, which I wouldn't have parted with for a thousand dollars, he smiled up at us and said, "This motorbike is worth twenty dollars; customs duty is two." After making out a check, he sent us on our merry way. Gyuszi and I concluded that the U.S. might very well be a biker's paradise.

Everything was strange and new to our eyes, starting with the white workers in the San Francisco Bay. We had, once again, grown so accustomed to seeing tiny Malaysian, Chinese, and Japanese men at work that the sight of hard-working white men was almost shocking. Even more interestingly, we found fellow white men to be unattractive, large and burly, overly tall and too red in the face. It wasn't hard to see why many Asians considered themselves superior to white men. Gyuszi and I recalled the words of a Japanese man who, dissatisfied with the tag "yellow" usually attached to Asians, had explained that Japanese skin color was natural, human color, and that white men were the color of spoiled meat.

Had someone asked us at the very start what our projected travel plans through the United States were to be, we would have been hard put for an answer. Our aim was to see as much as possible, not to content ourselves with the large cities, but to insist on our share of the Arizona deserts, the Texas plains, Hungarian-American communities, and glamorous Hollywood.

It was hard to believe our motorcycle was carrying us across the fifth of the six continents we were to visit. Our Harley proved its mettle on the roads of America, and, I am proud to say, so did we. The most dangerous parts of our journey were behind us, and our exhilaration at suddenly finding ourselves on the smooth roads of a real twentieth century place, with all its luxuries and modern comforts, was great.

San Francisco, one of the historical sites of the famous Gold Rush, turned out to be an excellent starting point, a yardstick for the rest of urban America. The city itself was by no means large, and everything worth visiting was concentrated about "downtown." Downtown was the heart of the city, home to shops, offices, hotels, and hospitals. Most of the theaters were also clustered in the downtown region; the only thing missing was private homes. As we found out later, the majority of San Franciscans lived in the sprawling suburbs, which consisted of endless rows of small, individual houses, making at least one car per family indispensable.

California had a population of six million, and these six million people owned a total of two million automobiles. That means every third Californian was a driver! Market Street featured four tramways in addition to the car lanes, and despite the chaos, everyone seemed to get where he was going. At the same time, had Gyuszi and I ever tired of walking on the ground, traffic was so heavy that we could have hopped from one car to the next at any time during the day without once touching the ground.

Americans drove on the right side of the road. There were very few policemen in sight, but traffic progressed just the same thanks to the ubiquitous traffic lights and white paint on the road indicating important forks and turns. The best thing about the American driving system was the STOP sign. When there were no traffic lights at a street juncture, there was always a round sign indicating that anyone wishing to turn onto or cross the main road was to stop for a second or two, size up the situation and then drive on. This concept was so ingrained in the heads of American drivers that they stopped at the proper moment even if the entire juncture was free of cars.

Parking spots were indicated by white paint (one minute limit), yellow paint (twenty or sixty minutes) and red (no parking.) The police took care that the system remained well-oiled and running smoothly. Once you parked your car or motorbike, a policeman would immediately show up and mark the tires with chalk indicating when you had stopped. If you exceeded the time indicated by the color of the paint, you could be sure of a hefty fine.

It didn't take us long to pick up and grow accustomed to the new driving rules. What's more, the sidecar of our motorbike was decorated with over eighty plaques and badges, attracting friendly honks and greetings wherever we went.

Sundays in San Francisco were unusually quiet. Traffic lights were turned off, there was virtually no traffic and everyone who had the opportunity vacated the downtown area. The most popular place for weekend excursions was Golden Gate Park, which featured few pedestrians but all the more cars and motorbikes. The alleys of the park were specially widened to allow for motor and equestrian sport. Towards evening, long columns of cars stood parked in the semi-darkness of the park. As hanging curtains from your car window was forbidden in California, young lovers had it rough.

The AAA or American Automobile Association was a model network of aid, with excellent coverage not only in the larger cities but small towns as well. There were over a million AAA members who enjoyed great maps and other excellent services.

Our visit to the United States, a land famous for wealth and bounty, began in the worst year of the Depression. The more we saw of America, the more obvious it became that the situation was far from cheery. Many shops were closed, the economy stagnant. American financial life had hit the rock bottom. Thank God, things have improved since then.

At that time, everyone was scared for himself and for his family. Most factories simply stopped production, the number of the unemployed soared to ten million, and countless banks closed their doors from one day to the next. Those unfortunate enough to have chosen the wrong bank lost money. Many people lost their entire life's savings, as the prevalent custom in America was to put your money in the bank upon receiving it. Many families were forced to sell their home, their car, their radio and piano, furniture, right down to the shirt on their backs. Most Americans had monthly installments of some kind to pay after purchases they had made. Wages were generally good, so that a working man had no problem paying his bills, but as soon as you lost your job, you were on your own. Bills piled up, the banks no longer gave out loans and many of the products people had bought, even if they had paid most of the installments, had to be returned to the seller. People had no buying power even as the market was flooded with goods. Many lost all they had.

Our first encounter with Hungarian-Americans came in San Francisco. Although we later made many good acquaintances from among them and, in hindsight, have a lot of reasons to be thankful to Hungarian expats, our first impressions were far from positive. There were approximately 3,000 Hungarians living in San Francisco, but there was no Hungarian life to speak of. Granted, there were Hungarian clubs, but people spoke mostly English and showed no appreciation or deeper knowledge of their Hungarian heritage. Exceptions were always refreshing, and we did meet a few Hungarian-Americans who were proud of who they were and did their best to preserve and cultivate their traditions.

Prohibition was still in full swing during the time of our visit. Upon arrival, we resigned ourselves to drinking no alcohol for as long as we were in the United States, but the very next day, we were already enjoying some fine wine at a Hungarian dinner. Most resourceful people had figured out how to make their own wine at home; Hungarian and Italian vintners were producing some of the best California wines in secret. Homemade beer, however, was a sore disappointment.

Those who weren't in America at the time of Prohibition would find it very difficult, if not impossible, to see through the maze of contradictions that such legislation inevitably produced. It was forbidden to produce, sell, or circulate alcoholic beverages, just as it was forbidden to buy and consume alcohol in public. On the other hand, people could drink whatever they chose in the privacy of their homes, and nobody seemed to care that alcohol didn't just flow from the faucet, that it had to be purchased somewhere and taken home.

Stepping into a small store, I noticed a row of what looked like smooth, black bricks. Taking one in hand, I stepped up to the shopkeeper to inquire what it was. "It's a 'wine brick,'" he answered, "sold everywhere." As it turned out, the wine brick was no less than a mass of wine grapes tightly compressed and ready for "home harvest." Selling wine bricks wasn't forbidden, but selling fake wine bricks was punishable by law. In other words, those who sold wine bricks that produced no wine were fined, while those shops carrying the real thing did rather well. Malt was sold in cans, accompanied by a set of thorough instruction on how to brew it into beer, and all this in a country where the sale and consumption of beer were against the law.

Drinking laws were in a class of their own; broken by nearly everyone, they were never quite taken seriously, even by the very people paid to enforce them. There was much the police overlooked; to tell the truth, they didn't have much choice.

We attended numerous dinners and banquets, hosted by Hungarian-Americans or university and motorist associations and attended by local dignitaries such as the mayor, police chief, and other notables. Wine and spirits flowed freely, and the policemen in attendance drank to our health with the best of them.

Hungarian events, especially when held in parks or other public places, always attracted a multinational crowd. Everyone knew Hungarians made good wine and expressed their newfound interest in Hungarian cultures by buying tickets to all the available get-togethers. We ourselves attended numerous picnics where wine, beer, even brandy were sold publicly, with signs advertising the drinks in question. Granted, the signs were in Hungarian.

Our every visit to a Hungarian home began with an aperitif of some kind. "I wish we were better drinkers," Gyuszi once exclaimed in response to the countless offers of fine spirits we received at every visit. It was only natural that people stocked up on alcohol during Prohibition. Even those who had never had so much as a sip before the new legislation was passed, now felt obliged to augment their personal wine and brandy collections.

And so we began our spirited journey through evergreen California. Although we had arrived in midwinter, the weather was mild, the sun constantly shining, and the oranges in the orchards lining the roads were gathering in sweetness. In the distance, we saw snow-capped mountains, but those living on the coastland or in the valleys never saw a speck of snow, unless they brought it home by car. This was something people actually did. They'd get in their cars, drive an hour or two to the mountains, pile their automobiles high with snow, and drive back down to the beach, where they played with great delight in a mixture of snow and ocean water.

To be quite honest, we experienced little of the famous natural beauties of California. Everything we saw worth noting was manmade and artificial. The orange orchards that went on for miles on all sides of the roads would hardly have been there if not for hundreds of diligent workers. When the heat was especially intense, orange farmers placed large blocks of ice among the trees; if there was a danger of frost, tiny stoves lit four to five trees apart kept the orchard warm. California farmers definitely had the upper hand. The fantastic little homes, even the villas of the rich, were somewhat artificial: white in color and overly eccentric in taste, they were mostly built in imitation of the prevalent Spanish style.

The United States was a bikers' and drivers' paradise. With years of experience behind us, we can honestly say that American roads are the best in the world, English roads being a close second. Wherever we went, and not only in California, but in the tremendous heartland of America, we encountered nothing but wide, smooth concrete roads. Not only did every individual state have a dense network of roads, but there were two or three massive highways of about 4-5,000 kilometers each connecting the Pacific and Atlantic Ocean. Good quality roads led from one tiny town to the next, and through the mountainous regions. The roads were as straight as circumstances allowed, twisting up the sides of mountains in ingenious curves peppered with bridges, tunnels, viaducts and other technological wonders. In many places, the roads were brown from all the oil that had trickled from passing cars. A good rule of thumb was: the browner the road, the steeper the climb.

Traffic was extremely busy. Cars regularly whizzed past even seemingly isolated country roads. In fact, an average American highway was generally more traffic-infested than the busiest boulevards of Budapest. American drivers were no fans of speeding; they generally progressed at no more than 70-80 kilometers per hour. Horse-drawn carts, motorbikes, even bicycles were rare; we often went for hundreds of kilometers without seeing a single one. Police and postal workers sometimes rode motorbikes, otherwise, bikers were looked down upon by the majority of car drivers. Americans were too comfortable for motorcycles; besides, a good motorbike cost much the same as a good car. Gyuszi and I often wondered where the money for these excellent roads had come from. Automobile tax was nonexistent, except for a minimal ten dollars a year. We finally discovered that the tax was included in gasoline prices; 3-4 cents per gallon resulted in a revenue of $500-600 million dollars a year.

While visiting San José, Gyuszi and I came face to face with the first

Hungarian-American career. Our man had been a world champion of wrestling, but his opponent managed to rip off his ear during an especially brutal match. He then stopped wrestling but remained in America and applied to a university instead. By the time we made his acquaintance, he was a wealthy and respected doctor.

We spent many nights in so-called "auto-camps," conveniently situated just outside most major cities. The auto-camps consisted of row upon row of fully furnished tiny houses, complete with showers, gas stoves, hot running water and electricity, as well as a small private garage for parking your vehicle. Auto-camps were excellent, cheap and comfortable. Visitors generally cooked their own meals in the pans provided, and the whole adventure cost only a single dollar per night.

The roads were lined with gas stations, which did much more than sell gas. Every station offered a range of services: tuning, a car wash, even buffet meals. Gasoline was cheap, no more than 20-25 cents a gallon. We found we had arrived in the middle of the so-called "gasoline wars." Small companies were selling their gasoline for so little that larger companies felt obliged to reciprocate. Then, afraid of going out of business, small companies cut back their prices even further. At one point, gasoline sold for a paltry five cents a gallon, while good drinking water cost ten. The gasoline wars naturally ended when the large companies ate the small companies alive and raised prices dramatically, but all California drivers retained fond memories of the days when California was a land flowing with oil and gasoline.

New oil wells were constantly being discovered. I spoke with a man who bought a seaside plot for a hundred dollars, discovered it gave oil, and was making five hundred dollars a day before he quite knew what had happened.

California was a fortunate land, seemingly free of all poverty and care. Factory towns in the East were stagnating even as wealthy pensioners or bored millionaires built up mansion after mansion on the California coast. Many people who had worked hard all their lives chose California as their place of retirement and moved out West to live out their days in peace and comfort. The other large group of seasonal visitors to California was the society of "hobos," mostly unemployed men who hitchhiked their way out West every winter to avoid the New England chill. In the spring, they migrated back East with the birds. Poor hobos had it tough; their hitchhiking methods had stood them in good stead for a while, but so many naïve drivers had been mugged or conned that fewer and fewer cars stopped at the wave of a hand.

While in Los Angeles, we went from sportsmen to spectators at the Tenth Olympic Games and rejoiced with local Hungarian-Americans at the victories of the Hungarian athletes. Although Hungarian organizations politely requested that the Hungarian athletes be able to stay a few weeks to celebrate

Rosita Morena, Spanish filmstar, Paramount Studios,
Hollywood

their victories in style, they were sent packing the very day after the closing ceremonies.

Still in Los Angeles, we took our time exploring the greatest film studios of the world, as I am sure anybody else would have done. We spent weeks visiting Hollywood, Culver City, National City, Burbank, Santa Monica, and Universal City, and I am proud to say we made time for almost every studio that would have us.

Although the studios had originally been built outside the city, Los Angeles had expanded to such an extent that all the neighboring studio towns suddenly found themselves within the L.A. city limit. When asked about their home town, people still referred to this smaller places by name. Hollywood was the best known studio town to have been engulfed by the L.A. conglomerate, and this was somewhat odd, because, as it turned out, none of the really famous studios were actually located in Hollywood.

As world travelers and bikers, we became instant V.I.P.'s and had free access to most of the studios around. Each film factory was like a tiny state within a state peopled by Arabs, Hindus, Africans, and slave traders who

Joan Blondell at Warner Studios, Burbank, California

were all average white men under all their make-up. The big stars had gorgeous cars, but our trusty old motorbike always attracted the most attention. There was no feeling of distance or hierarchy within the closed world of the studios. World-famous movie stars walked in and out of the cafeteria where we were stationed, stopping for a friendly chat when they saw us with our motorcycle. They were very interested in our travels and happy to oblige us with autographs, even private tours of studios, provided we gave them a ride on our bike. We even received a few lunch invitations and spent many pleasant hours in the spacious studio restaurant.

The various motorcycle companies went wild with the commercial possibilities of it all. They were constantly asking the stars to perch on our old machine for the space of a photograph. These were proud moments, and we made the acquaintance of Greta Garbo, Harold Lloyd, Charlie Chaplin, Douglas Fairbanks, Richard Dix, Edward Robinson, Joan Crawford, Clara Bow, Rosita Moreno and many other celebrities. We were often invited to visit the actors themselves in their homes and familiarized ourselves with the Hungarian film colony. Cecil de Mille, the famous director, and the actor John Barrymore showed special interest in our travels.

John Barrymore admiring our bike in Hollywood

The Hungarian actors, as a group, gave us a phenomenal and warm welcome. Mihály Kertész, Béla Lugosi, Pál Lukács, and Pál Fejős escorted us around their respective studios and invited us to their homes, each in turn. Other famous Hungarians in show business were Mihály Várkonyi, Ernő Vajda, and Gusztáv Pártos. They all made big money, but, like the rest of America, worked hard for their stellar wages. Besides, those in show business were socially expected to live a certain lifestyle. Ernő Vajda's stunning villa, Pál Lukács's small palace, and Mihály Kertész' Spanish-style residence were all located in the heart of Beverly Hills. Mihály Várkonyi and his wife lived high above Hollywood in a splendid mansion with a gorgeous view of the lights and sparkle of Tinseltown.

Those Hungarians who had made it in show business got along very well together. They spent a lot of time in each other's company and often made sumptuous Hungarian lunches and dinners to which they invited all their Hungarian friends. They showed us profound love and friendship, immediately accepting Gyuszi and me into the heart of their social circles. Pál Lukács insisted on riding our beat-up motorbike along the streets of Hollywood. To return the favor, he took us up in his private airplane to enjoy a glimpse of the Hollywood area from above.

An aerial excursion with Pál Lukács

Not only were many famous actors and directors Hungarian, but the movie industry was also chock full with Hungarian musicians, technicians, painters, extras, and simple laborers of all kinds, whose excellent work showed their studios to good advantage.

Hollywood was a fascinating and very beautiful city. Gorgeous young women from all over the world, but especially from within America, flocked to Hollywood to seek their fortunes. Very few made it; many returned home disappointed, realizing they would have to seek employment in more realistic and less glamorous fields. Hollywood must have been the only city in the world with a railroad but no railroad station. Not that there was any need for a railroad station. Everyone either drove or flew where he needed to go. If we were ever out on the street in need of directions, we'd have to wait quite a while before a pedestrian showed up.

There were, on average, three people to every automobile in Los Angeles. Prices were low; you could get incredible deals at any of the numerous second hand car dealerships. Gorgeous, quality cars, no more than two to three years old, sold for $200-300. Smaller vehicles went for a hundred bucks, while decent used cars more than three years old were available for $50. I even saw a few smaller, older cars, which sold for $15, even $10 dollars. I have to mention that these models were available only without a warranty, but were still

Automobile graveyard along the byways of America

in great shape, at least based on the test-drive. One Hungarian friend of ours bought his son an old Ford, its tires still in excellent shape, for a mere ten dollars. Another car owner we knew spent five dollars to have his old seven-seater towed from his garage. Had he done it through official means, he would have been charged at least $20.

Wherever we went in America, as soon as we were outside the city limit, we found ourselves surrounded by miles and miles of junkyards on every side. Hundreds upon hundreds of old cars had been carried off, whole or in pieces. Rusty and broken, these wrecks waited patiently for anyone with a keen sense of mechanics to sift through them and separate what could still be used from the utterly useless. Gyuszi and I saw perfectly good head- and rear-lights, individual leather seats and tires, all in excellent condition and eminently recyclable. The thought of how much money we could have made off them had we been back in Hungary refused to leave us alone. To prove that we weren't the only Hungarians with such thoughts on our minds, one of our new friends confessed to making a decent living scouring abandoned junkyards for reusable parts, which he then sold in Los Angeles.

To be completely fair, and for posterity's sake, I must mention that the people of Hollywood lived off of much more than just movies. Like in any other city on earth, Hollywood dwellers also subscribed to a variety of occupations, and some even insisted they had never seen a film star in person.

Of Hungarian-American Institutions

In Los Angeles, we saw some of the first Hungarian churches we had seen in years. Our delight at discovering these churches was heightened by the years of travel during which we hadn't once had the opportunity to worship in our own language. Sitting in on a service, our eyes filled with tears to hear the priest speak to Hungarians in Hungarian and address national issues that mattered to Hungarians.

California was home not only to numerous Hungarian churches but also to Hungarian newspapers, and it would be impossible for me to proceed without first describing the positive effect these two institutions had, not just on Hungarian-Americans but on Hungarians throughout the world.

Hungarian religious life in America was not to be measured with an old-country yardstick. Religious institutions received no financial support from the U.S. government, neither were there laws prescribing donations on the part of the parishioners. If a parish did spring up and managed to survive, it was entirely the result of the efforts of the pastor and his flock.

And how many Hungarians were there in the United States? Our data is fuzzy by necessity. After the Trianon Treaty, Hungarians not living within the newly drawn borders no longer counted as Hungarians if they chose to emigrate, but were listed in the Romanian, Czechoslovakian, etc. headcount. In the period between 1870 and 1920, when historical Hungary was still intact, approximately a million immigrants arrived in the United States from the Kingdom of Hungary, but only about 600,000 were ethnically Hungarian and spoke the Hungarian language. Many of these immigrants had died, others moved back to Europe or became entirely Americanized. American census takers counted everyone whose parents had been born in America as English-speaking, so the Hungarian thread was broken, at least at an official level, in the third generation. In 1930, there were 274,000 Hungarian speakers in the United States, who not only spoke the language but claimed to have been born in Hungary. Approximately 250,000 of them were ethnically Hungarian. Second-generation Hungarian speaking Americans numbered 316,000, with about 280,000 actually belonging to the Hungarian ethnic group. In other words, there were nearly 530,000 Hungarians in 1930 America. Seventy percent of them lived in four of the fifty states: Ohio, New York, Pennsylvania, and New Jersey. Most of the larger Hungarian communities were located on the East Coast, but there were Hungarians living in all fifty states in diasporic communities of various sizes. Hungarian immigrants generally lived in cities and worked in different industries, as artisans, or ran small businesses. The half a million Hungarian-Americans were decently employed and made a better living than they would have managed in the old country. Nevertheless,

Our first Hungarian-American church, Los Angeles, California

very few believed their dreams had come true, and precious few succeeded in making the fortune they had dreamed of.

I don't think there's a single Hungarian in the world who knows more about the Hungarian life worldwide than Gyuszi and I. There wasn't a single country on our travels where we didn't seek out the company of local Hungarians and listen to their stories. Regardless of where we were, at least one Hungarian always sought us out and told us not only his own story but the stories of countless others who were struggling along with him. Gyuszi and I visited Hungarians in their homes, in their offices, factories, churches, schools, and societies, growing in community with them, listening both to their success stories and complaints with discerning ears.

Hungarian-Americans worked hard for the financial edge they had over most other Hungarians in the world. Those working in the factories were especially drained; factory owners cultivated exploitation as an art. Many Hungarian immigrants to the United States had a very poor grasp of English and were therefore usually forced to perform menial tasks. American mines were filled with Hungarians. Hungarian workers, even after making enough money to buy their own small modest home, nevertheless always faced the haunting question of whether they wouldn't have done equally well had they persevered in Hungary. And even if their lot in America was better financially, wasn't relative poverty in your homeland worth more than modest wealth in a strange country? Hungarians all over the world were notorious for homesickness. They felt their immigrant status keenly, even if they managed to rise in the pecking order. Older Hungarians dreamt nightly of the villages they had left behind, villages where they had known everyone they met, where their neighbors had been just like them and had shared their mother tongue.

Hungarian-American life specifically had its own consolations. One was a robust democracy. Although they were immigrants, Hungarians did not feel oppressed or subordinated; they were respected, and, for the most part, treated like all other citizens. The other consolation stemmed from the sure knowledge that the future of their children was secure. Back in the old country, sons would rarely have surpassed their fathers in knowledge, social rank, or wealth, but in America, they had every opportunity of becoming proud, well-educated American citizens who would grow to prefer their adoptive country to all other nations on earth.

Grown children kept their aged parents from returning to Hungary once their life's work was done. Young Hungarian-Americans were not homesick for Hungary; they couldn't imagine their life anywhere outside America. In this regard, many Hungarian parents made a grievous mistake. Their children received an American education in school, and knew precious little about where their parents had come from and often spoke little or no Hungarian. Even those who had some Hungarian knew only basic expressions and were unable to read or write. Their understanding of Hungary and Hungarians was minimal and skewed. All they knew of the old country they learned through the stories their parents told, even if their parents had never left their natal village but to come to America. As a result of their ignorance, many young Hungarian-Americans were ashamed of their heritage and of their parents, especially those poor parents unable to master English. Most Hungarian parents didn't make a reasonable effort to teach their children the language. An entire generation grew up whose members were unable to communicate with their own parents. I saw many sad examples of Hungarian mothers attempting to talk to their infants in broken English.

No wonder then that members of the new generation often posed the silliest questions upon seeing us. "Are there motorcycles in Hungary?" was a perennial favorite, but their eyes also grew wide with wonder when we explained that there were radios and airplanes in Hungary, despite what their parents, who hadn't been to Hungary for twenty years, had told them. A college-educated youngster once brought me a picture article about Hungary and expressed his astonishment that Hungarian men actually wore tuxedos.

When parents failed at the task, it was up to Hungarian religious and social organizations to instill a little Hungarian-ness in the tender youths. To our greatest joy, we discovered that intelligent, schooled parents, unless they had personal reasons for wanting to forget Hungary, made sure their children spoke, read and wrote Hungarian. Many of these young people were indistinguishable from those raised in Hungary, at least as far as their mastery of Hungarian was concerned.

The Hungarian press also made heroic efforts to enrich the lives of Hungarian immigrants throughout the United States. Although there were many different Hungarian newspapers and journals in existence, theirs was a bitter struggle to stay alive. Hungarian immigrants who knew little or no English turned to these papers for information about local events, both Hungarian related and not, and news of the old country. I feel very strongly about the responsibility of all Hungarians to support the Hungarian media abroad. Were these newspapers and journals to cease being published, Hungarian life in the diaspora would shrivel up and disappear.

Hungarian religious organizations were especially in need of support. Priests and pastors, whether of the Roman Catholic, Protestant, or Byzantine Rite Catholic denominations, made superhuman efforts to keep the Hungarian communities together. Building their churches stone by stone, they often worked for many long years before a parish hall large enough to entertain the entire community could be raised. After the church and parish buildings were intact, most spiritual leaders dreamt up a Hungarian school and began a movement to turn their dreams into reality.

Everything they owned, they got from their parishioners, most of whom were far from wealthy. Donations were small, but they were all that the parish had. When the economy was especially bad, people were unable to pay even the tiniest installments for the upkeep of their religious institutions. Good priests and pastors often saw hunger but stayed with their flock, hoping and praying for a better future.

So-called church membership fees did not even come close to providing for the needs of the community, but Hungarian religious leaders gave evidence of their enthusiasm and creativity, organizing modest parties, theatrical performances, etc., to help raise funds for whatever the parish needed. Others took their flock bowling or planned card championships, anything to keep people involved and in attendance. Active from morning till night, Hungarian religious leaders worked tirelessly and selflessly for the improvement and longevity of Hungarian life in America. I have seen a Hungarian priest make rounds every morning with his own car to drive parishioners' children to the Hungarian school; I know how many nights our pastors spent, bowed over a writing desk, lost in thought, calculation and prayer, all for the good of their communities. Those not aware of the hardships the Hungarian religious faced and overcame would find it strange that a Hungarian priest should urge his flock from the pulpit to attend a traditional Hungarian dinner or take part in the weekly card games.

There was no religious instruction in public schools, and this lack of guidance made a pastor's job especially difficult. Because a strong theological grounding was unavailable to many, various sects and denominations seemed to spring up by the day. According to some sources, there were more than two hundred Christian sects in existence in 1930s America. It would be stating the obvious to explain that the founders, "saints" and "prophets" of many of these new religions were extremely business-minded. Americans were, because of the lack of religious instruction in school, extremely naïve and gullible in these matters. Phony preachers who would at best have been shunned in Europe, made it big in the States, gathering thousands upon thousands of enthusiastic believers willing to further their leader's cause both spiritually and financially. The more charismatic the leader, the more money he was able to con out of his credulous flock.

Amy McPhaerson, a self-proclaimed prophet living in Los Angeles, had made millions of dollars selling her ideas. She constructed a marble temple to house her theatrical services and even had a radio station of her own, which she used to urge her followers to greater heights of financial generosity. Those of her flock believed her to be a saint, capable of performing miracles. Some claimed to have seen her drown in the ocean and emerge live and well out of a nearby desert months later.

Here I would like to make a note about Hungarian clubs and civil institutions. There must have been more than a thousand such societies all over the United States with the purpose in mind of supporting Hungarian life financially, morally, and culturally. The sheer number of societies was mind-boggling. Had they all joined forces, they might have moved mountains! But the dream of the various Hungarian groups uniting under one banner was nothing but a mirage to a thirsty mind. There was too much infighting, disagreement, and selfish pursuing of individualistic goals for Hungarian-Americans to be able to realize the dream of perfect unity, but even a thousand institutions, each going after its own head, were better than none. A country that could support a thousand Hungarian institutions was a country with a breathing, feeling Hungarian presence. Every institution, after all, was founded with the basic idea of bringing Hungarians together and making sure they stayed together. Natural selection, or rather social selection, ensured that only the most vital and dynamic communities survived.

Many Hungarians complain that ours is a nation that doesn't know how to stick together. I don't see this as being necessarily true; the Hungarian community spirit is no greater and no weaker than that of other nations. While traveling the colonies, Gyuszi and I had encountered numerous tiny

Hungarian communities infested with gossip, back-stabbing, and ill-will. At the same time, wasn't this a natural human process to be constantly splitting into smaller groups and finding reasons to fight? This is the human curse, and not specifically the Hungarian curse. After all, Hungarian-Americans had founded the Verhovay Society with 20,000 members and almost two million dollars in funds. That had to be worth something.

I think that every decent Hungarian needs to look with admiration and appreciation at the untiring efforts of the Hungarian churches, societies, and press in the United States. After experiencing first hand the quality of life these institutions sought to uphold, I can safely say that Hungarian-Americans who subscribe to no Hungarian newspapers and weren't members of a Hungarian church or society might have been good Americans, but they certainly did not deserve the epitaph of Hungarian.

Our journey through America was made magical and unforgettable by the presence and hospitality of the Hungarian communities, whom I could never pass over without a few well-deserved words of appreciation. Although there were no Hungarians to be found between California and St. Louis, as we made our way east of St. Louis, we always became honorary members of the Hungarian communities we encountered. Every city we passed through, we stayed with fellow Hungarians; their hospitality amazed us with its warmth and insistence. These were the warmest welcomes we got anywhere and could be traced back to two sources: our own love and respect for fellow Hungarians, and our efforts, by our travels, to make our country better known world-wide.

American welcomes didn't lag far behind the Hungarian ones. The American press followed our movements with great interest, publishing a number of lengthy articles detailing our past travels and future plans. We always made sure to emphasize our nationality, even writing a few articles about Hungary for the American public.

Gyuszi and I soon realized that our American stay had great propaganda power, and we did our best to represent our country wherever we went. Sometimes we visited remote small towns and places not originally figuring in our travel plans just so the people living there would get a taste of Hungarian sportsmanship. It was a very big deal to Americans that we appeared on the front pages of their newspapers, many of which sold millions of copies. Our Hungarian-American friends were immensely proud of our achievements and took to carrying articles about Gyuszi and me around to show their Slovakian, Romania, Polish, Italian, and American neighbors.

During our U.S. visit, we also gave a number of lectures in English at a variety of venues: clubs, public schools, universities, and radio interviews, during which hundreds of thousands of American citizens were subjected to our

One of our countless talks addressed to Hungarian-Americans

poor pronunciation. We made a lot of new friends for our country and for Hungarians living abroad.

Our popularity may have been one cause of the warm hospitality we received everywhere we went, but I still believe that the warmth and friendship were genuine and not simply popularity-based. The entire American stretch of our travels was like a triumphant march. The Hungarian-American press, always a step ahead, took great care in organizing with whom we would be staying and where we would be giving one of our lectures or attending a reception held in our honor. The various societies, religious, and civil organizations competed for the right to house and feed us; we were constantly in and out of balls, banquets and large-scale parties given for our pleasure. The number of invitations to private homes was staggering, so much so, that we had incredible difficulties leaving any town with a decent-sized Hungarian population.

Using the money we had left, we published travelogues in Hungarian and English at the Hungarian publishing houses in San Francisco and Los Angeles. Fellow Hungarians were especially interested in what we had to say and purchased as many copies of our books as their budgets allowed. This initial generosity enabled us to print a new set of travelogues, which were, in turn, bought by other interested Hungarians, many of whom were otherwise unemployed.

Passing through larger towns, we always gave long talks peppered with a series of slides. People found our lectures and photographs to be so fascinating that we often found ourselves repeating what we had said the day before

at another gathering. Every Hungarian religious organization and social institution did its utmost to raise awareness of our talks by reserving lecture halls
and printing invitations. Those who did the most to help us wouldn't even
accept a complementary ticket.

Not even the warm and generous welcomes we received could cover up the
poverty that was rampant in all our communities. There was no employment
and no money. Poverty in the U.S. was different form poverty in the Old World.
Here, nobody went hungry and American children would have glibly turned
down an offer of bread and butter. Food was cheap and charitable organizations had a good grip on the situation. Every city, more or less, had the
resources to care for its poor.

American poverty had nothing to do with hunger. We often visited Hungarian families and had roast duck and strudel for dinner while the family sitting
around the table claimed total destitution. The quality of life in America was
much higher than that in Hungary. People's expectations were greater; if a
family were forced to sell their car, this was the equivalent of a Hungarian
worker being obliged to walk to work instead of taking the streetcar. If an
American had to miss his weekly jaunt to the movie theater, he experienced
this setback as a Hungarian would have experienced having to skip lunch or
dinner. Those who had to give up their telephones, and, God forbid, their radios, were true pariahs. Despite this widespread "misery," we often saw unemployed Americans get in their cars and go hunting, fishing, or sun-bathing
on the beach. The people lining up in front of soup kitchens often took their
cars there and drove off after enjoying their free meal.

It would be impossible for me to mention every single Hungarian institution and each Hungarian man, woman, and child deserving of our praise. I
cannot remember that we left a single Hungarian-American community behind with a bitter taste in our mouths. There were individual Hungarians,
however, who had distanced themselves from the rest of their nation and gotten mixed up in new political ideologies they themselves little understood.
They became the playthings of those who had managed to dupe them and
make a fortune off of their gullibility. These "lost sheep" hated everything
that had to do with Hungary or the Hungarian people. In their eyes, our country was a place of political terror and social oppression, all aimed at destroy-
ing the working class. These were people who hadn't been in Hungary, or in
Europe for that matter, for years, even decades, and no longer had any idea of
the state of things in that part of the world. I found it difficult to understand
why these radical Hungarian immigrants had taken it upon themselves to
save the American political soul. All they got in return for their pains was
time in prison or deportation.

One extreme example is the story of the Los Angeles Hungarian woman

314

who used the American flag to scrub the floor of her apartment, for which in-discretion she got to spend five years in jail. Others organized a protest against the Hungarian athletes arriving for the Olympic games and ended up severely beaten by the American police. Still others, believing the old adage that the pen is mightier than the sword, vented their rage by scribbling away at libelous articles about Gyuszi and myself to be published in the local news-paper. Gyuszi and I made sure he got Hungarian style thanks for his efforts, and the man was immediately fired by two of the Hungarian newspapers for which he wrote.

Fortunately, un-Hungarian Hungarians like the above were few and far be-tween. They had little, if any effect, on the decent, religious, and patriotic Hungarians who made up the majority of Hungarian-American communities. We had these good Hungarians to thank for the material success of the Amer-ican portion of our trip, which meant replenishing our financial sources to such an extent that we had no money-related worries whatsoever during our two years in South America. The Hungarian communities in the following cit-ies did the most to financially advance our cause: Bridgeport, Cleveland, Chi-cago area, New York, Pittsburgh area, Los Angeles, Bethlehem, Milwaukee, Buffalo, Detroit, Trenton, New Brunswick, South Norwalk, Perth Amboy, Youngstown, Passaic-Garfield, Carteret, Allentown, Phillipsburg, Easton, South Bend. The Hungarians living in the above towns supported us by buying our books and enthusiastically attending our lectures.

The Anti-pioneer Story: From the West to the East

The five thousand kilometers between California and New York passed like a dream on the smooth American roads. The first stretch of our trip was or-ange-scented and overshadowed by palms. Groves of the above trees alter-nated with vast dried up pastures. The road was fenced in on both sides by a maze of wires; not only was it impossible to veer off because of the fencing, it was also impossible to stop because of the thousands of automobiles stream-ing on behind us. There were no milestones, but the signposts generally told us all we needed to know. Reaching the border with Mexico, we saw with our own eyes to what lengths Americans went to get legally and properly drunk. Some drove all the way from San Francisco for their weekly fix. The gigantic signs posted all along the road leading to Mexico proclaimed "Drunk drivers will be prosecuted" to no avail. People figured if they had driven a thousand kilometers to the Mexican border, they owed it to themselves to get roaring drunk before beginning the arduous drive back. Just over the border, a variety of dubious pleasures awaited American visitors in the form of bars, dens, gambling joints, beautiful and ugly women. When the evening came,

Giant cactus in New Mexico

thousands of satisfied customers, some ruddy, others pale, made their gently swaying way back to the land of holy Prohibition.

Our trip through California was followed by the Arizona, New Mexico and Texas stretch. Gyuszi and I headed east on Route 80, popularly known as the "Old Spanish Trail." We were essentially retracing the steps, only in the opposite direction, of the heroic Franciscan padres who had made the grueling trek West. The blood-soaked Indian territories we crossed so glibly at a hundred kilometers per hour and on excellent roads had been the scenes of life-and-death encounters between the Spanish and Native Americans not so very long ago. Traffic steadily decreased as we left California until the roads were empty of all but transcontinental travelers.

Great desert roads in Arizona

We saw very little of the romance of the Wild West with its cowboys and Indians. Granted, there were cowboys in actual cowboy hats, but they mostly drove Fords on the country roads, even their horses rode trailers. Troops of wandering gypsies occasionally crossed our path; they traveled in "caravans" reminiscent of Hungarian gypsies, and otherwise resembled their European counterparts in their ragged attire and dirty faces, the disheveled hair of their women and the nakedness of their children. Nevertheless, these were American gypsies who rode dilapidated old Fords instead of horse-drawn carts. There were twenty gypsy passengers to every ten-dollar vehicle; crowded inside or balancing on top, they dried their clothing in the sun as they went, and the copper pans hanging down the sides of their cars clanked together to the rhythm of the moving vehicle.

It didn't take us long to cross the infamous "Desert Country," which, thanks to the excellent roads and modern amenities, no longer constituted a serious obstacle to travelers. The deserts of the Southwest were barren and monotonous, with only a scraggly cactus or two struggling to bring life to the arid landscape. The air was hot and dry; there was nothing but sand on all sides, the nearest town several days away. The state of our thermometer recalled summer in India, but despite the awful heat, we enjoyed first class roads all the way through with rest stops every fifteen minutes. Each rest stop doubled as a gas station and a buffet, with free ice water for everyone. The road the pioneers had traveled was still visible in the nearby sand and hauntingly reminiscent of the caravan routes of Syria and deep Africa. Wooden boards, wire netting and other clutter stuck out here and there from the quicksand.

We passed through several Native American villages. On the historical lands of the Apache tribe, we saw a copper-skinned people no longer dressed in bright plumage but sporting worn work clothes, no longer running about with bloody tomahawks or smoking peace pipes, but placidly tending their animals and living out their days in tiny houses of wood or corrugated iron. A few Indians clad in traditional tribal wear lined the roads hoping to make a few dollars by posing for photos with tourists. The proud descendants of once great tribes recited their history by rote; a single photo cost a quarter, but if you paid half a dollar, you got to pose three times with the braves.

The landscape changed drastically after we had crossed the Mississippi River. We could hardly hide our amused smiles when locals wonderingly inquired how on earth we had crossed the Arizona Desert. In reality, this stretch of road had been one of the most uneventful of all our travels; aside from a few rattlesnakes, nothing had impeded our speedy, even exhilarating, progress.

St. Louis was the first large city we encountered after leaving California, and, following a comfortable paved road, we made our way to Chicago and then on to the heavily populated East Coast. We made an effort to visit every notable city on the way, traveling tens of thousands of kilometers in the grip of our wanderlust, making two lengthier stops in Chicago and New York.

Chicago, notorious for crime throughout the world, seemed placid and steady to us. Gyuszi spent days on end in the most promising looking parts of town, trying desperately to get a taste of the gangster's life, but to no avail. After all, as we found out, the gangsters that really mattered lived in palaces, not dilapidated tenements. We never even heard a machine gun go off, yet it was enough to read the daily papers to size up the degree of corruption that had the city in its grip. Robbery and murder were all in a day's work, but what really made us blink was the news that the city of Chicago was near bankruptcy, when officially, it was known as one of the wealthiest cities in all of America. The city had no money. Top officials hadn't received their salaries in months, schools were closing down; some parts of town were in danger of losing their electricity. People with "typewriters," or small handheld automatics, roamed the streets, which were surprisingly poorly paved and neglected. Not only in Chicago were we surprised at the deplorable quality of urban roads, most other large American cities seemed to share the curse, which was a glaring blemish in our eyes, accustomed as they were to the smooth highways of the West. Loose bricks, potholes, and stone fragments impeded our progress on city roads where speed limits were truly superfluous. Chicago was a city of contradictions: even as the majority of its streets recalled small towns in the Balkans, it was also the proud home of Lakeside, where a superb broad boulevard ran the length of town, unbranching, and a motorist's delight.

The largest house in the world: the "Market House" in Chicago

There were approximately 800,000 automobiles in the Chicago area, with huge parking lots to accommodate factory workers attached to every working factory. At one point, we observed a line of cars parked at the side of the road. Wondering why they were there, we drove closer and soon found the solution to the mystery. The simple workers building the road drove their own cars to work every morning and parked close to the construction site for convenience's sake. A short distance separated the stunning skyscrapers of Chicago from the popular lake shore, which was available for public bathing in all its length. There were no cabins for dressing and undressing, so people either changed standing on the highway or commuted in their swimsuits. When it got especially warm, girls and young men walked around in pajamas and swimsuits, went in and out of restaurants and shops, and generally didn't show the least bit of embarrassment riding the bus or streetcar in their "light" attire.

Policemen, or officers, as they were popularly called, were specially selected for the job based on their height and fine body build. They were respected, cheerful, and rather lenient. It was easy to talk to them, and minor offenders, especially beautiful women with great smiles, often got off scot-free. There were plenty of bad drivers in the city of Chicago, which was only natural seeing as everyone from veritable children to little old ladies felt compelled to test his mettle on the road. "Sunday drivers," those who never used their cars during the week as their office was too close to their home, posed an additional threat. These notoriously bad drivers concentrated their efforts on Sunday afternoons, while young people, drunk and piled into cars six to eight at one time, often drove to their deaths at night heavily under the influence of alcohol.

Prohibition had done much to undermine respect and fear of the law. Bands of moonshiners often grew in power to such an extent that they waged small-scale wars on enemy bands. Those who've never been to America would find it hard to imagine that the shootings, car chases, and machine gun battles pictured in the movies actually took place on a daily basis. When it came to revenge or simply business, gangs didn't know the meaning of the word "mercy." Most murderers were never caught; those who were, rarely got a sentence. Criminals could be punished to the full extent of the law only if their guilt was proven without a doubt, and nobody was fool enough to stand up and witness against a mob leader. Most prosecutors threw up their hands in despair before the day of the trial; valid alibis sold for cheap. The crimes of some mob leaders were an open book to all, yet they continued to range free. Various gangs had representatives in political, governmental, or police circles; uprooting them had proven and was continually proving impossible. There were plenty of places to get alcohol, all of them known to the public at large, and though the police were well aware of most illegal activity, they contented themselves with a few round-ups and nothing more. A typical round-up meant the near destruction of an alcohol joint, with the owner paying for damages. A few weeks passed and the owner reestablished himself with the support of his faithful customers.

Alcohol was smuggled on land, by air and sea, by people of unseen creativity and daring. While driving at night, we often passed huge trucks, visibly carrying rows of barrels under their tarps. It wasn't hard to guess the contents of these barrels. These great bullies cut across towns and swept along highways at a hundred kilometers per hour disregarding all pertinent rules of traffic on their speedy way. Everyone knew very well what they were carrying, but nobody had the guts to stop them. The police generally chose not to notice such incidents.

The towns near the Canadian border were the real hotbeds of alcohol smuggling. Traveling through Buffalo, for example, we learned that our own compatriots had nothing against making a quick buck or two off the less-than-risky alcohol trade. There were fifty to sixty Hungarian-run pubs in Buffalo alone. There wasn't much mystery shrouding these places; once we were inside, all we had to do was knock on a certain side-door to be offered the alcoholic beverage of our choice, whether we were in the mood for wine, beer, brandy, Canadian whisky, even French spirits and champagne. There were some bars where beer flowed from the faucets from pipelines that had their source just over the border in Canada. Some faucets were so complex that they gave good beer only when you spun them a certain way; otherwise, all

Reception in front of City Hall, New York, N.Y.

you got was the virtually non-alcoholic and therefore harmless "near-beer."
Alcohol was regularly smuggled over the border under the strangest guises:
in gasoline cans, secret compartments, harmless-looking suitcases, even under ladies' skirts. I heard of a funeral procession with "nuns" and a "priest"
who crossed the border with a coffin full of booze. They were professional
smugglers who'd somehow gotten hold of the proper clothes but were caught
and arrested in the end.

Gyuszi would have a lot more to tell about the underworld than I. He spent
whole nights roaming the seediest parts of town and making the acquaintance of the petty thieves and small-scale gangsters inhabiting the local
parks. Pretending to be flat broke and Czech or Romanian (he never revealed
that he was actually Hungarian) he brewed plans with the best of them, often
returning from "work" with a dime one of his new "friends" had given him to
buy himself a cup of coffee. Some days he said he'd been given the task of buying revolvers, but on these "mission" days he always chose to stay at home.

The strangest gangster story I have to tell actually happened in the town
of Bridgeport, and I doubt I would believe it myself had I not been a part of it. I
was strolling about the harbor all by myself, when a freight ship weighing 2-
3,000 tons docked at one of the piers. A number of trucks carrying armed men
drove into the area and closed off the entire pier with everyone in it. Some
were carrying revolvers, others had them in their pockets, still others had
gotten hold of a few "typewriters." Those of us stuck on the pier were led to

Niagara Falls

the ship and forced to unload the "goods." We had no choice but to get to work and at top speed. Children and grown-ups, fishermen and businessmen, strolling ladies and gentlemen all began unloading the large crates and stacking them in the trucks. There was no escape; the mobsters were only too willing to use their weapons if something didn't go according to plan. People actually feared the arrival of the police, which would have resulted in a shooting spree that might have cost a number of innocent bystanders their lives. The gang in charge had planned the whole thing carefully; all nearby offices were being guarded; telephones had been switched off. And this is how it happened that an American gang had the public unpack a shipload of alcohol in the middle of a busy port in Prohibition America! I carried a number of crates myself; I had no choice. Nobody in the city had any idea of what was happening by the docks. We worked for three hours straight, and after the job was done, the ship left as quickly as it had come, the armed men got back in their trucks and drove off. Before they had quite left the scene, however, they handed out twenty-dollar bills to everyone who had participated. Twenty dollars for three hours of work was generous pay, even by American standards. When the people got the money, some actually began cheering. I thought to myself that I would gladly carry crates for twenty dollars a day. *Ecce homo!* The very next day, as luck would have it, I found myself loitering about the dock at about the hour the ship had arrived just the day before. I recognized a

The Capitol in Washington D.C.

number of my "co-workers" from the day before, and, exchanging embarrassed smiles, we waited for a ship that never came.

We found the big city skyscrapers endlessly fascinating and even climbed to the top of the Empire State Building in New York. Standing so many tens of stories high, we were under the impression that we were watching the pulsating life of the big city from an airplane. It took us a while to get used to such heights, especially on foggy, overcast days, when we had no choice but to call the doorman on the ground floor to inquire about the weather outside.

The only time we saw horses in New York was in the early mornings, when milkmen generally made their rounds. Children would leave their games and run to the windows to catch a glimpse of their horses; mothers held up their toddlers so the little ones could see the miracle: "Look, a horsie!"

Leaving the East Coast behind, we headed back west and then east again, as far as Texas. We made sure to see all the notable sights the continent had to offer, including a bit of Canada and the amazing Niagara Falls. Spending a number of days in Yellowstone National Park and driving through the pristine mountain passes of the Rocky Mountains, we marveled that despite a population of 120 million, there were still so many large territories of untamed wilderness. A few thousand kilometers later, on the shores of the Colorado River in the Grand Canyon, our eyes were opened to the smallness of man when placed next to the infinity of Nature. The greatest feats of human technology

William E. Borah, the Hungarophile senator

were nothing in comparison to the miracles the Colorado River had wrought on the colored soil of the canyon. Over the millennia, the river had created a diabolical labyrinth with fantastical peaks and hollows, jutting cliffs and a river valley as wide as forty kilometers in some spots. Had it not been for our knowledgeable tour guides, we never would have reached the hidden waters of the Colorado River for all the vast spaces surrounding it.

While in Washington, we were cordially received by President Hoover, whose autograph we still consider one of our prize souvenirs. We spoke with Senator Borah about all things Hungarian and Mayor Walker of New York exhibited great interest in Budapest. In our free time, we made sure to visit a number of factories and industrial plants, including Detroit's Ford conglomerate. Traveling 5-600 kilometers a day was child's play on the consistently excellent roads. The huge distances we traveled started making sense when we picked up the noon papers in California and were able to read what had happened that afternoon in New York. Four hours difference from coast to coast!

Our hopes for material support were dashed at the Harley-Davidson factory in Milwaukee, where we discovered the motorcycle business to be in shambles. Nevertheless, we received a warm welcome, attended a banquet held in our honor, and the C.E.O. and other leading figures in the motorcycle world expressed their admiration and astonishment at how far we had come.

Unexpected encounter in Canada

As a parting gift, they fixed up our motorcycle so that when we finally left, it was almost as good as new.

We quickly got over our disappointment at not receiving further financial recognition of our travels. By the time we arrived in Milwaukee, we had given so many successful talks and made so much money that our fiscal worries concerning the trip to South America became immaterial. Instead of worrying about how we would make ends meet, we were able to stock up on a few things we'd been needing for quite some time. Our Hungarian friends bought us a typewriter, an ammunition factory presented us with an excellent hunting rifle, and another thoughtful compatriot even gave us a small movie camera. We were very excited to be able to record the rest of our journey on film. Finally, we bought a few pieces of equipment for our motorcycle, had a new tent made, and installed a radio in our sidecar. The additions cost us a total of five hundred dollars, and it was with some heartache that we reflected how easy our previous few years would have been had we been as well stocked when we first left Budapest.

Although we appreciated the new equipment, the best development was still to come in the shape of a second German shepherd. We often thought about our faithful companion, Hadji, who had died back in Madras, India. While traveling through the town of Perth Amboy, we passed by the fence of a small family home and were arrested by the sound of barking coming from the other side. "Hadji," Gyuszi and I cried in unison, "good old boy!" And it was truly Hadji, or at least, the young German shepherd on the other side of the fence *looked* like Hadji, only he couldn't have been more than four to five months old. A young girl sat on the porch, reading. She got up, walked to the fence and said in Hungarian, *"Vigyék el, maguknak adjuk,"* "Take him, he's yours." It turned out we had happened on a Hungarian family. "May we come in?" we asked, sure of a warm welcome. The girl's parents quickly appeared and began complaining about the puppy, how he had a very bad nature, was constantly chewing everything apart and regularly ate the eggs from under the chickens. It all sounded too good to be true; this was precisely the kind of dog we were looking for!

After staying the night, we set out the next morning, no longer two friends, but three. Little Hadji had a hard time adjusting to riding a motorcycle at first, and he spent most of his first few days with us sleeping. Although we had no idea what he saw in his dreams, we could be fairly certain he couldn't foresee the four years of arduous travels awaiting him and his final arrival in Budapest, his new home, from which he was never to return. Hadji seemed a natural choice for his name, but, as a reference to his origins, we decided that his full name would be Mister Hadji. He retained the American part of his nature in that he never barked at cars or automobiles but went wild whenever he saw a cow or a horse.

Leaving the United States, we found ourselves already missing not just our Hungarian-American friends but the American people as a whole, whom we had grown to know and love. They had just taken a little getting used to. Raw and strange at first, they had proven to be straightforward, honest to a fault, and profoundly kind. Most Americans were selfish, but wholly aware of it and their businesslike manner never impeded them in seeking out what was good and beautiful in the world. They were also somewhat naïve. All American citizens insisted on their equality before the law and placed great emphasis on personal independence, in the spirit of which they raised their children. As a result of this independence, ties of respect between children and their parents or grandparents were loose at best. The American education system, although the country boasted extremely well-equipped schools, was also far from thorough, but somehow or other, American parents and schools managed to produce generation after generation of strong American citizens, which was the best thing they could do.

Sunny Mexico, Cuba, and Panama

The bridge in Laredo on the Rio Grande connected two worlds separated by at least a hundred years. From the lap of twentieth century modernity, we

326

Indians and their impromptu bridge in Mexico

tumbled into a backward region hauntingly reminiscent of the Balkans or the better-developed portions of Asia. Our unlimited freedom expired as abruptly as the good roads ended; we had to pay thirty dollars just to enter Mexico and were stranded at the border for four days, waiting for our travel permit. Despite all arguments to the contrary, the Mexican border patrol identified our trip as a business trip with the object in mind of advertising an American product, namely, the Harley-Davidson. As such, we needed a special permit to enter Mexico. The wealthy sons of Uncle Sam knew very well the welcome they would receive and rarely ventured onto the lands of their southern neighbor.

The further we got from the U.S. border, the greater our trepidation grew. The distance to the capital was 1,200 kilometers. Back in the States, it would have taken us no more than two days; in Mexico, we struggled on for a full twelve days before arriving at our destination. I wouldn't recommend this stretch of road to anyone but Olympic motorcycle champions. The roads were actual decent until the city of Monterrey, which was as far south as most Americans ever got, and the American presence was palpable in the streets of the small town. As for the other Mexican towns, they were a new world to us in the same way that they were entirely foreign territory to American visitors. The narrow streets were almost entirely void of cars, the bare and tumble-down walls of most Mexican buildings did a good job of hiding their friendly, and, in some cases, even luxurious interiors. The roads, paved with large, bulky stones were empty not only of cars but of carts as well. Those who had no car rode donkeys, horses or got where they needed to go on their own two

feet. Small towns were so shabby they looked like the whole area was the epicenter of a never-ceasing earthquake. The sight of the filth and sewage in the
streets was shocking at first, but we soon got used to these new facts of life,
which were to accompany us along our entire Middle and South American
journey.

The Mexican people didn't exactly inspire confidence. Men wore their sombreros and revolvers with equal pride. In most countries, revolvers were
tucked under belts or carried in a pocket; in Mexico, they dangled from the
belt, which was worn over the shirt, as if to say, "Look what I've got." We soon
got used to this manly business and strapped our revolvers to our own belts to
make sure everyone knew we had them, too!

We arrived in Victoria just in time for the evening stroll. At the same time
each evening, the young people of the city would gather on the main square
and form three lanes of amblers. Young women walked together in the middle;
young men kept to a separate aisle, unless they were officially engaged to one
of the ladies, in which case they were permitted to walk with their brides-to-
be. This method actually allowed for keen observation of the charms of the
opposite sex on both sides. Mexican girls were quite attractive, with their
thick black braids, brown faces, and dark eyes shadowed by long, smooth
lashes. They were entirely charming, but only the young ones; our illusions
fled when the mamas appeared. With regard to girls in Mexico, we had to proceed with extreme caution, because moral standards, or perhaps just fake
righteousness, were much higher than they had been in the north. And now
that I am on the subject of women, I feel now might be an appropriate time to
discuss our experience with the fair sex the world over.

It's obvious to everyone that our travels and the years spent in foreign
countries would give us a strong basis for comparing the women of one nation
with those of the next. Still, were we asked which country had the most beautiful women, we'd be hard pressed for a reply. We saw all kinds of women,
both attractive and unattractive, wherever we went. To further complicate
the question, a woman I find beautiful might seem ordinary, even unattractive
in another man's eyes, and vice versa. A good measure of beauty is disinter-
estedness. What I loved wholeheartedly and without looking to my interests
was truly beautiful to me. Unfortunately, on a trip around the world, one is often forced to show attraction where there was a great deal of interest mixed
in. Financial interest had a way of winning out over true attraction.

In countries and colonies with a colored population such as Arabia, Malaysia, China, and Japan, a white man had a good chance of making a conquest.
In most of these relationships, we acted out of attraction while women looked
to their interests. There were plenty of women to choose from, and as Gyuszi
and I spent the majority of our nights in hotels, we also had numerous

opportunities to make the acquaintance of white tourist women, who preferred us over colored men.

Some of the most beautiful women we saw were Arabian. Women of the Mediterranean, especially Spaniards, were equally attractive, but all of them proved to be hard to approach. It was easy enough to get close to white Englishwomen, Dutchwomen, and even Hungarian ladies in the colonies. Indian women belonging to the uppers castes were kept under lock and key; Malaysians were ugly; many Chinese women were attractive and good-natured, but the most beautiful women of all were always the half-bloods. Japanese-White and Dutch-Malaysian ladies were uniquely attractive, but simple Japanese women always seemed remote to me, somewhat shy and cold, at least by European standards. Their legs, figures, and clothing weren't according to Western tastes, and even those considered most beautiful in their own country were a far cry from Western ideals of feminine beauty.

American women were, in most respects, just the opposites of their Japanese counterparts. The per capita number of smart, pretty, and dynamic women was by far highest in the United States. American girls had great taste in clothing, were physically fit, confident and frank with everyone. They weren't puritanical but bold and independent, living the lives they wanted to live. Unashamed of their feelings, they would walk right up to the young man they liked and tell him so to his face. American women found men with special talents especially attractive; if you were a good dancer, for example, or a sportsman, or sang, played the piano, did anything that stood out, you were an instant ladies' man. Movie stars had more women than they knew what to do with. While we were in the States and appearing daily in various papers, our popularity index was stellar. We got several phone calls a day, and young ladies were constantly coming to take us for a ride in their cars. Sometimes it happened that we were too busy and had to physically hide from the eager crowd of girls. If we ever left our motorbike out on the street, we were sure to find our sidecar full of calling cards, phone numbers, and scribbled dinner invitations. We finally concluded that it was impossible not to like American girls at least as much as they liked us.

While in Mexico, we learned that Mexican women were possibly more beautiful than their northern sisters, but local social mores and our nonexistent Spanish kept us from getting to know them on more than a platonic level.

Unfortunately, we weren't able to admire the charms of Mexican women for long as the time soon came for us to resume our travels on the atrocious roads. The further south we got, the more deserted the roads became; some stretches reminded us of our jungle journeys. Occasionally coming across a rancho, we pressed on, knowing full well that our welcome would be less than cordial. Public safety on the roads of Mexico rivaled that of China, as evidenced by the high walls, complete with crenellations, that local rancheros put up to protect their turf.

The Almighty has blessed the backward land of Mexico with dreamlike beauty; it must be one of the most beautiful countries on earth. After reaching the mountains, we found ourselves driving amid lush tropical vegetation. In the plains region, huge portions of land the size of entire counties lay fallow, their fertile earth untilled. The people were incredibly lazy. They had few needs, and these could be satisfied with no work. The population of Mexico consisted of poor Indios and half-bloods; pure-blooded Spaniards were just as rare as authentic natives. At first glance, the people lived in extreme poverty. Perhaps, on a deeper level, they were wealthier than we, because, free of all unnecessary wants, they had all they needed through the graciousness of the natural world around them. There was no need for clothing in the tropical heat; a few patches of corn were enough to produce flour for tortillas, and oranges, tropical fruits, and coffee grew by themselves in the neighboring forests. There was no need to till the soil when it gave everything of itself. Nobody bothered to invest money in Mexico to found a large-scale plantation or farm because he could never be sure when all his wealth would be taken away from him. Simple people didn't even build proper houses; the walls of their huts were of bamboo, and once the roof-like structure was attached, construction was over. It was never cold; there was wood for cooking to be had from the forests, and kitchens were regularly located just outside the huts.

There were actually roads under construction in some parts of Mexico. The trucks aiding in the "construction" sunk into the black earth half a meter deep. Workers went ahead and piled the earth in embankments of two meters on either side. Frequent rains turned these earth roads into troughs of mud. The ruts left by the trucks were too deep for our motorcycle, and the quagmire in between didn't exactly speed our progress either. Sometimes we were stuck in the same place hours on end, trying desperately to dislodge our vehicle from the mud. There was little aid to be had, even for money. Our method was to unload the motorcycle and carry our belongings somewhat further down the road. Then, we would return to the vehicle, one of us insanely revving the engine while the other pushed, pulled, shoved, and cursed the bike out of one pothole into the next. Mister Hadji hated the roads of Mexico as much as we did, seeing as he was forced to trudge all day long through mud that often reached up to his belly. We spent our nights out in the open, which may or may not have been reckless. There were few wild animals, but Indian attacks were all the more to be feared.

We always made fires. Mister Hadji's great canine sense came in handy as he always let us know, kilometers in advance, if someone or something was

Mexican "highway" near Comoca

approaching our tent, giving us enough time to prepare a proper "welcome." When we slept, our dog lay sprawled across a hunting rifle at the opening of our tent, and we dozed inside, revolvers under our pillows, hunting knives within reach. Absolutely fastidious in our preparations, we never came face to face with any intruders; usually, by the time the sun set each night, we were too overcome with fatigue to mull over the possibility of a bandit attack.

Our motorcycle came across as a miracle to the villagers who saw it, although we were no more than a few hundred kilometers from the U.S. border and even closer to the Mexican capital, which was home to thousands of similar vehicles. People would approach us and wonderingly ask what our "apparatus" was called.

Mountain roads brought difficulties of their own. They were narrow and rocky; some jagged stones jutted out to such an extent that we had no choice but to get off and push our motorcycle again, as we had done back in the Mountains of Taurus. The carpets of wildflowers on both sides of the road were our sole source of solace. We were nearing the Equator, and snakes began appearing in large numbers. Not a day passed but we killed a few, along with poisonous centipedes, one of which I caught when it was already halfway up my leg, scorpions, and tarantulas. The knowledge that the nearest doctor was a few days' journey away was sobering. Reaching any river, we had to be especially careful of lurking alligators. I don't know how we would have survived had it not been for our trusty dog and rifle.

We pass a stranded car in Mexico

Most days we ate nothing but tortillas, oranges, and canned food. Tortillas, flat pancakes made of corn flour, were the Mexicans' daily bread. After passing through Valles, we reached the town of Comoca, where we made a rest stop of a few days, traveling ahead on horseback to size up the condition of the roads awaiting us. The muddy, flooded roads weren't an especially encouraging sight, but by the fourth day, we were on our way, armed with a number of wooden planks and four hired Indian guides. Our rate of progress was a hundred meters every few hours, but even that was much better than a large Buick we passed had done. We smiled to ourselves as we passed the envious American driver and passengers, who had been struggling in the same place for two days.

Our radio worked marvelously well. The people of Comoca spent several evenings listening to the "talking box," which often spoke in Spanish to their great delight. They enjoyed our radio so much that they gave us food and drinks and insisted we stay a few more nights and not deprive them of their newfound hobby. The radio had a few surprises in store even for us. One evening, we heard the Budapest Opera perform the famous Hungarian piece *Bánk Bán* on American radio. The opera *Bánk Bán* resounding through the streets of Comoca! Our new friends were surprised to see the tears glistening in our eyes.

By the time we reached Tamazunchale, we were driving at an elevation of

The Pyramid of the Sun in Teotihuacán, Mexico

2,300 meters. The mountain range, thankfully free of tropical heat and mud, led us all the way to Mexico City. Although the scenery on either side was picturesque, we had to remember to keep our eyes on the road ahead of us, which was so narrow that the outer wheel of our sidecar regularly balanced on the ledge, which overhung an abyss of hypnotic depth. Sometimes, there was more than a thousand meters of air separating us from the valley floor. Our fellow travelers all traveled by donkey, but the number of villages, and with it, the number of stone houses, was steadily increasing. Reaching the town of Pachuca, we were delighted to locate a hotel. A hundred kilometers of good road separated us from Mexico City.

Our drive into the capital was a far cry from a triumphal march. Filthy and exhausted, we suddenly found ourselves in a metropolis counting over a million inhabitants, 60,000 cars, and pulsating with urban rhythms. The streets of Mexico City were narrow, as if prefiguring those of South America, and policeman directed traffic in a singular way. Mexico must have been the only country in the world where a policeman facing you, his palm held out in your direction, meant it was your turn to step on the gas. Turning to the side was his way of signaling that we were expected to stop. "Go figure," Gyuszi wryly remarked.

Thousands upon thousands of dilapidated taxis and wrecks of buses filled the streets. Anybody who owned a taximeter could become a taxi driver, and so many people opted for this way of making a living that riding in a taxi was virtually free. With fares so low, taxi drivers began

Aztec monuments at Teotihuacan

experiencing difficulty buying gasoline even as the poorest citizens could afford to ride taxis all over town. Buses, known in Spanish as *camions*, filled the city with a cloud of stinking fumes and a screeching and grating that could be heard five streets over.

We were 2,300 meters above sea level. The climate was pleasant and healthy, with wildly fluctuating temperatures. Thirty degrees C by day alternated with near freezing temperatures at night. The inhabitants of Mexico City insisted theirs was the most beautiful town on earth; although we could have argued back, we kept our mouths firmly shut.

On fiesta days, *Charros* dressed in wildly colorful national costumes and wide-brimmed hats rode down the main streets of town. Their clothes were heavily embroidered and their ornamented saddles and horses worth a fortune.

Living costs were much lower than they had been in the U.S.; Mexicans literally lived off a few pennies per day. Their sense of community and solidarity were exemplary. Even those who had nothing could count on their relatives and friends for support. Far from depressed about their poverty, crowds of people filled the shops, theaters, and clubs. Everyone bought raffle tickets, especially for the Christmas raffle, which was always sold out by a few days before the holiday. Tickets to bullfights were another hot commodity. Gyuszi and I witnessed such a bullfight ourselves, during which a raging bull fought a life-or-death battle with a lion, both of them locked in a large cage. The bull ended up goring and trampling the King of Beasts to death, very much to the satisfaction of the audience.

Another Mexican peculiarity was the absence of uniforms in all areas of public life; taxi and bus drivers, railroad workers, and streetcar ticket controllers all went about in civilian clothes.

There were approximately 300 Hungarians living in Mexico City at the time, all of them enjoying a relatively high quality of life. Many of them were businessmen or factory owners; others ran their own restaurants or made their living as physicians, engineers, industrial workers, even film directors. The local Hungarian club was the site of numerous parties and related events. Hungarian immigrants, even those who were well-to-do, did not like Mexico and dreamt of the day they would return to Hungary, their hard-earned fortunes in hand. The Hungarian consul living in Mexico City happened to be a German businessman who didn't exactly make heroic efforts to promote Hungarian commerce in the region, which begs the question of why the Hungarian consulate was German in the first place and how it was possible that all local Hungarians had been found unfit for the job.

Our journey from Mexico City into Vera Cruz was brief but just as difficult as the previous stretch had been. Gyuszi and I both agreed we couldn't pass up an opportunity to see Cuba, and via Vera Cruz promised to be the shortest way. Our way to Vera Cruz was dotted with countless beautiful Aztec monuments. We spent an entire day admiring the pyramids at Teotihuacan, as well as other archeological wonders. Middle American archeology is a promising field; I'm convinced that if talented specialists with the time, money, and energy to penetrate even deeper into the more remote regions of the Mexican Peninsula, took the initiative to do so, the world archeology scene would be enhanced by numerous valuable sites. As it would have been impossible to ride our motorcycle all the way to Yucatan, we made our way in the direction of the small town of Cuernavaca, with the aim of visiting President Rodriguez and the de facto first man of Mexico, the "father of the revolution," General Calles.

Just before reaching Puebla, we climbed to an elevation of 3,500 meters. We hadn't been at such a height since our trip to Yellowstone National Park, but winter in the Mexican mountains was reminiscent of our August trip through Yellowstone. The only snow to be found had fallen around the well-known and beautiful volcanic peak of Popocatepetl. The entire region was volcanic; earthquakes were common. We ourselves "survived" a small one during our stay in Mexico City.

In the not so distant past, Mexico had been a country of priests. There were 300 churches in Puebla alone, and the priests running them seemed to run the entire country. Even villages consisting of nothing but a few huts of bamboo boasted a fine stone church. The tiny town of Cholula, population 8,000, was home to eighty churches. When we traveled through, we found most of the churches to be shut down. Priests were no longer allowed to wear their ecclesiastical garb, and very few had the permission to say mass, and only in select churches. Life in Mexico, especially for the religious, was hardly rosy; in fact, it was verging on Red.

The road from Cholula down to the sea took us through kilometer after kilometer of deserted countryside. There were so many stones and potholes, that we often had no choice but to push our motorcycle downhill.

The island of Cuba, known and loved the world over, made a sorry first impression. We arrived at the border after having traveled through fifty-one countries, our passports and papers in the highest order, but all this was not enough for the fastidious border guards. Convinced that we were there to stay, they demanded we pay a hefty deposit. To make matters even more complicated, it happened to be the time of day, sometime in the afternoon, when all available cashiers' desks were closed. Instead of being given the warm and ceremonious welcome we had been expecting, we were promptly arrested. They must have figured we would run and hide otherwise. The only way to keep us from wreaking havoc in Cuba was to seat us in a motorboat, and, after a short ride to the shore, carry us off by car to the nearby immigrant camp where we were to spend the night. Nobody spoke to us during the ride over, so we had to wait until our actual arrival in the camp to size up our situation. Once at the camp, we were forbidden to make phone calls or to contact the consulate. We spent the entire evening and night in a large building reminiscent of stables. One of the officers locked up poor Hadji in a separate room.

"Perhaps in your country, it is a custom to share a room with your dog; in Cuba, this is impossible," the uncomprehending officer explained. We had plenty of opportunities later on to experience the truth of his words. No nation on earth was more afraid of dogs than the Cubans, yet in the central and most backward parts of the island, people lived almost like animals and had no qualms about sharing a sleeping space with their cows, donkeys, chickens, even pigs. Poor Hadji howled the night away, despite our efforts to quiet him from the next building over. The unfortunate dog must have thought we had left him for good.

When morning came, we were released and made our way to the nearest cashier's desk to pay our deposit. Once that was done, and mountains of paperwork filled out, we were finally allowed into the country. But only we three, without the motorcycle. Our poor bike was a prisoner of the customs office.

"You either pay customs fees, or the bike stays with us," the officers explained.

"But tourists are allowed to bring their automobiles into the country free of charge," I argued back.

"Automobiles, yes," the stubborn guard insisted, "but this is not an automobile."

Despite my efforts to explain that a motorcycle was, indeed, an automobile from a strictly etymological point of view, the officers insisted that only vehicles with four wheels qualified. Turning to the official rule books, we noticed, to our horror, that automobiles were, indeed, the only foreign vehicles allowed into Cuba. The word "automobile" was everywhere, and it became very clear that an automobile was not a motorcycle, and a motorcycle not an automobile. After three days of tug-of-war with the customs officials, we were finally given our motorcycle, not as a result of our own efforts, of course, but in reaction to decisive intervention on the part of the Hungarian Embassy.

We had spent five days in Cuba before enjoying the privilege of riding through the beautiful city of Havana on our motorbike. It didn't take us long to forget how we had been inconvenienced upon entry into the country, and we spent a pleasant and memorable couple of days in the Cuban capital. The winds of revolution were blowing; bombings were relatively frequent, whether in ballrooms, drug stores, or on railway bridges, yet the people of Cuba continued to live life as they always had, carefree and Bohemian.

The entire population of Cuba had been living off of sugarcane and tourism for a very long time. Sugarcane was relegated to the rural areas, even as visitors crowded the cities. All of Havana seemed founded on a profound willingness to entertain and be entertained. It was a beautiful city, delighting mind, body, and soul. The large luxury hotels were always filled with guests; the forever pleasant weather made the seaside resorts inviting; theaters, cabarets, and hundreds upon hundreds of bars helped tourists while away their time in the American way, all the while immersed in a thick mist of Baccardi.

The Cuban golden age seemed to be in its declining phase by the time we reached the island. The American dollar, along with the naturally fertile Cuban soil, had brought great prosperity to the inhabitants of the island. Cubans had never been much for work, and the influx of American dollars and what their land gave of its own accord had been enough to support their happy-go-lucky lifestyle. Havana had lived off of American greed for pleasure and alcohol, the rest of the country off the world's sweet tooth. When the Depression struck, the price of sugar plummeted, leaving the Cuban economy defenseless. The sugar industry was in such bad shape that farmers threw up their hands in despair and stopped producing altogether. The uneasy political situation was a death sentence to tourism. There were no jobs to be had and very little money in circulation.

Despite the above economic and political troubles, however, Cuba

Across fields of sugarcane in Cuba

remained Cuba. Its many beauties were still intact, and there was much to remind one of the not-so-distant good old days. The evening streets were still filled with large crowds seeking entertainment; the horse races remained popular, and the lush, verdant natural beauty of the island continued to touch each heart. It was forbidden to gather in large groups, and for this reason, we left our motorcycle, which tended to draw huge crowds, in the garage. Policemen regularly patrolled the streets, beating on the pavement with their wooden batons to discourage any larger groups from gathering.

Havana was thoroughly urban. The sombreros and *serapas,* carpet-like ponchos so popular in Mexico, were nowhere to be seen. Cubans were generally very different from the people of Mexico. They wore clean, white clothing for one. There were restaurants belonging to many different nationalities all over town. To our greatest pleasure, we found three Hungarian establishments in Havana alone. While in Cuba, we did our utmost to avoid beans, as we'd had our fill of beans in all sizes and shapes while back in Mexico. Cubans, like Mexicans, drank their milk with salt, but in Cuba, we managed to order salt-free coffee, which had been impossible back in Mexico.

We loved the music of Cuba. Bands playing the latest exuberant rumba tunes showed their mettle both inside and on every café or bar terrace in town. "Troubadours" wandered from house to house, serenading the inhabitants, and the two of us reflected how many talented Cuban musicians, who

338

would have made it big in Europe, roamed the streets of Havana singing our favorite tunes for a few coins.

Our evenings were filled with dancing, not so much the rumba, but the *son*. Many people abroad mistake the *son* for the rumba, but it soon became clear that while the *son* was a popular dance, the rumba was mainly relegated to stage performances. Even if the rhythm and the music were the same, if people were dancing for their own pleasure, off-stage, they were dancing the *son* and not the rumba. We heard hundreds of traditional Cuban bands that went about town wildly shaking their rattle-like *maracas*.

The American influence on Havana was evident wherever we went. The narrow streets of the old city had managed to retain a feeling of the past, but the palaces that had recently sprung up in the newer districts, the marble walkway in Prado, or the seashore promenades in Malecon were distinctly modern and unforgettable.

The island of Cuba was a healthy place, entirely free of epidemic; Havana was the first mosquito-free city we had encountered in a long time. The heat was never oppressive, not even in the summer, and bathing season included practically all the days of the year.

There were 50,000 cars in Cuba, and 5,000 taxis on the streets of Havana alone. Taxi rides were hopelessly cheap; shorter distances cost no more than ten cents. Policemen directed traffic by clapping; we found this custom rather humorous and couldn't but feel sorry for the poor policemen, who returned home evening after evening, their palms raw with clapping.

We paid a memorable visit to the cigar factories. Although we only had time for the La Corona and Uppmann brands, there were plenty of other factories, their doors wide open to curious visitors. Besides, at the end of both visits, we got a small box filled with complimentary cigars. Cigarettes, on the other hand, tasted wretched all over Cuba. We figured the cigar companies were behind all this in some crafty way or other.

As in Mexico, we soon grew famous all over Cuba thanks to a film made with the intention of popularizing our journey around the world. We were very grateful as news of our arrival and Cuban stay spread, because it didn't take long before we began experiencing significantly greater goodwill on the part of the indigenous population.

In Cuba, all conflicts between foreigners and Cubans could only end one way. Taxi drivers ripped off their foreign passengers left and right, but even if the complaint made it to the policeman, it turned out that the cab driver was always right. Officials working for the regional or city government, or for the police hadn't received a salary in months. There was no money to go around. The only way these people could survive was to make sure foreigners got in some trouble serious enough to tempt them to smooth it over for a few

Rest stop at a small village in Cuba

dollars. If foreigners couldn't manage this on their own, there were plenty of corrupt officials around to help. For example, there were hundreds upon hundreds of dogs running around town, both without muzzles and without their owners. On the second day of our Cuban stay, we were obliged to bribe a policeman into not reporting us to the authorities, where we would have been heavily fined for not taking care to place a muzzle on Hadji. It was also advisable to pay cab fares before and not after the ride, when they suddenly became significantly higher. Although we stuck to paying in advance, cab drivers put one over on us when they stopped the car halfway and explained that the engine had suddenly shut down.

The president of Cuba, a certain Machado, was so well-hated that he surrounded himself with an army of bodyguards. It was literally impossible to approach him. Despite his caution, Machado's days were numbered; the winds of revolution were blowing strong all over Cuba. People were generally dissatisfied with the turn things had taken. For one, there were no schools in the villages and rural towns. Most Cubans grew to adult age without having received the most elementary schooling. The beautiful University of Havana had been closed for three years; Machado did his utmost to destroy the finest forum young intellectuals had.

We rode all over the island. The recently finished Carretera Central, an excellent paved road over a thousand kilometers long, made our journey a pleasure. The road had cost the country one hundred million dollars, but Cubans were well aware that not all of that hundred million had actually gone toward the building of the highway. We rode our motorcycle through the best-known cities in Cuba, passing hills and valleys, tropical forests, and immeasurable sugarcane plantations on our way to the other end of the island, the city of Santiago de Cuba. All things considered, the drive across the Cuban heartland was rather monotonous; there wasn't much to see inland. If Cuba is the Garden of Eden people often make it out to be, poor Adam and Eve must have been bored out of their minds, especially considering the infamous Molino Rojo, or Moulin Rouge, which offered cinematic experiences beyond one's wildest fantasies. The most decadent movie-goers in Paris would have blushed to see all there was to see at the Molino Rojo. Large posters lined the streets advertising the movies playing at the notorious cinema that American tourists, whether men or women, wouldn't have missed for a million dollars.

A few years before, there had been approximately 3,000 Hungarians living on the island of Cuba. Many had tried and failed to enter the United States and decided to bide their time in Cuba until the right moment arrived to try again. Some managed to enter the U.S. after a discreet waiting period, others were driven off by the poor economy, either deep into South America or back home to Hungary. At the time of our visit to Cuba, there were no more than 1,000 Hungarians living on the island. It was sad to see how many of them had failed to achieve their dreams. Very few had jobs, and the number of regular visitors to the Hungarian club founded by a Hungarian priest and a secretary at the consulate was smaller still.

The Hungarians living in Cuba ran restaurants or worked as waiters, barbers, photographers, beer brewers, and industrial workers. Some of these Hungarians gathered at the club occasionally to talk about their far-off homeland. There were even Hungarians living in rural towns; the workers at the Hershey sugar factory and the Hungarians living in Camagüey gave us an especially warm welcome. Most of our compatriots harbored hopes of returning to Hungary one day; very few were satisfied with their lot in life.

Cuban Hungarians had a lot to thank the Hungarian secretary at the consulate for. The Spanish count couldn't have cared less about his Hungarian "subjects," but his selfless secretary worked tirelessly to improve conditions for his compatriots, even sacrificing his free time to further the Hungarian cause. If our consulates all over the world were staffed with people like this generous secretary, Hungarians traveling abroad would enjoy constant support and security. Warm, welcoming consulates are of utmost importance; in the opposite case, people feel distant from and unwanted by their own motherland.

341

Bidding Cuba farewell, we took a short boat trip across to Panama. Although we had skipped a few smaller countries in Middle America, we felt that Cuba had been worth going out of our way for. Besides, sailing into Cuba and on to Panama was much more budget-friendly than paying unwilling natives to drag our motorcycle and belongings along the inhospitable Middle American terrain.

The Panama Canal is one of the wonders of the world. Most laypeople imagine it to be a simple channel between two large oceans, one that was created as teams of men cut through the thin sliver of land separating the two bodies of water. In reality, the Panama Canal is a miracle of engineering and the result of countless years of cruel, exacting labor.

We took our time visiting the canal, first riding the train around it, then driving our motorcycle along all the parts open to private vehicles. Later on, we took a short plane ride for a thorough aerial view and finally sailed across the canal itself, our belongings in tow.

The first plans regarding the Panama Canal were formulated in the year 1881, and the company in charge of the project had soon raised $260,000,000 and entrusted a certain Ferdinand Lesseps with the particulars of the undertaking. The project failed ten years later, in 1891. The actual results were so insignificant in comparison with the intentions of the investors that news of the failure spread like wildfire throughout the world. Reaching Hungary, it even left a permanent mark on the language, so that in Hungarian, the word "panama" is synonymous with "hopeless failure." The United States bought rights to the canal in 1903 from the government of Panama, which was discreetly recognized as a sovereign state to circumvent the annoying fact that the Colombians refused to sell their share in the venture. The Panama Canal was completed in 1914, its length an impressive 80 km, its cost an even more impressive $375,000,000.

Any ship sailing into the canal from the direction of the Atlantic is able to travel no more than 12 km at sea-level before an amazing piece of technology at Gatun raises it, and any vessel, regardless of its size, to 30 meters above the sea. The waters of the Chagras River are dammed up, creating an artificial lake thirty meters above sea level. Ships are raised as high as the lake in three stages, each consisting of a gigantic, hermeneutically secure lock. When the ship enters the first lock, the giant gates close around the vessel and water is allowed to flow into the sealed compartment until the ship is floating at the height of the water level in the next lock. Once the first step is complete, the gates of the initial lock open onto the second lock, the ship sails through, and the entire process begins all over again. Fifty kilometers from this set of three locks is a set of three more, which serve to gently lower ships into the waters of the Pacific Ocean.

The Panama Canal

Small electric engines tug ships from one lock into the next, seeing as these compartments are too narrow for the larger ships to move around in comfortably. The gates sealing off one lock from the next must withstand enormous pressure. They are approximately 25 meters, high, 20 meters wide, and 2 meters thick. All lock gates are opened and shut with the help of electronic devices, and there are two gates sealing off every aperture, just in case.

Most ships take nearly eight hours to traverse the canal. Ten to fifteen ships pass through each day, at the rate of $1 per metric ton. A 30,000-ton ship, for example, means $30,000 pure gain to the American government. Ship captains have no choice but to pay this hefty fee; the only other option is to circumnavigate the Tierra del Fuego, which is still more expensive. The Panama Canal means approximately $18,000,000 in profits every year; even disregarding military and strategic aspects, it has proven to be a highly successful venture.

Directly east of the canal, on the Atlantic side, lies the city of Colón. Panamá, the capital, is located on the other side. The entire Republic of Panama consists of these two cities; a strip of land 16 kilometers wide on either side belongs, according to the contract, to the United States of America. Cristóbal and Balboa, parts of Colón and Panamá that overlap with the American sector, continue to develop rapidly.

We spent some time in each of the four cities of the republic. Life on the

343

Panamá side, in Panamá and Colón, that is, was much more vibrant. These two port cities were no different from most other large, busy seaside towns the world over. Life in Colón resembled life on Malta, in Algiers, Port Said, or Havana. Chinese and Indian merchants flooded the streets; exuberant shop windows advertised Indian silk alongside French perfumes, American cigarettes, and Panama hats imported from Ecuador. Bars, drinking joints, cabarets, and nightclubs competed for clients, both from among tourists who happened to be passing through and the American sailors and soldiers stationed in the U.S. sector. The amount of alcohol and number of women consumed by ten thousand American soldiers was mind-boggling. To make things easier, American soldiers had excellent wages and limitless credit at all the pubs and joints; American police trucks patrolled the streets every night in an effort to collect drunken sailors and deposit them at the nearest prison, where they were expected to sober up by the morning. The memory of our nights in Colón will remain fresh on my mind forever. Drunken soldiers brawling, broken records playing, sailors' catcalls, and women's screams filled the night air. The U.S. Army and Navy seemed to care very little for its reputation throughout the region.

The Americans stationed in Panama enjoyed decent wages with extraordinary buying power. Living costs were significantly lower than in the U.S. There were two price tags on every item for sale, one stating the price in gold (this was for white men) the other in silver (for the blacks.) Cigarettes that had cost fifteen cents back in the States sold for seventy-five in Cuba, but only eight (in gold) in Panama, and five cents only, if you were a soldier. The government ended up reimbursing the cigarette factories for their losses, seeing as production costs exceeded sale prices.

The canal and its surroundings were heavily fortified by high walls, visible and hidden cannons, a legion of trucks and military vehicles, gigantic storage areas, radio stations, a dense network of searchlights, and a number of airplanes.

There was no road between the cities of Colón and Panamá; as countless artificial lakes lay in between, the best way to get from one city to the other was by train. Another option would have been to take a slow ride along the canal to Gatun, where we would have had no choice but to switch to a railroad car for the last forty kilometers until Gamboa.

There were Hungarian communities established even in the Republic of Panama. Fifty of our compatriots lived in Colón, another twenty in Panamá. They made a living working as bakers, furniture makers, barbers, beauticians, dancers, waiters, doctors, vets and butchers. There were a few second-generation Hungarians among the American soldiers stationed in the region. We were delighted one day by friendly greetings in Hungarian from a group of

American soldiers and sailors. Their parents were Hungarian, and they spoke the language, although they had never set eyes on the old country. Other Hungarians we met made a decent living as factory workers; good technicians had no trouble finding very satisfactory jobs. Despite the pleasures of a booming job market, the heat in Panama grew increasingly unbearable. The single white guard at the Gamboa Penal Colony was Hungarian, as was the owner of the canteen and the coin laundry frequented by the soldiers.

Panama is the last bulwark of Northern civilization in South America, and we keenly felt the need to prepare both ourselves and our vehicle for the long journey south. Our first task was to make sure our papers were in order; there is nothing like an expired passport to make life miserable in South America. While in Havana, we waited three whole weeks for our passports to return from Washington. When they did finally make it back to Havana, we were disappointed to learn that because they hadn't yet expired, it was impossible to renew them, and whenever the proper time to extend our passports would come, the fees would be hefty. Fortunately for us, we had the good sense to approach the Italian embassy in Panama, who were kind enough to renew our passports for us in two minutes and entirely without cost.

After securing our newly validated passports, we turned to our motorbike and welded a few cracks on the frame, which were reminders of our bumpy ride through Mexico. Following minor repairs on our motorcycle, we went shopping for water bags, mosquito netting, basic medications, and a set of pulleys, all of which proved to be indispensable on our journey through South America.

The dense rainforests to the south of Panama were impossible to cross by foot; riding a motorcycle across them was out of the question. Our first impulse was to sail into Colombia, but news from the consulate of the war raging between Peru and Colombia quickly put an end to that idea. Even if we managed to avoid the line of fire the Peruvians weren't about to let anybody coming from the direction of Colombia into their country. We finally decided to sail to Colombia, stop over as long as the ship was docked and continue our journey by sea into Ecuador, where we could finally disembark and begin our trek down south.

Two Years in South America

Along the Coast of the Pacific

Our small boat skirted the coast of Colombia and soon docked in the northern-most harbor of Ecuador, Esmeraldas. We stayed on the boat after finding out that it was to continue up the Esmeraldas River to another riverside town, where we could then disembark and safely ride our motorcycle to Quito.

It was in Buenaventura, Colombia that we finally set our feet and wheels on dry land. As we later learned, it would have been impossible to get to Ecuador by land, so our boat trip had proven to be a very fortunate choice.

From Esmeraldas, we started up dizzyingly narrow, stony mountain paths hauntingly reminiscent of the roads of Mexico. To make matters worse, the roads wound through terrain populated by unfriendly natives who were hardly to be counted on should anything go wrong. They hated all white men and refused even to sell them food or to work for them, however decent the wages offered. Rumor had it that Peruvian natives were just as unfriendly, so Gyuszi and I made up our minds to be wholly self-supporting. We crossed the Equator yet again. Quito lay right next to the imaginary line, only 3,000 meters above sea-level. This was a land of eternal spring, at an elevation too high for tropical heat. The town was backward and poor, very unlike a capital city.

And so we began our land journey across South America, and we are very proud that we managed to finish what we started, even though it took us pre-cisely two years instead of the projected one. These were two years of great physical exertion, hunger, and danger lurking around every corner. The knowledge that the South American stretch was the last long chapter in our odyssey gave us strength, which was just as well, because we were in need of all the strength and perseverance we could muster.

Although we had traversed five continents already, our ride across South America brought new, unexpected challenges. Back in Panama, we had stocked up on all things necessary, but upon our arrival in Quito, we found ourselves in need of additional gear: large containers for motor oil and gas, a pickaxe to compliment our handy spade, and another large container for drinking water. We also secured four new boards, two short and two long, in the sizes that had proven to be most useful back in Mexico. A piece of rope five to six meters in length, plenty of canned food, and film for our camera completed our inventory. With all our new supplies in tow, Hadji, Gyuszi, and I safely installed on the vehicle, we calculated the engine was forced to carry a full 800 kg.

It was nearly impossible to determine the direction of travel, seeing as nobody seemed to know where the roads came from and where they led. Even in hindsight, I cannot determine our route with greater precision than simply listing the countries we passed through: Ecuador, Peru, Chile, Argentina, Uruguay, and Brazil. The lack of a dependable map was a huge hindrance in our travels. Maps of any kind were only available in the capitals of the respective countries and only covered the territory of that single state. Getting to the capital, however, often posed the greatest difficulty. Even the maps we bought in the large cities were far from dependable, at least with regard to the direction and existence of rural roads. We quickly gave up trying to squeeze information out of the various consuls. The Ecuadorian consul stationed in Panama admitted he'd never actually been to Ecuador, and the Peruvian representative in Quito, anxious to help, turned to his thirty-year-old encyclopedia for guidance.

Our way was far from clear, and we clearly perceived the ludicrous nature of our venture. We felt ourselves to be, and later found that we were indeed, the first to ever travel this way by motorbike. The only people able to give us relatively accurate information and directions were the foreigners. Locals weren't to be depended on, because their concept of "good roads" or "roads" in general differed dramatically from ours. They were never able to gage, for example, the quality of the roads they were sending us onto. For example, one helpful native informed me that the road to city so-and-so was quite good, except for a two-kilometer stretch, which could only be crossed by swimming.

Such discrepancies weren't to be wondered at: South America is a strange continent, and although the people were homogenous and spoke roughly the same language everywhere, a few hundred kilometers in either direction could make the difference between 20th century modernity and near-medieval backwardness. Carts of all kinds were unknown on the western coast, so how could we expect even dirt roads. And if there were no dirt roads, there were, logically, no roads fit for automobiles. While there were approximately 400,000 automobiles in Argentina, there were less than 1,000 in Ecuador and not more than 10,000 in Peru. Automobile drivers rarely left the cities to venture into the countryside. Those who were obliged to travel generally traveled by boat across the sea or along one of the numerous waterways that crisscrossed the continent. Otherwise, people rode horses or went by foot. The twentieth century had burst into South America so fast that airplanes

Primitive Indians in Northern Ecuador

appeared before the people had even managed to build up a railroad or a decent infrastructure. Airplanes zoomed across the skies of South America carrying mail, packages, and passengers, who got where they needed to go in a few hours instead of a few weeks. Simple villagers, who'd never seen a motorbike in their lives or sat on a train, sent their mail by airplane. A road to them was anything that could be traveled sitting on a horse or donkey or by foot. There were many adventures in store before we were to reach central Peru, with its properly paved roads.

There were two wars raging at the time; one between Colombia and Peru, the other between Bolivia and Paraguay. Fortunately, the front line was generally located far from the cities, on deserted, neglected terrain.

The people, as I have said, were generally homogenous. There were very few pure whites or pure natives; most South Americans were mixed and somewhere in between. Far from amiable, they were lazy and careless, reminding us of the people of Cuba. In fact, the inhabitants of Mexico, Cuba, and Middle America as well as Colombia, Ecuador, Peru, Uruguay, and Argentina were much the same in this respect. Chileans and Brazilians, however, were in a class of their own. There was something of the Spanish grandee in all South Americans, combined with a palpable disdain for all things foreign. Not only were the sons of far-off continents of little worth in their eyes, but

Indian girls near the Amazon River

Peruanos, Argentinos and Bolivianos respectively looked down on citizens of neighboring South American lands.

South American bureaucracy exceeded anything we had run across in Europe. Before entering South America, all foreigners should ask God's help in avoiding the need to take care of any official business. Knowing the right people in the right places is the only way to get things done. Accustomed to North American precision, we were shocked to find high-ranking officials "missing in action" during prime working hours. The most popular word in Latin America seemed to be *manyana*, tomorrow. It occurred at the rate of at least once per minute in everyday conversations. South America was true "manyana-land," a place where people postponed until tomorrow everything they could easily have accomplished today. Nothing was certain; promises, agreements, and appointments had to be taken and met with a grain of salt.

Here we were in a truly destitute and backward country, where 40 percent of the population consisted of members of the Qechua, Zaparo, and Jivaro tribes, another 40 was of mixed origins, 15 percent was pure black and only the remainder white. We had to content ourselves with being able to reach their only reasonably-sized seaport, Guayaquil. The city itself wasn't much to look at; it was more like an overgrown village, but the moment we parked our motorcycle on the main street, which was inhabited by a few stray donkeys and a dilapidated car or two, we were approached by a policeman, who asked us to kindly remove ourselves to a side street. "Why can't we park here?" we inquired. "Because there's too much traffic, and such crowding will result in an accident," the officer explained. The side-streets, as we soon found out, were either unpaved and therefore inundated by mud and out of the question for parking, or paved, in which case the locals made good use of the smooth, flat surfaces by placing their cocoa beans out to dry. The beans were spread out all over the street and occasionally mixed and turned to make sure they dried thoroughly and evenly.

There were plenty of sickly, stray dogs abroad, so we took additional care of our canine companion. Here, I must digress and make a note of Hadji's adventures back in Esmeraldas. Before disembarking the boat, we were told Hadji couldn't enter the country until he had been checked by a vet. After all, if English and American vets had a say in which dogs could enter their respective countries and which dogs could not, why shouldn't Ecuadorian vets have the same kind of power?

To our greatest surprise, the weather in Guayaquil was far from sweltering. Although we were a few kilometers from the Equator, the summer days were pleasantly warm and the evenings cool, even on the coast. This cool weather, a result of the cold offshore sea currents, was to accompany us as we made our way south along the coast of the Pacific. Our first thoroughly pleasant surprise!

Another unexpected pleasure was the sight of the snow-capped peak of the volcano Chimborazo, with simple workers sitting close by, weaving away the world-famous Panama hats. Try as we might, Gyuszi and I could not resist the temptation to buy a few hats, especially of the well-known Montechristi variety. We spent fifty *sucre,* or the equivalent of five American dollars on hats that would have sold for at least fifty dollars a piece in the United States and perhaps even more on the streets of Budapest.

The inhabitants of Guayaquil put on brilliant red uniforms each evening and crowded the streets of their town, waiting for the nightly military drills to begin. The winds of war had even swept through the quiet streets of Guayaquil.

Leaving Guayaquil, we soon found ourselves fighting our own personal war against the deplorable roads in the region. In reality, there were no roads to speak of, so we ended up painstakingly inching our way along, using the tentative and often unreliable guidelines we had been given. We were well into the rainy season, and the seas of rainwater and mud would have flooded the roads, even if they had existed. Wherever our engine could not move the bike along of its own accord, we rented horses and donkeys and made good use of the rope and spades we had bought before setting out.

Somehow or other, we made our way to the village of Santa Rosa only to be told that although we were very close to the Peruvian border, we would never be allowed to cross in that direction. Our best bet was to travel on to Arenillas and attempt to enter Peru there. Although Arenillas was a mere twenty-six kilometers away, it took us another two miserable days wading through seas of mud to get there. Upon reaching our destination, we ran into a border patrol guard on horseback, who reported that it had taken him a full eight hours to travel fifteen kilometers from the border into Arenillas. What's more, he and his horse had been obliged to swim at least six times, and the waters had lapped at the horse's belly a full quarter of the way.

Crossing into Peru from Arenillas was out of the question. The only viable option was to retrace our steps, something we detested, and make the miserable return trip to Santa Rosa. From Santa Rosa, we planned to ride to the sea, to the town of Puerto Bolivar, where a small boat was to take us to our next destination.

After much spirited haggling, we managed to locate a boat whose owner was willing to take us on board for a day or two and sail up and down the rivers and their deltas by the sea in an effort to locate the spot of our entry into Peru. The boat we opted for sported a sail and small engine, but it was so small that we were forced to hire a group of lookers-on to help us take our motorbike apart and secure the various parts to the vessel.

Had the possibility of huge waves and our dread of sharks not kept us in a constant frenzy, we might even have called our boat journey enjoyable. At the very least, it was physically restful. The weather was mild, the water quiet, and our little boat puffed along peacefully, ever on the lookout for the perfect landing. As we made our way upriver, even the tiniest ruffles in the water disappeared, until we were under the impression that we were gliding along the surface of a mirror. The rainforests on both sides of the river were profoundly quiet; the branches of nearby trees trailed in the water, and, because the forest floor was entirely flooded, there were no animals to disturb the supreme hush. A few monkeys frisked about the branches of the trees; occasionally, colorful tropical birds tempted us to pull our rifles. The alligators sleeping on the shore didn't show the least sign of disturbance as we passed by. Hadji, however, wasn't quite at peace with the scaly creatures and barked at them furiously as we passed by.

Our little boat took us to the village of Hualteco, which consisted of no more than a cluster of houses. Its inhabitants crowded around us as we disembarked and soon helped unload our motorcycle as well. To our greatest joy, we found there was a pair of dry wheel-ruts leading all the way to the Peruvian border!

Our sudden joy was short-lived, however, because a new obstacle soon reared itself in the form of the actual border between the two states, the

Crossing the Zarumilla River in Ecuador, Peru

swollen Zarumilla River. There were no ferries or rafts in sight; the only vessel remotely capable of crossing the swollen river was a small canoe manned by a single native. Parking our motorbike on the shore, we asked him to carry us across and marveled at the dexterity and courage with which he maneuvered our way despite the whirlpools, hidden undercurrents, and other dangers of the Zarumilla. Since the river had overflowed its banks and flooded the nearby forest, we saw that building a raft large enough to carry our bike but narrow enough to pass through the openings between the trees was impossible. Seeing as our boat had left, returning to Puerto Bolivar was entirely out of the question. Our only choice seemed to go forward, not backward, and the only aid in sight was our Indian. We finally agreed to take the motorcycle apart, spend the night on the riverbank, and have our friend row us over in installments the next day. The Indian boatman seemed to like the idea as much as we did. The very next day, I floated across first, with our packages, rifles, a bit of food, and good old Hadji. The sidecar and chassis came next, then the wheels, the motorcycle frame, and miscellaneous equipment. Gyuszi rode across last, sharing his seat with the engine. The river was so wide that it was impossible to see from one bank to the next. Each transport filled us with dread. Gyuszi fired his rifle each time the boat took off, and I kept peering at my watch and the placid waters alternately until the joyful moment the canoe would appear among the trees. Then it was my turn to fire a salvo of relief.

The road to Peru

Gyuszi took care to bind all the parts of our motorcycle to the boat; we were well aware that the tiny canoe, a mere fifty centimeters wide, was our sole hope of continuing our journey. Had a single part of our bike fallen into the water, we would have been unable to go on.

It was our desperation at the prospect of never reaching Peru that had urged us on to such a bold solution. The number of things that might have gone wrong frightens me to this day, yet our luck held out, as it had all along. By that very evening, we were swatting Peruvian mosquitoes to our greatest delight. Our Indian guide stood uncomprehending, both upon seeing our joy and after receiving the generous reward he more than deserved. That evening, we were too tired to do more than cover the individual motorcycle parts with tarps and set up our own tent. The next morning, however, we reassembled our vehicle and headed off in the direction of the first Peruvian town from the border, Tumbes, leaving behind what possibly had been the world's cheapest country, a place where a single American dollar had purchased us room and generous board for two, and five American cents had gotten us movie tickets at the Guayaquil cinema.

Our first night in Peru held its own share of perils. We had tied Hadji to a stake, as usual, to protect him from wandering off and running into large wild animals. Gyuszi and I awoke to barking sometime around midnight. We'd hardly had time to realize what was happening when a group of men pulled away the mosquito netting at the opening of our tent. By the light of our flashlights, which I shone at them, we could clearly see the revolvers pointing at us. I could also make out their soldiers' uniforms and began breathing easier despite the guns still pointed at us. The men belonged to the border guard and had been passing through on their horses when they spotted the tarps and huge mounds under them. They must have figured we were smuggling cannons into Peru and gotten terribly scared; the man holding the revolver trembled so violently that I was afraid the gun would go off of its own accord. I immediately handed him the flashlight to aid him in his search.

"Who are you, and what are you doing here?" asked the man with the revolver. His companions had begun searching under the tarps, their movements accompanied by Hadji's furious barking. It took us a great deal of time and effort to calm the border patrol and explain the situation in our broken Spanish. Showing them our valid passports helped, but we still had to promise we would report to them as soon as we reached Tumbes the next day.

Roughly an hour later, they woke us again to ask where their companion had gone. There had been four of them, but the one they were looking for had ridden off after seeing our tent. Gyuszi and I agreed he was a real warrior.

Try as we might, we didn't reach Tumbes the next day. We spent the night at the Zarumilla police station instead, which we deemed the safest spot in the village. That it was, and we continued the next morning with all our supplies intact, discounting our oranges, which the brave Peruvian policemen had made off with in the night.

It took us two days to travel the thirty kilometers to Tumbes. Those were two days to remember. As in old Indian stories, we were constantly stopping in our tracks to kneel on the ground in an effort to try to make out the direction we were to take. The painstaking pace was the lesser of two evils. Small rivers, ravines, and gullies blocked our path; sometimes the way was so steep that we descended into a gully only to find ourselves unable to ascend the other bank.

We finally had a chance to pull our pulleys, without which we would have found it impossible to proceed. "Pulleying" our way along the road was tiring beyond measure. Wherever possible, sturdy trees were our Archimedean fixed points, but if our motorcycle was stuck in a rut, and the nearest tree was thirty-forty meters off, we were forced to use our longer stretches of rope and pull, both of us with all our strengths, just to move the bike a few centimeters in the right direction. This work was unbelievably tiring; we were forever stopping for breaks, and by the end of the day, had run out of drinking water. Setting out, we had believed the journey to Tumbes would take us a few hours, and we were hardly prepared for the heat and physical exertion. Neither were the pulleys, it seemed, and they kept snapping to show their displeasure. We finally decided to unload all our equipment and try merely to move the motorcycle along.

It took us a full day to travel ten kilometers. When the sun set, we put up our tent and prepared dinner. Food we still had, but we had drunk all our water during the day. The riverbeds around us were dry; there wasn't a soul in sight to give us a drop to drink. Our throats parched with thirst, we seriously considered walking back to the village for a drink of water. In the end, we decided to stay, hoping all the while that somebody with water would come along by the morning.

Nobody came, and our second day passed much like the first, only that we were thirstier and weaker. Nobody who hasn't experienced it himself knows what it's like to toil away in the tropical heat without a drop of water the whole day long. Sometime during the day, we spotted a small puddle. Disregarding all rumors of infection and parasites, we strained the muddy water through a layer of silk and fell to drinking. At that moment, the few drops of lukewarm, smelly water were heaven to us.

Our savior arrived that afternoon in the form of a small man perched on a donkey. He gave us his liter of cold tea immediately; I'm afraid we would have knocked him down had he not been so obliging. When we offered him a few coins, he even offered to escort us back to Tumbes, helping us past every obstacle on the way.

By that evening, we had reached the town of Tumbes. It would be impossible to give a true description of what we looked like; our shirts hung in shreds, our beards were caked with mud, and the inhabitants of the town could probably smell us from a mile away. We hardly made a positive first impression after our two days on the Zarumilla and two more days of "pulleying." The owner of the stable-like inn where we first stopped eyed us warily, insisting we pay before moving into our rooms. We finally had a room, our own beds, a bath, and iced drinks. Gyuszi and I agreed that all this bliss was almost worth the suffering that had preceded it. That same day we heard that the president of the republic had just been assassinated. This was hardly a good omen, and we hoped it wouldn't bode darkly for the rest of our trip.

We spent the next day in the company of our native and half-blood friends. The local police had taken issue with our visas and showed an overwhelming willingness to take us back to the border and send us packing. That was one border we never wanted to see again! Gyuszi and I pleaded with them, explaining that the entire region was flooded, that there were swollen rivers blocking our path to the border. The root of the trouble was that we had bought our visas in Cuba, and this was a type of visa they had never seen. Why, the police reasoned, had we not purchased visas in Ecuador when we claimed to have just passed through?

The sandy pampas of Peru

We sent a telegram of a hundred words to Lima, explaining our desperate situation. Just when all seemed lost, we got the go-ahead from the capital. Our joy knew no bounds. Setting out from Tumbes, we still knew very little of the road that lay ahead, but we made sure to pack two gallons of drinking water.

The road from the Peruvian border to Lima was 2,000 kilometers long, and our impression after completing those 2,000 kilometers is that anybody with the energy and patience to ride a motorbike across that terrain deserves the highest honor in Peru as well as a comfortable pension for the rest of his life. It took us four weeks to get to Lima, averaging seventy kilometers a day. What tortured us more than the poor roads under our wheels was our complete ignorance of the roads that lay ahead. Not knowing when a better stretch would come, we always expected the best and got the worst, making for a rather discouraging experience. We went from valley to valley, into one village and out of the next, hoping. This is the most accurate description I can give of those four weeks. Flooding gradually ceased to be a problem; the rivers disappeared, and after a few days' journey, we found ourselves in the middle of the sandy pampas of Peru. All the way south, from Tumbes to Lima and into the heart of Chile, we encountered nothing but pampa terrain.

With the less-than-Pacific Ocean at our right and the barren red peaks of the Cordilleras brushing the sky to our left, we made our way along a ribbon of land sometimes as wide as fifty kilometers, sometimes as narrow as five. This was an isolated and desert land of shifting sands. Called a pampa by the locals, it reminded us of the Sahara Desert in Africa. At least in the Sahara

357

there had been some life in the form of snakes, scorpions, vultures, and the occasional lion or camel; the pampas of Peru were utterly hostile to life. No rain ever fell; no plants or animals were hardy enough to survive. An uneasy silence reigned over all. Occasionally, we'd come across a river valley without a river. Despite the lack of visible water, a bit of green, a few stray signs of life, had sprung up in the sands. These river valleys were also home to the rare village, where we stopped for food, water, gasoline, and much needed rest. There were very few such river valleys, and we occasionally went on for days without seeing a single soul, twisting our way along the foothills or riding across the sands of the deserted beach. Only someone with the art of motorcycling in his blood could make out the path he was to follow in the pathless sands. Upon closer look, the sand itself was varied. There was living sand and dead sand; ranging in color and texture from yellow, gray, red, alkaline, claylike, pebbly, even the notorious quicksand. Some types of sand preserved tire marks for months; others swallowed them up in a matter of minutes.

Fruit was amazingly cheap in Ecuador: we once bought two pineapples, two papayas, and twenty oranges for the equivalent of twenty Hungarian Fillér. Had there been fruit in Peru, which there wasn't, it would have been ten times as expensive.

We rarely hit a stretch of road smooth enough to proceed at full speed. The pampas reminded us most of large pastures, only without sheep or grass. There were hundreds upon hundreds of tire-marks in the sand; some of them many years old. Every new traveler felt a need to forge a path of his own across the solid terrain. In the sand, however, there were fewer tracks, and new generations of travelers seemed only too happy to follow tried and true paths across the frightening sand. The one usable track was so deep in some places that our motorcycle sank up to its chassis, and we were forced to proceed at a snail's pace along a track of our own.

We were traveling across very unfriendly terrain; there wasn't a blade of grass in sight; the silence was often sepulchral and skeletons, both human and animal, dotted the sand. The occasional bleached skull was gruesome testimony to a traveler who had succumbed to engine trouble and perished in the Peruvian sands. Those who got lost or ran out of food and water had no choice but to accept their fate. Waiting for help was not an option; it often took weeks for the next "traveler" to pass by.

The Piura-Chiclayo-Trujillo-Casma-Huacho stretch was nothing but sand. One of us usually walked next to the motorcycle accompanied by Hadji, while the other attempted to balance the vehicle on top of the shifting sands. Hadji was confident and carefree; he didn't worry much about the scarcity of food and drinking water. The gentle melancholy he did exhibit most likely stemmed from the lack of interesting things to bark at. His sense of smell

Grisly finds in the Peruvian desert

never ceased to amaze us. We might be trudging through a stretch of seemingly unchanging sand when our dog would perk its ears, sniff around and generally start fidgeting. Approximately an hour later, we would encounter the object of his sniffing: a fellow traveler, a small village, or a source of water.

Gyuszi and I had no time for sniffing the sand; we had our work cut out for us. The deep and loosely layered sands formed hills and valleys, and the only way to progress on such uneven terrain was with the help of our trusty boards. We'd lay the boards down in front of the bike, drive to the very edge of the foremost board, pick up the boards behind the vehicle and carry them to the front. These steps could then be repeated ad infinitum until we found ourselves once again on solid terrain. The pampas of Peru gave us ample opportunities to master the art of "boardwalking," so that by the end of our journey, we felt confident enough to challenge anyone to beat us at our newfound sport. Driving through kilometer after kilometer of sand, we found that the most important thing was to keep up our speed and inertia. If we were unfortunate enough to stop in loose sand, we had no choice but to resort to the boards. Once the motorcycle picked up speed, whoever happened to be holding on to the last board would have to make a running leap for the sidecar, unless he wanted to walk to the next spot of solid land. Whenever the wind picked up, the air filled with fine sand, the dunes suddenly grew "wrinkled," and made for a magnificent sight with their ruffled sides and sharp profiles.

Fifty to sixty kilometers a day was the best we could do on the pampas. There were days when we were glad to have progressed ten, and our record slow came somewhere near Huarmey, where we spent a full three hours "boarding" across a hundred-meter dune.

Our nights, at least, were wholly tranquil. There was nobody and nothing to fear; there wasn't so much as an insect hiding in the desert sand. Although we were close to the Equator, nights were cold. Lighting a fire was out of the question as there was no wood in sight.

Not even human settlements brought us any ease. We were forced to keep to the soft earthen roads to avoid trampling the crops. The streets of most towns were so sandy that it was easy enough to get stuck merely crossing from one house to another. Each bridge we encountered had to be repaired before it could be crossed. Dry riverbeds often proved to be the best roads; pebbly and sandy, occasionally slightly wet, they at least meant a slight change after the monotony of the sand.

Occasionally, we caught a glimpse of the giant bird of the Cordillera Mountains: the majestic condor. Its shadow as it flew past overhead was as expansive as that of an airplane.

In the vicinity of Lima, we encountered a whole new category of Peruvian road: the paved road that had never seen a steamroller. This Peruvian specialty shook the daylights out of us; our teeth and all the nuts and bolts in our motorcycle rattled as we road across the tiny waves of sand the wind had graciously swept across the road in an effort to hide the obvious. We'd had our share of bumpy roads throughout the world, but Liman road, surpassing them all in that it looked smooth and promising from far off, was really rough and treacherous. To make matters worse, we had no choice but to follow the road. In our desperation, we began wishing we were back in the pampa sands. At the Budapest Amusement Park, the Haunted Castle, as I remember, featured an electric bench that best approximated our Liman experience. And to make us feel as if we were truly at an amusement park, the Peruvian government exacted hefty fees for the ride.

Ocean Waves

Traveling on the beach brought challenges of its own. Our general tactic was to keep as close to the water as possible. The hard sand beaten down by the waves was the best of possible roads, only the beaches of Peru were no Lido or Daytona Beach. The Pacific Ocean was forever on the move, and the "road" along the shore, instead of being wide and flat, was narrow, especially as travelers were only allowed to make use of the firm coastal sands during low-tide. There were plenty of travelers, ourselves included, who threw all caution to the winds and pressed on even during high tide. Traveling when the water level was on the rise meant making constant semi-circles to avoid driving into the waves. We kept a delicate balance trying to avoid both the deep water and the dry, shifting sands on the shore. Getting mired in seawater was just as time-consuming as sinking in the loose sand. Trucks had been lost this way; their drivers, anxious to get to their destination had driven on in high-tide, only to find themselves suddenly surrounded by water and without enough time to save the cargo. The pull of the ocean was strong enough to swallow entire trucks, cargo, engine and all.

If our motorbike got stuck in the water during high-tide, we had to wait until low-tide to remove the wheels from the mire. Our *playa,* or seaside journey, almost cost us our Harley. I was driving the bike one day at a speed of roughly seventy kilometers per hour. The tide had just begun to rise, and we weren't about to stop our bike when we were making great strides at about a kilometer per minute. Suddenly, the sand under the front wheel felt unusually soft. "Watch out!" screamed Gyuszi, but it was too late. To avoid sinking in the soft sand, I veered to the right, directly into the waves. The maneuver would have been successful had a large wave not come and swept over the engine, shutting it off and leaving us stranded. Gyuszi and I jumped off the bike immediately and exerted all our strength to push it out of the water, but our efforts were in vain. The water was already up to our knees and rising. Aware of the grave danger we were in, my companion and I dove for the wheels and began feverishly scraping away the wet sand that had gathered about them. We were hardly done with one wheel when another huge wave came and swept back the sand we had just removed. Even our trusty boards proved to be useless; the ocean waves tossed them this way and that, and we were unable to keep them on the ground in front of the bike, where they were needed. In the meantime, the water rose steadily and soon began seeping into our sidecar. At this point, we grabbed whatever came into our hands and began methodically throwing the contents of the sidecar onto the dry sand. A few minutes later, our sidecar was completely empty but still impossible to budge.

There was no tree in sight to which we could have bound our motorbike, waiting until low tide to reclaim it. There was only one way out of this fiasco, but panic had driven it from our minds. Gyuszi and I struggled desperately even as the water rose to our waist and waves crashed in our faces, but the Harley could not be moved. "Let's detach the sidecar!" I shouted into the roaring waves as the last, saving idea illumined my mind. We fumbled for the screws under the water, but at last managed to separate the two halves of the vehicle. Quickly pushing the motorbike, then the sidecar, onto dry land, we sank to our knees in the sand and lay there for some time in shocked silence.

It took hours for everything to dry thoroughly in the merciless heat of the sun. We made solemn vows never to ride the *playa* at high tide, and broke them in turn the next time we were forced to travel on the coast. To Hadji, our feverish scramble in the Pacific Ocean had seemed like an amusing game; he'd taken the opportunity to splash around himself and bark cheerfully at our efforts.

Once in Lima, we finally had a chance to rest. It was the only civilized spot in all of Peru, yet even during our Liman stay, we found it impossible to grow to love the Peruvian people. They were the epitome of everything that was negative, even repulsive, in South Americans (discounting Chileans and Brazilians.) Although they were terribly behind when compared to European civilization, they still imagined themselves to be superior to all the nations of the world. Many Americans complained about the rules and regulations, passport and visa troubles that prevented them from enjoying their time in Europe. I wonder what they would have said had they suddenly found themselves in Peru! Courtesy was not a Peruvian virtue. Upon our arrival in any new town or village, our first visit invariably was to the police station. The Peruvian police were rude and arrogant; foreigners simply didn't count. Hotel keepers gave us the worst rooms available; whenever we entered a shop, the shopkeeper would leave in the middle of serving us each time a native stepped inside. In sharp contrast to how foreigners were treated was the degree of influence foreigners had over the Peruvian economy; the railroad, the mines, banks, large firms were mostly in Asian hands, and Peruvians saw this as an insult to their nation.

We crossed a number of rivers by ferry. Pedestrians paid ten cents, those riding horses or donkeys thirty, only we were forced to pay three *sols*, the price of ten horsemen or thirty pedestrians. Although Peruvians were well aware of the poor quality of the roads in their country, nobody seemed amazed that we had come all the way from Ecuador on a motorbike. They probably hadn't believed us when we told them. Lima was the only real city in Peru; what the Peruvians called towns were actually villages, and so-called villages were *haciendas*, consisting of a farmhouse or two. Most of the land in Peru belonged to a small group of oligarchs who had their seat in Lima. These wealthy landowners depended on a network of supervisors and overseers to keep their property in order. The streets in Lima hadn't changed much since the time of Pizarro.

Most of the villages were inhabited by natives; the poverty was appalling. People lived in dirty, stuffy huts, whose walls were constructed of reeds and clay. Most hotels lacked windows entirely; those who wished for air had merely to open the door; lighting a candle was the only way to create light. In most of the restaurants we visited, there was a single glass placed on every table, regardless of the number of people sitting around it.

Hospitality was unknown in Peru. Shifty eyes gazed at us warily, as if we'd been spies or their enemies. At one restaurant we visited, the owner insisted we eat in the kitchen. Truth be told, we weren't exactly dressed to kill, but even so, we were the most elegant men in the entire village.

While in Piura, we even managed to get arrested. This happened after a heated argument with the chief of police. After routinely checking our passports, he reached for his stamp set to leave his mark on one of the pages. I tried to explain that our passports had already been stamped at the border, and that there was very little space left for additional stamps.

"Let me do my job; I know what I'm doing," said the officer in an angry voice.

"I think I've seen just a little more of the world and would know better," I retorted.

"You don't know anything," the officer shouted, *"Usted no sabe nada."*
"You know even less than I do," I shouted back.

It was at this point in the conversation that I was arrested and led off to the parish hall, where I was locked up in the yard. Gyuszi ran off to round up the local journalists with the prospect of a promising tidbit of news. After visiting the journalists, he headed to city hall to speak with the mayor. As soon as the journalists began streaming into the parish hall, the obstinate officer saw it best to set me free. Gyuszi and I were always so polite and respectful with whomever we met that we felt we had a right to a similar level of courtesy and decent treatment.

The outskirts of Lima were the best things about the entire country. Development was slow and fitful. The few tourists who did come to Peru never got further than Lima, Cuzco and a few other significant Inca sites. It was hardly a wonder, then, that Peruvians weren't used to visitors and considered us charlatans or speculators of some sort. Life in Lima was picking up speed; concrete office buildings spring up across from the old Spanish houses, carved wooden porches met neon lights head on. Lima was the crossroad of two civilizations, and this confusion was duly reflected in the life of the people. Peruvians were religious and highly moral, but at the time of revolution, entertained no scruples about stepping out of the confessional at church only to shoot someone. Six thousand Peruvians had lost their lives for political reasons under the regime of the recently assassinated president. At the same time, women kept to their homes after dark, and there wasn't a single bar or dance club in all of Lima.

While in Lima, we encountered another distinctly Peruvian solution to an everyday problem. Peruvians did not receive mail, at least not in the same way as most Europeans and Americans do. Instead of checking their private mailboxes, those expecting letters were obliged to walk to the post office and scan the voluminous lists of names nailed to the walls. Only if their name was on the list could they apply for their letter. Those expecting telegrams had it easy. Instead of running to the post office, they simply bought a copy of the morning papers, which included the texts of all the telegrams that had arrived in a given city that day. Most people bought newspapers only when they were waiting for a telegram.

It was difficult to leave the relative comfort of Lima for what might lie beyond. We finally managed to buy a map of Peru. The sandy way from Ecuador to Lima was marked as the same kind of road that would take us to Chile, and the map was right. The road from Lima to Arica, and into Chile was just as miserable as the Ecuador-Lima stretch had been. Only our experience with sand made the journey somewhat easier.

The country of Chile is a narrow strip of land between the ocean and the snow-capped peaks of the Cordillera Range. Standing at an elevation of some height in the middle of Chile, we could easily make out the two natural borders of the country. The western and eastern borders of Chile were intimately close; the northern- and southernmost parts of Chile, however, were 5,000 kilometers apart. We had to travel more than 2,000 kilometers to reach Valparaiso.

Chilean roads were far superior to those we had encountered in Peru. Chile, on the whole, seemed much more developed than its northern neighbor. Chilean concepts of what constituted a road and what made a road good or bad also seemed to match ours much more closely. What the Chileans called an impasse, Peruvians would have shrugged off as a bad road; a bad road in Chile was the equivalent of the better roads in Peru; a truly great Chilean road was without its Peruvian equivalent.

Although we traversed all of Chile, from the northern border down to Tierra del Fuego, it took us very little time to grow to love the Chilean people. Their friendly, open faces were a welcome change after the suspicious glances and grudging hospitality we had experienced in Peru. There were many foreigners in Chile, and they were, for the most part, well-respected. Precisely for this reason, those immigrants settling in Chile immediately felt at home, and their children and all generations thereafter were proud to call themselves Chilean. Although Chile was the fifty-ninth country on our world trip, it would have been difficult to name any place where the welcome had been warmer.

Our journey through Chile might be divided into two portions. The cold, barren pampas of the north held out for roughly 1,200 kilometers, until the city of La Serena. South of La Serena, the somewhat more fertile soil was tilled and green with crops, but it wasn't until we had passed Santiago that we felt we were in the green heart of the country.

Travel in the north was difficult, and we encountered no large towns. A

A night on the pampas of Chile

few years before, the north of Chile had been a land of prosperity; the famous Chilean saltpeter and numerous mines had provided hundreds of thousands of people with a steady income. When we were passing through, poverty seemed to be the supreme lord. Saltpeter was no longer good business; the production of artificial saltpeter and the recession in the global economy had taken its toll even in remote Chile. We rode our motorbike across the saltpeter beds; the once invaluable white mineral glittered and blazed in the heat, like rows of crops planted in a field plowed by giants. The furrows and white mineral blossoms were the work of nature, but man was not there to harvest what nature gave. The large factories lining the beds were closed; the machinery eaten by rust. All of the old workers had long moved to neighboring cities, where the slums were full to overflowing with the unemployed. Even the railroad station was boarded up; a train passed through once a week, its passengers visibly anxious to spend as little time as possible in this desolate place.

As we continued south, the Andes posed another formidable challenge. The road through the Andes took us to elevations of 2,000–3,000 meters, from which vantage point the masses of clouds below us looked like a vast silver sea. Then, in a few hours, we would find ourselves back at sea level, only to begin another steep climb somewhat later. The pampas of Chile were located on high plateaus; we occasionally traveled thirty, even forty, kilometers to reach the seaside towns that figured in our travel plans. As in Peru, the pampas of Chile were dotted with animal and human remains. Occasional grisly clusters of eight to ten human skulls called to mind our human frailty and the dire fate of those who had attempted and failed to cross the Andes.

Giant condors circled just a hundred meters above us, yet try as we might, we were unable to shoot a single one.

We passed through numerous sleepy towns. In most places, trade and much of the economy was in the hands of Dalmatian immigrants. We were surprised to see so many Dalmatians living so comfortably in Chile. Most of them had gotten rich before the economic slump; those who came too late found the *rottos* to be poor clients. Chile's poor were called *rottos*, from the word for "broken" or "ruined." There were more *rottos* in Chile than non-*rottos*; they wandered the streets in their filthy rags covered with parasites. As a journalist we'd met had warned us, the only dangerous animals in Chile were lice, which were carriers of typhoid fever.

The northern cities had no water. Trains brought transports of soil for northern gardens as well as large containers of drinking water. We found it especially difficult to buy gasoline. The government tried wisely to limit consumption of this most precious material. Gas station owners sold what they had quickly; we were constantly running from one official body to another to collect permits for more rations of gas. Such permits were only available in the morning, so running out of gasoline in the afternoon hours meant a day's delay in our plans.

The countryside south of Antofagasta was sandy. Although we had a set of new boards ready for the occasion, they turned out not to be necessary. Although stray rumors of this sandy stretch had been grave, we literally flew across it without once having to employ our brand new boards. Who was to stop us after Peru? The next day, we met a Chilean motorist who claimed it had taken him three days to cross the twenty-kilometer sandpit.

Much worse than Chilean sand was our constant fear of getting lost. Old mining roads twisted this way and that, mazelike and unintelligible. We relied heavily on our compass and sharpened instincts. Despite our best efforts, we managed to lose our way shortly after leaving Pueblo Hundido. Climbing hill after hill and descending into valley after valley, we soon found ourselves at higher and higher elevations without the least idea of where we were going. The thought that we would soon run out of gas without a soul in sight to help froze the blood in our veins. We couldn't make up our minds whether to persist or turn back. Our doubts and excitement overwhelmed even as our gas level decreased hour after hour. We spent the night in our tent, under the stars, but it was a night of worried sleeplessness.

Dawn brought relief in the form of two *rottos* riding donkeys. Our shouts of joy upon seeing them were so loud that one of the donkeys became uncontrollable and ran off with its helpless rider. The other *rotto* told us the unpleasant truth. We were headed towards Argentina, but in the wrong direction, and were in that precise moment at an elevation of 3,000 meters. We had no choice but to retrace our steps for sixty kilometers. Our good luck held out, however, because most of our return trip consisted of speeding downhill, so the amount of gasoline used was minimal. Had the two *rottos* not come trotting along on their donkeys, our bleached bones might be glittering in the Cordillera Mountains today.

The mountains of Chile were rich to overflowing with natural resources; poor Chile might very well have been the wealthiest country in the world. It didn't take an expert to see that the multi-colored strata in the stone were goldmines of various precious minerals. The mountainside looked like a giant had taken a ruler and divided it into stripes of various widths, which he'd then imaginatively proceeded to dye in various colors. Green stones held rich deposits of copper dotted with gold. Soil with a high sulphur content was yellow; black meant coal. Iron painted rocks a bright red while further on, we saw pure white strata of fine marble and mounds of gray rock, which was famously rich in silver. The seemingly inexhaustible wealth of Chile waited patiently for someone with the vision, initiative, and resources necessary to make the best of it. In the meantime, the downward spiral of the world economy and the lack of proper infrastructure in Chile hindered what might have been booming progress.

The Chilean government had designed and printed thousands of posters with the same inspiring image of a *rotto* clutching a fistful of gold nuggets with the inscription: Go find gold! And they did. Some *rottos* struck it rich, but pure gold was a rare find, and separating gold from the stone in which it was lodged required a set of expensive machinery that few *rottos* could afford. Chileans didn't know what to do with their gold ore; they generally exported gold ore, which was then processed and refined in the countries of destination. Gold ore naturally sold for less than pure gold, so mining gold in Chile only made sense if the mines were located close to the railroad tracks or a road leading directly to the sea. Another huge problem for would be gold-miners was the lack of capital. Even those who owned their own mines found it difficult to get started; they simply didn't have the money to buy enough donkeys to transport the gold to its destination. The Chilean business world was cursed with a general lack of trust. Those who owned a mine were automatically granted rights to dig. Once a mine was established, it would be visited by experts who would gage and record the percentage and quality of gold to be found in that particular mine. The lack of trust was so widespread, however, that even official papers were disregarded more often than not. Chile must have been the only country in the world where someone could own a gold mine and go hungry at the same time. Geologists with expertise and some capital would have limitless possibilities in Chile.

A fellow Hungarian living in Chile climbed into the crater of a volcano and,

Panning for gold in Northern Chile

at a height of 4,000 meters, found a source of pure sulphur. If there were a way to get the sulphur down from the mountain and to the harbor, he would be offered forty dollars a ton. Although he had the rights to the volcano, he had no money to hire men and donkeys to transport his wealth from the volcano crater to civilization. His was another example of success crowned by failure.

Some opted for gold pans over pick axes and headed for the rivers of Chile to make their fortunes there. Certain sarcastic persons have quipped that Chilean gold-washers had two big problems: there was no gold to be panned and there was no water for it to be panned from. Passing through a number of gold-panning camps, we were greeted with hostile glances left and right. People were afraid we'd come to make off with their gold and made it quite obvious that we were unwanted. It wouldn't have been a good idea to stay anyhow, seeing as where gold was concerned, human lives were of little value.

The landscape changed gradually as we continued south. There were more and more creeks and rivers; crops were sprouting and the untilled countryside was filled with flowers. It was September, the beginning of the Chilean spring!

Mud, not sand, became our worst enemy. We'd meander down lazy serpentine roads leading deep into the riverbeds. It was in southern Chile that we first made good use of the siren we had received as a gift from the Chicago police. With our sirens blaring, we could be sure that everyone within five to six kilometers of where we were would pull off to the side and wait anxiously for the strange noisy vehicle to pass. Our motorcycle did very well on the roughest hillsides and riverbeds; aside from a few cracks in the chassis, which we temporarily fixed with wire and welded together at an appropriate time, nothing hindered our progress. Sand, water, and mud were nothing to our motorbike, which was still in such good shape that we felt like it would go on forever. The only palpable consequence of the heavy strain on our motorcycle was the wearing away of the coupling gear, which meant ignition troubles. This meant we had no choice but to push our motorcycle a ways each time we meant to get going. Bikers know the joys of pushing a fully laden motorcycle and sidecar through a sea of mud. Once we managed to get the bike rolling, we found it best to keep it in low gear much of the day.

We weren't ashamed to give gold-panning a try. Passing by a promising looking mountain stream, we'd stop our motorbike, clamber up the hillside, and search the water for little glints of gold. We never found a thing, except for donkey scat and tracks, reminders that the Chileans had been there before us.

Hadji enjoyed Chile much more than he had Peru. He had plenty of opportunities to guard the bike and lots of unprotected animals to chase. Sheep and goats seemed to be his special favorites. Although we did our best to keep him away from all animals, he still managed to get away from us once and severely maul a large goat. It was only with great difficulty that we were able to free the unfortunate animal from Hadji's grasp. Needless to say, we left as quickly as we could to avoid an encounter with the angry goatherd.

The last large river we crossed was the Aconcagua before heading on to the two largest cities in Chile: Valparaiso and Santiago. The roads leading to these large towns were excellent. Valparaiso was nestled in a crescent of mountains with its houses dotting the hills on every side. Santiago was a great deal closer to the Cordillera Range; the snow-capped mountain peaks were visible from almost every street in town. Santiago felt much more European than American. Nobody was in a hurry; people worked and lived at a comfortable pace. Peace and quiet was all these people wanted. There were plenty of foreigners, especially of the German variety.

While in the Chilean capital, we gave a number of talks both in Spanish and Hungarian. Our story and the motorcycle itself attracted larger crowds than ever. One day the president of the republic, Senor Alessandri himself, elbowed his way through the crowd just to take a closer look at our bike and ask us a few questions about our travels.

We soon learned that we would have to wait until January in order to cross the Andes. To while away the time, we opted for a 3,000 kilometer "excursion" in the south of Chile. Riding to Osorno, to the foothills of the Andes, we had an opportunity to marvel at the unique beauties of southern Chile. The roads were dusty and bumpy, but the hospitality and warm friendship of the Chilean people made it all worthwhile. We soon got used to Chilean cuisine and enjoyed *cazuela*, a hearty soup each day. On the road, the best choice was *empanadas*, meat-filled dumplings. Along with a new taste in food, we also acquired middle names. Everyone in Chile had at least one, and we would have been ashamed to admit that we, in fact, had nothing but a single first and last name. When we signed our names on official documents, we were expected to do so with a great deal of curly-cues and underlines. The first time we handed over a plain signature, we got the document back with the request that we sign our names properly.

Living costs in Chile were even lower than they had been in Ecuador, possibly making Chile the cheapest country on earth. The price of food, clothing, nearly everything, was so laughably low that many Americans who had lost their jobs during the Depression moved to Chile, where the little money they had could be expected to tide them until their affairs took a better turn. Although living costs were low, it was next to impossible to grow rich. That is why Hungarian immigrants to Chile rarely returned home. Travel costs to Europe exceeded the price of a house in Chile, and nobody was fool enough to spend his hard-earned wages on a boat trip when he could invest in a house. Besides, life in Chile was comfortable and pleasant. Most immigrants grew to know and love their new homeland and didn't much regret having left home.

Prices in Valparaiso and Santiago were immobile, despite the fluctuations of the money-market. A single *peso* was worth approximately twenty Hungarian Fillérs, or four American cents. Gyuszi and I paid 100 pesos for a fully furnished room with three meals a day for an entire month. Back in the States, that was how much we had paid for a single day. For a single American dollar, you could travel 500 kilometers on the Chilean railroad. The most expensive tickets at the best cinema cost a single Hungarian Pengő, but there were tickets available for a fifth of that price. Twenty average quality cigarettes cost 15 Fillérs, while forty Fillérs got you afternoon tea at an elegant German patisserie.

Wages were low. Higher officials were paid approximately a thousand *pesos* a month, but this was enough for the upkeep of a car and lackey. A simple working man earned five *pesos* a day.

The number of Hungarians on the west coast of South America was noticeably smaller than on the Atlantic side. While in Ecuador, we met only two Hungarians in the city of Guayaquil, both of them mechanics. There were only two Hungarians we knew of living in rural Peru. The twelve Hungarians in Lima worked in a variety of professions: medicine, architecture, transportation, and trade. Chile seemed more hospitable to our compatriots. We met a Hungarian tailor in Tocopillo, and a very dynamic, multi-faceted Hungarian man in Iquique. This man had spent the past forty years of his life engaged in a heroic effort to better the lot of South Americans. He'd started a number of colonies, successfully introduced a set of innovations in agriculture and founded a settlement, which had grown into a small town. There were a few Hungarians in Antofagasta and Valparaiso as well, a notable painter among them. The biggest Hungarian community in Chile was located in Santiago. They were well situated and contented for the most part. There must have been approximately two hundred of them, and they worked in a variety of different fields, although the majority tended towards industry and trade. The Hungarian Club in Santiago was home to Hungarian-related events of various kinds, including, as usual, one of our talks detailing our travels.

The Highest Highway in the World

As the month of December drew to a close, Gyuszi and I finally felt prepared for the journey across the Cordillera Mountains, which was to become one of the most difficult and beautiful portions of our trip. The Cordilleras were impregnable except for the three warmest months of the year. The road from Chile to Argentina led through a mountain pass located at the height of 4,000 meters, a pass that had most likely never been crossed by motorcycle. We left the small town of Los Andes to head for the snow-capped peaks. The pass was a mere eighty kilometers off, but the road was mercilessly steep and the thinning air and danger of snow impeded our progress. It was only December, and we couldn't be sure whether the snow had melted enough to let us pass. Before we left town, the police took our fingerprints, which didn't bode well for us. The road wound up the mountain along a small river, and we experienced no serious difficulties until we had reached a height of about 1,500 meters. Annoyingly enough, the Chilean government had just finished "repairing" the roads, which meant they had been covered with a fresh layer of earth and pebbles—hardly conducive to successful climbing. The engine would periodically get overheated, at which point we'd all stop to rest. After a few such rest stops, Gyuszi came up with a new tactic. Perched on the edge of the sidecar, he'd jump off and push each time we came to a turn in the road. After a while, he was jumping off to push so often that he stayed off, and the two of us ended up pushing the motorbike and sidecar much of the way.

The road was rather primitive, narrow and too steep for either automobile or motorcycle. The heavy labor of pushing the bike and sidecar made us sweat profusely, and we were only too glad when the wind picked up. Our carburetor wheezed and spluttered as the air around us grew thinner and thinner. Towards the evening of the first day, we reached a military shelter by the name of Juncal. Juncal was positioned halfway up the slope. We were at an elevation of 2,200 meters and still had forty kilometers to go. We'd managed the first twenty kilometers in about two hours; the next twenty had taken us six. At this rate, who knew how long it would take us to reach the mountain pass?

371

Prepared for all eventualities, we spent the night in the company of the Chilean soldiers, and rented one of their horses when we set out in the morning.

The second half of the climb was clearly the more difficult. For as long as possible, we followed the route of the famous Transandino Railroad. The trouble was that the tracks stopped at an elevation of 3,000 meters where trains continued their comfortable way through a tunnel cut in the mountainside. Most tourists had the train carry their cars through the tunnel. Hitching ourselves to the train was not an option for us, however. We insisted on reaching the "top of the world" ourselves and planned to take a number of spectacular photos once we were there.

The road ahead grew steeper and steeper until it reminded us more of American "hill climb" motorcycle races rather than a run-of-the-mill highway. We had no choice but to hitch the horse to our motorcycle, tying the free end of the rope to a fixed point on the chassis. One of our soldier guides sat on the horse, urging it on, while the other walked behind the bike, accompanied by Gyuszi and Hadji. The motorcycle creaked, groaned, and spluttered; the soldier astride the horse did all that was humanly possible to convince the poor animal to take just a few more steps. I didn't know whom to pity more: the horse, the bike, or those who were forced to walk. I myself was safely installed on the motorcycle, holding on to the steering wheel and keeping a wary eye on the abyss below. The tiniest slip might have been fatal. Additionally, it was my job to switch the engine on and off; the unfortunate horse would have been unable to pull a stopped engine. I knew the gears weren't going to thank me for it, but this was our only way to get to the top. Our path twisted and turned on the brink of the abyss. Each time I revved the engine, the poor horse gave the rope an enormous tug. If the horse fell, we knew he'd take the bike with him; if the bike had slid over the ledge, the horse wouldn't have been far behind.

Temperatures dropped dramatically. A strong, chill wind was blowing, sometimes helping our progress, sometimes impeding it. I put on all the layers within reach and started enviously eyeing those who had managed to keep warm by walking. The landscape in front of us was magnificent. Mountain creeks rumbled their way into the water of a small river, taking with them rocks and stones of various sizes. Tall, jagged cliffs reached for the skies; the shadows of the silhouettes showed in fantastic shapes against the brilliant white background of the snow. The Cordilleras were very different from the mountains of Hungary. They were entirely barren, impossibly wrinkled and without so much as a tree, shrub, or blade of grass to serve as a sign of life. Neither were there animals near the peaks; even lizards and birds had been left far behind. Dizzying heights revealed their aching beauties; there was snow above us, below us, and snow surrounded us on all sides.

The border patrol at Caracoles cheered when we came in sight of their outpost. We were at a height of 3,000 meters, not far from the entrance to the railway tunnel. Pausing for a few hours, we took care of paperwork, drank hot tea, and gathered our strength for the remaining eight kilometers that would take us to the top. We got another taste of Chilean hospitality when the commander of the guard sent horsemen ahead with all our equipment. It took us three hours to reach the peak by the serpentine road. Man, horse, and machine strove with the remainder of their waning strength to climb the incredibly steep path. With the fury of the cold winds raging about us, we no longer sensed the heat of the sun. The air was thinning fast. Those obliged to walk grew pale, found it more and more difficult to breathe. Their hearts often skipped a beat, unable to adjust to the physical strain. The oxygen content of the air at 4,000 meters is so low that even experienced climbers were known to faint. Few men would be capable of what Gyuszi accomplished; to climb, on his own two feet and in two days, to an elevation of 4,000 meters. Near the peak, the engine threatened to give out; we were actually climbing in a deep rut as glaciers flowed by on both sides.

Our walkers arrived shortly after the horse and motorcycle made it to the top. They were swaying left and right, breathing hard, their arms and legs swollen. Hadji was the only living creature undaunted by the distance run; he frisked about at an elevation of 4,000 meters, not comprehending why his human companions were so blue in the face. Once we had located the shelter on the peak, we huddled inside for a well-deserved drink of hot tea.

We had never been so high up in our entire lives. The view from the top of the world was enthralling. Not far from where we were stood the giant statue of Jesus Christ marking the border between Chile and Argentina. A plaque at the foot of the statue assured the world that this giant monument of stone would have to crumble to dust before the people of Chile and Argentina rose up in arms against one another. We soon forgot our fatigue and physical discomfort as we realized the dignity and importance of what we had done. The giant statue and the beauty of the snowy peaks filled us with quiet wonder.

No statue could have been more welcome on that mountain peak than the image, carved in stone, of the Savior of the World. There he stood in the snow-capped Andes, immobile, proud yet tender, the symbol of peace and goodness without end. The beautiful view, the gigantic peaks encircling us made us aware of the frailty of man in the face of nature's might.

Only a few steps separated us from Argentina, and a downhill road into the sun. The walk downhill posed its own challenges. It took us three days to reach the nearest Argentine town, Uspallata, located approximately 100 kilometers from the border. The road took us through a tunnel carved into the snow and ice, a tunnel so narrow that our motorcycle barely fit through. Snow

The border between Argentina and Chile lies in the Cordillera Mountains

had piled up eight to ten meters high; it would have been impossible for the border guard to clear it away in so short a time. An hour after entering the tunnel, we arrived in Las Cuevas, elevation 3,200 meters. Those eight hundred meters really made a difference!

Our relief didn't last long, as we soon realized that the road into Argentina was to be filled with its own, very literal, ups and downs. Uphill stretches were just as difficult as they had been in Chile, except that we no longer had a horse and all our equipment had been reloaded into the sidecar. We tried many different methods from carrying our equipment ahead and catching up with the motorbike to leaving equipment behind to be picked up later as our vehicle was secure. In the end, we spent two nights under the stars in the less than hospitable and hauntingly isolated Cordillera Mountains.

Once in Uspallata, we took the opportunity to repair our worn bike and soon reached sunny, mid-summer Mendoza. While in Mendoza, we got news of a fierce storm and heavy rainfall in the mountains. As a result of the unusual amounts of rainfall, the tiny Mendoza River became a raging cataract, its water level rising dramatically by twenty meters. The waters of the swollen river destroyed everything and everyone in its path; the flooding that year most likely meant the end of the Transandino Railway. A few days before the storm, Gyuszi and I had spent two nights on the banks of the Mendoza River. The thought of what might have happened had we set out from Chile a mere three days later chilled us to the bone.

Along the Eastern Coast

We had arrived in yet another powerful and wealthy country, but the power and wealth were well hidden from our eyes. Argentina, with a population of only twelve million, covered a territory 3,500 kilometers long and 1,500 kilometers wide. Most Argentines were white; natives were extremely rare. The entire country exhaled an air of modernity. The first sign of said modernity was the large number of cars. While there had been no more than 2,000 automobiles in Ecuador, 14,000 in Peru, and 35,000 in Chile, the Argentine nation was outfitted with 400,000. Argentines drove on the left side of the road, which soon became as natural to us as being served cheese as an appetizer.

Coming from the direction of Chile, we had to cross the entire country to get to the capital. Our route traced the Mendoza-Córdoba-Santa Fé-Rosario-Buenos Aires line. We were in the middle of the Argentine summer; January temperatures were in the forties centigrade. Near the Atlantic Ocean, temperatures rose to a boiling 45 degrees C. To make matters worse, we couldn't get away with wearing our tropical shorts in Argentina. Collared shirts with ties were the norm. After attempting to enter restaurants dressed in our tennis shirts, we finally put on our striped pajamas, which had the advantage of being collared and long-sleeved, and our entry was suddenly ensured.

Those who think we had an easy time traveling in Argentina have it all wrong. The country is indescribably vast and had no proper roads to speak of. Those who had managed to cross Argentina on a motor vehicle could expect to make the headlines of all major papers. The dirt roads that were the only avenues of travel proved decent enough in the summer, but travelers unfortunate enough to be caught out in the rain faced dire consequences.

The country, large as it was, held nothing we hadn't seen before. Our two-thousand kilometer journey led us along dusty flatlands dotted with cattle and small farms, and not much else. Farms were separated from the road by a wire fence; the road was usually very wide and unnecessarily twisted, as if we had been continually dodging imaginary trees. Expansive puddles and potholes brimming with water were the sole signs of what Argentine roads could be in the rainy season. *Barrancas,* deep gorges, were relatively frequent and provided us with additional opportunities to make use of our pulleys. We ran over a number of snakes as we traveled, most of them harmless. Birds and rabbits were the only other "wild animals." While in Argentina, we averaged approximately 200 kilometers a day.

The barren peaks of the Sierra de Córdoba were a popular Argentine resort, drawing visitors from all over the country. We reflected, a bit smugly perhaps, that in Hungary, people living in a barren and unpleasant landscape such as this would feel the need to seek out resorts themselves. Fresh

A typical wide Argentine road

mountain air seemed to be the only real attraction of the place. The Villa Turul, a Hungarian hotel, crowned one of the many hillsides we passed.

After reaching the city of Santa Fé on the river Paraná, we enjoyed excellent roads all the way to the town of Rosario. Although Rosario was the second largest city in all of Argentina, it had a distinctly small-town feel. Rosario was large and populated by half a million people, but the buildings were small and traffic virtually non-existent.

We spent a great deal of time in Buenos Aires. The largest city in South America seemed the perfect place to rest after a year of inhuman struggles and physical exertion. The longer we stayed, the more our eyes were opened to the fact that Buenos Aires was hardly the city of riches, beautiful women, and nights of tango that people generally made it out to be.

The Argentine capital was undeniably a metropolis, so expansive that it took hours by motorbike to get from one end to the other. It had very few thoroughly cosmopolitan boulevards, however, discounting the beautiful and imposing Avenida de Mayo. The other streets were far too narrow for existing traffic, which didn't bode well for the future, seeing as the capital was becoming more car-infested by the day.

Traffic rules in Buenos Aires were the perfect example of how not to do things in a busy capital. Everything that could go wrong did, and many times over. Instead of yielding to those arriving from the right, people sped on or stopped at random. Speed was of the essence, and the smaller your vehicle, the better your chances of twisting and turning your way through the columns of cars that lined the streets at all times of the day. Taxis, buses, and so-called *collectivos* seemed to be the most popular modes of transportation. There were no parking rules; drivers felt at ease stopping on the sidewalk, next to the curb or in the middle of the road, depending on where the passengers wished to get out. And what were *collectivos?* The name says it all. *Collectivos* actually developed out of taxis. When cabdrivers realized there were too many cars running about town, they turned their own vehicles into tiny buses capable of carrying eight to ten passengers at once. *Collectivo* drivers, once they had the proper vehicle, simply established a route, gave it a number, and were, from that moment on, official providers of public transportation. Most *collectivo* routes were one-man businesses, with the owner doubling as a chauffeur. *Collectivos* were cheap, quick, available around the clock, and, for the above reasons, wildly popular. *Collectivos* had no official stops; passengers simply let the driver know where along the established route they wished to get off. *Collectivos*, then, were collective taxis that sped passengers from one end of town to the other faster than any other vehicle could have done.

There were no rules and regulations pertaining to *collectivos,* which came in all shapes, sizes, and physical conditions. The numbering system was so complicated that the best way to tell routes apart was by the color and shape of the vehicles. In some cases, the color and style of the driver's hat was indicative of the direction in which he was traveling. *Collectivos,* once they had picked up speed, rarely stopped for male passengers. Men were expected to leap on to the moving vehicles. As soon as a lady made a sign that she wished to get on, the driver would stop in the middle of a busy street and graciously wait until the lady passenger had made herself comfortable. The people of Buenos Aires seemed engaged in a giant game of hide-and-go-seek among the thousands of various vehicles filling their streets. Nobody seemed stressed or even mildly annoyed by the impossible traffic situation. Streetcars took up a large portion of the street. Cars parked next to the sidewalk often blocked the streetcar's way, at which point the driver would simply get out, push the parked car off to the side with the help of a few passengers, and continue on his way. Police had no control over traffic whatsoever. Drivers blatantly breaking the most basic traffic rules would drive on with impunity. Police officers would never even attempt to stop them; the best they could do was scream at the delinquent driver as he sped by. There were no traffic lights in Buenos Aires. Upon asking a citizen of Buenos Aires why this was so, I got the following answer: "We had them once, but they only made things worse. Buenos Aires traffic is so busy that traffic lights did nothing but mix things up."

Vehicles swept past each other at amazing speeds, regardless of which side of the road they happened to be on. Cars sped past streetcars at a hundred kilometers per hour, and nobody seemed to care. When we spoke about the lack of respect for rules of traffic in Buenos Aires, we got nothing but scornful smiles; people would then condescendingly explain that we were no longer in Europe, where everything was over-regulated, that we were in fact in a free republic, where everyone did as he pleased.

This very same free republic demanded of its male citizens that they wear suits in 40 degrees C heat. Policemen would actually stop those driving without suits anywhere in the city, and men were forbidden to enter the downtown area if they weren't wearing ties.

We found it difficult to like the Argentine people. Few Argentines had ever been abroad, and therefore nobody in Argentina could imagine a country better and more beautiful than theirs. Just like the Peruvians, Argentines looked down on all foreigners. European tourists, the few that made it this far, were seen as intruders whose sole purpose in life was to steal Argentine jobs and deprive the Argentine people of what was rightfully theirs. The people were raw and uncultured; one out of twelve was completely illiterate. Stylish clothes were more important than true value; young men who couldn't spell their own names went about in fine silk shirts and ties. We were often asked whether the roads of any other country on earth were as fine as those in Argentina. Patriots compared the grim peaks of the Sierra Córdoba to the mountains of Switzerland without having any idea of where Switzerland was located. Asking for directions in our heavily accented Spanish, we were often rudely shrugged off or simply ignored. Once on a streetcar, I had the effrontery to ask the driver whether he was headed in the direction I wished to travel. He sized me up, then condescendingly explained that I should ask about the route before I actually got on the streetcar.

Fortunately both for us and the Argentines, there were plenty of exceptions to the rule of rudeness. We made a number of new friends from among polite, interested Argentines; officials, journalists, members of various clubs, and even everyday people showed friendly interest in our travels, and our days in Buenos Aires passed pleasantly, for the most part. As our Spanish was quite good by then, we gave a number of highly successful talks about our travels and about Hungary at the Automobile Club.

The position of women in Argentina, and throughout South America, for that matter, deserves a digression. According to good Spanish custom, women rarely showed themselves on the street, especially towards the evening. The promenades in small towns especially were reserved for males. The sexes were separated at public baths and most movie theaters. Cafés, unless there was a room reserved for ladies, were off limits to female customers.

Rural towns were, of course, more conservative in this regard than the capital. Small town cafés were filled with men, except for a single lady in elegant attire who either sat at the piano and played, or kept busy switching the records in the gramophone. All the men in the café kept their eyes glued on the single female. Men brave enough to woo a young woman weren't allowed to enter her house; the best they could do was talk to her through the bars of an open window or chat on the staircase or in a dark doorway. One young Argentine friend of ours rented a room with a family for a few years. He was evicted the moment he asked the young lady of the house to marry him, and from then on, wasn't even allowed to talk to her unless she was accompanied by a chaperone. These strict rules held throughout the duration of the engagement, and it often took years before a young couple could get married.

Women walking on the streets by themselves received a great deal of attention in the form of loud and whispered comments and compliments. This way of treating ladies was so widespread and so much the norm that only foreigners considered it odd. Argentine girls were distinctly unhappy if they did not get enough compliments on the street. Not getting any male attention convinced them that they were wholly undesirable. On the other hand, it was rare for a woman to get no compliments at all. Even ugly old women were whispered a sweet word or two. For a long time, women hadn't been allowed to travel on buses, because it was considered improper. Ladies had been forced to content themselves with the streetcar.

Our stay in Buenos Aires was made even more pleasant by the presence of a sizeable Hungarian community. Hungarian colonies in Argentina were so large that it would have taken us a considerable time to get to know everyone personally. Immigrants disregarded Argentine social norms pertaining to women. Hungarian wives would never have allowed their husbands to spend entire evenings at the movies or the theater while they sat at home. Argentine women had no choice.

Hungarians in Argentina were different from those we had met in the United States. Most of them had left Hungary and the neighboring areas after the First World War with the intention of settling in the United States. When the U.S. closed its doors, approximately ninety percent of Hungarian immigrants settled in Argentina, Uruguay, and Brazil. It would have been difficult to estimate their precise numbers, seeing as many had been registered as native Czechs or Romanians. The Hungarian community in Buenos Aires numbered approximately 10,000 members; Hungarian communities outside the capital were tiny. The number of Hungarians in rural Argentina couldn't have exceeded a few hundred.

The Hungarians in neighboring Uruguay had restricted themselves to the capital, Montevideo. Argentine Hungarians didn't form communities as close-knit as we had encountered in other parts of the world. One of the main reasons for this was the rightful suspicion directed towards those who had been forced out of Hungary for political reasons. Many of these politically-minded Hungarians took it upon themselves to influence Argentine politics, giving free reign to their Communist and other radical tendencies. Many of these radicals were otherwise uneducated and completely devoid of a conscience, but Argentina being a "free republic," as its citizens liked to advertise, anyone with a talent for propaganda could very soon find himself in the political spotlight. Hungarian communities were divided along political, religious, and class lines. Wealthy Hungarians strove against the poor, industrial workers against businessmen, Jews against Christians, those of one political party against those of the next. The proletariat was divided between Communists and patriots, each political conglomeration consisting of both working men and the unemployed.

There must have been ten to twelve Hungarian societies in existence, but differences were so irreconcilable that there wasn't a single club with more than two hundred members. Nobody had yet managed to sponsor a Hungarian-related event that brought together more than three or four hundred participants. Most of the hostility was incited by a small group of about twenty public figures, without whom Hungarian life in Buenos Aires might have been a great deal more harmonious. Despite their differences, Hungarian immigrants were well-situated; unemployment rates among our compatriots were low. We found Hungarian restaurants, cafés, patisseries, and shops; Hungarians worked in a variety of fields from banking to transportation. Most Hungarians were satisfied with their lot in life, except perhaps those from Transylvania, whose eyes inevitably filled with tears when we talked of home. They were the real outcasts of the Hungarian community, unable to find support either at the Hungarian or the Romanian embassy.

Hungarians in South America faced another serious problem. With the exception of Brazil, whose official language is Portuguese, the citizens of Cuba, much of Middle America, Mexico, and all of Latin America, in other words, of every country where Spanish is spoken, considered Hungarians to be Gypsies.

The first time we heard of this error, we simply laughed it off, but soon learned that the situation was indeed graver than we had thought. Hungarians were called *húngaros* in Spanish, which incidentally was the same word used to mark Gypsies. In other words, the people of South America thought Hungarians the equivalent of the vagabond Gypsies who'd immigrated from Spain and the Balkans and often made a living stealing. Even educated, refined Argentines used the word *húngaro* indiscriminately to mean both Hungarians and Gypsies, as did journalists in all major newspapers. Hungarians struggled hard against this etymological legacy, but there really wasn't much to be done.

Whenever we told someone we were from Hungary, the best we got was disbelieving smiles. When we tried to explain that Gypsies and Hungarians were separate people, they would make the concession that we might be "better" *húngaros* than your average *húngaro,* but still refused to believe that the Gypsies settling in their country in ever larger numbers had not, in fact, come from Hungary. Argentine Gypsies didn't speak a word of Hungarian, nevertheless, when asked their nationality, they would glibly reply that they were *húngaros.*

Confusion bred more confusion. Although we published articles in the local papers explaining the difference between Hungarians and Gypsies, the headlines the very next day would be filled with news of a *húngaro* caravan that had passed through such and such a town stealing everything in their wake, or a recent traditional *húngaro* wedding, which was actually Gypsy and had nothing to do with Hungarians. At a revue in Buenos Aires, I myself witnessed a show consisting of a Gypsy *voivod,* or chief, driving a group of girls from his tent with a whip, insisting they dance a Hungarian *csárdás.* The Gypsy chieftain was named Budapest; the girls, named for our rivers, were called Duna (Danube), Tisza, Dráva, and Száva.

One smaller newspaper published an article about Gyuszi and myself explaining that our wanderlust stemmed from our restless Gypsy blood. Educated Hungarians at important social events could never be sure when they would be asked to tell someone's fortune. Our first day in Mexico, we'd asked a local whether there were any Hungarians in that town. "Sure there are," was his answer, and he promptly led us to the local Gypsy camp.

The ignorance of South Americans in this matter was appalling. Once at the Peruvian beach, we were changing for a dip in the ocean when we heard someone from the cabin next to ours call out to his friends, "Make sure you lock the door properly; our neighbors are *húngaros.*" In the Chilean capital, we had a long chat with the chief of police. One of our topics of discussion was the *húngaro*/Gypsy question, which had become one of the stumbling blocks of our South American journey. I tried to explain as clearly as possible who Hungarians were, who the Gypsies were, and why it wasn't proper to confuse the two.

"Hungarians have a state of their own," I began. "They have been living in the same place for a thousand years, and they are an educated people like the French, the Germans, and the British. Gypsies don't have a country of their own. They wander from place to place, and your country, incidentally, is home to many more of them than Hungary ever was."

"Now I understand," the officer exclaimed, "Gypsies are none other than the Jews."

The real trouble was that Hungarian immigrants, instead of fighting against prevalent stereotypes and misunderstanding, often chose the easy way out and made themselves out to be German or Austrian. Their shops bore the Dutch, Viennese, or International label. How could Argentines be expected to form a clear idea of who Hungarians were if members of the sizeable Hungarian community in their midst denied their Hungarian heritage. Gyuszi looked upon such "traitors" with bitter disapproval.

"No worries," he used to say, "they're wormy apples anyhow. We're better off without them."

In a short book we published about our travels, we devoted a whole chapter to clarifying, once and for all, the Hungarian/Gypsy question. We made sure to bring up the problem in our talks, as well as radio and newspaper interviews. Each time we passed a school, we gave teachers short Hungarian histories along with lists of famous Hungarians, asking them to pass it all on to the children. In our remaining time, we wrote a number of articles on the issue, fought with various journalists and raised a rumpus with the Gypsy chief named Budapest. We even placed a large sign on our bike stating that we were Hungarians, and only the completely ignorant could confuse us with Gypsies. It was evident to us that we were furthering the cause of Hungarians throughout South America, and most Hungarians understood what we were doing for them and showed gratitude and appreciation. I still remember one unfortunate Hungarian who couldn't get a job because of his origins. No employer would have him once his nationality was known.

Leaving Argentina, it took us a mere two hours to cross the La Plata River, following which we found ourselves in the small country of Uruguay. Uruguay consisted of little else than its charming capital, Montevideo. Arriving at the border on a Sunday, we were forced to wait until the next day as customs was closed. Uruguay seemed no different from Argentina in our eyes, except that Montevideo was much smaller than Buenos Aires. We felt as if we'd arrived in the town of Szeged, Hungary, after a long sojourn in Budapest. Orderly traffic and improved road quality were the only signs that we were indeed in a different country. Uruguay, roughly the size of Hungary, had a population of two million, half of which lived in the capital. It was a fertile land, but farmers were few. People preferred the comforts of town life to the hard work and uncertainties of agriculture. Uruguay was much poorer than its northern neighbor, but Uruguayan men seemed preoccupied with much the same things as Argentines: politics, women, horse races, gambling, and soccer.

The love of soccer wasn't constrained to men alone. Men, women, and children, from the very old to the very young, were all diehard fans of the sport. Soccer was the national pastime par excellence. We attended a "derby," or game, between the two most popular teams, the Penarol and Nacional. All

Uruguayan mud, not much different

shops were closed for the occasion, the streets empty. Nacional won, which made us happy, as their coach was Hungarian.

Soccer games were somewhat stormy in nature. At one game we attended, a referee was beaten half to death, while five policemen had to be rushed to the hospital as the consequence of a fight at another game. Uruguayan police, in general, enjoyed no respect. They were often beaten on the street by groups of displeased civilians.

There were approximately 4,000 Hungarians living in Montevideo. Most of them worked in the beauty industry as women's hairstylists. Walking along the street, we often listened in on Hungarian conversations and attended amateur performances at the local Hungarian theater, which would have held their own on the Budapest stage. Even the milkmen were Hungarian; their trucks were painted red, white, and green after the Hungarian flag. Montevideo's only raffle-ticket agent was also Hungarian. Hungarian Reds faithfully sent their hard-earned money to Moscow, even as their local leaders grew shamefully rich. The Hungarian Club and Jewish Hungarian Club were the picture of cooperation and noble competition. Wages weren't bad; even the simplest workers made the equivalent of three Hungarian Pengős a day, while trained workers made the equivalent of five or six.

Although the rainy season was upon us, we pressed on towards Brazil, the last country in Latin America that we were to visit. The Brazilian border was a mere 340 kilometers from Montevideo, but the first larger Brazilian town, Porto Alegre, was over a thousand kilometers off. As in Peru, nobody seemed to be able to tell us anything with regard to the quality of the roads.

We'd gotten as far as San Carlos when we were told it was impossible for us to proceed because of the mud and the best we could do would be turn back. Knowing that muddy roads were no laughing matter, we had another set of boards prepared for the next stretch of our journey. Struggling towards the border through a mixture of water and mud, we couldn't be too thankful that water prevailed in most places. The roads of Uruguay were so isolated that we had to measure out each puddle carefully, making sure we'd be able to cross it on our boards. Had we gotten stuck, there would have been nobody to turn to for help.

From Castillos to the border was no more than 70 kilometers, but those 70 kilometers took us a full three days. Our progress was impeded by a thick, sandy mush reminiscent of oatmeal. Gorges were deep, some the equivalent of small canyons. Horsemen passing by helped us along out of empathy, or, if that didn't work, a few pesos always did the trick. The Zeppelin headed towards Buenos Aires elicited envious glances and sighs on our part; how fortunate they were not to have to go rooting through the mud! In Castillos, we hired guides and horses to take us to the border. As luck would have it, the stretch to the border was dry and decent, so money spent on the horses had gotten us no more than walking companions.

We crossed the border into Brazil at the village of Chuy, which became the first stop in our 5,000 kilometer tour through the largest and friendliest of all Latin American countries. Southern Brazil was backward and deserted, not the most welcoming region, but we had no choice but to cross it in order to arrive in the central, populated, and flourishing states.

People talk of Brazil the world over. Most educated people can name its larger cities; immigrants sigh for an opportunity to settle in the heart of the country, but few, if any, have ridden across the southern wilds on a motorcycle in the middle of the rainy season.

Our welcome at the border was warm and friendly. The border guards wished us all the best on the remainder of our journey and either forgot or thought it beneath them to ask for our passports. Our first destination was the town of Rio Grande, roughly 300 kilometers from the village of Chuy. The *playa* or *praya* in Portuguese, which always sounded to us like inside-out Spanish, was eleven kilometers off. Our spades stood us in good stead as we made our slow way to the firm sands of the coast. The beaches of Brazil proved to be the best roads we had traveled in a long time. To our left, at a distance of a hundred meters, sand hill followed sand hill, but the space between this row of hills and the water was packed down and hard as stone. With the sand's surface smooth as a mirror, we felt like we were riding along the best racetrack on earth. The Pacific coast had been smooth but soft; the sands of the Brazilian coast stayed hard wherever the waters of the Atlantic kept them reasonably wet. To make our joy more complete, we never had to wait for low tide, and could make good progress regardless of where the waters stood.

Making excellent progress on the wet beach sands

We traveled 200 kilometers on the coast without the least obstacle to block our way. There wasn't a single tidepool in our way; we simply had to take care to follow the curves of the coast, and, if we chose to stop, to stop in a spot where the sand was especially hard to avoid our wheels sinking and some hefty digging. The road was so monotonous that I often found myself accidentally driving into the waves, which was no serious matter as the sand under the water was hard and the waves gentle. Discounting the delta of the lake at Rio Grande and another small river, these 700 kilometers of the Brazilian coast were a biker's paradise, excelling the best American highways in that we had this road all to ourselves. There wasn't much to see, except for a few gulls and the occasional lighthouse dotting the coast.

A few old shipwrecks brought some excitement into our otherwise monotonous trip. We found all sorts of vessels; sometimes, the complete ship or fishing boat lay on the sand for our perusal, other vessels were more hidden, with only their two ends and chimneys sticking out of the ground. These weathered witnesses to violent storms were usually surrounded by crates and barrels. In our initial excitement, we stopped regularly to inspect the contents of all old containers but found nothing worth salvaging. Most of the wrecks had been there for decades, from before the lighthouses were constructed.

The dangerous accident we'd had on the Peruvian coast repeated itself in Brazil when we carelessly stopped on a bit of land that was more broken shells than sand. Our wheels sank into the shifty substance, but, prepared for all such eventualities after our experience in Peru, we knew exactly what to do to save the day. After ascertaining that digging and pushing were in vain, we began systematically unloading the sidecar and finally unhitched it from the bike itself and pushed both to dry land. Far from easy, the unloading and salvaging took us hours. Every piece of equipment had been firmly bound to the sidecar, and we were soaked to the bone by the time we managed to unpack our tent, stores of food, gasoline containers, and additional belongings.

We traveled the last forty kilometers enveloped in darkness. I wouldn't recommend a nighttime seaside journey to any but the most experienced bikers. Our headlights were worse than useless; having them off and keeping our eyes on the moonlight reflected in the water was actually the better choice. When the moon was out of sight, we drove by sound. If we heard water splashing beneath the wheels, we knew we had gone in too far. On the other hand, if the sand under the bike grew soft and dry, it was time to steer in the direction of the sea.

At the village of Casino, we left the beach in anticipation of a wide delta to come. This was the delta that later almost swallowed us whole, motorcycle and all, and became one of the most exciting and dangerous adventures of all our travels.

There wasn't the tiniest speck of light anywhere to indicate that we were nearing a village. We slowed our motorcycle to a comfortable pace, often stopping on sandbanks to take a look around. In the inky darkness we failed to make out the silhouette of the village. We knew we had gone too far, but kept driving on just the same, unsure of where we had missed the road to Casino. After some time, we ran up against a small pier, which was highly suspect, seeing as no such embankments figured on our maps. Crossing the pier with the help of our boards, we drove on through a shallow river, its sandy bottom packed hard as rock. The next river was a bit more difficult to ford, but we pressed on in the hopes of finding the sandbank we were looking for. We found water instead, and lots of it. Gyuszi walked ahead with a flashlight, trying to find our way out. We could never be quite sure whether we were driving through the ocean shallows or the waters of the river delta. As the water rose higher and higher, we realized we'd have to get out as soon as possible. Spending the night in the waters of the bay would have been too great a risk. Leaving our bike on a bit of solid ground, Gyuszi and I hurried ahead. The small light burning on our motorcycle was to ensure our way back.

The further we walked the deeper the water around us became. After a while, all we could see was water, whichever direction we looked. To make matters worse, the ground under our feet changed from hard sandbank to a marshy mush that could easily swallow a motorcycle.

The harsh truth dawned on us. We had passed the village, and were wading through the waters of an inland sea, a lagoon of whirlpools and squelching mud, dangerous even by day, but potentially fatal by night.

We decided to go back. Strangely enough, the water level seemed much higher on our way back than we remembered it being on the way out. Were we walking in the wrong direction? No, it was high tide, and the waters were rising so fast that we could no longer locate the tire marks we were hoping to follow back to relative safety.

We struggled feverishly to retrace our steps, knowing full well that the waters of all the tiny creeks and rivers filled the bay to overflowing at high tide. At the bare minimum, we had to make it back to the pier. Checking our compass, we headed back in the right direction step by excruciating step. One step in the wrong direction could have meant getting irretrievably stuck. Feeling before us for firm ground, we laid down our boards whenever we felt the slightest justification for extra caution. We held our breaths while crossing every stream and sighed with relief after each successful crossing.

We never would have made it had Hadji not been there with us. His instincts and excellent sense of smell led us back to safety better than our compass would have done. We arrived back at the pier after tracing Hadji's steps for two whole hours. We were saved, and Hadji was our savior!

Back on the pier, we set up our tent and caressed our faithful dog, giving him the best dinner he'd had in a long time. Our night on the pier was restless; we kept waking up and glancing at the sea to make sure the water wasn't about to swallow us, tent and all. To make matters worse, there was a horrible stench in the air, which made it very difficult to breathe easily.

The next morning was a morning of discoveries. The first discovery came with regard to the source of the stench. Daylight revealed to us the half-rotten carcass, ten to twelve meters long, of a dead whale that had been washed ashore. We also found out that we had passed the village of Casino by a distance of ten kilometers. Although it was a large village, there hadn't been a single lamp burning the previous night by the light of which we might have located and rejoined civilization. Traveling on through the village of Casino, we soon found ourselves in Rio Grande, the largest seaport in South Brazil.

There were many Germans living in the southern states of Brazil, and we encountered a number of German colonies on our way north. After passing through Rio Grande, we headed back to the *praya*, giving thanks that we were safely past the marshy delta. Our journey north was pleasant and uneventful. At night, we either slept in our tents, or, more often than not, enjoyed the hospitality of the lighthouse keepers, who were kind enough to give us a warm dinner and a bed to sleep in. Traveling along the shore, we saw a number of runaway pigs. Once domesticated, they had somehow managed to escape from various farms along the shore and were living out their lives

The roads of Southern Brazil

undisturbed. We often felt tempted to shoot one and enjoy a dinner of roast pork, but we promptly lost our appetites when we discovered that the runaway pigs fed off the dead fish that had been washed ashore.

Following our speedy journey along the praya, we headed inland towards the town of Porto Alegre, approximately 150 kilometers from the shore. A sea of mud separated us from our destination. Our progress was painfully slow. We made only six kilometers the first day. The second day, we rented a cart and loaded our disassembled bike and sidecar onto it. The third day, one of the carts broke, and we were forced to push the motorbike and empty chassis along after the cart carrying the rest of our equipment. We must have been quite a spectacle as we entered the villages, Gyuszi walking in front with Hadji, both bespattered with mud, Gyuszi holding on to a giant walking stick, myself pushing the bike behind them, then the owner of the cart beating his black oxen with a stick of his own. Our sidecar rattled along on the cart, the countless plaques and decorations shining in the sun, a large sign proclaiming to all we passed that we were the first to travel "Around the World on a Motorcycle!"

It took us six days to reach Porto Alegre. A pedestrian passed us the first day, but we caught up with him on the sixth, a hundred kilometers later, proving that motorcycles were faster after all! Our August journey took us from Porto Alegre through Vacaria, Lages, Florianópolis, Curity, and Sao Paulo.

We were into the Brazilian spring; the countryside was green, the tiny forest we crossed as full of snakes as the orange trees with pale yellow fruit.

The journey to Sao Paulo lasted two months, although the distance was merely 2,000 kilometers. The rain accompanied us wherever we went. Rain clouds were insistent companions, impossible to evade.

Brazilian roads were no more than Brazilian cart ruts. Where one pioneering cart had gone before, many others followed, until the rut was deep enough to be called an established road. "You'd best turn back, Senores," warned nearly everyone we met on the way. Perhaps they were right, but where could we go? What kept us going was the thought that our struggles would soon be at an end.

The rut-road led into the mountains, where we encountered huge carts drawn by as many as five to six oxen at a time. The number of oxen before a cart was a pretty good indication of the quality of the roads to come. "Brown" roads were best; in dry weather, they were hard as stone with a network of cracks; when it rained, they became soft and slippery. The so-called "red" roads were treacherous. In dry weather, they were smooth and dust-free, but the lightest rainfall turned them into bogs reminiscent of a giant bowl of oatmeal. Ten minutes of rain were enough to trap us in the sticky substance for days. When it rained on a red road, we had no choice but to set up camp and wait until the weather was dry. If we got stuck in a village, at least we had a roof and four walls about us as we whiled away time. Far from civilization, we had no choice but to sit in our tent for days on end, waiting for the rain to abate. The rule of thumb was to wait two days after the last rainfall to give the roads ample time to dry. Sometimes, the rain would return on the second "dry day," and we'd have no choice but to begin our wait all over again.

We passed many poverty-ridden villages; wealthier farmers lived on their own land a ways off. People traveled by foot, on horseback, or two-wheeled carts. Even doctors, many of whom were Hungarian in South Brazil, rode horses when making their rounds.

Crossing the Rio Pelotas, we finally arrived in the state of Santa Catharina. *Campo* roads gave way to *sierra,* or mountain, paths. The number of trees increased steadily as we made our way towards the northern rainforests. These were virgin forests, untouched by the corrupting presence of man. The road through the forest was narrow and muddy; even so, we had no choice but to follow it. Rainwater mingled with mud flowed down the hillsides, and we made every effort to reach a higher elevation as soon as possible. We climbed up the hillsides, so high that the river Pelotas was no larger than a narrow ribbon winding through the valley. Three kilometers from the peak, our way was blocked by a deluge of mud and water as well as the occasional tumbling rock. Climbing further was out of the question. We decided to

Camping out with our newfound friends, Brazilian road construction workers, near the Pelotas River

return to the river valley, where we had seen the tents of a small group of men engaged in building the road. Descending into the river valley meant it would be days until we made it back up the hill, but staying on the hill was too risky for our motorcycle.

It took us an hour of concentrated effort to turn our bike in the other direction on the narrow hillside path. We did our best to prop up the wheels with sticks and stones, anything and everything available to keep it from tumbling into the gorge. In the meantime, the rain continued to pour, and a deluge of mud swept down the hill, bringing with it entire clumps of trees.

The five workers, one white and four natives, gave us a warm welcome. They knew very well we'd be imposing on their hospitality as long as the inclement weather lasted, but did their best to cheer us up, explaining that their tent was large enough for us all, and there was plenty of food to go around.

We spent a week stranded in the rainforest, eating beans with rice for lunch and rice with beans for dinner. Gyuszi and I were worried for the first day or so; the grim expressions and rugged features of our hosts were far from reassuring, but we soon became good friends, sitting by the campfire at night, talking and listening to the radio. The radio was something entirely new to them; they couldn't comprehend how it was that we could sit in

Seven days of twiddling our thumbs near the flooded roads by the Pelotas River

the middle of the jungle at Pelotas and listen in on a conversation in Rio de Janeiro.

It was only after the rain stopped that the majestic beauty of the place shone through. We were in the heart of the rainforest. Monkeys leapt from tree to tree, grimacing wildly at poor Hadji, whose patience for the jumpy creatures was just as short-lived as our first Hadji's had been back in India. Hadji was a smart dog, with plenty of experience tucked under his belt one could say, if he'd worn a belt, that is. Everyone we met marveled at his many skills. He found hidden objects in a matter of minutes, and knew how to follow tracks and what tracks to follow infinitely better than we ever could have. When Gyuszi and I got separated, Hadji was the perfect messenger and go-between. At a single word from us, Hadji would pounce on the strongest man and quickly lay him low. He also knew to attack if he saw a gun or revolver pointed in our direction. Our motorcycle was the apple of his eye; he never faltered in guarding it; even if we left for the space of a few hours, we could be sure Hadji would be sitting on the motorbike when we got back. He knew how to walk on his hind legs and could jump as much as two meters high. Hadji had a keen sense of sight and seemed to observe and understand everything. His excellent instincts helped him discern between potential friends and enemies, so much so that he wagged his tail when he recognized Hungarians by the way they spoke. Hadji kept us safe from snakes and other wild animals, watched through the night and signaled the coming of any intruder, even if he was still far away. Gyuszi and I often conversed with Hadji as if he'd been human; he understood our commands and signals and obeyed unquestioningly.

Although he understood commands spoken in Hungarian best, he still recognized a few English words and was rapidly picking up Spanish and Portuguese.

Hadji was altogether priceless, and we wouldn't have parted with him for all the money in the world. We had a feeling that the affection was mutual; I doubt Hadji would have survived separation from us and the motorcycle. He'd grown up on the motorcycle; that was his home. He only walked when Gyuszi or I were forced to get out and push, or when he felt he needed exercise, at which point he'd leap from the bike and trot next to us for a distance of four to five kilometers. Hadji lived the good life in South America. He could wander off as he pleased; we never had to worry he'd get run over. On the busiest city streets, he knew to keep to the sidewalk. In some towns, there was a custom of killing stray dogs by strewing poison meat on the street. Hadji never ate a bite, however tantalizing, without our permission. Sometimes gone for a whole day, we'd return to our hotel room in the evening only to find Hadji sitting next to a portion of meat. The meat remained untouched until we had made sure it was safe for him to eat. Meat was very cheap in South America, and we generally bought Hadji half a kilo or a kilo of meat. This he ate raw and got little else. Gyuszi and I had almost a father's affection for Hadji, and wouldn't have parted with him for all the riches in the world. I would never leave on an expedition without Hadji or a similar companion.

There was a pristine creek flowing at a short distance; we walked over to bathe and wash our clothes. Afterwards, we went hunting in the forest, but found no game, so we returned after shooting a few monkeys. Our goal was to shoot and capture a monkey, then heal it and domesticate it. We had heard they made excellent companions, but each monkey we shot died of its wounds. Only one recovered and lived with us for three days before disappearing into the woods.

Spending six days in Lages, we struggled on for another difficult 300 kilometers. Despite the red clay lining our way, we made it down to Florianópolis on the seacoast within four days. The citizens of Florianópolis were rather liberal in their thinking. The town had boasted a fine horse-drawn train, but Florianópolis illuminati decided one night that horse-drawn trains were a thing of the past, banded together and, lifting the cars off the tracks, pushed them into the sea. From that day forward, the people of Florianópolis went by foot.

There were no cigarettes available in the villages we passed through. Tobacco was sold in sausage-shaped packets; smokers used their pocket knives to snip off the right amount and rolled up the scented substance, not in cigarette paper, but corn leaves. This was something that took getting used to, as was the lack of bread. All food in Brazil was sprinkled with flour from the

Hunting trophies from Paraná, Brazil

roots of the mandioca plant. This thin layer of flour was the local substitute for bread.

Blumenau, Joinville, and area were almost entirely German. The Germans living in town, within the German colony, were clean and preserved their language and culture. Germans who, for one reason or another, became separated from their fellows sank to the level of the natives, forgetting even their mother tongue. The single white man among the road builders wasn't even aware that his father had been German until he showed us a photo of his father with the name and address of the photographer who had made it in Hamburg. Lone Germans lived and worked like the most primitive natives, spending their lives dirty and ragged on small, isolated farms. These out-of-the-way settlements were often full of beautiful blonde children who spoke nothing but Portuguese.

The next stretch of road took us through the lovely rainforests of Paraná. Giant butterflies in a myriad of colors waltzed past tiny hummingbirds, while the orchids poured forth their fragrance from where they grew twined on the trees. Spotted leopards and Brazilian tigers, or *onsahs,* were common. The forest was also home to the *sucurri,* or boa constrictor, which we spotted only once and at a respectful distance. We killed three leopards and skinned them; the best skin we sent home by ship, while the other two stood us in good stead on the seats of our motorcycle, where the skin of our Sumatran tiger had begun to show signs of falling apart.

The roads progressively improved, even as we continued through the rainforest. Our last exciting nighttime adventure came just before reaching the

Farmlands slowly replace the rainforests

Sao Paulo coffee plantations. Gyuszi and I were dozing in our tent, when I suddenly woke to a loud hissing not far off. Hadji was in the sidecar, and I lay as if paralyzed, knowing the least movement on my part could be fatal. I reflected that South American snakes were braver than their Indian counterparts. In India, we had learned the trick of surrounding our tent with rope. Natives had explained to us that coiled rope was the best snake deterrent. We'd been conscientiously using the same method throughout South America, but this particular snake in the forest of Paraná seemed unperturbed.

I woke Gyuszi and quietly explained the danger we were in. Suddenly pointing our flashlight at the entrance of our tent, I grabbed my revolver and Gyuszi took hold of a knife. There the snake was, its first fifty centimeters swaying left and right. It had broken through the mosquito netting but was momentarily blinded by strong rays of the flashlight. Without a moment to lose, I fired my gun at the ugly reptile. At the sound of the shot—I don't know to this day whether I actually hit it—the snake began to withdraw from the tent. Following the second shot, it disappeared entirely. Grabbing sticks, Gyuszi and I attempted to chase it off, but try as we might, we were unable to locate the *yarará*. I had recognized the creature by the light of our flashlights; it was a two-meter specimen of a highly dangerous species of snake. Hadji barked into the night, but we wouldn't let him go after the snake, even though he probably could have caught it with little trouble.

The Rua Paysandú in Rio de Janeiro

Our cheerful way into Sao Paulo and on to Rio de Janeiro led us through endless coffee plantations. During an excursion to Santos, we saw plantation workers burn a portion of the surplus coffee, while remaining vast quantities were simply thrown into the ocean. Rio de Janeiro, the capital of Brazil, was surrounded by rainforests. Sao Paulo was the livelier of the two, but Rio was far more beautiful. The economy of both cities was booming; there was virtually no unemployment, and new shops and businesses sprang up by the day. Nobody complained. New immigrants found it easier to find jobs in the industrial sector and therefore settled in large cities, leaving much potentially fertile land untilled. Nobody seemed anxious to cut additional rainforest acreage and turn it into farmland. Such a venture would have required thousands upon thousands of determined farmers. Brazil was developing fast; it was rapidly becoming a land of unlimited possibilities. The whole country seemed under construction, new cities and communities sprung up overnight. Streetcars and modern buses whipped along the still unfinished streets. You could travel all over town for next to nothing.

The famous peak at Rio de Janeiro

Living costs in Brazil were amazingly low, as they had been in Ecuador and Chile, possibly making these three countries the cheapest places on earth. One *milreis*, the equivalent of a single Hungarian Fillér, paid for a complete lunch, while twenty five Hungarian Pengős got you room and board at a decent hotel for an entire month. The price of a cup of espresso was five Fillérs, while a glass of excellent, ice-cold beer cost only ten. Menial laborers made the equivalent of twenty five to thirty Hungarian Fillérs an hour, but this was more than enough for a comfortable living. The excellent climate in Rio de Janeiro kept clothing prices down as well. Most people wore white linen all year round. It was never unbearably hot, except perhaps in the northern, tropical cities, yet the waters of the Atlantic remained warm enough for bathing year-round.

A little while back, a Hungarian singer returning from her concert tour through Brazil had mentioned gangsters and boa constrictors in her interviews with the Budapest papers. The people of Rio were deeply insulted, yet they really had no reason to be angry, because the part of Rio de Janeiro that lay between Urca and the famous Pao de Acugar was still impenetrable rainforest. The final stop on the tram route to Alto Boa Vista was located in the heart of the rainforest, with nothing but narrow walkways leading into the dense woods. I'm sure there was no lack of snakes in the vicinity of that tram station. Nowhere in the world could half an hour by streetcar take you from

A Rio de Janeiro statue commemorates the noblest canine qualities

among the skyscrapers of a dynamic capital into the trackless heart of the jungle. Surely this was something to be proud of.

The Brazilians were an amazing people; hospitable, friendly, enthusiastic, and open, they did their best to make every visitor and new immigrant feel at home. There was also a certain naïveté about Brazilians that made them all the more charming. Sitting in movie theaters, they were capable of completely losing themselves in the story unfolding on the screen, so much so that the more exciting moments of the movie would often elicit cries of "Hurry, Senor," or "Watch out, Senor!" Police officers left their posts every half an hour for a cup of coffee. During a strike, three soldiers were stationed at the post office to guard it from intruders. One sat in an easy chair, smoking a cigarette. The other haggled with a fruit vendor, while the third had disappeared for his umpteenth espresso. Their arms were stacked six feet away against the side of the building.

The motorized police force in Rio turns out to bid us farewell

Signs of prohibition were blatantly disregarded. People smoked everywhere, even if there were a dozen signs strictly prohibiting the act. Brazil, like Argentina, was a "free republic." The police searched everyone entering bars and clubs, requesting those with revolvers to kindly leave them at the door and pick them up once the evening's revels were through.

Here I must make mention of the world famous carnival at Rio de Janeiro. The carnival was a national holiday throughout Brazil, lasting a full four days. Although there were celebrations throughout the country, those in the capital were the best-attended by far. The entire city turned out for the festivities. Men and women, from the very old to the very young, decked themselves out in the most varied and colorful costumes. There was music and dancing in the streets; various drinks flowed in rivers. Even automobiles and streetcars were decorated; rides were free, and ticket controllers drank along with the passengers. Bands of lively carousers filled the streets day and night. Brazilians laid aside money each month so they would have something to spend at the carnival.

All "serious" life ceased for the duration of the carnival. Stores, schools, and offices were closed. Even the post office shut down; no letters or packages left or entered Rio for four whole days. State employees and government officials got two months' salary in advance to ensure they would have plenty of money to spend at the festival.

There were 60,000 Hungarians living in Brazil, 40,000 of whom had settled in Sao Paulo, the only city in Brazil with distinct Hungarian quarters. Hungarians were in the majority in the towns of Anastacio, Moóca, Ipojuca, Ypiranga, and Indianapolis, the suburbs of which looked recognizably

Hungarian. Rio de Janeiro had a small Hungarian community counting no more than 2,000–3,000 members; other Hungarian immigrants had simply passed through the capital on their way to being scattered in the remoter corners of Brazil. There were three entirely Hungarian villages by the name of Árpádfalva, Szentistvánkirályfalva, and Boldogasszonyfalva. Hungarians were, for the most part, contented with life in Brazil. Their communities were much more close-knit than those in Argentina; their clubs and schools flourished.

On our last day in Rio de Janeiro, which coincided with our last day in South America, I barely escaped being killed by a falling leaf. The incident was no laughing matter! One of the gigantic leaves of a royal palm tree approximately ten stories high detached itself from the branch and crashed to the ground at my feet as I was peacefully strolling through the park next to our hotel. The huge leaf falling sounded like an earthquake and brought with it various smaller twigs and branches foolish enough to try to arrest it in its fall. My head, had it been in the way, would have met a similar fate!

Gyuszi and I had grown to love Brazil and the Brazilian people. Parting was sweet sorrow in that we regretted leaving them behind, but nevertheless breathed a sigh of contentment and relief when our motorcycle disappeared in the belly of the giant ocean liner that was to take us to old Europe.

Fifty to sixty police officers riding motorcycles, the same who had welcomed us upon our arrival into Rio, escorted us to the harbor as the crowds in the streets waved and cheered in friendly farewell to the two Hungarian bikers.

Once on the ship, we marveled at the beauties of Rio de Janeiro only visible from the ocean. Although Gyuszi and I had seen many cities, we both agreed that Rio de Janeiro is the most beautiful city in the world, but only because the old Danube cutting through Budapest wasn't quite as monumental as the vast Atlantic Ocean.

Jewel-like islands without number dotted the many bays along the Atlantic shore. The emerald green of the islands alternated with larger swathes of green on the peninsulas and carpeting the mountains surrounding the Brazilian capital. The surface of the ocean reminded us of shattered glass; in its grandeur, the bay at Rio could have harbored all the ships of all the nations of the world.

The tall mountains reached down to the sea, their lower halves covered with houses, which seemed to flow down the hillsides and stop abruptly where the water began. The city of Rio de Janeiro was a thin curve of civilization between the green of the mountains and the blue of the sea.

We were slowly leaving the city of colors, marble, palm trees, and joyful people behind. The yellow sands of the beach traced the outlines of the water;

above the sand was the green of trees, then the pink and blue of houses, red roofs, and the solid gray of mountains crowning the whole scene. The jutting cliffs cast fantastical shadows and silhouettes in the sunlight. There was more imagination in these bold curves than in all of human art. Rio de Janeiro is nature's masterpiece, not man's, and would win any competition among beautiful cities with flying colors.

"Addio, Rio de Janeiro!" we shouted, "Go with God, South America!"

MEGHIVO

Az Elgini elso Magyar Ev. Ref.
Egyhaz Junius ho 21-en nagy
szabasu Picnic et tart a
Hickoryville Park Helyisegben
Melyre tisztelettel meg hivja
Elgini es kornyeke Magyarsagat
a rendezoseg.

Yjdonsag! Elginben eloszor
Kovacs Zenekara huzza a talp
ala valot. Yo etelekrolk es
italokrol gondoskodva van.

COMMUNIST TERROR IN KIANGSI

Monetary Loss $214,000,000;
37,000 Homes Destroyed;
87,000 Killed

Hsien	Loss of Property	Houses Burnt	People Killed
Yungfoong	$ 2,000,000	510	1,150
Suiswei	30,000,000	2,000	3,000
Taichee	100,000	4,000	100
Tehshing	35,000,000	4,000	5,000
Wuning	5,000,000	500	300
Loping	400,000	5	120
Yungshui	500,000	400	1,000
Leechuan	50,000	—	7
Nichuan	20,000,000	700	100
Tungsiang	10,000	22	50
Fengnee	1,000,000	—	200
Chungjen	5,900,000	100	1,000
Shihkiang	383,600	290	131
Shangyao	500,000	200	200
Kanshan	50,000	10	20
Kiukiang	1,000,000	500	1,000
Chingkiang	(few thousand)	20	10
Kingchee	300,000	20	10
Wan Nee	600,000	500	1,000
Wan An	2,400,000	5,000	3,470
Nanchang	300,000	50	9
Sweichuen	5,000,000	6,600	27,600
Chingyen	12,730	45	100

A Unique Opportunity To Visitors to Malaya. For $1,000.

Shooting a Tiger in His Natural Haunts!!

Have His Skin and a Cine-Kodak Film as a Souvenir.

CHOLERA IN DELHI

REVENUE MEASURES

(ASSOCIATED PRESS OF INDIA.)
NEW DELHI. April. 22.

CHOLERA IN ALLAHABAD

(ASSOCIATED PRESS OF INDIA.)
ALLAHABAD. April. 20

Epidemics in the Presidency.—During the week ending March 30 there were 129 deaths from cholera in the Presidency, 103 from smallpox and 18 from plague. The figures for the previous week were, cholera 204, smallpox 120 and plague 27. There

ALL-INDIA WEATHER.

The following table gives the details of the weather for the 24 hours ended at 8 a.m. on Tuesday, together with the rainfall departure from normal since April 1:—

	Maximum.	Minimum.	Past 24 hours.	Since 1st April.	Departure from normal.
Agra	113	77	..	0.1	—9.2
Ahmednagar	103	80	..	1.8	+1.5
Ahmedabad	108	79	..	0.7	+0.6
Ajmer	107	86	..	0.2	—0.1
Akola	112	93	..	0.3	+0.1
Allahabad	115	78	..	0.1	—0.1
Ambala	105	75	..	0.6	—0.2
Bangalore	92	69	0.2	7.1	+5.0
Bareilly	112	75	..	..	—0.4
Benares	103	75	..	..	—0.2
BOMBAY	92	82	..	..	..
Calcutta	101	85	..	2.1	—0.9
Calicut	93	77	0.1	7.7	+3.1

"Old Curiosity Scrapbook:" (from top to bottom, left to right) American invitation—Indian personals—Trouble in Kiangsi—Tiger Hunting in Malaysia—Cholera, smallpox and plague death tolls in India—Indian weather report: April in Agra, temperature: 113 F

Back in Europe

We could hardly wait for our two-week journey across the Atlantic to be over. We had been away from Europe for seven long years of danger and discovery, and we cried to see the cliffs of England emerge from the mist. We were back in Europe!

Proud Albion gave us an unexpectedly warm welcome. Our goal upon arriving in England was to pass through those European countries we hadn't touched on our outward journey, and spent the whole summer touring England, Wales, Scotland, and Ireland. As winter was not a good time to arrive in Hungary, we made our way to the South of France and crossed into Spain, spending the winter months in Mediterranean climes only to return to Hungary via Belgium, Switzerland, Germany, and Austria in the spring.

This was our first visit to England, and we finally discovered for ourselves the small kingdom that ruled over a colonial empire spanning the globe. We got to know the English, and, by the end of the summer, most of England knew the two Hungarian bikers.

We had nearly forgotten the ways of Europe, being away so long. Our first few days in England felt like the initial steps on a vast new continent. We had left Rio de Janeiro in the middle of a tropical autumn and arrived in England in the cool springtime of the year. Our light tropical wear was unfit for English weather, so we quickly acquired a whole new wardrobe.

Our stay in England was a triumphal march. Talks, movie clips, long articles published in major papers, radio interviews, and the publication of a small English-language volume passed like a dream. The English, reputedly cool and aloof, exhibited incredible enthusiasm and excitement over our accomplishments.

The English in the colonies were very different from those living in the mother country. There were millions upon millions of Englishmen living in the British Isles who had never made it even so far as London. The British, upon closer examination, had their strengths, weaknesses, and strange customs; they were no better and no worse than other nations.

The smooth roads of England were an added treat. Although we traveled thousands of kilometers on our tour of the British Isles, never once did we see a stretch of road being repaired or under construction. It seemed that English roads had been built to perfection and built to last. English driving rules were practical, logical, and even more surprisingly, universally observed. Those who broke them were immediately taken to court.

British weather was the real killjoy of our tour. Although we were there in the summer and spent the entire season traveling from one seaside resort to the next, there wasn't a single day warm enough to persuade us to take a dip. The entire summer was chilly, windy, even rainy, and we spent most days huddled in our leather jackets. There were no cafés, no outdoor pubs, or roadside restaurants. Whenever we felt it was time for a drink of tea or more "spirited" beverages, we had no choice but to enter a rigid, somewhat unpleasant bar, inn, or hotel. When England began looking much the same in our eyes, we crossed the border into Scotland and later sailed to Ireland to stir things up a bit. Scots and Irishmen were somehow more European than the English. What's more, the English were much more frugal, even to a fault, than the proverbially miserly Scots. The Irish knew surprisingly much about Hungarian culture and history, and showed a warm affinity towards all things Hungarian.

It's part of Hungarian nature to admire, even idolize, foreign countries and people. No people in the world are better at this mild form of self-deception than our own compatriots. Travelogues written by Hungarians tend to praise the achievements of other nations to the skies while forgetting about our own. I believe Hungarians should continue to respect and love foreigners, while keeping their eyes open for what is less than perfect in other nations. When traveling abroad, we hardly need to marvel, out of sheer politeness, at things we would consider perfectly ordinary in our own country. I speak from experience when I say that we, Hungarians, aren't inferior to the nations of the world, and that, were we to set up some kind of order, we would be closer to the front than we imagine.

After our British tour, we rediscovered Spain, visiting those areas we had missed our first time through. At the beginning of our world trip in 1928, Alfonso XIII was king. Many things had changed since then. Roads were better, Spanish money was losing its value, and living costs were significantly lower than they had been. Spanish towns were growing up to become Spanish cities; whole new quarters, modern and distinctly beautiful, had sprung up in the space of seven years.

Despite the positive developments, Spain was engaged in a bloody power struggle. The nights were lit by burning cloisters and churches; shootings and murders had become mundane events. Although much had changed in Spain, the Spanish soul had not. Neither had Spanish poverty. Even as modern new buildings sprung up overnight, the Spanish people continued to live in poverty and dream of better days to come. The monarchy had brought them

Some of our most prized autographs: Herbert Hoover, President of the United States of America; Y. Hamaguchi, Prime Minister of Japan; Benito Mussolini, Prime Minister of Italy; William E. Borah, American senator; John Barrymore, filmstar; the Maharaja of Kapurthala; Douglas Fairbanks, film star; and T. Chaliapin, opera singer.

little alleviation of their troubles, so people's hopeful glances turned towards the republic. When the republic failed them, they placed their hopes in the Popular Front. And after they became dissatisfied with the Popular Front, what then?

The Spanish people had preserved their simplicity, goodness, and nobility of heart despite the turbulent political changes. Because of their backwardness and passionate temperaments, they were just as easy to influence as ever. The people dreamt of one thing and one thing alone: a better, easier, and more peaceful Spain and showed every willingness to follow whoever made the most impassioned promises. Spain was quickly becoming a land of clenched fists and bloody demonstrations, and we soon found ourselves seeking more peaceful climes.

We literally sped through the cities of the French Riviera, along the gorgeous lakes of Northern Italy, and crossed tiny Switzerland in the space of two days. Germany, much changed, held no attractions for us; not even Vienna, with all its charms, could detain us from flying to our final destination. As if drawn by a magnet, we urged our motorcycle to even greater speeds, using all our resources, intelligence, and driving experience to arrive, as fast as humanly possible, at the one place in the world where we

405

Back in Budapest with 170,000 kilometers behind us

could kneel down and give thanks to God for bringing us to that day: the Hungarian border!

Back on Hungarian soil, our restless yearning changed to a profound and calm joy. The road to Budapest was lined with friends, relatives, and well-wishers all eager to embrace the two world travelers. Our entrance into Budapest was something of a spiritual triumphal march; our eyes streamed with tears as we scanned the houses and read each sign in every single shop window.

Good God, how good it was to be back on the shores of the Danube, to drive across the Chain Bridge and along Kossuth Lajos Street. Surely this was the happiest moment in our lives. I don't think I could recall a single word of the speeches given at the Automobile Club; the journalists' questions seemed irrelevant. We had difficulty recognizing even our closest friends in the all-consuming joy of having come home at last.

Concluding Remarks Written upon our Arrival into Hungary

We have visited sixty-eight countries on six different continents, traveling over 170,000 kilometers in the process. Our trip around the world took us eight years to complete, but after those eight years were up, we returned to Hungary with the happy knowledge of having accomplished what we set out to do. Nobody asked us to attempt the voyage; we set out of our own accord and returned of our strength. We set our own goals and strove hard to accomplish them. Not all our goals were sport-related. Our greatest wish, one that I feel has come true, was to make the name of Hungary known and loved throughout the world. Our travels have won our homeland many new friends.

The short volumes we published in a number of languages throughout the world were dedicated to relaying a sense of Hungarian history and culture, with special attention to the beauties of our capital, Budapest. All volumes we published ended with a warm invitation to the reader to come and discover our beautiful capital for him- or herself.

We have a large collection of souvenirs: autographs, more than two thousand photographs, an album of more than a thousand newspaper articles written about us and short amateur movies we filmed to record memorable portions of our journey. These we will cherish for a lifetime. Our motorcycle, with 270 plaques and stickers of the various Automobile Clubs of the world, is unique throughout the world and a very precious piece of machinery.

What have we lost? Gyuszi and I have both sacrificed eight years of our lives, but I think we would both agree that the eight years spent discovering the world were hardly a painful sacrifice. These eight years coincided with a worldwide economic recession, and I doubt we would have advanced much had we stayed in Hungary and attempted to work in our own field. Our eight years abroad wore us out somewhat, both mentally and physically, but the experience, knowledge, and vision of the world that rises above the boundaries of our own small country, more than make up for the time and strength we have lost. What's more, our circle of friends, numbering in the thousands, encircles the world.

Here I must make special mention of my companion and friend, Gyula Bartha, who was with me from start to finish, and without whose dedication, loyalty, and support I hardly could have completed what I set out to do. Many great plans have flopped and visions faded because those who set out to accomplish something could not or would not stay together. Gyula Barta was an exemplary travel companion and friend throughout eight challenging and beautiful years, and I commend and thank him for that.

Our dog Hadji now feels very much at home in Hungary. Surprised at first that all the humans around him speak Hungarian, he has made peace with his new home and is enjoying a well-deserved vacation from world travel.

Many people ask us, "What now?" "Where will you go from here?" Gyuszi and I would like to stay home. We are brimming with plans and good intentions. Knowing full well that nobody is a prophet in his own land and that achieving success and happiness will be more difficult for us in Hungary than it might have been in many other countries of the world, we are inclined to stay. During our travels, we would have had many opportunities to begin a new life thousands of kilometers from our home, but our dream is and always has been to use the experience and vision we have gained to better our own lot and the lot of our nation.

And if someone were to ask whether it was all worth it after all, I would answer, although I would never make the same journey again, that it was!

Index